The General Windows Classes

CApplication

- Manages the application
- Stores information on the current program instance
- Loads accelerator tables

CMLDialog

- Manages the main program window and modeless dialog boxes
- Creates a main window or a modeless dialog box based upon a dialog box template designed in an interactive resource editor
- Assigns icons to a main window
- Handles messages sent to a main window or modeless dialog box
- Destroys a main window or modeless dialog box

CMDialog

- Manages modal dialog boxes
- Displays a modal dialog box based upon a dialog box template created in a resource editor
- Handles messages sent to a dialog box
- Hooks F1 keystrokes to provide context-sensitive dialog box help

For every kind of computer user, there is a SYBEX book.

All computer users learn in their own way. Some need straightforward and methodical explanations. Others are just too busy for this approach. But no matter what camp you fall into, SYBEX has a book that can help you get the most out of your computer and computer software while learning at your own pace.

Beginners generally want to start at the beginning. The **ABC's** series, with its step-by-step lessons in plain language, helps you build basic skills quickly. Or you might try our **Quick & Easy** series, the friendly, full-color guide.

The **Mastering** and **Understanding** series will tell you everything you need to know about a subject. They're perfect for intermediate and advanced computer users, yet they don't make the mistake of leaving beginners behind.

If you're a busy person and are already comfortable with computers, you can choose from two SYBEX series—**Up & Running** and **Running Start**. The **Up & Running** series gets you started in just 20 lessons. Or you can get two books in one, a step-by-step tutorial and an alphabetical reference, with our **Running Start** series.

Everyone who uses computer software can also use a computer software reference. SYBEX offers the gamut—from portable **Instant References** to comprehensive **Encyclopedias, Desktop References,** and **Bibles**.

SYBEX even offers special titles on subjects that don't neatly fit a category—like **Tips & Tricks**, the **Shareware Treasure Chests**, and a wide range of books for Macintosh computers and software.

SYBEX books are written by authors who are expert in their subjects. In fact, many make their living as professionals, consultants, or teachers in the field of computer software. And their manuscripts are thoroughly reviewed by our technical and editorial staff for accuracy and ease-of-use.

So when you want answers about computers or any popular software package, just help yourself to SYBEX.

For a complete catalog of our publications, please write:
SYBEX Inc.
2021 Challenger Drive
Alameda, CA 94501
Tel: (510) 523-8233/(800) 227-2346 Telex: 336311
Fax: (510) 523-2373

SYBEX is committed to using natural resources wisely to preserve and improve our environment. As a leader in the computer book publishing industry, we are aware that over 40% of America's solid waste is paper. This is why we have been printing the text of books like this one on recycled paper since 1982.

This year our use of recycled paper will result in the saving of more than 15,300 trees. We will lower air pollution effluents by 54,000 pounds, save 6,300,000 gallons of water, and reduce landfill by 2,700 cubic yards.

In choosing a SYBEX book you are not only making a choice for the best in skills and information, you are also choosing to enhance the quality of life for all of us.

Mastering Windows Utilities Programming with C++

Mastering Windows™ Utilities Programming with C++

Michael J. Young

SYBEX®

San Francisco • Paris • Düsseldorf • Soest

ACQUISITIONS EDITOR: Dianne King
DEVELOPMENTAL EDITOR: Gary Masters
PROJECT EDITOR: Kristen Vanberg-Wolff
EDITOR: Mark Woodworth
TECHNICAL EDITOR: Amrik Dhillon
BOOK SERIES DESIGNER: Suzanne Albertson
PRODUCTION ARTIST: Charlotte Carter
SCREEN GRAPHICS: John Corrigan
TYPESETTER: Dina F Quan
PROOFREADER/PRODUCTION ASSISTANT: Kristin Amlie
INDEXER: Matthew Spence
COVER DESIGNER: Archer Design
COVER PHOTOGRAPHER: Richard Wahlstrom

Screen reproductions produced with Collage Plus
Collage Plus is a trademark of Inner Media Inc.

Library of Congress Card Number: 93-87024
ISBN: 0-7821-1286-2

Manufactured in the United States of America

10 9 8 7 6 5 4 3 2 1

WARRANTY AND DISCLAIMER

Warranty

SYBEX warrants the enclosed disk to be free of physical defects for a period of ninety (90) days after purchase. If you discover a defect in the disk during this warranty period, you can obtain a replacement disk at no charge by sending the defective disk, postage prepaid, with proof of purchase to:

> SYBEX Inc.
> Customer Service Department
> 2021 Challenger Drive
> Alameda, CA 94501
> (800) 227-2346
> Fax: (510) 523-2373

After the 90-day period, you can obtain a replacement disk by sending us the defective disk, proof of purchase, and a check or money order for $10, payable to SYBEX.

Disclaimer

SYBEX makes no warranty or representation, either express or implied, with respect to this software, its quality performance, merchantability, or fitness for a particular purpose. In no event will SYBEX, its distributors, or dealers be liable for direct, indirect, special, incidental, or consequential damages arising out of the use or inability to use the software even if advised of the possibility of such damage.

The exclusion of implied warranties is not permitted by some states. Therefore, the above exclusion may not apply to you. This warranty provides you with specific legal rights; there may be other rights that you may have that vary from state to state.

Copy Protection

None of the programs on the disk is copy-protected. However, in all cases, reselling these programs without authorization is expressly forbidden.

ACKNOWLEDGMENTS

T<small>**HIS**</small> book is the result of the efforts of many dedicated and talented people at SYBEX. First, I would like to thank Gary Masters, developmental editor, for helping to define the initial concept of the book and for offering his continued enthusiasm and support throughout the project. I would also like to thank Mark Woodworth, editor, for carefully working through each of these chapters and improving their consistency and style. Thanks, too, to Kristen Vanberg-Wolff, project editor, for coordinating the entire effort; and to Amrik Dhillon, technical editor, for verifying the technical accuracy of the text and testing the utility programs. Finally, I would like to express my gratitude to all of the other people at SYBEX whose names appear at the front of the book, for their important roles in the project.

Contents

AT A GLANCE

CONTENTS

PART THREE   **PERSONAL INFORMATION UTILITIES**

INTRODUCTION

FEW of us have all the utility programs that we need to make working in Microsoft Windows thoroughly productive and enjoyable. Although many utilities are available—both brilliant and ill-conceived—it is difficult to find one that does exactly what we want and that works precisely the way we want it to. On the other hand, writing custom utilities from the ground up can be a difficult and time-consuming task.

Mastering Windows Utilities Programming with C++ is a book/software package that was written to solve this dilemma. It not only provides a set of ready-to-run Windows utilities, but also includes complete source code and programming instructions so that you can modify the utilities to suit your needs or develop your own programs. The following is a list of the components that are included:

- *Seven ready-to-run Windows utilities.* These programs include Windows desktop utilities as well as personal information utilities and are described later in the introduction. (The utility ideas originated from my own wish list.)

- *Full instructions for using each utility,* supplied both as online help and printed in the book.

- *The complete, thoroughly commented C++ source code for each utility,* both printed in the book and provided on the companion disk. Also included is the source code for a utility program template, which you can use as the starting point for developing your own utilities or other types of Windows programs.

- *Step-by-step explanations* on how each utility is programmed, *suggestions* for enhancing each utility, and many Windows programming *tips and techniques.*

- *A set of general C++ classes* that I designed to simplify writing utilities and other types of Windows programs. The complete source code for these classes is provided, as well as documentation on how the classes are used and an explanation of how they are programmed.

Mastering Windows Utilities Programming with C++ was written for a variety of audiences. Whether or not you are a programmer, you can use these utilities just as they are written (I find myself using them every day). If you are a beginning Windows programmer, you can tinker with the utility source code, adding new features or experimenting with programming techniques. If you are an intermediate or advanced Windows programmer, you can make extensive modifications to the utilities, or you can use the resources provided in this package to develop your own utility programs.

What Is Required

To run the utility programs, you need Microsoft Windows version 3.1 or later. To modify the utility source code, you need a compiler that can generate Windows applications. All of the utilities in the book were prepared and tested using *both* Microsoft Visual C++ version 1.0 *and* Borland C++ version 4.0; the source files are therefore completely compatible with these two development systems. Furthermore, the companion disk provides project files for these two products, which automate the preparation of the programs if you modify the source code.

The code was kept as portable as possible; for example, the programs do *not* use proprietary class libraries provided with specific compilers (such as the Microsoft Foundation Classes or the Borland Object Windows Library). Therefore, you should have no difficulty using compilers from other companies or other versions of the Microsoft or Borland compiler. However, you may need to make minor changes to the source code, and you will need to prepare your own project files (as discussed in Chapter 1).

If you want to modify the online help for the utilities (as described in Chapter 2), you will also need the Microsoft Help Compiler (provided with the professional editions of Microsoft Visual C++ and Borland C++, and available separately from Microsoft).

The background knowledge that you require depends upon how you are using the book. To *run* the utilities, you need only know basic Windows techniques, such as starting programs, manipulating windows, and choosing commands. To tinker with the source code, you will need a rudimentary understanding of C++ and Windows programming. To fully understand the programming techniques (some of which are relatively advanced) or to make major modifications to the source code, you should have a rudimentary knowledge of C++ and an intermediate level of understanding of Windows programming. Because the code in this book does not use advanced C++ features (such as multiple inheritance), you can learn everything you need to know about C++ from a primer, such as the *C++ Tutorial* provided with Microsoft Visual C++ or *Mastering C++ (From C to C++ in Two Weeks)* by Nathan and Ori Gurewich, published by SYBEX. You can learn all you need to know about Windows programming by reading a comprehensive introduction, such as *Programming Windows* by Charles Petzold, published by Microsoft Press. You can also learn *both* C++ *and* Windows programming by reading my book *Mastering Microsoft Visual C++ Programming*, published by SYBEX (although this book emphasizes Windows programming using the Microsoft Foundation Classes, which are *not* employed in the utilities given here).

An Overview of the Book

Part One of the book (Chapters 1 and 2) presents the background information that will enable you to run the utilities, to understand how they are programmed, and to modify their behavior. Chapter 1 explains how to install the companion disk and describes the files it contains, which include the utility programs as well as all of the source code files. This chapter provides general instructions for running the utilities and shows you how to use your programming environment to modify the utilities.

Chapter 2 presents a simple Windows program template, which forms the basis for all of the utility programs in the book. This chapter explains the general programming techniques used in developing the utilities.

The chapters in Parts Two and Three of the book then present the utilities themselves. Each chapter describes in detail how to run a particular utility, and explains the specific programming techniques used in its development.

Part Two (Chapters 3 through 6) presents a set of utilities designed to enhance your Windows desktop and to help you manage your Windows programs. Chapter 3 presents a Resource Viewer, which monitors important Windows resources and automatically warns you if a given resource drops to a dangerously low level. This utility also allows you to increase the amount of memory available to your programs by compacting memory or by releasing the contents of the Clipboard.

The Setup Saver given in Chapter 4 allows you to save and restore desktop setups. A setup stores the state of an entire collection of Windows programs; when you restore it, each program is run and each window is assigned its original size and position. This utility also allows you to automatically save and restore the set of programs you are using whenever you quit and restart Windows.

Chapter 5 provides a Task Scheduler, which allows you to run a program (or a set of programs, using the Setup Saver) at a predesignated time. You can also have the utility run a Windows Recorder macro after it runs the program, so that you can fully automate a simple or complex task, such as performing a backup, printing a series of files, or downloading information from an online service.

Chapter 6 presents a Screen Saver that you can add to your collection. When this screen saver is activated, it turns your Windows screen into an animated sliding-tile puzzle. You can also use the program code to create your own custom screen savers.

Part Three (Chapters 7, 8, and 9) presents a collection of personal information utilities. These utilities can be used together as an integrated set, or they can be used individually or with other Windows programs. Chapter 7 presents an Address Manager, which allows you to store and quickly retrieve names, addresses, telephone numbers, and free-form information for your friends, family members, and business contacts. Chapter 8 provides an Envelope and Label Printer, designed to quickly print envelopes or labels on any printer that is supported by Windows; this program permanently stores the return address, font, and format to be used for printing envelopes and labels. Chapter 9 offers a Phone Dialer, which dials phone numbers automatically using your modem and will automatically redial phone numbers to help you get through busy phone lines.

When you use the Envelope and Label Printer, you can enter the recipient's address manually, or you can use an address that you have copied into the Windows Clipboard from another program. Similarly, when you run the Phone Dialer, you can either enter a number manually or use a number in the Clipboard. Alternatively, once you have retrieved a record in the Address Manager, you can simply click a button to automatically run the Envelope and Label Printer and print an envelope or label using the displayed address. Likewise, you can click a different button in the Address Manager to run the Phone Dialer and dial the selected phone number.

Finally, the Appendix explains how to use the General Windows Classes (GWC) to write Windows programs. It also presents the GWC source code and describes the inner workings of these classes. The General Windows Classes are a collection of C++ classes that make it easier to write utility-like Windows programs. The source code for the GWC is provided on the companion disk and is printed in the Appendix. All of the utility programs presented in this book make use of these classes; you can also use them when writing your own utilities or other types of Windows programs.

The Companion Disk

The disk provided with this book includes the following components:

- All of the utility programs and online help files

- The complete source code required to create each utility program

- An automated installation program, which allows you to install the utilities, the source code, or both (see the instructions for running the installation program in Chapter 1)

How to Use the Book

To learn how to run a particular utility, either you can read the first section of the chapter that presents the utility (the "How to Use..." section), or you can read the program's online help (see Chapter 1 for instructions on accessing online help).

To understand how a utility is programmed, you should read the "How the Program Works" section in the chapter that presents the utility. The discussions in the chapter focus on the overall organization of the source code, the general programming strategies, the reasons for the programming choices that were made, and the advanced or interesting programming techniques that were used. For more detailed information on specific lines of code, see the comments in the source code listings. The source code files are printed in the chapter and are included with the companion disk files. If you are at your computer while reading the book, it might be easiest to open the relevant source files in an editor and browse through the source code.

While reading through the programming explanations, you should have your run-time library and Windows API documentation available (either the printed or online version). The discussions in the book assume that you have this information available and do not needlessly duplicate the material.

The utilities presented in the book use a wide variety of programming techniques. The book explains each technique *only when it is first encountered* in one of the utility programs. Thus, for example, if a particular technique is used in the utility given in Chapter 3 *and* in the utility given in Chapter 5, it is explained only in Chapter 3. Ideally, therefore, you should read all of the chapters in order. If, however, you are reading a particular chapter out of sequence, you can refer back to previous chapters to obtain additional information on some of the programming techniques (the Index and the cross-references given in the text will help).

Also, the source code includes detailed comments for a particular programming technique only when the technique is *first used* in a source code file. For example, the source files presented in Chapter 2 (for the TEMPLATE program) include comments for the basic programming techniques that are used in all of the utilities; these comments are *not* duplicated in the source files presented in subsequent chapters.

Contacting the Author

You can send me E-mail via CompuServe (75156.2572), or via Internet (75156.2572@compuserve.com). I welcome your technical questions, feedback, and ideas. If you have questions about ordering books or disks, please contact the publisher.

The Basics

This part of the book presents the background information that will enable you to run the utilities, to understand how they are programmed, and to modify their behavior. Chapter 1 explains how to install the companion disk and describes the files it contains, which include the utility programs as well as all of the source code files. This chapter provides general instructions for running the utilities and shows you how to use your programming environment to modify the utilities.

Chapter 2 presents a simple Windows program template, which forms the basis for all of the utility programs in the book. This chapter explains the general programming techniques used in developing the utilities.

The chapters in Parts Two and Three of the book then present the utilities themselves. Each chapter describes in detail how to run a particular utility and explains the specific programming techniques used to develop it.

Windows Utilities in C++

Template

Resource Viewer

Setup Saver

Task Scheduler

Address Manager

Envelope & Label Printer

Phone Dialer

CHAPTER

1

Installing and Using
the Software

THE software provided on the companion disk includes the utility programs, the online help files, and the complete source code for each utility. This chapter describes how to install the companion disk and gives an overview of the files that are copied to your hard disk. It then provides general instructions for running the utility programs and tells you how to access detailed help information. Finally, the chapter explains how to use a project file from the companion disk to rebuild a utility program if you have modified its source code. A description of the inner workings of the program source code is postponed until Chapter 2.

Installing the Disk

Because the files on the companion disk are compressed, you must use the automated Install program to copy them to your hard disk. Install is a Windows program; to run it, perform the following steps:

1. Insert the companion disk into a floppy disk drive.

2. From the Windows Program Manager or Windows File Manager, choose the Run... command on the File menu. Windows will display the Run dialog box.

3. If you placed the companion disk in drive A, type the following text into the Command Line: text box, and click the OK button:

   `A:\INSTALL`

   If you placed the companion disk in a different drive, substitute the appropriate drive letter. The Install window will appear on your screen, as shown in Figure 1.1.

4. Choose *one* or *both* of the following options, which are displayed in the Install program window:

   - Install the utilities and online help files
   - Install the utility source code

5. If you wish, change the directory path displayed in the Target Directory: text box. This text box specifies the hard disk directory to which Install will copy the companion disk files. The default directory is C:\WUC (for "Windows Utilities in C++"). If you specify a different directory, be sure to enter the *full directory path*, including the drive specification. If the specified directory does not exist, Install will create it.

6. Click the OK button in the Install window. The Install program will begin copying files.

NOTE

Installing the utility programs and help files requires approximately 0.5MB of free space on the hard disk. Installing the source code requires approximately 1.5MB of additional free space.

If you selected the "Install the utilities and online help files" option in step 4, the Install program does the following:

- It copies the executable file (.EXE) and the online help file (.HLP) for each utility to the directory you specified in step 5.

- It copies the Screen Saver program presented in Chapter 6 (SLIDER.SCR) and its help file (SLIDER.HLP) to your Windows directory.

- It creates a program group in the Windows Program Manager named "Windows Utilities in C++" and installs an icon within this group for each utility, so that you can readily run the programs. This group is shown in Figure 1.2.

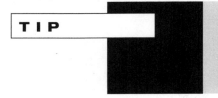

TIP

If you did *not* install one of the companion disk components (either the programs or the source code), you can later run Install again to add the missing component.

If you selected the "Install the utility source code" option in step 4 of the installation process, Install copies the source code files for each utility to a separate subdirectory within the directory you specified in step 5. Additionally, Install copies the source code for the General Windows Classes to a separate subdirectory (these general-purpose source code files are used by all of the utilities, and are described in Chapter 2 and the Appendix).

For each utility, Table 1.1 lists the name of the executable file and the name of the help file, as well as the name of the subdirectory containing the program source code. Table 1.1 assumes that you have accepted the

FIGURE 1.2

The Windows Program
Manager group that
the Install program
creates

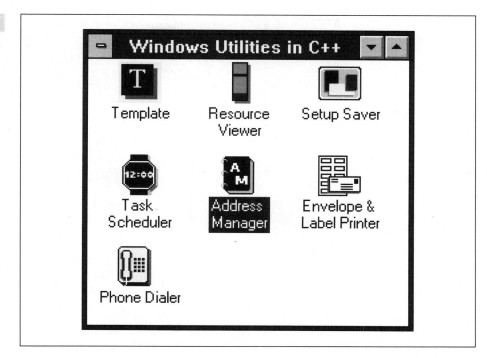

default target directory, \WUC; if you specified a different directory, substitute the directory name that you selected. The different file types that
constitute the source code are described later in the chapter (in the section "Modifying the Programs").

TABLE 1.1: Utility Files Copied by Install*

UTILITY	CHAPTER PRESENTED	EXECUTABLE AND HELP FILES COPIED TO \WUC	SUBDIRECTORY CONTAINING SOURCE CODE
Template	2	TEMPLATE.EXE, TEMPLATE.HLP	\WUC\TEMPLATE
Resource Viewer	3	RESVIEW.EXE, RESVIEW.HLP	\WUC\RESVIEW
Setup Saver	4	SETSAVE.EXE, SETSAVE.HLP	\WUC\SETSAVE

TABLE 1.1: Utility Files Copied by Install* (continued)

UTILITY	CHAPTER PRESENTED	EXECUTABLE AND HELP FILES COPIED TO \WUC	SUBDIRECTORY CONTAINING SOURCE CODE
Task Scheduler	5	SCHEDULE.EXE, SCHEDULE.HLP	\WUC\SCHEDULE
Screen Saver	6	SLIDER.SCR, SLIDER.HLP (copied to Windows directory!)	\WUC\SLIDER
Address Manager	7	ADDRESS.EXE, ADDRESS.HLP	\WUC\ADDRESS
Envelope and Label Printer	8	ENVELOPE.EXE, ENVELOPE.HLP	\WUC\ENVELOPE
Phone Dialer	9	DIAL.EXE, DIAL.HLP	\WUC\DIAL
General Window Classes	2 and Appendix	(none)	\WUC\WCLASSES

*Assuming that you accepted the default target directory, \WUC

NOTE

If you want to copy one or more individual files from the companion disk, you can use the Microsoft EXPAND utility, which is an MS-DOS program included with Windows 3.1 and with MS-DOS 6.0. To copy a file, type EXPAND at the MS-DOS prompt, and the program will prompt you for the required information. Note that the compressed files are named by replacing the last letter of the file name with the '_' character. For example, the compressed version of TEMPLATE.EXE is named TEMPLATE.EX_.

Running the Programs

To run one of the utilities, you need only double-click the program icon within the "Windows Utilities in C++" group that was added to the Windows Program Manager. Full instructions for using each utility are given at the beginning of the chapter that presents the utility (in the "How to Use..." section). These instructions are also available as online help.

NOTE Unlike the other utilities, the Screen Saver presented in Chapter 6 is run through the Windows Control Panel. See the instructions given in Chapter 6.

When the program's main window is active, you can access the online help by choosing one of the commands on the Help menu; all utilities have the standard Help menu shown in Figure 1.3. You can view a list of available help topics either by choosing the Contents... command on the Help menu or by pressing F1.

FIGURE 1.3

The standard Help menu provided by the utilities

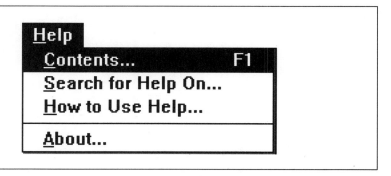

TIP

You can have Windows automatically run a utility when Windows first starts by placing a copy of the utility icon in the StartUp group of the Windows Program Manager. (To copy an icon from the "Windows Utilities in C++" group, hold down the Ctrl key and drag the icon into the StartUp group.)

Help is also available for many of the dialog boxes displayed by the utility programs. Each of these dialog boxes contains a Help button; an example is shown in Figure 1.4. When the dialog box is displayed, you can view an explanation of the dialog box controls either by clicking the Help button or by pressing F1.

FIGURE 1.4

A dialog box with online help available

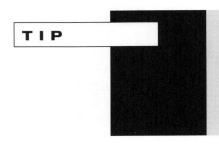

Set Red Lines

USER Resources: [20] %

GDI Resources: [20] %

Global Memory: [15] %

Disk Space: [5] %

OK

Cancel   Help

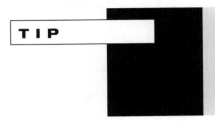

TIP You can change the background color displayed in the utility program windows by running the Windows Control Panel, double-clicking the Color icon, and adjusting the color for the Application Workspace screen element.

Modifying the Programs

As you work through this book, you may decide to modify one or more of the utility programs. You might simply want to adjust minor program features to learn more about some of the programming techniques discussed in the book; you might decide to enhance a utility, either by using the suggestions given at the end of each chapter or employing your own ideas; or you might wish to use a utility or some of its code to develop an entirely different program. To modify a utility, you must edit the program source code and then rebuild the program. This section briefly describes the source code files provided on the companion disk and explains how to rebuild a utility after you have changed its source code. Explanations of the programming techniques required for modifying the source code are postponed until Chapter 2 (Chapter 2 explains the general programming techniques, while the subsequent chapters explain techniques specific to each utility).

If you chose the "Install the utility source code" option when running the Install program, the complete source code for both the program template given in Chapter 2 and the utilities presented in Chapters 3 through 9 is copied to your hard disk; the code for each program is copied to a separate subdirectory within the target directory; see Table 1.1.

The companion disk provides all of the source code files that are printed in the book, plus all other files that are needed to prepare the utility programs and their online help files. Table 1.2 briefly describes the different types of source files that are provided; in this table, each type of file is identified by its file extension. These file types will be explained more fully in the following chapters.

TABLE 1.2: The Types of Source Code Files Provided on the Companion Disk

FILE EXTENSION	DESCRIPTION OF FILE
.BMP	Bitmap file, which stores a drawing used in the online help file. When the help file is created, the Help Compiler incorporates the bitmap within the help text.
.CPP	C++ source code file.
.DEF	Module-definition file, which defines several properties of the program, such as the heap and stack size, and is used when linking the program.
.H	Header file, which contains definitions of classes or symbolic constants and is included within the C++ source code file or resource-definition file.
.HPJ	Help project file, which describes features of the online help file and is used when creating the online help with the Help Compiler.
.ICO	Icon file, which stores the data for the program icon. The resource-definition file contains an ICON statement that causes this data to be included in the program resources.
.IDE	Project file for building the program, using the Borland C++ Integrated Development Environment.
.MAK	Project file for building the program, using the Microsoft Visual C++ Visual Workbench.
.RC	Resource-definition file, which defines the program resources (menus, dialog boxes, icons, accelerators, and so on).
.RTF	Text for the online help file, in *Rich Text Format*.

To make it easy for you to modify the utilities, the companion disk provides a set of project files; a project file automates the process of rebuilding a program after you have modified its source code. For each utility, the disk includes a project file for Microsoft Visual C++ version 1.0 (which has the .MAK extension), as well as a project file for Borland C++ version 4.0 (which has the .IDE extension). For example, the Install program copies the project files ADDRESS.MAK and ADDRESS.IDE into the \ADDRESS subdirectory together with the other source code files for the Address Manager utility; you can use these files to build the Address Manager program. If you are using a compiler from another company, or another version of the Microsoft or Borland Compiler, you will need to create your own project files (as will be discussed in the section "Using Other Compilers").

NOTE

You will need to rebuild the program if you have edited any of the source code files within the integrated environment editor, or if you have modified the program resources, using a resource editor (such as the Microsoft App Studio or the Borland Resource Workshop).

A project file lists the program source files and describes each of the steps required to build the program. In general, to modify a program, you load the project file into your development environment (for example, the Microsoft Visual Workbench or the Borland Integrated Development Environment), make any desired changes to the program source code, and rebuild the program by issuing the Build, "Make all," or other appropriate command (as described later). When using a project file, the development environment performs only those steps required to prepare an up-to-date version of the program. For example, if you have modified only a single C++ source file since the last time you built the program, the environment will compile only that file and then will relink the program. The following sections give more detailed steps for using a project file with Microsoft Visual C++ version 1.0, Borland C++ version 4.0, and other development systems.

TIP If you change compilers (for example, from Borland C++ to Microsoft Visual C++) or if you modify the project file itself (by adding or removing source files or by changing options that affect the way the program is built), you must rebuild *all* of the source code files. To do this with Microsoft Visual C++, choose the "Rebuild All" command on the Project menu; to do this with Borland C++, choose the "Build all" command on the Project menu.

NOTE The project file and integrated environment are used for building the executable program file (.EXE), *not* the online help file (.HLP). The procedure for creating the online help file is discussed in Chapter 2.

Using Microsoft Visual C++ Version 1.0

To load one of the project files into the Microsoft Visual Workbench, choose the Open... command on the Project menu. Then, in the Open Project dialog box, select the desired project file and click OK. The project file provided for each utility has the .MAK extension and is stored in the directory containing the utility's source code files (see Table 1.1 for the location of the source files for each utility).

After you have made the desired modifications to the source code, you can prepare an up-to-date version of the program by choosing the Build command on the Project menu or by pressing Shift+F8.

NOTE To build the programs using the project files presented in this book, you must have installed the appropriate run-time library version. When you run the Visual C++ Setup program, install this library by choosing the following options in the Library Options dialog box (in addition to any other options that you want): the "Small/Tiny"-memory model, the "Windows .EXE" target, and one of the math support options. Also, if you want to modify the help files or create your own help files, you should choose the Help Compiler option in the Tool Options dialog box.

Creating the Microsoft Project Files

This section explains how the Microsoft Visual C++ project files for the utilities in this book were created. Because the project files are provided on the companion disk, you do not need to create them yourself; however, this procedure may be of interest if you need to create your own project files for other programs. For each project file, the following steps were performed:

1. The New command on the Project menu was chosen.

2. In the New Project dialog box, the full path name of the project file was entered into the Project Name: text box, the "Windows application (.EXE)" option was selected in the Project Type: list, and the Use Microsoft Foundation Classes option was turned off. An example of a completed New Project dialog box is shown in Figure 1.5. (In this example, a project is being created for the Address Manager program, ADDRESS. Note that in this figure the text in the Project Name: text box has scrolled and is therefore not completely visible.)

FIGURE 1.5

The completed New Project dialog box for creating a project file for the ADDRESS program

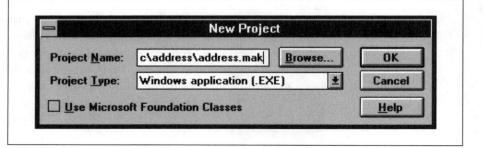

3. In the Edit project dialog box, each of the utility source files was added to the Files in Project: list. Note that the WCLASSES.CPP source file (stored in the \WCLASSES subdirectory) was added to *all* of the projects (this file contains the source code for the General Windows Classes, which are described in Chapter 2 and the Appendix).

4. The small-memory model run-time library was selected for the project as follows: The Project... command on the Options menu was chosen, the Compiler... button was clicked, the Memory Model category was selected, and the Small model was selected.

5. The stack size specification was eliminated as follows: The Project... command on the Options menu was chosen, the Linker... button was clicked, the Memory Image category was selected, and the contents of the Stack Size: text box were erased. This step was performed because the stack size is specified in the module-definition file (which will be described in Chapter 2), as required for Borland C++; if the size were specified in both places, the linker would issue a warning.

6. For the Resource Viewer utility only, the TOOLHELP Windows library was added to the project, as follows: The Project... command on the Options menu was chosen, the Linker... button was clicked, the Windows Libraries category was selected, and the TOOLHELP "import library and DLL" was selected. For more information, see Chapter 3 (the section "How the Resource Viewer Works").

Using Borland C++
Version 4.0

To load one of the project files into the Borland Integrated Development Environment (IDE), choose the "Open project…" command on the Project menu. Then, in the Open Project File dialog box, select the desired project file and click the OK button. The project file provided for each utility has the .IDE extension and is stored in the directory containing the utility's source code files (see Table 1.1 for the location of the source files for each utility).

N O T E

Borland C++ project files store the location of both the include files and the library files. The project files supplied on the companion disk specify the directory C:\BC4\INCLUDE for the include files and the directory C:\BC4\LIB for the library files. If your include or library files are contained in a different directory, you must change the path specification for each project file. You can do this as follows: Load the project, choose the Project… command on the Options menu, select the Directories topic, and enter the correct paths into the Include: and Library: text boxes.

After you have made the desired modifications to the source code, you can prepare an up-to-date version of the program by choosing the "Make all" command on the Project menu.

NOTE

To build the programs using the project files presented in this book, you must have installed the appropriate run-time library version. When you run the Borland C++ Install program, install this library by choosing the following options in the "C++ RTL Model Selection" dialog box (in addition to any other options you want): 16-BIT Small Library, and 16–32 BIT Header Files. Also, if you want to modify the help files or create your own help files, you should choose the "Install MS Windows Dev. Kit" option in the Select Borland C++ Tools dialog box.

Creating the Borland Project Files

This section explains how the Borland C++ project files for the utilities in this book were created. Because the project files are provided on the companion disk, you do not need to create them yourself; however, this procedure may be of interest if you need to create your own project files for other programs. For each project file, the following steps were performed:

1. The "New project..." command on the Project menu was chosen.

2. The New Project dialog box was completed as shown in Figure 1.6 (in this figure, the "Project path and name:" and the "Target name:" text boxes were assigned the appropriate names for the Address Manager program, ADDRESS).

3. The IDE automatically adds many of the source code files to a new project. The remaining C++ source files were now added to the project (including WCLASSES.CPP, which was added to *all* projects). Each source file was added as follows: The right mouse button was clicked while the pointer was on the "address (.exe)" line at the top of the Project window, causing this line to be selected and a floating menu to appear. Then, the "Add node..." command on the floating menu was chosen and the source file was selected in the Add to Project List dialog box. The completed

FIGURE 1.6

The completed New
Project dialog box, for
creating a project for
the ADDRESS program

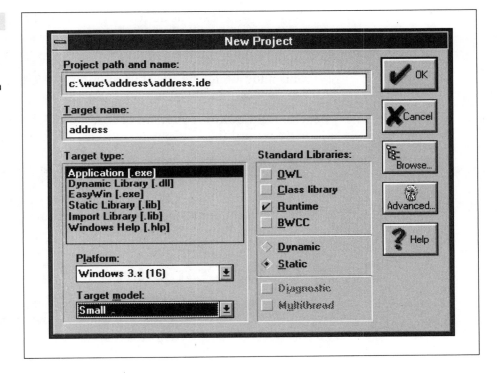

Project window (for the ADDRESS program) is shown in Figure 1.7.

4. The right button was clicked on the top line in the Project window and the "Edit local options..." command on the floating menu was chosen. Then, the Directories topic was selected and

FIGURE 1.7

The completed Project
window for the
ADDRESS program

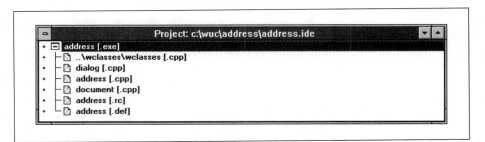

the following text was added to the *end* of the existing text in the Include: text box:

```
;..\wclasses
```

This addition allows the IDE to find the WCLASSES.H header file.

5. The right button was again clicked on the top line in the Project window and the "Edit local options..." command on the floating menu was again chosen. Then, the Messages topic was chosen and the Selected option was selected. Next, the Inefficient Coding subtopic was chosen, and the "Parameter 'ident' is never used" option was turned off. This change prevents Borland C++ from generating warning messages for unused parameters, which are quite common in Windows programs.

Using Other Compilers

If you are using a development environment from a company other than Microsoft or Borland, or if you are using a version of the Microsoft or Borland compiler other than the ones described above, you will have to create your own project files.

To create your own project file for a program, follow the instructions supplied with your compiler, and make sure that you include all of the program source files in the project file list. For a utility in this book, you must include the following source files in the project:

- All files with the .CPP extension in the project subdirectory
- The file WCLASSES.CPP in the \WCLASSES subdirectory
- The file with the .DEF extension in the project subdirectory
- The file with the .RC extension in the project subdirectory

See Table 1.2 for a brief explanation of these types of files.

Load the project file and build the program, using the appropriate commands provided by the development environment. You may also need to make minor revisions to the program source code to eliminate warning or error messages generated during the build process.

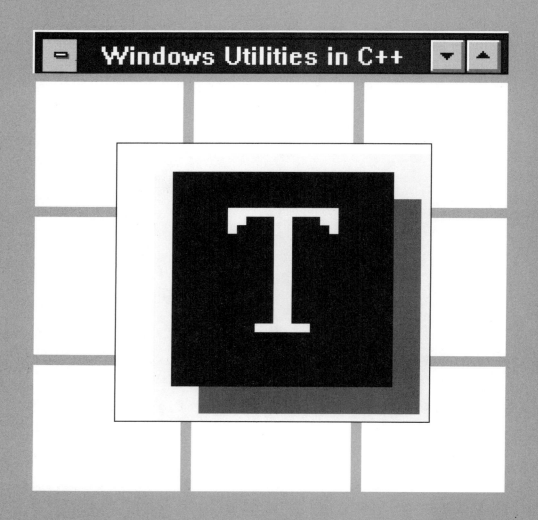

CHAPTER

2

A C++ Windows Program Template

THE previous chapter explained how to install the utility source code from the companion disk, it briefly described the different types of source files provided, and it showed you how to rebuild a program using your C++ development environment after modifying the source code. In this chapter, you will learn the most basic, general programming techniques that are used in all of the utilities. The following chapters in the book will explain the techniques that are specific to each utility.

The chapter explains these general techniques by presenting a simple template program. Unlike the general Windows program templates provided elsewhere (for instance, in the manuals and example code provided with Microsoft Visual C++), this template is designed specifically for writing utility programs. In fact, it was used as the starting point for writing all of the utilities in this book (except the Screen Saver presented in Chapter 6). You can also use this template for writing your own utilities.

The program template presented here—as well as all of the utilities in the book—makes extensive use of the General Windows Classes (GWC) that are provided with the book. The Appendix lists the source code for these classes, describes how to use them, and explains how they are programmed.

How to Run the Template Program

The Template program demonstrates many of the basic features of the user interface that is common to the utility programs given in this book.

Run the program by double-clicking the program icon that was installed in the "Windows Utilities in C++" group of the Program Manager:

The Template program window displays a text message and the program icon. The window background is filled with the color that is currently assigned to the Application Workspace screen element in the color scheme set through the Windows Control Panel. The window is shown in Figure 2.1.

If you select the Always on Top item on the Options menu, the Template program window will always appear on top of other windows that occupy the same screen space, even if the program window is inactive or has been reduced to an icon. (The following is an exception: if another window has *also* been assigned the "always on top" property, the option will have no effect.) All of the utility programs in the book provide the Always on Top option; selecting it can make it easy to quickly access the utility.

FIGURE 2.1

The Template program window

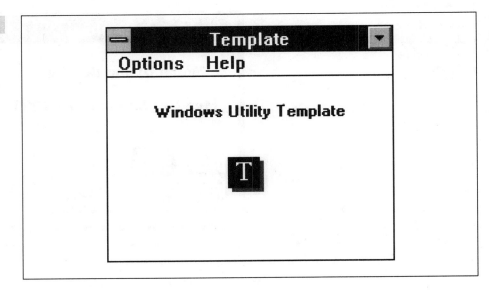

If you choose the Dialog... command on the Options menu, the Template program displays the "Dialog" example dialog box. This dialog box displays the current date and time and is shown in Figure 2.2. You must click the OK or Cancel button or choose the Close command on the system menu to close the dialog box and reactivate the main program window (such a dialog box is termed *modal* and is typical of many of the dialog boxes displayed by the utility programs).

If you choose the About... command on the Help menu, the Template program displays a typical About dialog box, which is shown in Figure 2.3 (this dialog box is also modal).

Finally, the Template program provides online help, as described in Chapter 1. When the main window is active, you can access the online help by choosing a command on the Help menu, or by pressing F1 to view the help contents. When the "Dialog" dialog box is displayed, you can access context-sensitive help by clicking the Help button or by pressing F1. The help text provided for the Template program contains examples of many of the elements used in the utility help files (titles, paragraphs of text, lists, bitmaps, and so on).

FIGURE 2.2

The example modal dialog box displayed by the Template program

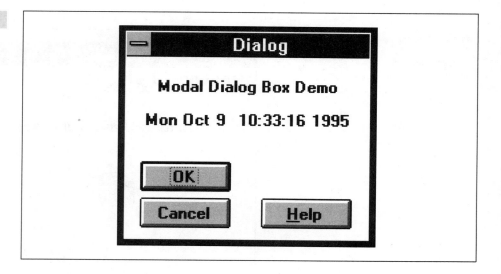

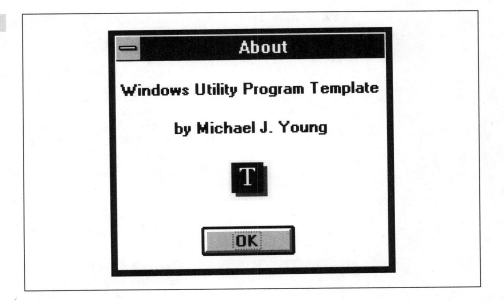

The Template Source Code

Table 2.1 lists and briefly describes all of the source code files for the Template program. Following the convention in this book, the technical discussions will refer to the program as TEMPLATE, because this is the name used for the executable file as well as many of the source code files.

TABLE 2.1: The Source Code Files for the TEMPLATE Program

FILE	DESCRIPTION
DIALOG.CPP	The C++ source code file that defines the member functions belonging to the main window class (CMainDialog) and the class that manages the "Dialog" example dialog box (CDemoDialog).
HELP.RTF	The document (in Rich Text Format) that supplies the text for generating the online help file.

TABLE 2.1: The Source Code Files for the TEMPLATE Program (continued)

FILE	DESCRIPTION
HELP01.BMP	A bitmap file containing a drawing that is incorporated into the online help file.
RESOURCE.H	The resource header file generated by the Microsoft App Studio program, which contains constant definitions for accessing the program resources (specifically, the menu commands and buttons). This file is included in the resource-definition file (TEMPLATE.RC) and in both of the main C++ source files (TEMPLATE.CPP and DIALOG.CPP; it is actually included in TEMPLATE.H, which is included in the .CPP files).
TEMPLATE.CPP	The C++ source code file that contains the program entry function, WinMain, and declares the global program objects (App and MainDialog).
TEMPLATE.DEF	The module-definition file, which defines several properties of the program such as the heap and stack size and is used when linking the program.
TEMPLATE.H	The main program header file, which defines all the classes used in the program and is included in both of the main C++ source files (TEMPLATE.CPP and DIALOG.CPP). It includes the header files WCLASSES.H and RESOURCE.H so that these two files will also be included in the main C++ source files.
TEMPLATE.HPJ	The help project file, which describes features of the online help file and is used when creating the online help with the Help Compiler.
TEMPLATE.ICO	The program icon file, which stores the data for the program icon. The resource-definition file contains an ICON statement that causes this data to be included in the program resources.

TABLE 2.1: The Source Code Files for the TEMPLATE Program (continued)

FILE	DESCRIPTION
TEMPLATE.IDE	The project file for building the program, using the Borland C++ Integrated Development Environment.
TEMPLATE.MAK	The project file for building the program, using the Microsoft Visual C++ Visual Workbench.
TEMPLATE.RC	The resource-definition file, which defines the program resources (specifically, the menu, dialog boxes, icon, and accelerator table).
WCLASSES.CPP	The C++ source file that defines the member functions of the General Windows Classes, which are used by the Template program and all of the other utilities in the book. A single copy of this file is stored in the \WCLASSES subdirectory and is shared by all of the utilities.
WCLASSES.H	The header file that contains the class definitions for the General Windows Classes, which are used by the Template program and all of the other utilities in the book. A single copy of this file is stored in the \WCLASSES subdirectory and it is included in all C++ source files.

The primary source files for the TEMPLATE program are given in Listings 2.1 through 2.6. These listings are provided for quick reference as you work through the book. (As an alternative to referring to the printed listings, you can load the source files from the companion disk into your editor and browse through them as you read the book.)

Listing 2.1 (TEMPLATE.H) is the main header file for the program; it contains the definitions of all of the classes used in the program and it is included within both of the main C++ source files (TEMPLATE.CPP and DIALOG.CPP). TEMPLATE.H also includes the WCLASSES.H and RESOURCE.H header files so that the definitions in these two files will be available to both of the source files.

Listing 2.2 (TEMPLATE.CPP) contains the C++ source code for the program entry function, `WinMain`, as well as the declarations for both of the global program objects (`App` and `MainDialog`). Listing 2.3 (DIALOG.CPP) defines the member functions belonging to the class that manages the main window (`CMainDialog`) and the class that manages the "Dialog" dialog box (`CDemoDialog`). To make it easier for you to locate specific member functions, the member functions for a particular class are arranged in alphabetical order within the source file. Listing 2.4 (TEMPLATE.DEF) is the program module-definition file.

Finally, Listing 2.5 (RESOURCE.H) contains the constant definitions that are used for accessing the program resources (specifically, the menu commands, buttons, and text controls), and Listing 2.6 (TEMPLATE.RC) defines all of the program resources. Note that Listings 2.1 through 2.4 were manually typed into an editor. Listings 2.5 and 2.6, however, were generated by the Microsoft App Studio program, although they were edited slightly to make them conform to the standard format of the text listings in this book.

Listing 2.1

```
/////////////////////////////////////////////////////////////////
//                                                             //
// TEMPLATE.H:  Header file for the TEMPLATE program.          //
//                                                             //
/////////////////////////////////////////////////////////////////

#include "..\wclasses\wclasses.h"  // general header files to
#include "resource.h"              // include in all source files

// constant for help topic:
#define HELPDEMODLG 100


/////////////////////////////////////////////////////////////////
// main dialog box class definition:                           //
/////////////////////////////////////////////////////////////////

class CMainDialog : public CMLDialog
{
    HBRUSH HBrushWorkSpace;
```

```
    int OnTop;

    virtual BOOL DialogProc (UINT Msg, WPARAM WParam,
                             LPARAM LParam);

    BOOL OnCommand (int IDItem, HWND HWndCtl, WORD NotifyCode);
    BOOL OnCtlColor (HDC HDCChild, HWND HWndChild, int CtlType);
    BOOL OnDestroy ();
    BOOL OnInitDialog (HWND HWndFocus, LPARAM Data);
    BOOL OnSysColorChange ();
    void WrapUp ();

public:
    CMainDialog ();
};



//////////////////////////////////////////////////////////////
// 'Dialog' demo modal dialog box class definition:         //
//////////////////////////////////////////////////////////////

class CDemoDialog : public CMDialog
{
    virtual BOOL DialogProc (UINT Msg, WPARAM WParam,
                             LPARAM LParam);
};
```

Listing 2.2

```
//////////////////////////////////////////////////////////////
//                                                          //
// TEMPLATE.CPP:  Global object declarations and program entry //
//                point for the TEMPLATE program.           //
//                                                          //
//////////////////////////////////////////////////////////////

#include "template.h"
```

```
/////////////////////////////////////////////////////////////////
// global object declarations:                                  //
/////////////////////////////////////////////////////////////////

CApplication App;
CMainDialog MainDialog;

/////////////////////////////////////////////////////////////////
// program entry function:                                      //
/////////////////////////////////////////////////////////////////
int PASCAL WinMain
   (HINSTANCE HInstCurrent,
   HINSTANCE HInstPrevious,
   LPSTR CmdLine,
   int CmdShow)
   {
   MSG Msg;

   if (HInstPrevious)
      {
      // an instance of the program is already running; because
      // only ONE instance should be running, activate the
      // previous instance and exit:

      HWND HWndPopup;

      // obtain the main window handle for previous instance:
      GetInstanceData
         (HInstPrevious,
         (BYTE *)&MainDialog.mHDialog,
         sizeof (HWND));

      // display the main window of previous instance in its
      // normal size (in case it is minimized):
      ShowWindow (MainDialog.mHDialog, SW_SHOWNORMAL);

      // if the previous instance is currently displaying a
      // dialog box, get the dialog box handle:
      HWndPopup = GetLastActivePopup (MainDialog.mHDialog);
```

```
    // activate both the main window and any dialog box that
    // is displayed by the previous instance:
    BringWindowToTop (MainDialog.mHDialog);
    BringWindowToTop (HWndPopup);

    return (FALSE);  // terminate current instance
    }

// initialize the application class:
App.Initialize (HInstCurrent, HInstPrevious, CmdLine,
            CmdShow);

// load the table of accelerator keystrokes:
if (!App.LoadAccel ("TemplateAccel"))
    return (FALSE);

// assign icon to the main window:
if (!MainDialog.SetIcon ("TemplateIcon"))
    return (FALSE);

// create and display the main program window:
if (!MainDialog.Create ("MainDlg"))
    return (FALSE);

// MAIN MESSAGE LOOP: extract messages from the queue and
// dispatch them:
while (GetMessage (&Msg, NULL, NULL, NULL))
    // special processing for accelerator keystrokes:
    if (!TranslateAccelerator (MainDialog.mHDialog,
                        App.mHAccelTable,
                        &Msg))
        // special processing for dialog box messages:
        if (!IsDialogMessage (MainDialog.mHDialog, &Msg))
            {
            // translate virtual-key messages into character
            // messages (WM_CHAR):
            TranslateMessage (&Msg);

            // invoke window procedure to process the message:
            DispatchMessage (&Msg);
            }
```

```
        return (Msg.wParam);
        }
```

Listing 2.3

```
//////////////////////////////////////////////////////////////////
//                                                                //
// DIALOG.CPP:  Dialog class member functions for the             //
//              TEMPLATE program.                                 //
//                                                                //
//////////////////////////////////////////////////////////////////

#include "template.h"
#include <time.h>

// make the global objects accessible in this source file:
extern CApplication App;
extern CMainDialog MainDialog;

//////////////////////////////////////////////////////////////////
// CMainDialog member functions:                                  //
//////////////////////////////////////////////////////////////////

CMainDialog::CMainDialog ()
   {
   HBrushWorkSpace = 0;
   }

BOOL CMainDialog::DialogProc (UINT Msg, WPARAM WParam,
                              LPARAM LParam)
   {
   switch (Msg)
      {
      case WM_CLOSE:
      // user chose the Close command on system menu
         Destroy ();    // destroy the main window, which
         return (TRUE); // terminates the application

      case WM_COMMAND:
```

```
    // user chose a menu command or clicked a button
        return OnCommand ((int)WParam, (HWND)LOWORD (LParam),
                          HIWORD (LParam));

    case WM_CTLCOLOR:
    // a dialog box or control is setting its color
        return OnCtlColor ((HDC)WParam, (HWND)LOWORD (LParam),
                           (int)HIWORD (LParam));

    case WM_DESTROY:
    // the main window has been destroyed
        return OnDestroy ();

    case WM_ENDSESSION:
    // the user has ended the Windows session
        if (WParam)
            WrapUp ();
        return (TRUE);

    case WM_INITDIALOG:
    // the main window has just been created, but not yet
    // displayed
        return OnInitDialog ((HWND)WParam, LParam);

    case WM_SYSCOLORCHANGE:
    // the user has chosen the color scheme through the
    // Windows Control Panel;
        return OnSysColorChange ();

    default:
    // all other messages: allow the system to perform default
    // processing
        return (FALSE); // returning FALSE means that the
    }                   // program has NOT processed the message
  }

BOOL CMainDialog::OnCommand (int IDItem, HWND HWndCtl,
                            WORD NotifyCode)
  {
  switch (IDItem)
    {
```

```
case IDM_ABOUT:   // Help/About menu command
   {
   // display the 'About' dialog box:
   CMDialog MDialog;
   MDialog.Create ("AboutDlg", mHDialog);
   return (TRUE);
   }

case IDM_SHOWDIALOG:   // Options/Dialog menu command
   {
   // display the demo dialog box:
   CDemoDialog DemoDialog;
   DemoDialog.Create ("DemoDlg", mHDialog);
   return (TRUE);
   }

case IDM_HELPCONTENTS:   // Help/Contents menu command
   // display the "contents" topic in the online help file:
   WinHelp (mHDialog, "TEMPLATE.HLP", HELP_CONTENTS, OL);
   return (TRUE);

case IDM_HELPHELP:   // Help/How to Use Help menu command
   // display the "help on help" online help topic:
   WinHelp (mHDialog, "TEMPLATE.HLP", HELP_HELPONHELP, OL);
   return (TRUE);

case IDM_HELPSEARCH:   // Help/Search for Help On menu
                       // command
   // display the help Search dialog box:
   WinHelp (mHDialog, "TEMPLATE.HLP", HELP_PARTIALKEY,
            (DWORD)(LPCSTR)"");
   return (TRUE);

case IDM_ONTOP:   // Options/Always on Top menu command
   // toggle OnTop flag:
   OnTop = !OnTop;

   // check or uncheck menu command:
   CheckMenuItem (GetMenu (mHDialog), IDM_ONTOP,
                  OnTop ? MF_CHECKED : MF_UNCHECKED);
```

```
        // set "on top" property of main window:
        SetWindowPos (mHDialog,
                      OnTop ? HWND_TOPMOST : HWND_NOTOPMOST,
                      0, 0, 0, 0, SWP_NOMOVE | SWP_NOSIZE );
        return (FALSE);


    default:
        return (FALSE);


    }
  }

BOOL CMainDialog::OnCtlColor (HDC HDCChild, HWND HWndChild,
                             int CtlType)
  {
  COLORREF WorkSpaceColor;

  switch (CtlType)   // CtlType is the type of control that
     {               // is being redrawn
     case CTLCOLOR_BTN:    // redrawing button or group box
     case CTLCOLOR_STATIC: // redrawing text
        // set text to color contrasting Application Workspace:

        WorkSpaceColor = GetSysColor (COLOR_APPWORKSPACE);
        if (GetRValue (WorkSpaceColor) * 2 +
            GetGValue (WorkSpaceColor) * 5 +
            GetBValue (WorkSpaceColor) > 1020)
           // Application Workspace color is light; therefore
           // set text color to black:
           SetTextColor (HDCChild, RGB (0, 0, 0));
        else
           // Application Workspace color is dark; therefore
           // set text color to white:
           SetTextColor (HDCChild, RGB (255, 255, 255));
        // draw text over existing background color:
        SetBkMode (HDCChild, TRANSPARENT);
        // supply brush for drawing background color:
        return ((BOOL)HBrushWorkSpace);

     case CTLCOLOR_DLG:    // redrawing dialog box itself
        // supply brush for drawing background color:
```

```
            return ((BOOL)HBrushWorkSpace);

        default:
            return (FALSE);
        }
    }


BOOL CMainDialog::OnDestroy ()
    {
    WrapUp ();   // save settings

    // delete the brush used for painting the window background:
    if (HBrushWorkSpace != 0)
        DeleteObject (HBrushWorkSpace);
    // close the help window in case it is still displayed:
    WinHelp (mHDialog, "TEMPLATE.HLP", HELP_QUIT, OL);
    // cause the main message loop to exit and the program to end:
    PostQuitMessage (0);
    return (TRUE);
    }


BOOL CMainDialog::OnInitDialog (HWND HWndFocus, LPARAM Data)
    {
    // read the setting of the "on top" option saved in the
    // program initialization file:
    OnTop = (int)GetPrivateProfileInt
        ("options",     // section of initialization file
        "ontop",        // item within this section
        O,              // default value
        "TEMPLATE.INI"); // name of initialization file
    if (OnTop)
        {
        // the "on top" option was selected; therefore, check the
        // menu command and assign the "on top" property to the
        // main window:
        CheckMenuItem (GetMenu (mHDialog), IDM_ONTOP, MF_CHECKED);
        SetWindowPos (mHDialog, HWND_TOPMOST, 0, 0, 0, 0,
                    SWP_NOMOVE | SWP_NOSIZE);
        }

    // create a brush for drawing the window background; the color
```

```
    // of the brush matches the color that the user assigned to
    // the Application Workspace element in the Control Panel:
    HBrushWorkSpace = CreateSolidBrush
       (GetSysColor (COLOR_APPWORKSPACE));

    return (TRUE);
    }

BOOL CMainDialog::OnSysColorChange ()
    {
    // because the user has selected a new Application Workspace
    // color, delete the old background brush and create a new
    // one that has the selected color:
    if (HBrushWorkSpace != 0)
       DeleteObject (HBrushWorkSpace);
    HBrushWorkSpace =
       CreateSolidBrush (GetSysColor (COLOR_APPWORKSPACE));

    return (TRUE);
    }

void CMainDialog::WrapUp ()
// performs final tasks that are always required when the program
// is terminated (even when the user is exiting Windows)
    {
    // save the current setting of the "on top" option:
    WritePrivateProfileString
       ("options",
        "ontop",
        OnTop ? "1" : "0",
        "TEMPLATE.INI");
    }

/////////////////////////////////////////////////////////////////
// CDemoDialog member function:                                  //
/////////////////////////////////////////////////////////////////

BOOL CDemoDialog::DialogProc (UINT Msg, WPARAM WParam,
                                LPARAM LParam)
    {
    switch (Msg)
```

```
    {
case WM_COMMAND:      // the user clicked a button, pressed
    switch (WParam) // Enter or Esc, or chose Close command
        {              // on system menu
        case IDCANCEL:
            // user clicked Cancel button, chose Close command
            // on system menu, or pressed Esc; therefore,
            // close the dialog box:
            EndDialog (mHDialog, IDCANCEL);
            return (TRUE);

        case IDC_HELP:
            // user clicked Help button or pressed F1; display
            // context-sensitive help information on the
            // current dialog box:
            WinHelp (MainDialog.mHDialog, "TEMPLATE.HLP",
                     HELP_CONTEXT, HELPDEMODLG);
            return (TRUE);

        case IDOK:
            // user clicked OK button or pressed Enter;
            // therefore, close the dialog box:
            EndDialog (mHDialog, IDOK);
            return (TRUE);

        default:
            return (TRUE);
        }

case WM_INITDIALOG:
    // dialog box has just been created (and not yet
    // displayed); display current time and date:
    {
    time_t Time = time (0);
    SetDlgItemText (mHDialog, IDC_TEXT,
                    asctime (localtime (&Time)));
    return (TRUE);
    }

default:  // all other messages sent to dialog box
    if (Msg == mHelpMessage)
```

```
                    // user pressed F1; therefore send the dialog box the
                    // same message that is sent when the Help button is
                    // clicked:
                    {
                    SendMessage (mHDialog, WM_COMMAND, IDC_HELP, OL);
                    return (TRUE);
                    }
                else
                    // have system perform default processing on all
                    // other messages:
                    return (FALSE);
            }
        }
```

Listing 2.4

```
;;;;;;;;;;;;;;;;;;;;;;;;;;;;;;;;;;;;;;;;;;;;;;;;;;;;;;;;;;;;;;;;;;;;;;;;
;                                                                      ;
; TEMPLATE.DEF:  Module-definition file for the TEMPLATE               ;
;                program.                                              ;
;                                                                      ;
;;;;;;;;;;;;;;;;;;;;;;;;;;;;;;;;;;;;;;;;;;;;;;;;;;;;;;;;;;;;;;;;;;;;;;;;


NAME TEMPLATE

DESCRIPTION  'Windows Utility Template'

EXETYPE WINDOWS

CODE PRELOAD MOVEABLE DISCARDABLE

DATA PRELOAD MOVEABLE MULTIPLE

HEAPSIZE 1024

STACKSIZE 10240
```

Listing 2.5

```
//////////////////////////////////////////////////////////////
//                                                            //
// RESOURCE.H:  Constant definitions for the TEMPLATE program //
//              resources (generated by Microsoft App Studio).//
//                                                            //
//////////////////////////////////////////////////////////////

//{{NO_DEPENDENCIES}}
// App Studio generated include file.
// Used by TEMPLATE.RC
//
#define IDC_HELP                        100
#define IDC_TEXT                        101
#define IDM_ABOUT                       1000
#define IDM_HELPHELP                    1001
#define IDM_HELPSEARCH                  1002
#define IDM_HELPCONTENTS                1003
#define IDM_SHOWDIALOG                  1004
#define IDM_ONTOP                       1005

// Next default values for new objects
//
#ifdef APSTUDIO_INVOKED
#ifndef APSTUDIO_READONLY_SYMBOLS

#define _APS_NEXT_RESOURCE_VALUE        101
#define _APS_NEXT_COMMAND_VALUE         1006
#define _APS_NEXT_CONTROL_VALUE         102
#define _APS_NEXT_SYMED_VALUE           101
#endif
#endif
```

Listing 2.6

```
//////////////////////////////////////////////////////////////////
//                                                                //
// TEMPLATE.RC:  Resource-definition file for the TEMPLATE        //
//                   program (generated by Microsoft App Studio). //
//                                                                //
//////////////////////////////////////////////////////////////////

//Microsoft App Studio generated resource script.
//
#include "resource.h"

#define APSTUDIO_READONLY_SYMBOLS
//////////////////////////////////////////////////////////////////
//
// Generated from the TEXTINCLUDE 2 resource.
//
#include "windows.h"


//////////////////////////////////////////////////////////////////
#undef APSTUDIO_READONLY_SYMBOLS


//////////////////////////////////////////////////////////////////
//
// Accelerator
//

TEMPLATEACCEL ACCELERATORS DISCARDABLE
BEGIN
    VK_F1,            IDM_HELPCONTENTS,         VIRTKEY,NOINVERT
END


//////////////////////////////////////////////////////////////////
//
// Dialog
//

MAINDLG DIALOG DISCARDABLE  14, 36, 122, 88
```

```
STYLE WS_MINIMIZEBOX | WS_POPUP | WS_VISIBLE | WS_CAPTION |
    WS_SYSMENU
CAPTION "Template"
MENU TemplateMenu
FONT 8, "MS Sans Serif"
BEGIN
    CTEXT           "Windows Utility Template",-1,0,12,122,14
    ICON            "TEMPLATEICON",-1,50,37,18,20
END

DEMODLG DIALOG DISCARDABLE  12, 24, 105, 87
STYLE DS_MODALFRAME | WS_POPUP | WS_VISIBLE | WS_CAPTION |
    WS_SYSMENU
CAPTION "Dialog"
FONT 8, "MS Sans Serif"
BEGIN
    DEFPUSHBUTTON   "OK",IDOK,7,50,39,14
    PUSHBUTTON      "Cancel",IDCANCEL,7,67,39,14
    CTEXT           "Modal Dialog Box Demo",-1,0,10,105,12
    PUSHBUTTON      "&Help",IDC_HELP,59,67,39,14
    CTEXT           "Static",IDC_TEXT,0,26,105,11
END

ABOUTDLG DIALOG DISCARDABLE  12, 24, 116, 100
STYLE DS_MODALFRAME | WS_POPUP | WS_VISIBLE | WS_CAPTION |
    WS_SYSMENU
CAPTION "About"
FONT 8, "MS Sans Serif"
BEGIN
    CTEXT           "Windows Utility Program Template",-1,0,10,
                    116,8
    CTEXT           "by Michael J. Young",-1,0,28,116,8
    ICON            "TemplateIcon",-1,48,48,18,20
    DEFPUSHBUTTON   "OK",IDOK,36,80,40,14
END

#ifdef APSTUDIO_INVOKED
/////////////////////////////////////////////////////////////
//
// TEXTINCLUDE
//
```

```
1 TEXTINCLUDE DISCARDABLE
BEGIN
    "resource.h\0"
END

2 TEXTINCLUDE DISCARDABLE
BEGIN
    "#include ""windows.h""\r\n"
    "\0"
END

3 TEXTINCLUDE DISCARDABLE
BEGIN
    "\r\n"
    "\0"
END


/////////////////////////////////////////////////////////////////
#endif    // APSTUDIO_INVOKED


/////////////////////////////////////////////////////////////////
//
// Icon
//

TEMPLATEICON           ICON    DISCARDABLE    "TEMPLATE.ICO"

/////////////////////////////////////////////////////////////////
//
// Menu
//

TEMPLATEMENU MENU DISCARDABLE
BEGIN
    POPUP "&Options"
    BEGIN
        MENUITEM "Always on &Top",              IDM_ONTOP
        MENUITEM "&Dialog...",                  IDM_SHOWDIALOG
    END
```

```
    POPUP "&Help"
    BEGIN
        MENUITEM "&Contents...\tF1",            IDM_HELPCONTENTS
        MENUITEM "&Search for Help On...",      IDM_HELPSEARCH
        MENUITEM "&How to Use Help...",         IDM_HELPHELP
        MENUITEM SEPARATOR
        MENUITEM "&About...",                   IDM_ABOUT
    END
END


#ifndef APSTUDIO_INVOKED
/////////////////////////////////////////////////////////////////////
//
// Generated from the TEXTINCLUDE 3 resource.
//


/////////////////////////////////////////////////////////////////////
#endif    // not APSTUDIO_INVOKED
```

The following sections will explain each of these listings. As in the other chapters in the book, the discussions focus on the key programming techniques, on general strategies, and on the reasons for the programming decisions that were made. You will find information on many of the programming details in the comments within the source files.

Note that the listings do *not* include some of the program source files. Specifically, they do not include the project files (TEMPLATE.IDE and TEMPLATE.MAK), the icon file (TEMPLATE.ICO), the files for creating the online help (HELP.RTF, HELP01.BMP, and TEMPLATE.HPJ), and the General Window Classes source files (WCLASSES.CPP and WCLASSES.H).

The project files are used for building the program, as explained in Chapter 1, in the section "Modifying the Programs." The creation and use of the icon file will be explained later in the chapter (in the section "Defining the Resources"). The source files for creating the online help will be described in the section "Creating the Online Help File." Finally, the source code for the General Windows Classes is printed and explained in the Appendix.

The Program Entry Function, WinMain

The program entry function, WinMain, is defined in the source code file TEMPLATE.CPP (Listing 2.2). This file begins by including the general program header file, TEMPLATE.H, which will be described later (in the section "The Window Code"). TEMPLATE.CPP then declares the global objects that are used in the program: App and MainDialog. App is an instance of the class CApplication, which is one of the General Windows Classes. Each program declares a single global instance of CApp, which serves primarily to store information on the current program instance.

MainDialog is an instance of the class CMainDialog. CMainDialog is *derived* from another of the General Windows Classes, CMLDialog, which is a general-purpose class designed for managing modeless dialog boxes. MainDialog is used specifically for creating and managing the main program window (as will be explained later, the main program window is a modeless dialog box).

NOTE

In general, a *modeless* dialog box is one that can be displayed while the main program window remains active and continues to process commands. A modeless dialog box can also serve as a main program window. In contrast, displaying a *modal* dialog box disables the main program window; the user must close the modal dialog box before the main window can resume processing commands.

Activating the Previous Program Instance

To simplify the operation of the utilities, the user is permitted to run only a single instance of a given utility at a time. To prevent the user from loading more than one instance, the WinMain function begins by testing the value of the parameter HInstPrevious. If HInstPrevious is zero, then no other instance of the program is currently running; in this case, WinMain proceeds to initialize the program. If HInstPrevious is nonzero, however, then an instance of the program is already running (HInstPrevious contains the handle of the previous instance); in this case, WinMain performs the following main steps:

1. It calls the Windows API function GetInstanceData to obtain the handle of the main window belonging to the previous instance. GetInstanceData allows a program instance to access the data belonging to another concurrent instance (each instance of a program has a separate data segment, and therefore program instances do not normally have access to each other's data).

2. It restores the main window of the previous instance to its normal size (in case it has been minimized) and activates this window. If the previous instance is currently displaying a dialog box, it also activates the dialog box.

3. It issues a return statement, thus terminating the new program instance.

NOTE

The book uses the term *Windows API function* or simply *API function* to indicate a function that belongs to the Windows Application Program Interface as well as to distinguish it from a function that is defined within the program or provided by the C++ run-time library.

As a result, if the user attempts to run a second instance of the program, rather than displaying an annoying error message or simply exiting, the program activates the window belonging to the previous instance before it exits, allowing the user to immediately begin working with the program.

Initializing the Application

WinMain next initializes the application object, App, by calling the CApplication member function Initialize. Initialize stores—within CApplication public data members—the information on the current program instance that is passed to WinMain. Because the data members are public and App is a global object, all parts of the program have access to this information (the GWC also uses some of this information internally).

WinMain then calls the CApplication::LoadAccel function, which loads the program's *accelerator table* and stores a handle to this table in the public data member CApplication::mHAccelTable. An accelerator table is a program resource that defines a set of shortcut keystrokes, normally used for activating menu commands. The TEMPLATE program accelerator table defines only a single keystroke, F1, which activates the Contents... command on the Help menu. You will learn how the table is defined in the section "Defining the Resources," and you will learn how the handle to the accelerator table is used to activate the accelerator keystroke in the section "The Main Message Loop."

N O T E

Throughout the book, the :: operator is used as a shorthand way of showing that a data item or function is a member of a particular class. For example, the expression CApplication::mHAccelTable is equivalent to "the mHAccelTable data member of the CApplication class", and CApplication:: LoadAccel is equivalent to "the LoadAccel member function of the CApplication class". Also, the terms instance of a class and object are used synonymously.

Creating the Main Window

WinMain now proceeds to set the program icon and to create the main program window by calling two member functions of the CMainDialog class: SetIcon and Create (these two functions are inherited from CMLDialog, which is described in the Appendix).

It sets the icon by passing the name of the icon resource to SetIcon:

```
if (!MainDialog.SetIcon ("TemplateIcon"))
   return (FALSE);
```

The icon name, TemplateIcon, was chosen when the icon was designed using the Microsoft App Studio, as described later in the chapter (in the section "Defining the Resources"). As a result of this function call, the specified icon will be displayed whenever the window managed by the MainDialog object is minimized.

WinMain creates the main window by passing the name of a dialog box template to Create:

```
if (!MainDialog.Create ("MainDlg"))
   return (FALSE);
```

The dialog box template, MainDlg, is a program resource that specifies the size, position, contents, and styles of the main program window. It was created and named using the interactive dialog box editor provided by the Microsoft App Studio, as will be explained in the section "Defining the Resources."

Many Windows programs create the main program window by calling either the CreateWindow or the CreateWindowEx API function, passing it the desired size, position, and styles of the window as parameters. This method is suitable for creating a typical sizable window that consists largely of an open area in which the program can display text and graphics.

All the utilities in this book (except the Screen Saver), however, call the Create function (inherited from CMLDialog) to create a modeless dialog box that is used as the main program window. (Because a modeless dialog box is a type of window, the terms *main window* and *main dialog box* are used synonymously in the book.) For a typical utility in this book, there are three important advantages to using a dialog box as the main window rather than creating a main window by calling `CreateWindow`:

- The main window of the utility has a fixed size and is filled with a collection of controls (such as buttons, text controls, and list boxes). Designing such a window is quite easy, using an interactive dialog box editor. (If the window were created with `CreateWindow`, each control would have to be created and positioned with a separate call to `CreateWindow`).

- When you display a dialog box, Windows automatically handles the special keystrokes that the user types, such as Tab and Shift+Tab for moving the focus from control to control, and Enter for activating the default push button.

- Windows automatically scales the size of the dialog box and all its controls according to the actual size of the font used to display text in the dialog box. Thus, the text always fits properly within the dialog box and within controls such as push buttons.

The Main Message Loop

`WinMain` now enters the main message loop, which is responsible for obtaining and dispatching messages; this loop continues running until the program is terminated. The essential features of the message loop are a call to the `GetMessage` API function and a call to the `DispatchMessage` API function:

```
while (GetMessage (&Msg, NULL, NULL, NULL))

    // other code ...

    {

    // other code ...

    DispatchMessage (&Msg);
    }
```

Whenever an important event occurs that affects the program window (for example, the user clicks the mouse in the window, or the window needs redrawing), Windows places a data structure known as a *message* into the program's message queue. The call to GetMessage extracts the next message from the queue, assigning the message data to the fields of the MSG structure passed as a parameter, Msg. GetMessage does not return until a message is available. The call to DispatchMessage causes Windows to call the *window procedure* belonging to the window, passing it the message data in Msg. The window procedure then processes the message, control returns from the call to DispatchMessage, and the loop continues.

In the TEMPLATE program, the window procedure is defined as a member function of the CMainDialog class and is named DialogProc; in the following sections, you will see how it is defined and how it processes each type of message. Invoking the window procedure to process a message is known as *sending a message to the window*. (Because DialogProc handles messages for a dialog box, it is more accurately termed a *dialog procedure*.)

When GetMessage extracts a message with the identifier WM_QUIT (each type of message has a unique identifier, which is part of the data assigned to the MSG structure), it returns 0, causing the message loop to exit and the program to terminate. Later, you will learn how the WM_QUIT message is placed in the queue to end the program.

Figure 2.4 illustrates the main message loop. In this diagram, notice that when the program calls GetMessage, other Windows programs are allowed to run (although Windows is a multitasking system, other programs are permitted to run only when an application yields control by calling a function such as GetMessage).

The message loop is actually a bit more complex than indicated in Figure 2.4 because it also contains three calls to API functions for filtering or translating certain messages. The complete message loop is as follows:

```
while (GetMessage (&Msg, NULL, NULL, NULL))
    if (!TranslateAccelerator (MainDialog.mHDialog,
                               App.mHAccelTable,
                               &Msg))
        if (!IsDialogMessage (MainDialog.mHDialog, &Msg))
            {
            TranslateMessage (&Msg);
            DispatchMessage (&Msg);
            }
```

The main message loop

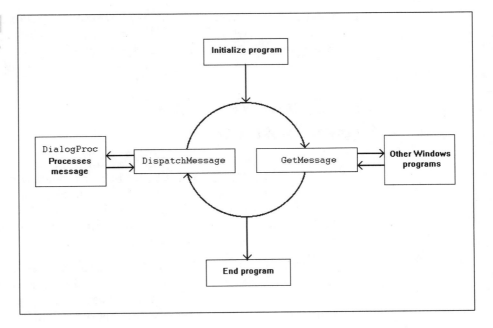

Briefly, `TranslateAccelerator` translates accelerator keystroke messages into the appropriate menu messages, `IsDialogMessage` processes special dialog box keystrokes such as Tab and Shift+Tab (as mentioned in the previous section), and `TranslateMessage` translates the messages sent when keys are pressed (virtual-key messages) into the appropriate character (`WM_CHAR`) messages, which indicate the ANSI value of the key that was pressed.

The Window Code

As explained, the `CMainDialog` class is used for managing the main program window; its `Create` member function is used to create the main window, using a dialog box template, and its `SetIcon` member function is used to assign an icon to the main window (both of these member functions are inherited from `CMLDialog`). In the following sections, you will learn how the `CMainDialog` class is defined and how its `DialogProc` function processes the messages that are sent to the window.

The Main Window Class Definition

`CMainDialog` is defined in TEMPLATE.H, the general program header file (Listing 2.1). TEMPLATE.H begins by including several header files that need to be included in all of the source code files: WCLASSES.H, which contains the definitions of the General Windows Classes, and RESOURCE.H, which defines constants used for identifying menu commands, buttons, and text controls.

`CMainDialog` is derived from the `CMLDialog` class, which belongs to the General Windows Classes and is designed for managing modeless dialog boxes. The program derives a new class (rather than simply using an instance of `CMLDialog`) because it needs several additional members; these members fall into the following two categories:

1. Data members for storing information on the window:

   `HBrushWorkSpace`

   and

   `OnTop`

   The purpose of these members will be described later.

2. Member functions for processing messages. These functions consist of

   `DialogProc`

   which is called whenever a message is sent to the window, plus a set of helper functions that are called by

   `DialogProc`

   to complete the processing of the messages. The implementation of these functions is described in the next section.

The Main Window Class Member Functions

The new member functions belonging to the CMainDialog class—that is, the functions that it does not inherit from its base class, CMLDialog—are implemented in the DIALOG.CPP source file (Listing 2.3). These functions are used for processing the messages that are sent to the main program window. The following sections describe the main tasks performed by these member functions in response to various messages.

Identifying the Messages

When the main program window is sent a message, CMainDialog::Dialog-Proc receives control (the mechanism that routes control to this function is explained in the Appendix). The first parameter passed to DialogProc, Msg, is an identifier for the particular type of message that is being sent. DialogProc tests Msg and branches to the appropriate routine to handle the message. For messages that require custom processing, DialogProc processes the message itself (or calls a helper function to do so); for all other types of messages, it simply returns FALSE so that Windows will provide default message processing. Returning FALSE from DialogProc tells Windows that the message has *not* been processed; Windows therefore provides default processing. Returning TRUE from DialogProc tells Windows that the message *has* been processed; Windows therefore provides no further processing.

Initializing

When Windows first creates the dialog box (just before it becomes visible), it sends it the WM_INITDIALOG message. In response to this message, DialogProc calls the CMainDialog::OnInitDialog function to perform initialization tasks.

The CMainDialog class maintains a flag, OnTop, which is set to 1 when the window is assigned the "always on top" property (which was described in the section "How to Run the Template Program") and is set to 0 when this property is not assigned. Whenever the program exits, it saves the current value of this flag in the program's private initialization file, TEM-PLATE.INI (which is contained in the Windows directory). OnInit-Dialog begins by calling the GetPrivateProfileInt API function to read this value from the initialization file, so that it can restore the option to its former setting (most of the utility programs save an entire group of settings in their initialization files). If the initialization file does not exist (that is, if the program is being run for the first time or the user has deleted the file), GetPrivateProfileInt returns the default value, 0, which it is passed as the third parameter.

If the retrieved value of OnTop is 1, OnInitDialog checks the Always on Top menu item and assigns the "always on top" style to the main window:

```
if (OnTop)
    {
    CheckMenuItem (GetMenu (mHDialog), IDM_ONTOP, MF_CHECKED);
    SetWindowPos (mHDialog, HWND_TOPMOST, 0, 0, 0, 0,
                    SWP_NOMOVE | SWP_NOSIZE);
    }
```

If the last parameter passed to the SetWindowPos API function includes the SWP_NOMOVE and SWP_NOSIZE flags, the function merely adjusts the style of the window according to the value of the second parameter (that is, it does *not* move or change the size of the window). The HWND_TOPMOST style causes the window (and any windows that it owns) to always appear on top of other windows, even when the window is inactive (unless the other window has also been assigned the HWND_TOPMOST style!).

When the user chooses the Always on Top menu option, Windows sends the main window a WM_COMMAND message, accompanied by the identifier of the menu command, IDM_ONTOP (an identifier is assigned to each menu command when the menu is designed in the resource editor). The Dialog-Proc function calls CMainDialog::OnCommand to process the message. On-Command (the IDM_ONTOP branch) toggles the value of the OnTop data member, checks or unchecks the menu command, and then calls the Set-WindowPos API function to adjust the window style according to the new value of OnTop:

```
case IDM_ONTOP:
    OnTop = !OnTop;

    CheckMenuItem (GetMenu (mHDialog), IDM_ONTOP,
```

```
                    OnTop ? MF_CHECKED : MF_UNCHECKED);

    SetWindowPos (mHDialog,
                  OnTop ? HWND_TOPMOST : HWND_NOTOPMOST,
                  0, 0, 0, 0, SWP_NOMOVE ¦ SWP_NOSIZE);
    return (FALSE);
```

Note that the HWND_NOTOPMOST style turns off the "always on top" feature, restoring the standard window behavior.

Just before the program terminates, the CMainDialog::WrapUp function (described later) calls the WritePrivateProfileString API function to *save* the current value of OnTop in the TEMPLATE.INI initialization file.

Finally, OnInitDialog creates the brush used for drawing the window background color. This step will be described later, in the section "Managing Colors."

Displaying the About Dialog Box

When the user chooses the About... command on the Help menu, Windows sends the window a WM_COMMAND message with the IDM_ABOUT identifier. To process this message, DialogProc calls CMainDialog::OnCommand. The IDM_ABOUT branch of OnCommand then displays the About dialog box (shown in Figure 2.3), using only two lines of code:

```
CMDialog MDialog;
MDialog.Create ("AboutDlg", mHDialog);
```

The first line creates an instance of the CMDialog class, which is one of the General Windows Classes and is designed for managing modal dialog boxes. The call to CMDialog::Create then displays the dialog box; the size, position, contents, and styles of the dialog box are specified by the dialog template AboutDlg, which was designed and named using App Studio. Because the dialog box is modal, control does not return from Create until the user closes the dialog box. The CMDialog class provides a default dialog procedure that closes the dialog box when the user clicks the OK button, presses the Enter or Esc key, or chooses the Close command on the system menu.

Displaying the Demo Dialog Box

When the user chooses the Dialog... command on the Options menu, the IDM_SHOWDIALOG branch of the OnCommand function displays the "Dialog" example modeless dialog (shown in Figure 2.2), as follows:

```
CDemoDialog DemoDialog;
DemoDialog.Create ("DemoDlg", mHDialog);
```

Notice that rather than simply using an instance of CMDialog to display the dialog box, OnCommand uses an instance of CDemoDialog, which is *derived* from CMDialog. The program derives a new class because the default message processing provided by CMDialog (which sufficed for the About dialog box) is *not* adequate. The CDemoDialog class definition is at the end of the program header file, TEMPLATE.H (Listing 2.1), and the implementation of its only member function, DialogProc, is at the end of DIALOG.CPP (Listing 2.3). CDemoDialog::DialogProc overrides the default dialog procedure provided by CMDialog (which is a virtual member function with the same name). CDemoDialog::DialogProc provides the following two features that are *not* provided by the default dialog procedure:

- It provides a handler for the WM_INITDIALOG message, which displays the current date and time in the dialog box.

- It provides message handlers for displaying context-sensitive help in response to the Help button and F1 key. The techniques will be explained in the section "Displaying Online Help."

Managing Colors

Rather than displaying its window using the default colors (black letters on a white background), the TEMPLATE program—together with the other utility programs in the book—uses the following color scheme:

- The window background is painted, using the color that is currently assigned to the Application Workspace element in the color scheme that the user sets through the Windows Control Panel.

- If the Application Workspace color is light, the text is displayed in black, and if the Application Workspace color is dark, the text is displayed in white. Thus, the text is always visible.

The code for implementing this color scheme is spread throughout the
DIALOG.CPP source file (Listing 2.3). First, the CMainDialog::OnInit-
Dialog function assigns a handle to a *brush* for drawing the background
color to the data member CMainDialog::HBrushWorkSpace (a brush is a
Windows data item that stores a color that is used for painting areas):

```
HBrushWorkSpace = CreateSolidBrush
   (GetSysColor (COLOR_APPWORKSPACE));
```

Then, whenever the main window or one of its controls is about to paint
itself, it sends the window a WM_CTLCOLOR message, which allows the program to set the background color and other attributes that will be used
for drawing the window or control. CMainDialog provides a function for
handling this message, OnCtlColor, which performs the following primary
tasks:

- It calls the API function SetTextColor to set the text color to
  black or white, depending upon the relative brightness of the current Application Workspace color.

- It passes the flag TRANSPARENT to the API function SetBkMode,
  which causes Windows to draw the text directly on top of the existing background color, without filling in the current text background color around the letters.

- It returns the brush handle stored in HBrushWorkSpace, which
  causes Windows to draw the dialog box background, using the
  color that is associated with this brush.

Also, if the user *changes* the color scheme through the Control Panel while
the program is running, Windows sends a WM_SYSCOLORCHANGE message.
The function that processes this message, CMainDialog::OnSysColor-
Change, deletes the old brush and then creates a new brush that matches
the newly set Application Workspace color:

```
if (HBrushWorkSpace != 0)
   DeleteObject (HBrushWorkSpace);
HBrushWorkSpace =
   CreateSolidBrush (GetSysColor (COLOR_APPWORKSPACE));
```

Finally, before the program terminates, the `CMainDialog::OnDestroy` function (described in the section "Terminating the Application") deletes the brush:

```
if (HBrushWorkSpace != 0)
   DeleteObject (HBrushWorkSpace);
```

The brush is deleted before the program exits to release the resources that it consumes; Windows does *not* automatically release these resources on program exit.

Displaying Online Help

The TEMPLATE program demonstrates the two ways that the utility programs in this book display online help; namely:

- When the main window is active, the user can choose one of the topics on the Help menu to view the desired help topic (the F1 key is a shortcut for choosing the Contents... command).

- When the "Dialog" dialog box is displayed, the user can click the Help button or press F1 to view context-sensitive help (that is, the program immediately displays the help topic that describes the opened dialog box).

Processing the Help Menu Commands When the user chooses one of the commands on the Help menu (other than About...), the `CMainDialog::OnCommand` function displays the online help file by calling the API function `WinHelp`. `WinHelp` loads the Windows Help program (WINHELP.EXE)—if is not already running—and causes the Help program to display the help file and topic specified by the parameters the program passes to `WinHelp`.

In response to the Contents... command or the F1 accelerator key, `OnCommand` passes `WinHelp` the flag `HELP_CONTENTS`,

```
case IDM_HELPCONTENTS:
   WinHelp (mHDialog, "TEMPLATE.HLP", HELP_CONTENTS, OL);
   return (TRUE);
```

which causes it to display the "Contents" topic. This topic lists all other available topics and allows the user to jump to any of these topics. (The "Contents" topic is designated when the help text is created.)

In response to the Search for Help On... command, OnCommand passes WinHelp the flag HELP_PARTIALKEY and assigns an empty string to the fourth parameter,

```
case IDM_HELPSEARCH:
    WinHelp (mHDialog, "TEMPLATE.HLP", HELP_PARTIALKEY,
            (DWORD)(LPCSTR)"");
    return (TRUE);
```

which causes WinHelp to display the Search dialog box. This dialog box permits the user to find topics based upon key words. (The key words are specified when the help text is created.)

Finally, when the user chooses the How to Use Help... command on the Help menu, OnCommand passes WinHelp the flag HELP_HELPONHELP,

```
case IDM_HELPHELP:
    WinHelp (mHDialog, "TEMPLATE.HLP", HELP_HELPONHELP, OL);
    return (TRUE);
```

which causes it to display the standard "How to Use Help" help file that is provided by Windows.

In the section "Creating the Online Help File" you will learn how to create a help file and how to designate individual topics within this file.

Displaying Context-Sensitive Help When the user clicks the Help button in the "Demo" dialog box, the CDemoDialog::DialogProc function passes WinHelp the flag HELP_CONTEXT, which causes it to display the specific help topic that is identified by the fourth parameter, HELPDEMODLG:

```
case IDC_HELP:
    WinHelp (MainDialog.mHDialog, "TEMPLATE.HLP",
            HELP_CONTEXT, HELPDEMODLG);
    return (TRUE);
```

(IDC_HELP is the identifier of the Help button, which was assigned when the dialog box was designed in App Studio.) The constant HELPDEMODLG (which is defined in TEMPLATE.H and equals 100) contains the identifier of the help topic that describes the dialog box; this identifier was assigned to the topic when the help file was created.

When the user presses the F1 key while the "Dialog" dialog box is open, the dialog box receives a message that has the identifier stored in the `CMDialog::mHelpMessage` data member. (While the dialog box is displayed, the F1 key is *not* processed as an accelerator key.) When `CDemoDialog::OnCommand` receives this message, it calls the API function `SendMessage` to send itself the message that is normally sent when the user clicks the Help button, thus causing the context-sensitive help to be displayed:

```
default:
   if (Msg == mHelpMessage)
      {
      SendMessage (mHDialog, WM_COMMAND, IDC_HELP, OL);
      return (TRUE);
      }
   else
      return (FALSE);
```

The mechanism that sends the `mHelpMessage` message in response to the F1 key is explained in the Appendix.

Closing the Help Program   Once a program has loaded Windows help, the Help program normally remains running until the user closes it. To avoid leaving the Help program running after the TEMPLATE program ends, the `CMainDialog::OnDestroy` function (described in the next section) passes `WinHelp` the flag `HELP_QUIT`,

```
WinHelp (mHDialog, "TEMPLATE.HLP", HELP_QUIT, OL);
```

which causes it to terminate the Help program, provided that no other programs are using it. (If the user never displayed help or has already ended the Help program, this function call is unnecessary but harmless.)

Terminating the Application

The TEMPLATE program is terminated normally in one of two ways: first, when the user chooses the Close command on the system menu (or double-clicks the system menu) and, second, when the user terminates Windows itself.

Closing the Application When the user chooses the Close command on the system menu or double-clicks the system menu, Windows sends the main window a WM_CLOSE message. In response to this message, the CMainDialog::DialogProc function calls the CMLDialog::Destroy function to destroy the main window:

```
case WM_CLOSE:
    Destroy ();
    return (TRUE);
```

When the main window is destroyed, Windows sends it a WM_DESTROY message. In response to this message, DialogProc calls CMainDialog::OnDestroy, which performs the following final cleanup tasks:

- It calls CMainDialog::Wrapup to save the current value of the OnTop data member in the initialization file.
- It deletes the brush used to paint the window background color.
- It closes the Windows Help program.
- It calls the API function PostQuitMessage.

The first three tasks were already discussed. The fourth task, calling PostQuitMessage, places the WM_QUIT message in the program's message queue. When GetMessage extracts this message from the queue, it returns 0, which causes the main message loop (described previously) to exit and the program to terminate.

Terminating Windows When the user terminates the Windows session, Windows sends the main window of each running program the WM_END-SESSION message, with the WParam parameter set to TRUE. To process this message, the DialogProc function calls WrapUp to save the value of the OnTop data member.

The two ways of terminating the TEMPLATE program are illustrated in Figure 2.5. Notice that the WrapUp function is called regardless of the way that the program is terminated. In the TEMPLATE program and in the other utilities in the book, WrapUp performs only the essential tasks that must always be completed before the program exits (it does not include such tasks as deleting brushes or closing the Help program, which do *not* need to be performed if the Windows session is ending).

FIGURE 2.5

The two ways of terminating the TEMPLATE program

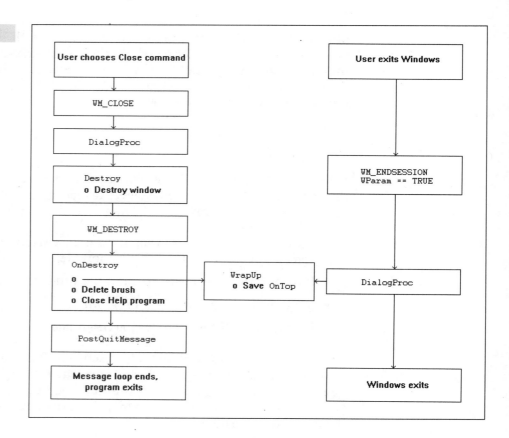

Defining the Resources

The following are the resources used by the TEMPLATE program:

- The templates for creating the three dialog boxes displayed by the program: the main window, the "Dialog" dialog box, and the About dialog box
- The menu that is displayed in the main window
- The accelerator table
- The program icon

The resources are defined within the text file TEMPLATE.RC, which is known as the resource-definition file. When the program is built, this file is processed by the Microsoft Resource Compiler, and the resulting resource data is stored within a special, read-only segment within the executable file. You do not need to perform any special steps to prepare the resource data; the integrated environment performs all steps automatically under the direction of the project file (provided that the resource-definition file is included in the list of source files in the project). Each resource has an identifier that allows the program to load it from the resource segment at run time.

Although you could manually type the definitions into the resource-definition file, following the syntax explained in the Resource Compiler documentation, it is *much* easier to define the resources, using an interactive editor such as the Microsoft App Studio or the Borland Resource Workshop.

The resources for the TEMPLATE program were designed using the Microsoft App Studio. App Studio generated the two source files TEMPLATE.RC (Listing 2.6) and RESOURCE.H (Listing 2.5). TEMPLATE.RC contains the resource definitions and RESOURCE.H defines the constants used to identify the individual resource elements, such as the specific menu commands and buttons.

All of the resources except the program icon are fully defined within the resource-definition file. The data for the program icon (which is binary) is stored in a separate file, TEMPLATE.ICO (also generated by App Studio). The resource-definition file contains an ICON statement that causes the Resource Compiler to include the data from TEMPLATE.ICO within the resource segment. The program icon, as it appears in the App Studio icon editor, is shown in Figure 2.6.

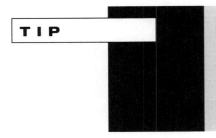

T I P

To view the appearance of the other resources within the resource editor, and to ascertain the properties assigned to each resource element, you can load the resource-definition file provided on the companion disk, TEMPLATE.RC, into your resource editor.

The TEMPLATE program icon, as it appears in the Microsoft App Studio icon editor

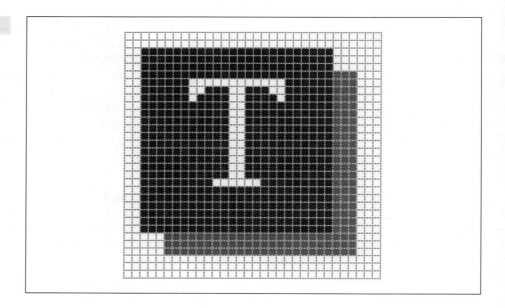

The Module-Definition File

The TEMPLATE module-definition file, TEMPLATE.DEF (given in Listing 2.4), defines several properties of the program's executable file. The module-definition file is read by the linker when it prepares the executable file. Table 2.2 briefly describes each of the statements contained in TEMPLATE.DEF. Note that the module-definition files for all of the utilities are almost identical (only the NAME and DESCRIPTION statements differ).

TABLE 2.2: Statements Used in the TEMPLATE program's Module-Definition File, TEMPLATE.DEF

STATEMENT	PURPOSE
NAME	Specifies the name of the executable program (without the .EXE file extension).
DESCRIPTION	Inserts the specified text directly into the executable file. You can use this statement, for example, to insert a program description, a version number, or a copyright notice.
EXETYPE	Indicates the type of the executable file header. All programs written for Windows must include the statement EXETYPE WINDOWS.
CODE	Defines the attributes of the program code segment. PRELOAD causes the code segment to be loaded when the program is first run. MOVEABLE allows the code segment to be moved—if necessary—to compact memory. DISCARDABLE allows the system to discard the code segment when it is not being used (the segment can then be reloaded when it is required).
DATA	Defines the attributes of the program data segment. PRELOAD and MOVEABLE have the same effects as for the CODE statement. MULTIPLE causes each program instance to have a separate data segment.
HEAPSIZE	Specifies the size of the program heap in bytes.
STACKSIZE	Specifies the size of the program stack in bytes.

Creating the Online Help File

The help file for the TEMPLATE program, TEMPLATE.HLP, was created using the Microsoft Help Compiler. The following are the main steps for creating an online help file such as TEMPLATE.HLP:

- Enter the help text (along with special commands and labels, which will be described later) into a word processor and save the document in Rich Text Format (the Rich Text Format file for the TEMPLATE program is named HELP.RTF).

- Create any drawings you want to display in the online help, using a bitmap editor such as Microsoft Paintbrush (the TEMPLATE online help uses an example drawing stored in HELP01.BMP).

- In a text editor, create a help project file that tells the Help Compiler how to create the help file, and save it in a file with the .HPJ extension (the project file for the TEMPLATE help file is TEMPLATE.HPJ).

- Run the Help Compiler, passing it the name of the project file.

These steps (as performed for creating the TEMPLATE.HLP help file) are illustrated in Figure 2.7, and are explained in more detail in the

FIGURE 2.7

Preparing the TEMPLATE.HLP help file for the TEMPLATE program

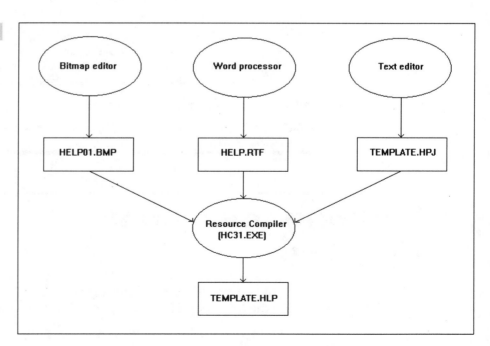

following sections. Note that the TEMPLATE program uses only a small portion of the features provided by the Windows 3.1 Help program. You can use the information presented in this chapter as a quick introduction to designing simple help files; for more information, see the Windows Software Development Kit documentation on creating online help and on using the Help Compiler.

Entering the Help Text

You must enter the help text into a word processor (such as Microsoft Word for Windows) that is capable of saving documents in Rich Text Format. The text in a help file is divided into *topics*; when the file is displayed, the user views only a single topic at a time, but can readily jump from topic to topic.

Individual topics are separated within the help text by page breaks. Each topic should be labeled by inserting a series of footnotes at the beginning of the topic's text. The following are three different types of footnotes you can insert:

- If the footnote uses the # character as the footnote mark, the footnote text indicates the topic's *context string*, which is used to identify the topic. Every topic must have a context string.

- If the footnote uses the $ character as the footnote mark, the footnote text specifies the topic's title. Topic titles are displayed when the user employs the Help program's Search dialog box to find a particular topic.

- If the footnote uses the K character as the footnote mark, the footnote text provides one or more key words, which the user can employ when finding topics in the Search dialog box. Individual key words are separated in the footnote text by semicolons.

You can also create a link that allows the user to jump from one topic to another. To create a link, you mark a sequence of characters by assigning them the double-underlined character format. Immediately following these characters, you type a context string, using hidden text. When the text is displayed by the Help program, the double-underlined text is printed in green single-underlined characters, and the hidden text (the context string) is invisible. If the user clicks on the green text, the Help program immediately switches to the topic identified by the context string.

Figure 2.8 shows the first screen of the TEMPLATE help text entered into Microsoft Word for Windows, and illustrates all of the features discussed so far in this section.

To insert a drawing in bitmap format, you can use the bmc statement, as follows:

```
{bmc HELP01.BMP}
```

This statement inserts the bitmap contained in the file HELP01.BMP; the Help program will display the bitmap centered within the window.

FIGURE 2.8

The first screen of the TEMPLATE help text entered into Microsoft Word for Windows

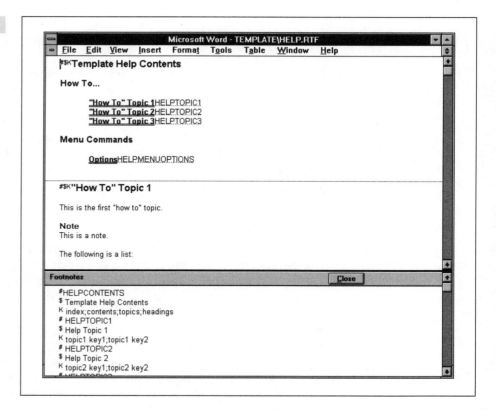

You can use TEMPLATE.RTF as a template for creating simple help files for your own programs.

Creating the Project File

The following are the contents of the file TEMPLATE.HPJ, which is the project file for creating the TEMPLATE program help file:

```
[OPTIONS]
CONTENTS=HELPCONTENTS
TITLE=Template

[FILES]
HELP.RTF

[MAP]
HELPDEMODLG 100

[BITMAPS]
HELP01.BMP
```

The help project file is a script that tells the Help Compiler how to prepare the online help file. The project file is divided into sections.

In the [OPTIONS] section, the CONTENTS statement specifies the context string of the help topic that displays the help file contents. When the program passes WinHelp the flag HELP_CONTENTS, the Help program shows this topic. In the TEMPLATE program, the HELPCONTENTS context string is assigned to the first topic in the help file (shown in Figure 2.8) and this context string is specified in the CONTENTS statement; as a result, when the program passes the HELP_CONTENTS flag to WinHelp, the Help program displays the first topic.

The TITLE statement in the [CONTENTS] section specifies the title that is displayed in the Help program window when the help file is viewed.

The [FILES] section lists the names of the Rich Text Format files that contain the help text. For the TEMPLATE program, there is only one such file, HELP.RTF.

The [MAP] section assigns numeric values to one or more of the context strings. Assigning a numeric value to a topic's context string allows the program to display that topic by passing the numeric value to WinHelp. The TEMPLATE program displays context-sensitive help, using the following sequence of assignments:

- In the help text, the context string HELPDEMODLG is assigned to the topic describing the "Dialog" dialog box.

- In the help project file, the context string HELPDEMODLG is given a numeric value of 100.

- In the TEMPLATE.H header file, the symbolic constant HELP-DEMODLG is also assigned the value 100.

- When the user requests help while the dialog box is open, the program displays context-sensitive help by passing the symbolic constant HELPDEMODLG to WinHelp:

```
WinHelp (MainDialog.mHDialog, "TEMPLATE.HLP",
    HELP_CONTEXT, HELPDEMODLG);
```

(Having the symbolic constant match the context string for a topic is not required, but simply makes it easier to write the help code.)

Finally, the [BITMAPS] section lists the names of any bitmap files that are to be inserted into the help text. The TEMPLATE program includes only one bitmap file, HELP01.BMP, by means of the bmc statement described previously.

NOTE You can specify many additional features in a help project file. For information on these features, see the documentation on the Microsoft Help Compiler.

Running the Help Compiler

The Help Compiler is an MS-DOS program named HC31.EXE. To prepare the help file, you run the Help Compiler from the MS-DOS prompt, passing the name of the help project file on the command line. The following is the command for preparing the help file for the TEMPLATE program:

```
HC31 TEMPLATE.HPJ
```

This command causes the Help Compiler to generate the help file TEMPLATE.HLP.

PART TWO

Windows Desktop Utilities

This part of the book presents a set of utilities designed to enhance your Windows desktop and to help you manage your Windows programs.

Chapter 3 presents a Resource Viewer, which monitors important Windows resources and automatically warns you if a given resource drops to a dangerously low level. This utility also allows you to increase the amount of memory available to your programs by compacting memory or by releasing the contents of the Clipboard.

The Setup Saver given in Chapter 4 allows you to save and restore desktop setups. A setup stores the state of an entire collection of Windows programs; when you restore it, each program is run and each window is assigned its original size and position. This utility also allows you to automatically save and restore the set of programs you are using whenever you quit and restart Windows.

Chapter 5 provides a Task Scheduler, which enables you to run a program (or a set of programs, using the Setup Saver) at a predesignated time. You can also have the utility run a Windows Recorder macro after it runs the program, so that you can fully automate a simple or complex task, such as performing a backup, printing a series of files, or downloading information from an online service.

Finally, Chapter 6 presents a Screen Saver that you can add to your collection. When this screen saver is activated, it turns your Windows screen into an animated sliding-tile puzzle. You can also use the program code to create your own custom screen savers.

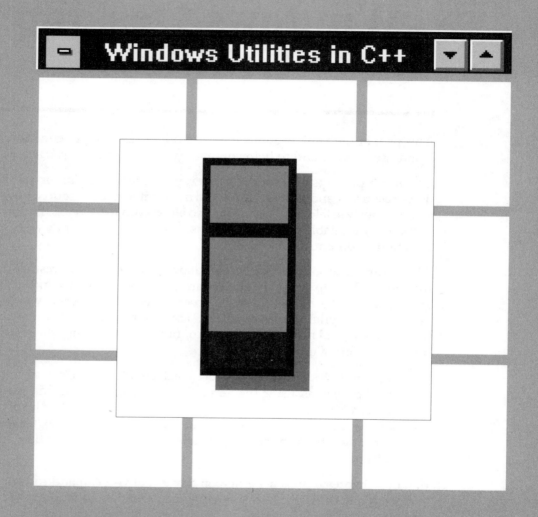

CHAPTER

3

Resource Viewer

THE Resource Viewer presented in this chapter monitors the most important resources that can be consumed during a Windows session: USER and GDI system resources, global memory, and disk space. The utility displays the percent and amount of each resource that is free; it also warns you when the free percent of a resource has dropped below the "red-line" level (which you can adjust). Additionally, you can use the Resource Viewer to increase the amount of free memory, either by compacting global memory or by releasing the contents of the Clipboard.

The source code for the Resource Viewer illustrates many Windows programming techniques, including using a Windows timer, drawing within a normal or minimized program window, compacting memory, and detecting mouse clicks within specific areas of the window. The program also shows how to obtain information on system resources by calling Windows API functions, by calling C++ run-time library functions, and by reading information stored in the computer's permanent RAM (that is, the CMOS RAM).

How to Use the Resource Viewer

This section explains how to use each of the features of the Resource Viewer. Note that most of this information is also included in the online help provided with the program.

Chapter 1 described how to install the utilities from the companion disk, how to run them, and how to access the online help.

The Resources

The Resource Viewer monitors four different Windows resources: USER resources, GDI resources, global memory, and disk space.

USER and GDI System Resources

The term *USER resources* refers to the heap space available to the Windows USER module (that is, USER.EXE, which is one of the core files containing the Windows system code). Windows uses this memory area to store data for program windows and menus. The percent of free USER resources decreases as programs create new windows and menus.

The term *GDI resources* refers to the heap space available to the Windows GDI module (that is, GDI.EXE, which is another of the Windows core files; it contains the code that supports the Windows graphics device interface). This area is used to store data for *GDI objects* (fonts, brushes, pens, bitmaps, and regions) as well as device context handles. The percent of free GDI resources decreases as programs create GDI objects and obtain device context handles for displaying text or graphics on devices.

It is important to monitor the percent of free USER and GDI resources; if one or both of these resources falls to a low level, you may get an unexpected out-of-memory error message, or Windows programs may fail in various ways without warning. Note that the total amount of space available for these resources is fixed under a particular version of Windows; the space does *not* depend upon the amount of memory installed in the machine. Therefore, even if you have a large amount of memory, the number of programs you can run may be limited by the available USER and GDI resources.

NOTE

The *system resources* percent that Windows reports when you choose the About command from the Program Manager or the File Manager is either the percent of free USER resources or the percent of free GDI resources, whichever is currently lower.

Global Memory

Global memory is the total amount of memory in your system. *Free* global memory is the amount of memory currently available for loading Windows and DOS applications and for providing global memory allocations that are requested by Windows programs.

If you are running Windows in Standard mode, the total global memory reported by the Resource Viewer is the total amount of physical memory—Conventional plus Extended—that is installed in your machine, and the free global memory is the amount of physical memory that is still available.

If, however, you are running Windows in Enhanced mode, the total global memory reported by the Resource Viewer is the total size of the virtual memory space provided by the Windows virtual memory manager (VMM), and the free global memory is the amount of virtual memory that is still available. By using a swap file (temporary or permanent) the virtual memory manager is able to create an effective memory space that is considerably larger than the amount of physical memory installed in your machine.

NOTE

The *memory* amount that Windows reports when you choose the About command in the Windows Program Manager or File Manager is the same as the amount of free global memory reported by the Resource Viewer.

Disk Space

Finally, the Resource Viewer reports the total amount of space, as well as the amount of free space, on any disk (floppy or hard) that is installed in your machine. As you will see later, you can select the disk that is monitored.

Viewing the Resources

The Resource Viewer provides three different ways to view the resources that it keeps track of. First, the main program window, shown in Figure 3.1, provides a bar chart indicating the free percent of each resource. The percent of the resource that is currently free is printed above each bar. Also, the position of the horizontal black line within the bar visually indicates the free percent: if the line is at the top, the resource is 100% free, and if it is at the bottom, the resource is completely exhausted.

FIGURE 3.1

The Resource Viewer
main program window

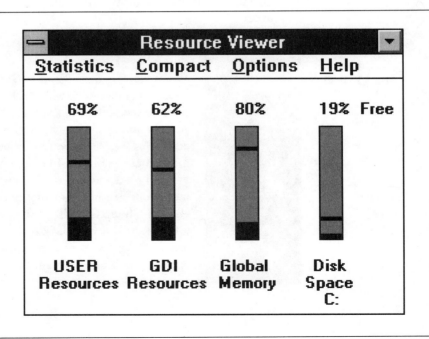

If, as the resource is depleted, the black line descends into the red zone at the bottom of the bar, the program beeps and displays a warning message (as you will see later, you can adjust the height of the red zone). The Resource Viewer will generate the warning even if it is *not* the active program and even if it has been reduced to an icon. After the warning appears, you can take action to replenish the depleted resource before problems arise. If you are out of USER or GDI system resources or system memory, you might close one or more applications. If you are out of global memory, you might close applications or attempt to release memory using the commands on the Resource Viewer's Compact menu (described later, in the section "Freeing Memory"). If you are out of disk space, you might back up and delete unnecessary files.

As a second method of viewing resources, you can view more detailed information on a particular resource by choosing one of the commands on the Statistics menu, or by clicking on one of the bars displayed in the main window. The Statistics dialog box will appear, showing the total amount of the resource, the amount free, the amount used, as well as the percents free and used. Figure 3.2 shows the Statistics dialog box for the disk space resource.

NOTE

When viewing the USER and GDI resources, you should pay more attention to the free *percents* than the free amounts. The Resource Viewer obtains the percent values directly from Windows; it then calculates the free amounts by assuming that the total amount of free GDI resources is 64KB (since the GDI module uses a single heap and the maximum size of a memory segment that can contain a heap is 64KB), and it assumes that the total amount of free USER resources is 128KB (since the USER module uses two heaps, one for program windows and one for menus).

The Statistics dialog box for the disk space resource

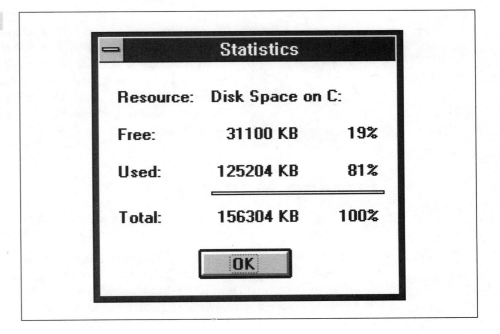

Third, when you minimize the Resource Viewer window, the program icon displays a bar for one of the resources. You can designate the particular resource that is shown by choosing one of the items on the Icon Shows: submenu of the Options menu. For instance, the icon shown below displays the free global memory.

Global Memory

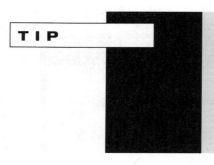

TIP

If you choose the Always on Top feature on the Options menu, the program icon will remain visible even if another window is placed over it. You can then easily monitor the level of a particular resource. Of course, you can move the icon to whatever position on the screen suits your needs at the moment.

Freeing Memory

You might be able to increase the amount of free global memory by choosing one of the commands on the Compact menu.

If you choose the Compact Memory command, Windows will rearrange global memory to provide larger blocks of contiguous memory and at the same time it will eliminate discardable memory segments. This command is especially useful when running Windows in Standard mode, which does not provide a large virtual memory space.

You can choose the Free Clipboard command to free the contents of the Clipboard, thereby freeing global memory (Clipboard data items are stored in global memory segments). If the Clipboard contains data when you choose this command, the program asks you to confirm that you want to erase the data.

Setting Options

You can set various program options by choosing commands on the Options menu. The option settings are saved in the program initialization file, and they remain in effect even after you quit and restart the program.

The Set Red Lines... command allows you to specify the free percent of each resource that will cause the Resource Viewer to issue a warning; see Figure 3.3. For example, if you set the red-line level for global memory to 15%, the program will warn you when the amount of free global memory first goes below 15%; also, the red zone will fill the bottom 15% of the bar for the global memory resource. If you assign a negative red-line

FIGURE 3.3

The Set Red Lines
dialog box

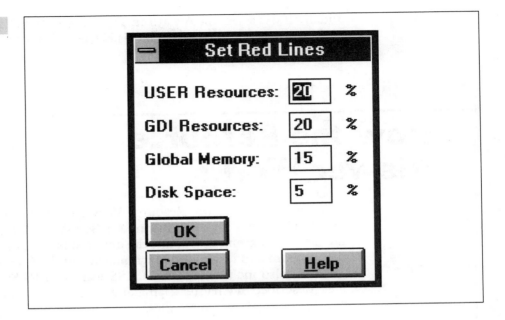

value, the Resource Viewer will *not* issue a warning (even if the resource level goes to 0%), and the red zone will be removed from the bar.

The Select Disk... command allows you to choose the disk drive that is to be monitored. You can select any of the drives—floppy or hard—that are installed on your system.

By choosing the Set Update Frequency... command, you can specify the number of seconds that elapse between each time the Resource Viewer checks the resources and updates the bar chart. You may enter a value between 1 second and 65 seconds. Specifying a small duration causes the Resource Viewer to monitor the resources more closely. Specifying a large duration reduces the program overhead. If you are monitoring disk space on a floppy disk, you will probably want to enter a large value (up to 65 seconds), since the program spins the disk each time it checks for free space.

You can specify the resource that is displayed within the program icon by choosing one of the items on the Icon Shows: submenu. If you choose the USER/GDI Resources item, the icon will display the USER *or* the GDI resource level, whichever is currently lower.

Finally, if you select the Always on Top menu option, the Resource Viewer main window or icon will remain visible, even if another window is placed over it.

How the Resource Viewer Works

The source code for the Resource Viewer program, RESVIEW, is given in Listings 3.1 through 3.7. Listing 3.1 (RESVIEW.H) is the main header file for the program; it contains the definitions of all of the classes used in the program and it is included within each of the C++ source files. RESVIEW.H also includes the WCLASSES.H and RESOURCE.H header files (described in Chapter 2), making the definitions in these two files accessible to all of the source files.

Listing 3.2 (RESVIEW.CPP) contains the C++ source code for the program entry function, WinMain, as well as the declarations for several global program objects (App and MainDialog). Listing 3.3 (MAINDLG.CPP) defines the member functions belonging to the class that manages the main window (CMainDialog), and Listing 3.4 (MODALDLG.CPP) defines the member functions for the classes that manage the modal dialog boxes. Listing 3.5 (RESVIEW.DEF) is the program module-definition file (explained in Chapter 2).

Finally, Listing 3.6 (RESOURCE.H) contains the constant definitions for the program resources, and Listing 3.7 (RESVIEW.RC) defines all of the program resources. Both of these files were generated by the Microsoft App Studio program, as explained in Chapter 2.

Figure 3.4 shows the program icon as it appears within the Microsoft App Studio, which was used to design the icon. Note that the project files required to build the program (RESVIEW.MAK for Microsoft Visual C++, and RESVIEW.IDE for Borland C++) are provided on the companion disk.

FIGURE 3.4

The RESVIEW program
icon, as it appears in
the App Studio

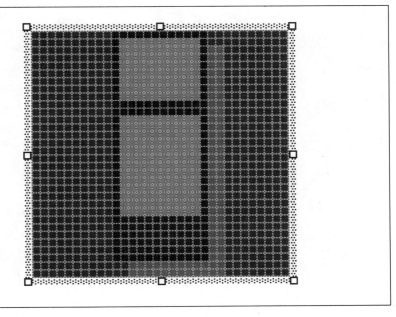

NOTE

The RESVIEW program uses a function (`MemManInfo`) belonging to the Windows TOOLHELP library. Accordingly, when the Microsoft Visual C++ project file (RESVIEW.MAK) was prepared, the file TOOLHELP was added to the list of Windows libraries linked to the program (this list is accessed by choosing the Project... command on the Visual Workbench Options menu, clicking the Linker... button, and selecting the Windows Libraries category). The TOOLHELP library is automatically included in a Borland C++ project. Also, the TOOLHELP.H header file is included in the source file that calls the `MemManInfo` function (MAINDLG.CPP).

Listing 3.1

```
////////////////////////////////////////////////////////////////
//                                                              //
// RESVIEW.H:  Header file for the RESVIEW program.             //
//                                                              //
////////////////////////////////////////////////////////////////

#include "..\wclasses\wclasses.h"
#include "resource.h"

// constants for help topics:
#define HELPSETREDDLG 100
#define HELPDISKDLG    101
#define HELPUPDATEDLG 102


////////////////////////////////////////////////////////////////
// main dialog box class definition:                            //
////////////////////////////////////////////////////////////////

class CMainDialog : public CMLDialog
{
    HBRUSH HBrushWorkSpace;
    int IconRes;
    int OnTop;
    RECT RectDisk;
    RECT RectGdi;
    RECT RectGlobal;
    RECT RectUser;

    virtual BOOL DialogProc (UINT Msg, WPARAM WParam,
                             LPARAM LParam);
    BOOL OnCommand (int IDItem, HWND HWndCtl, WORD NotifyCode);
    BOOL OnCtlColor (HDC HDCChild, HWND HWndChild, int CtlType);
    BOOL OnDestroy ();
    BOOL OnInitDialog (HWND HWndFocus, LPARAM Data);
    BOOL OnLButtonDown (int XPos, int YPos);
    BOOL OnPaint ();
    BOOL OnSize (int SizeType);
    BOOL OnSysColorChange ();
    BOOL OnTimer ();
```

```
        void WrapUp ();

public:
    CMainDialog ();
    char Disk [2];
    unsigned long FreeDisk;
    unsigned long FreeGlobal;
    int PercDisk;
    int PercGdi;
    int PercGlobal;
    int PercUser;
    int RedDisk;
    int RedGdi;
    int RedGlobal;
    int RedUser;
    UINT TimeOut;
    unsigned long TotalDisk;
    unsigned long TotalGlobal;

};

//////////////////////////////////////////////////////////////////
// 'Statistics' dialog box class definition:                     //
//////////////////////////////////////////////////////////////////

class CStatDialog : public CMDialog
{
    virtual BOOL DialogProc (UINT Msg, WPARAM WParam,
                             LPARAM LParam);

public:
    int ResourceType;
};

//////////////////////////////////////////////////////////////////
// 'Set Red Lines' dialog box class definition:                  //
//////////////////////////////////////////////////////////////////

class CRedLineDialog : public CMDialog
{
    virtual BOOL DialogProc (UINT Msg, WPARAM WParam,
```

```
                                           LPARAM LParam);
};


/////////////////////////////////////////////////////////////////
// 'Select Disk' dialog box class definition:                   //
/////////////////////////////////////////////////////////////////

class CSetDiskDialog : public CMDialog
{
   virtual BOOL DialogProc (UINT Msg, WPARAM WParam,
                                   LPARAM LParam);
};


/////////////////////////////////////////////////////////////////
// 'Set Update Frequency' dialog box class definition:          //
/////////////////////////////////////////////////////////////////

class CUpdateDialog : public CMDialog
{
   virtual BOOL DialogProc (UINT Msg, WPARAM WParam,
                                   LPARAM LParam);
};
```

Listing 3.2

```
/////////////////////////////////////////////////////////////////
//                                                             //
// RESVIEW.CPP:  Global object declarations and program entry  //
//               point for the RESVIEW program.                //
//                                                             //
/////////////////////////////////////////////////////////////////

#include "resview.h"


/////////////////////////////////////////////////////////////////
// global object declarations:                                 //
/////////////////////////////////////////////////////////////////

CApplication App;
CMainDialog MainDialog;
```

```
//////////////////////////////////////////////////////////
// program entry function:                               //
//////////////////////////////////////////////////////////

int PASCAL WinMain
    (HINSTANCE HInstCurrent,
    HINSTANCE HInstPrevious,
    LPSTR CmdLine,
    int CmdShow)
    {
    if (HInstPrevious)
        {
        HWND HWndPopup;

        GetInstanceData
            (HInstPrevious,
            (BYTE *)&MainDialog.mHDialog,
            sizeof (HWND));
        ShowWindow (MainDialog.mHDialog, SW_SHOWNORMAL);
        HWndPopup = GetLastActivePopup (MainDialog.mHDialog);
        BringWindowToTop (MainDialog.mHDialog);
        BringWindowToTop (HWndPopup);
        return (FALSE);
        }

    App.Initialize (HInstCurrent, HInstPrevious, CmdLine,
                    CmdShow);

    if (!App.LoadAccel ("ResViewAccel"))
        return (FALSE);

    if (!MainDialog.Create ("MainDlg"))
        return (FALSE);

    MSG Msg;
    while (GetMessage (&Msg, NULL, NULL, NULL))
        if (!TranslateAccelerator (MainDialog.mHDialog,
                                   App.mHAccelTable,
                                   &Msg))
            if (!IsDialogMessage (MainDialog.mHDialog, &Msg))
                {
```

```
                    TranslateMessage (&Msg);
                    DispatchMessage (&Msg);
                    }

        return (Msg.wParam);
        }
```

Listing 3.3

```
/////////////////////////////////////////////////////////////////
//                                                               //
// MAINDLG.CPP:  Member functions of the CMainDialog class       //
//               for the RESVIEW program.                        //
//                                                               //
/////////////////////////////////////////////////////////////////

#include "resview.h"
#include <bios.h>
#include <ctype.h>
#include <dos.h>
#include <stdio.h>
#include <stdlib.h>
#include <toolhelp.h>


// define __max and __min because some C++ run-time libraries
// don't include them:
#define __max(a,b)  (((a) > (b)) ? (a) : (b))
#define __min(a,b)  (((a) < (b)) ? (a) : (b))
CMainDialog::CMainDialog ()
    {
    FreeDisk = 0;
    FreeGlobal = 0;
    HBrushWorkSpace = 0;
    PercDisk = 999;
    PercGdi = 999;
    PercGlobal = 999;
    PercUser = 999;
    }


BOOL CMainDialog::DialogProc (UINT Msg, WPARAM WParam,
                              LPARAM LParam)
```

```
    {
switch (Msg)
    {
    case WM_CLOSE:
        Destroy ();
        return (TRUE);

    case WM_COMMAND:
        return OnCommand ((int)WParam, (HWND)LOWORD (LParam),
                          HIWORD (LParam));

    case WM_CTLCOLOR:
        return OnCtlColor ((HDC)WParam, (HWND)LOWORD (LParam),
                           (int)HIWORD (LParam));

    case WM_DESTROY:
        return OnDestroy ();

    case WM_ENDSESSION:
        if (WParam)
            WrapUp ();
        return (TRUE);

    case WM_INITDIALOG:
        return OnInitDialog ((HWND)WParam, LParam);

    case WM_LBUTTONDOWN:  // left mouse button pressed
        return OnLButtonDown (LOWORD (LParam), HIWORD (LParam));

    case WM_PAINT:  // main window or icon needs repainting
        return OnPaint ();

    case WM_SIZE:  // window has been iconized or restored
        return OnSize (WParam);

    case WM_SYSCOLORCHANGE:
        return OnSysColorChange ();

    case WM_TIMER:  // Windows timer message
        return OnTimer ();
```

```
        default:
           return (FALSE);
        }
    }


BOOL CMainDialog::OnCommand (int IDItem, HWND HWndCtl,
                                 WORD NotifyCode)
    {
    int Result;

    switch (IDItem)
        {
        case IDM_ABOUT:
           {
           CMDialog MDialog;
           MDialog.Create ("AboutDlg", mHDialog);
           return (TRUE);
           }

        case IDM_CLIPBOARD:  // Compact/Free Clipboard menu command
           if (!OpenClipboard (mHDialog))
              {
              MessageBox
                 (mHDialog,
                 "Cannot open Clipboard.",
                 "Free Clipboard",
                 MB_ICONEXCLAMATION | MB_OK);
              return (TRUE);
              }
           if (CountClipboardFormats ())
              {                                // Clipboard contains data
              Result = MessageBox
                 (mHDialog,
                 "Are you sure you want to delete the "
                 "Clipboard contents?",
                 "Free Clipboard",
                 MB_ICONQUESTION | MB_YESNO);
              if (Result == IDYES)
                 EmptyClipboard ();    // delete Clipboard contents
              }
```

```
    CloseClipboard ();

    return (TRUE);

case IDM_DISK:      // commands on Statistics menu
case IDM_GDI:
case IDM_GLOBAL:
case IDM_USER:
    {
    CStatDialog StatDialog;
    // 'ResourceType' tells dialog code which command was
    // chosen:
    StatDialog.ResourceType = IDItem;
    StatDialog.Create ("StatDlg", mHDialog);
    return (TRUE);
    }

case IDM_HELPCONTENTS:
    WinHelp (mHDialog, "RESVIEW.HLP", HELP_CONTENTS, OL);
    return (TRUE);

case IDM_HELPHELP:
    WinHelp (mHDialog, "RESVIEW.HLP", HELP_HELPONHELP, OL);
    return (TRUE);

case IDM_HELPSEARCH:
    WinHelp (mHDialog, "RESVIEW.HLP", HELP_PARTIALKEY,
            (DWORD)(LPCSTR)"");
    return (TRUE);

case IDM_ICONDISK:      // options on Icon Shows: submenu
case IDM_ICONGLOBAL:
case IDM_ICONUSERGDI:
    // IconRes indicates which resource to show on icon:
    CheckMenuItem (GetMenu (mHDialog), IconRes,
                MF_UNCHECKED);
    IconRes = IDItem;
    CheckMenuItem (GetMenu (mHDialog), IconRes, MF_CHECKED);
    return (TRUE);

case IDM_MEMORY:  // Compact/Compact Memory menu command
```

```
      GlobalCompact (OxffffffffL);
      return (TRUE);

   case IDM_ONTOP:  // Options/Always on Top menu option;

      OnTop = !OnTop;  // toggle flag

      // set 'topmost' property of main window:
      SetWindowPos
         (mHDialog,
         OnTop ? HWND_TOPMOST : HWND_NOTOPMOST,
         0,
         0,
         0,
         0,
         SWP_NOMOVE ¦ SWP_NOSIZE);  // don't move or size

      // maintain menu check mark:
      CheckMenuItem
         (GetMenu (mHDialog),
         IDM_ONTOP,
         OnTop ? MF_CHECKED : MF_UNCHECKED);

      return (TRUE);

   case IDM_REDLINES:  // Options/Set Red Lines... menu cmd
      {
      CRedLineDialog RedLineDialog;
      RedLineDialog.Create ("RedLineDlg", mHDialog);
      return (TRUE);
      }

   case IDM_SETDISK:  // Options/Select Disk... menu command
      {
      CSetDiskDialog SetDiskDialog;
      SetDiskDialog.Create ("SetDiskDlg", mHDialog);
      return (TRUE);
      }

   case IDM_UPDATE:  // Options/Set Update Frequency...
                     // menu command
```

```
                   {
                   CUpdateDialog UpdateDialog;
                   UpdateDialog.Create ("UpdateDlg", mHDialog);
                   return (TRUE);
                   }

               default:
                   return (FALSE);

               }
          }

BOOL CMainDialog::OnCtlColor (HDC HDCChild, HWND HWndChild,
                                    int CtlType)
     {
     COLORREF WorkSpaceColor;

     switch (CtlType)
          {
          case CTLCOLOR_BTN:
          case CTLCOLOR_STATIC:
              WorkSpaceColor = GetSysColor (COLOR_APPWORKSPACE);
              if (GetRValue (WorkSpaceColor) * 2 +
                  GetGValue (WorkSpaceColor) * 5 +
                  GetBValue (WorkSpaceColor) > 1020)
                  SetTextColor (HDCChild, RGB (0, 0, 0));
              else
                  SetTextColor (HDCChild, RGB (255, 255, 255));
              SetBkMode (HDCChild, TRANSPARENT);
              return ((BOOL)HBrushWorkSpace);

          case CTLCOLOR_DLG:
              return ((BOOL)HBrushWorkSpace);

          default:
              return (FALSE);
          }
     }

BOOL CMainDialog::OnDestroy ()
     {
```

```
      WrapUp ();
      if (HBrushWorkSpace != 0)
         DeleteObject (HBrushWorkSpace);
      KillTimer (mHDialog, 1);    // remove the timer
      WinHelp (mHDialog, "RESVIEW.HLP", HELP_QUIT, OL);
      PostQuitMessage (0);
      return (TRUE);
      }

BOOL CMainDialog::OnInitDialog (HWND HWndFocus, LPARAM Data)
      {
      char Buffer [16];
      struct diskfree_t DiskSpace;
      MEMMANINFO MMInfo;
      int Result;
      unsigned int TotalExtended = 0;

      // get screen coordinates of bars:
      GetWindowRect (GetDlgItem (mHDialog, IDC_DISK), &RectDisk);
      GetWindowRect (GetDlgItem (mHDialog, IDC_GDI), &RectGdi);
      GetWindowRect (GetDlgItem (mHDialog, IDC_GLOBAL),
                     &RectGlobal);
      GetWindowRect (GetDlgItem (mHDialog, IDC_USER), &RectUser);

      // convert screen coordinates to client coordinates:
      MapWindowPoints (NULL, mHDialog, (POINT FAR *)&RectDisk, 2);
      MapWindowPoints (NULL, mHDialog, (POINT FAR *)&RectGdi, 2);
      MapWindowPoints (NULL, mHDialog, (POINT FAR *)&RectGlobal, 2);
      MapWindowPoints (NULL, mHDialog, (POINT FAR *)&RectUser, 2);

      // read option settings from INI file:

      RedUser = (int)GetPrivateProfileInt
         ("redlines",
         "reduser",
         20,
         "RESVIEW.INI");

      RedGdi = (int)GetPrivateProfileInt
         ("redlines",
         "redgdi",
```

```
      20,
      "RESVIEW.INI");

RedGlobal = (int)GetPrivateProfileInt
      ("redlines",
      "redglobal",
      15,
      "RESVIEW.INI");

RedDisk = (int)GetPrivateProfileInt
      ("redlines",
      "reddisk",
      5,
      "RESVIEW.INI");

Result = GetPrivateProfileString
      ("options",
      "disk",
      "",
      Disk,
      sizeof (Disk),
      "RESVIEW.INI");
if (Result == 0)
      {
      // by default, monitor the disk containing the Windows
      // directory:
      char Path [_MAX_PATH];
      GetWindowsDirectory (Path, _MAX_PATH);
      Disk [0] = toupper (Path [0]);
      Disk [1] = '\0';
      }

// call DOS to get total free space on disk:
_dos_getdiskfree (Disk [0] - 64, &DiskSpace);

// calculate free space in bytes:
TotalDisk = (unsigned long)DiskSpace.total_clusters *
            (unsigned long)DiskSpace.sectors_per_cluster *
            (unsigned long)DiskSpace.bytes_per_sector;
// convert to KILObytes:
TotalDisk /= 1024;
```

```
// display label under disk bar:
sprintf (Buffer, "Disk Space %c:", Disk [0]);
SetDlgItemText (mHDialog, IDC_DISKT, Buffer);

OnTop = (int)GetPrivateProfileInt
    ("options",
    "ontop",
    0,
    "RESVIEW.INI");
if (OnTop)
    {
    // set the 'ontop' property of the main window:
    SetWindowPos (mHDialog, HWND_TOPMOST, 0, 0, 0, 0,
                  SWP_NOMOVE | SWP_NOSIZE);
    CheckMenuItem (GetMenu (mHDialog), IDM_ONTOP, MF_CHECKED);
    }

IconRes = (int)GetPrivateProfileInt
    ("options",
    "iconres",
    IDM_ICONUSERGDI,
    "RESVIEW.INI");
CheckMenuItem (GetMenu (mHDialog), IconRes, MF_CHECKED);

TimeOut = GetPrivateProfileInt
    ("options",
    "timeout",
    5000,
    "RESVIEW.INI");

// determine total global memory:
if (GetWinFlags () & WF_ENHANCED)  // running in Enhanced mode
    {
    // get information on the virtual memory manager:
    MMInfo.dwSize = sizeof (MEMMANINFO);
    MemManInfo (&MMInfo);

    // calculate and save total virtual memory size in kilobytes:
    TotalGlobal = (  min (MMInfo.dwTotalLinearSpace,
                         MMInfo.dwTotalPages +
```

```
                    MMInfo.dwSwapFilePages *
                    MMInfo.wPageSize) / 1024;
    }
else                                 // running in Standard mode
    {
    // get total conventional memory:
    TotalGlobal = _bios_memsize ();

    // get total extended memory by directly reading the CMOS:
    _asm {
        xor   ax, ax
        mov   al, 17h
        out   70h, al
        nop
        in    al, 71h
        mov   TotalExtended, ax
        mov   al, 18h
        out   70h, al
        nop
        in    al, 71h
        xchg  al, ah
        or    TotalExtended, ax
        }

    // total global memory = Conventional + Extended:
    TotalGlobal += TotalExtended;
    }

HBrushWorkSpace = CreateSolidBrush
    (GetSysColor (COLOR_APPWORKSPACE));

// start WM_TIMER messages:
Result = SetTimer (mHDialog, 1, TimeOut, NULL);
if (!Result)
    {
    MessageBox
        (mHDialog,
        "Could not create timer!",
        "Resource Viewer",
        MB_ICONEXCLAMATION | MB_OK);
    Destroy ();
```

```
        }

    // manually send first WM_TIMER message so that it is received
    // without delay:
    SendMessage (mHDialog, WM_TIMER, O, OL);

    return (TRUE);
    }

BOOL CMainDialog::OnLButtonDown (int XPos, int YPos)
    {
    POINT Point;

    Point.x = XPos;
    Point.y = YPos;

    // determine whether mouse pointer is within one of the
    // bars; if so, send a Statistics menu command:

    if (PtInRect (&RectUser, Point))
       SendMessage (mHDialog, WM_COMMAND, IDM_USER, OL);
    else if (PtInRect (&RectGdi, Point))
       SendMessage (mHDialog, WM_COMMAND, IDM_GDI, OL);
    else if (PtInRect (&RectGlobal, Point))
       SendMessage (mHDialog, WM_COMMAND, IDM_GLOBAL, OL);
    else if (PtInRect (&RectDisk, Point))
       SendMessage (mHDialog, WM_COMMAND, IDM_DISK, OL);

    return (TRUE);
    }

BOOL CMainDialog::OnPaint ()
    {
    HBRUSH HBrush;
    HDC HDc;
    HBRUSH HOldBrush;
    HPEN HPen;
    HPEN HPenOld;
    unsigned long John;
    int PercFree;
    unsigned long Percent;
```

```
PAINTSTRUCT PS;
RECT Rect;
RECT RectTemp;
int Red;
int Y;

HDc = BeginPaint (mHDialog, &PS);

// if window is iconic, draw bar chart within icon:
if (IsIconic (mHDialog))
    {
    // calculate bar dimensions:
    GetClientRect (mHDialog, &RectTemp);
    Rect = RectTemp;
    Rect.left += (RectTemp.right - RectTemp.left) / 3;
    Rect.right -= (RectTemp.right - RectTemp.left) / 3;

    // create & select green brush:
    HBrush = CreateSolidBrush (RGB (0, 255, 0));
    HOldBrush = (HBRUSH)SelectObject (HDc, HBrush);

    // draw green-filled rectangle:
    Rectangle
        (HDc,
        Rect.left,
        Rect.top,
        Rect.right,
        Rect.bottom);

    SelectObject (HDc, HOldBrush);
    DeleteObject (HBrush);

    // determine red-line percentage (Red) and
    // percentage of free resources (PercFree):
    switch (IconRes)
        {
        case IDM_ICONDISK:
            Red = RedDisk;
            PercFree = PercDisk;
            break;
```

```
              case IDM_ICONGLOBAL:
                 Red = RedGlobal;
                 PercFree = PercGlobal;
                 break;

              case IDM_ICONUSERGDI:
                 // display whichever resources is the lower:
                 if (PercGdi < PercUser)
                    {
                    Red = RedGdi;
                    PercFree = PercGdi;
                    }
                 else
                    {
                    Red = RedUser;
                    PercFree = PercUser;
                    }
                 break;
              }

           // draw red zone if defined:

           if (Red > 0)
              {
              // create red brush:
              HBrush = CreateSolidBrush (RGB (255, 0, 0));

              // calculate distance of red from TOP of bar:
              Percent = 100 - Red;
              John = ((unsigned long)Rect.bottom -
                     (unsigned long)Rect.top) * Percent;
              John /= 100;

              // calculate dimensions of red zone:
              RectTemp = Rect;
              RectTemp.top += (int)John;
              RectTemp.left += 1;
              RectTemp.right -= 1;
              RectTemp.bottom -= 1;

              // draw red color:
```

```
    FillRect (HDc, &RectTemp, HBrush);

    DeleteObject (HBrush);
    }

// draw horizontal black line indicating percent of free
// resource:

// create and select 2-pixel wide pen:
HPen = CreatePen (PS_SOLID, 2, 0);
HPenOld = (HPEN)SelectObject (HDc, HPen);

// calculate distance of line from TOP of bar:
Percent = 100 - PercFree;
John = ((unsigned long)Rect.bottom -
        (unsigned long)Rect.top) * Percent;
John /= 100;

// calculate vertical position of line:
Y = Rect.top + (int)John;

// draw line:
MoveTo (HDc, Rect.left + 1, Y);
LineTo (HDc, Rect.right - 2, Y);

SelectObject (HDc, HPenOld);
DeleteObject (HPen);

EndPaint (mHDialog, &PS);
return (TRUE);
}

// window is normal size, draw the bar chart:

// draw the green zones:

// create green brush and draw the color:
HBrush = CreateSolidBrush (RGB (0, 255, 0));

FillRect (HDc, &RectUser, HBrush);
FillRect (HDc, &RectGdi, HBrush);
```

```
FillRect (HDc, &RectGlobal, HBrush);
FillRect (HDc, &RectDisk, HBrush);

DeleteObject (HBrush);

// draw the red zones:

// create red brush:
HBrush = CreateSolidBrush (RGB (255, 0, 0));

// draw red in USER bar if red-level has been defined:
if (RedUser > 0)
    {
    Rect = RectUser;

    // calculate the distance of red from top of bar and
    // adjust 'top' dimension of Rect:
    Percent = 100 - RedUser;
    John = ((unsigned long)Rect.bottom -
            (unsigned long)Rect.top) * Percent;
    John /= 100;
    Rect.top += (int)John;

    // draw the red:
    FillRect (HDc, &Rect, HBrush);
    }

// draw GDI red if level defined:
if (RedGdi > 0)
    {
    Rect = RectGdi;
    Percent = 100 - RedGdi;
    John = ((unsigned long)Rect.bottom -
            (unsigned long)Rect.top) * Percent;
    John /= 100;
    Rect.top += (int)John;
    FillRect (HDc, &Rect, HBrush);
    }

// draw Global Memory red if level defined:
if (RedGlobal > 0)
```

```
   {
   Rect = RectGlobal;
   Percent = 100 - RedGlobal;
   John = ((unsigned long)Rect.bottom -
          (unsigned long)Rect.top) * Percent;
   John /= 100;
   Rect.top += (int)John;
   FillRect (HDc, &Rect, HBrush);
   }

// draw Disk Space red if level defined:
if (RedDisk > 0)
   {
   Rect = RectDisk;
   Percent = 100 - RedDisk;
   John = ((unsigned long)Rect.bottom -
          (unsigned long)Rect.top) * Percent;
   John /= 100;
   Rect.top += (int)John;
   FillRect (HDc, &Rect, HBrush);
   }

DeleteObject (HBrush);

// draw the horizontal black lines:

// create and select 3-pixel wide pen:
HPen = CreatePen (PS_SOLID, 3, 0);
HPenOld = (HPEN)SelectObject (HDc, HPen);

// draw USER line:

// calculate vertical position of line (Y):
Percent = 100 - PercUser;
John = ((unsigned long)RectUser.bottom -
        (unsigned long)RectUser.top) * Percent;
John /= 100;
Y = RectUser.top + (int)John;

// draw line:
MoveTo (HDc, RectUser.left + 1, Y);
```

```
LineTo (HDc, RectUser.right - 2, Y);

// draw GDI line:
Percent = 100 - PercGdi;
John = ((unsigned long)RectGdi.bottom -
        (unsigned long)RectGdi.top) * Percent;
John /= 100;
Y = RectGdi.top + (int)John;
MoveTo (HDc, RectGdi.left + 1, Y);
LineTo (HDc, RectGdi.right - 2, Y);

// draw Global Memory line:
Percent = 100 - PercGlobal;
John = ((unsigned long)RectGlobal.bottom -
        (unsigned long)RectGlobal.top) * Percent;
John /= 100;
Y = RectGlobal.top + (int)John;
MoveTo (HDc, RectGlobal.left + 1, Y);
LineTo (HDc, RectGlobal.right - 2, Y);

// draw Disk Space line:
Percent = 100 - PercDisk;
John = ((unsigned long)RectDisk.bottom -
        (unsigned long)RectDisk.top) * Percent;
John /= 100;
Y = RectDisk.top + (int)John;
MoveTo (HDc, RectDisk.left + 1, Y);
LineTo (HDc, RectDisk.right - 2, Y);

SelectObject (HDc, HPenOld);
DeleteObject (HPen);

EndPaint (mHDialog, &PS);
return (TRUE);
}

BOOL CMainDialog::OnSize (int SizeType)
{
char Buffer [16];

// if window has been minimized, set label to indicate the
```

```
      // resource that is displayed within the icon:
      if (SizeType == SIZE_MINIMIZED)
         switch (IconRes)
            {
            case IDM_ICONDISK:
               sprintf (Buffer, "Disk Space %c:", Disk [0]);
               SetWindowText (mHDialog, Buffer);
               break;

            case IDM_ICONGLOBAL:
               SetWindowText (mHDialog, "Global Memory");
               break;

            case IDM_ICONUSERGDI:
               SetWindowText (mHDialog, "USER/GDI Resources");
               break;
            }

      // if window has been restored, set window label to name of
      // program:
      else if (SizeType == SIZE_RESTORED)
         SetWindowText (mHDialog, "Resource Viewer");

      return (TRUE);
      }

BOOL CMainDialog::OnSysColorChange ()
   {
   if (HBrushWorkSpace != 0)
      DeleteObject (HBrushWorkSpace);
   HBrushWorkSpace =
      CreateSolidBrush (GetSysColor (COLOR_APPWORKSPACE));
   return (TRUE);
   }

BOOL CMainDialog::OnTimer ()
   {
   char Buffer [5];
   BOOL Change = FALSE;
   struct diskfree_t DiskSpace;
   unsigned long Percent;
```

```
RECT Rect;
BOOL RedReached = FALSE;

// get percent of free USER resources:
Percent = (int)GetFreeSystemResources (GFSR_USERRESOURCES);

// test whether free percent has changed:
if ((int)Percent != PercUser)
   {
   // test whether percent has just gone below the red-line
   // level:
   if ((int)Percent <= RedUser && PercUser > RedUser)
      RedReached = TRUE;

   // store new percent:
   PercUser = (int)Percent;

   // update label above bar:
   sprintf (Buffer, "%d%%", PercUser);
   SetDlgItemText (mHDialog, IDC_USERP, Buffer);

   // invalidate bar so it can be redrawn:
   Rect = RectUser;
   Rect.top -= 2;     // adjustments in case previous line
   Rect.bottom += 2;  // extends outside of bar area
   InvalidateRect (mHDialog, &Rect, TRUE);
   Change = TRUE;
   }

// get percent of free GDI resources:
Percent = (int)GetFreeSystemResources (GFSR_GDIRESOURCES);
if ((int)Percent != PercGdi)
   {
   if ((int)Percent <= RedGdi && PercGdi > RedGdi)
      RedReached = TRUE;
   PercGdi = (int)Percent;
   sprintf (Buffer, "%d%%", PercGdi);
   SetDlgItemText (mHDialog, IDC_GDIP, Buffer);
   Rect = RectGdi;
   Rect.top -= 2;
   Rect.bottom += 2;
```

```
    InvalidateRect (mHDialog, &Rect, TRUE);
    Change = TRUE;
    }

// get percent of free global memory:

// calculate kilobytes of free memory:
FreeGlobal = GetFreeSpace (0) / 1024;

// calculate percent of free memory:
Percent = FreeGlobal * 100;
Percent /= TotalGlobal;

if ((int)Percent != PercGlobal)
    {
    if ((int)Percent <= RedGlobal && PercGlobal > RedGlobal)
        RedReached = TRUE;
    PercGlobal = (int)Percent;
    sprintf (Buffer, "%d%%", PercGlobal);
    SetDlgItemText (mHDialog, IDC_GLOBALP, Buffer);
    Rect = RectGlobal;
    Rect.top -= 2;
    Rect.bottom +=2;
    InvalidateRect (mHDialog, &Rect, TRUE);
    Change = TRUE;
    }

// get percent of free disk space:

// call DOS to get bytes of free disk space:
_dos_getdiskfree (Disk [0] - 64, &DiskSpace);
FreeDisk = (unsigned long)DiskSpace.avail_clusters *
           (unsigned long)DiskSpace.sectors_per_cluster *
           (unsigned long)DiskSpace.bytes_per_sector;

// convert bytes to kilobytes:
FreeDisk /= 1024;

// calculate percent of free disk space:
Percent = FreeDisk * 100;
Percent /= TotalDisk;
```

```
        if ((int)Percent != PercDisk)
            {
            if ((int)Percent <= RedDisk && PercDisk > RedDisk)
                RedReached = TRUE;
            PercDisk = (int)Percent;
            sprintf (Buffer, "%d%%", PercDisk);
            SetDlgItemText (mHDialog, IDC_DISKP, Buffer);
            Rect = RectDisk;
            Rect.top -= 2;
            Rect.bottom +=2;
            InvalidateRect (mHDialog, &Rect, TRUE);
            Change = TRUE;
            }

        // if percent of any resource has changed, force Windows to
        // send a WM_PAINT message so bar(s) can be redrawn:
        if (Change)
            UpdateWindow (mHDialog);

        // if a resource has just gone below red-line level, warn
        // the user:
        if (RedReached)
            {
            MessageBeep (-1);
            MessageBox
                (mHDialog,
                "A Windows resource has dropped\n"
                "below the red-line level!",
                "Resource Viewer",
                MB_ICONEXCLAMATION | MB_OK);
            }

        return (TRUE);
        }

void CMainDialog::WrapUp ()
    {
    char Buffer [8];

    WritePrivateProfileString
```

```
      ("options",
      "disk",
      Disk,
      "RESVIEW.INI");

sprintf (Buffer, "%u", TimeOut);
WritePrivateProfileString
   ("options",
   "timeout",
   Buffer,
   "RESVIEW.INI");

sprintf (Buffer, "%c", OnTop ? '1' : '0');
WritePrivateProfileString
   ("options",
   "ontop",
   Buffer,
   "RESVIEW.INI");

sprintf (Buffer, "%d", IconRes);
WritePrivateProfileString
   ("options",
   "iconres",
   Buffer,
   "RESVIEW.INI");

sprintf (Buffer, "%d", RedUser);
WritePrivateProfileString
   ("redlines",
   "reduser",
   Buffer,
   "RESVIEW.INI");

sprintf (Buffer, "%d", RedGdi);
WritePrivateProfileString
   ("redlines",
   "redgdi",
   Buffer,
   "RESVIEW.INI");

sprintf (Buffer, "%d", RedGlobal);
```

```
WritePrivateProfileString
    ("redlines",
    "redglobal",
    Buffer,
    "RESVIEW.INI");

sprintf (Buffer, "%d", RedDisk);
WritePrivateProfileString
    ("redlines",
    "reddisk",
    Buffer,
    "RESVIEW.INI");


}
```

Listing 3.4

```
/////////////////////////////////////////////////////////////////
//                                                               //
// MODALDLG.CPP:  Member functions of the modal dialog boxes     //
//                for the RESVIEW program.                        //
//                                                               //
/////////////////////////////////////////////////////////////////

#include "resview.h"
#include <ctype.h>
#include <dos.h>
#include <stdio.h>
#include <stdlib.h>

extern CMainDialog MainDialog;


/////////////////////////////////////////////////////////////////
// CRedLineDialog member function:                               //
/////////////////////////////////////////////////////////////////

BOOL CRedLineDialog::DialogProc (UINT Msg, WPARAM WParam,
                                 LPARAM LParam)
    {
    char Buffer [8];
```

```
switch (Msg)
   {
   case WM_COMMAND:
       switch (WParam)
          {
          case IDCANCEL:
              EndDialog (mHDialog, 0);
              return (TRUE);

          case IDC_HELP:
              WinHelp (MainDialog.mHDialog, "RESVIEW.HLP",
                      HELP_CONTEXT, HELPSETREDDLG);
              return (TRUE);

          case IDOK:
              // assign new red-line values to MainDialog
              // member functions:
              GetDlgItemText (mHDialog, IDC_USER, Buffer, 3);
              MainDialog.RedUser = atoi (Buffer);
              GetDlgItemText (mHDialog, IDC_GDI, Buffer, 3);
              MainDialog.RedGdi = atoi (Buffer);
              GetDlgItemText (mHDialog, IDC_GLOBAL, Buffer, 3);
              MainDialog.RedGlobal = atoi (Buffer);
              GetDlgItemText (mHDialog, IDC_DISK, Buffer, 3);
              MainDialog.RedDisk = atoi (Buffer);

              // setting free percents to 999 and posting
              // WM_TIMER causes OnTimer function to test
              // whether each resource has gone below the new
              // red-line level, and to force redrawing of
              // the bars:
              MainDialog.PercDisk = 999;
              MainDialog.PercGdi = 999;
              MainDialog.PercGlobal = 999;
              MainDialog.PercUser = 999;
              PostMessage (MainDialog.mHDialog, WM_TIMER,
                          0, 0L);

              EndDialog (mHDialog, 0);
              return (TRUE);
```

```
                    default:
                        return (TRUE);
                    }

            case WM_INITDIALOG:
                // limit length of strings that can be entered:
                SendDlgItemMessage (mHDialog, IDC_USER, EM_LIMITTEXT,
                                    2, OL);
                SendDlgItemMessage (mHDialog, IDC_GDI, EM_LIMITTEXT,
                                    2, OL);
                SendDlgItemMessage (mHDialog, IDC_GLOBAL, EM_LIMITTEXT,
                                    2, OL);
                SendDlgItemMessage (mHDialog, IDC_DISK, EM_LIMITTEXT,
                                    2, OL);

                // display current values:
                sprintf (Buffer, "%d", MainDialog.RedUser);
                SetDlgItemText (mHDialog, IDC_USER, Buffer);
                sprintf (Buffer, "%d", MainDialog.RedGdi);
                SetDlgItemText (mHDialog, IDC_GDI, Buffer);
                sprintf (Buffer, "%d", MainDialog.RedGlobal);
                SetDlgItemText (mHDialog, IDC_GLOBAL, Buffer);
                sprintf (Buffer, "%d", MainDialog.RedDisk);
                SetDlgItemText (mHDialog, IDC_DISK, Buffer);

                return (TRUE);

            default:
                if (Msg == mHelpMessage)
                    {
                    SendMessage (mHDialog, WM_COMMAND, IDC_HELP, OL);
                    return (TRUE);
                    }
                else
                    return (FALSE);

            }
        }
```

```
////////////////////////////////////////////////////////
// CSetDiskDialog member function:                     //
////////////////////////////////////////////////////////

BOOL CSetDiskDialog::DialogProc (UINT Msg, WPARAM WParam,
                                  LPARAM LParam)
    {
    char Buffer [32];
    struct diskfree_t DiskSpace;
    int Result;

    switch (Msg)
        {
        case WM_COMMAND:
            switch (WParam)
                {
                case IDCANCEL:
                    EndDialog (mHDialog, 0);
                    return (TRUE);

                case IDC_DISK:
                    // allow user to choose disk and close dialog
                    // box by double-clicking:
                    if (HIWORD (LParam) == LBN_DBLCLK)
                        SendMessage (mHDialog, WM_COMMAND, IDOK, OL);
                    return (TRUE);

                case IDC_HELP:
                    WinHelp (MainDialog.mHDialog, "RESVIEW.HLP",
                            HELP_CONTEXT, HELPDISKDLG);
                    return (TRUE);

                case IDOK:
                    EndDialog (mHDialog, 0);

                    // get letter of disk that is selected in
                    // list box:
                    Result = (int)SendDlgItemMessage (mHDialog,
                        IDC_DISK, LB_GETCURSEL, O, OL);
                    if (Result == LB_ERR)
                        return (TRUE);
```

```
                        Result = (int)SendDlgItemMessage (mHDialog,
                           IDC_DISK, LB_GETTEXT, (WPARAM)Result,
                           (LPARAM)(LPCSTR)Buffer);
                        if (Result == LB_ERR)
                           return (TRUE);
                        MainDialog.Disk [0] = toupper (Buffer [2]);

                        // update label under disk bar:
                        sprintf (Buffer, "Disk Space %c:",
                              MainDialog.Disk [0]);
                        SetDlgItemText (MainDialog.mHDialog, IDC_DISKT,
                                    Buffer);

                        // update total space on disk:
                        _dos_getdiskfree (MainDialog.Disk [0] - 64,
                                    &DiskSpace);
                        MainDialog.TotalDisk =
                           (unsigned long)DiskSpace.total_clusters *
                           (unsigned long)DiskSpace.sectors_per_cluster *
                           (unsigned long)DiskSpace.bytes_per_sector;
                        MainDialog.TotalDisk /= 1024;

                        return (TRUE);

                  default:
                     return (TRUE);
                  }

            case WM_INITDIALOG:
               // display disk drives in list box:
               Buffer [0] = '\0';
               DlgDirList
                  (mHDialog,
                  Buffer,
                  IDC_DISK,
                  0,
                  DDL_DRIVES);

               // select the list box item corresponding to the current
               // monitored disk:
               sprintf (Buffer, "[-%c-]", MainDialog.Disk [0]);
```

```
            SendDlgItemMessage (mHDialog, IDC_DISK, LB_SELECTSTRING,
                            -1, (LPARAM)(LPCSTR)Buffer);
        return (TRUE);


    default:
        if (Msg == mHelpMessage)
            {
            SendMessage (mHDialog, WM_COMMAND, IDC_HELP, OL);
            return (TRUE);
            }
        else
            return (FALSE);


    }
  }


///////////////////////////////////////////////////////////////////
// CStatDialog member function:                                   //
///////////////////////////////////////////////////////////////////

BOOL CStatDialog::DialogProc (UINT Msg, WPARAM WParam,
                              LPARAM LParam)

  {
  int AmtFree;
  char Buffer [32];

  switch (Msg)
      {
      case WM_COMMAND:
          EndDialog (mHDialog, O);
          return (TRUE);

      case WM_INITDIALOG:

          // calculate and display statistics for the appropriate
          // resource (a code for the resource is stored in the
          // ResourceType data member):

          switch (ResourceType)
              {
              case IDM_DISK:
```

```
                              sprintf (Buffer, "Disk Space on %c:",
                                      MainDialog.Disk [0]);
                              SetDlgItemText (mHDialog, IDC_RESOURCE, Buffer);

                              sprintf (Buffer, "%lu KB", MainDialog.FreeDisk);
                              SetDlgItemText (mHDialog, IDC_FREE, Buffer);

                              sprintf (Buffer, "%d%%", MainDialog.PercDisk);
                              SetDlgItemText (mHDialog, IDC_FREEP, Buffer);

                              sprintf (Buffer, "%lu KB", MainDialog.TotalDisk -
                                      MainDialog.FreeDisk);
                              SetDlgItemText (mHDialog, IDC_USED, Buffer);

                              sprintf (Buffer, "%d%%",
                                      100 - MainDialog.PercDisk);
                              SetDlgItemText (mHDialog, IDC_USEDP, Buffer);

                              sprintf (Buffer, "%lu KB", MainDialog.TotalDisk);
                              SetDlgItemText (mHDialog, IDC_TOTAL, Buffer);

                              break;

                      case IDM_GDI:
                              SetDlgItemText (mHDialog, IDC_RESOURCE,
                                                "GDI Resources");

                              AmtFree = 64 * MainDialog.PercGdi;
                              AmtFree /= 100;
                              sprintf (Buffer, "%d KB", AmtFree);
                              SetDlgItemText (mHDialog, IDC_FREE, Buffer);

                              sprintf (Buffer, "%d%%", MainDialog.PercGdi);
                              SetDlgItemText (mHDialog, IDC_FREEP, Buffer);

                              sprintf (Buffer, "%d KB", 64 - AmtFree);
                              SetDlgItemText (mHDialog, IDC_USED, Buffer);

                              sprintf (Buffer, "%d%%",
                                      100 - MainDialog.PercGdi);
                              SetDlgItemText (mHDialog, IDC_USEDP, Buffer);
```

```
        SetDlgItemText (mHDialog, IDC_TOTAL, "64 KB");

        break;

    case IDM_GLOBAL:
        SetDlgItemText (mHDialog, IDC_RESOURCE,
                        "Global Memory");

        sprintf (Buffer, "%lu KB", MainDialog.FreeGlobal);
        SetDlgItemText (mHDialog, IDC_FREE, Buffer);

        sprintf (Buffer, "%d%%", MainDialog.PercGlobal);
        SetDlgItemText (mHDialog, IDC_FREEP, Buffer);

        sprintf (Buffer, "%lu KB", MainDialog.TotalGlobal
                 - MainDialog.FreeGlobal);
        SetDlgItemText (mHDialog, IDC_USED, Buffer);

        sprintf (Buffer, "%d%%",
                 100 - MainDialog.PercGlobal);
        SetDlgItemText (mHDialog, IDC_USEDP, Buffer);

        sprintf (Buffer, "%lu KB",
                 MainDialog.TotalGlobal);
        SetDlgItemText (mHDialog, IDC_TOTAL, Buffer);

        break;

    case IDM_USER:
        SetDlgItemText (mHDialog, IDC_RESOURCE,
                        "USER Resources");

        AmtFree = 128 * MainDialog.PercUser;
        AmtFree /= 100;
        sprintf (Buffer, "%d KB", AmtFree);
        SetDlgItemText (mHDialog, IDC_FREE, Buffer);

        sprintf (Buffer, "%d%%", MainDialog.PercUser);
        SetDlgItemText (mHDialog, IDC_FREEP, Buffer);
```

```
                            sprintf (Buffer, "%d KB", 128 - AmtFree);
                            SetDlgItemText (mHDialog, IDC_USED, Buffer);

                            sprintf (Buffer, "%d%%",
                                    100 - MainDialog.PercUser);
                            SetDlgItemText (mHDialog, IDC_USEDP, Buffer);

                            SetDlgItemText (mHDialog, IDC_TOTAL, "128 KB");

                            break;
                        }
                    return (TRUE);

                default:
                    return (FALSE);
                }
        }


///////////////////////////////////////////////////////////////////
// CUpdateDialog member function:                                  //
///////////////////////////////////////////////////////////////////

BOOL CUpdateDialog::DialogProc (UINT Msg, WPARAM WParam,
                                    LPARAM LParam)
    {
    char Buffer [3];
    int Result;

    switch (Msg)
        {
        case WM_COMMAND:
            switch (WParam)
                {
                case IDCANCEL:
                    EndDialog (mHDialog, 0);
                    return (TRUE);

                case IDC_HELP:
                    WinHelp (MainDialog.mHDialog, "RESVIEW.HLP",
                            HELP_CONTEXT, HELPUPDATEDLG);
                    return (TRUE);
```

```
case IDOK:
    // get string entered by user, convert to integer,
    // and test whether it is in valid range:
    GetDlgItemText (mHDialog, IDC_FREQ, Buffer,
                    sizeof (Buffer));
    Result = atoi (Buffer);
    if (Result < 1 || Result > 65)
        {
        MessageBox
            (mHDialog,
            "Must enter a value between 1 and 65.",
            "Set Update Frequency",
            MB_ICONEXCLAMATION | MB_OK);
        SetFocus (GetDlgItem (mHDialog, IDC_FREQ));
        return (TRUE);
        }

    // exit immediately if timeout value is unchanged:
    if (MainDialog.TimeOut == (unsigned)Result * 1000)
        {
        EndDialog (mHDialog, 0);
        return (TRUE);
        }

    // timeout value has changed

    // update data member:
    MainDialog.TimeOut = (unsigned)Result * 1000;

    // delete old timer:
    KillTimer (MainDialog.mHDialog, 1);

    // create new timer using new timeout value:
    Result = SetTimer (MainDialog.mHDialog, 1,
                       MainDialog.TimeOut, NULL);
    if (!Result)
        {
        MessageBox
            (mHDialog,
            "Could not create new timer!",
```

```
                              "Set Update Frequency",
                              MB_ICONEXCLAMATION | MB_OK);
                     MainDialog.Destroy ();
                     }

                 EndDialog (mHDialog, O);
                 return (TRUE);

             default:
                 return (TRUE);
             }

         case WM_INITDIALOG:
             SendDlgItemMessage (mHDialog, IDC_FREQ, EM_LIMITTEXT,
                               2, OL);
             sprintf (Buffer, "%d", MainDialog.TimeOut / 1000);
             SetDlgItemText (mHDialog, IDC_FREQ, Buffer);
             return (TRUE);

         default:
             if (Msg == mHelpMessage)
                 {
                 SendMessage (mHDialog, WM_COMMAND, IDC_HELP, OL);
                 return (TRUE);
                 }
             else
                 return (FALSE);

         }
     }
```

Listing 3.5

```
;;;;;;;;;;;;;;;;;;;;;;;;;;;;;;;;;;;;;;;;;;;;;;;;;;;;;;;;;;;;;;;;;;;;;;;;;;
;                                                                        ;
; RESVIEW.DEF:  Module-definition file for the RESVIEW program. ;
;                                                                        ;
;;;;;;;;;;;;;;;;;;;;;;;;;;;;;;;;;;;;;;;;;;;;;;;;;;;;;;;;;;;;;;;;;;;;;;;;;;

NAME RESVIEW
```

```
DESCRIPTION  'Resource Viewer/Compactor'

EXETYPE WINDOWS

CODE PRELOAD MOVEABLE DISCARDABLE

DATA PRELOAD MOVEABLE MULTIPLE

HEAPSIZE 1024

STACKSIZE 10240
```

Listing 3.6

```
///////////////////////////////////////////////////////////////
//                                                             //
// RESOURCE.H:  Constant definitions for the RESVIEW program   //
//              resources (generated by Microsoft App Studio). //
//                                                             //
///////////////////////////////////////////////////////////////

//{{NO_DEPENDENCIES}}
// App Studio generated include file.
// Used by RESVIEW.RC
//
#define IDC_RESOURCE                    101
#define IDC_FREE                        102
#define IDC_USED                        103
#define IDC_TOTAL                       104
#define IDC_FREEP                       105
#define IDC_USER                        106
#define IDC_USEDP                       107
#define IDC_HELP                        108
#define IDC_DISKT                       109
#define IDC_USERP                       110
#define IDC_GDIP                        111
#define IDC_GLOBALP                     112
#define IDC_GDI                         113
#define IDC_GLOBAL                      114
#define IDC_DISK                        115
#define IDC_DISKP                       116
```

```
#define IDC_FREQ                        117
#define IDM_ABOUT                       1000
#define IDM_CLIPBOARD                   1001
#define IDM_DISK                        1002
#define IDM_HELPCONTENTS                1003
#define IDM_HELPHELP                    1004
#define IDM_HELPSEARCH                  1005
#define IDM_GDI                         1006
#define IDM_GLOBAL                      1007
#define IDM_ICONDISK                    1008
#define IDM_ICONGLOBAL                  1009
#define IDM_ICONUSERGDI                 1010
#define IDM_MEMORY                      1011
#define IDM_ONTOP                       1012
#define IDM_REDLINES                    1013
#define IDM_SETDISK                     1014
#define IDM_UPDATE                      1015
#define IDM_USER                        1016


// Next default values for new objects
//
#ifdef APSTUDIO_INVOKED
#ifndef APSTUDIO_READONLY_SYMBOLS

#define _APS_NEXT_RESOURCE_VALUE        101
#define _APS_NEXT_COMMAND_VALUE         101
#define _APS_NEXT_CONTROL_VALUE         1000
#define _APS_NEXT_SYMED_VALUE           101
#endif
#endif
```

Listing 3.7

```
//////////////////////////////////////////////////////////////////
//                                                                //
// RESVIEW.RC:  Resource-definition file for the RESVIEW          //
//              program (generated by Microsoft App Studio).      //
//                                                                //
//////////////////////////////////////////////////////////////////

//Microsoft App Studio generated resource script.
```

```
//
#include "resource.h"

#define APSTUDIO_READONLY_SYMBOLS
/////////////////////////////////////////////////////////////////////////////
//
// Generated from the TEXTINCLUDE 2 resource.
//
#define APSTUDIO_HIDDEN_SYMBOLS
#include "windows.h"
#undef APSTUDIO_HIDDEN_SYMBOLS


/////////////////////////////////////////////////////////////////////////////
#undef APSTUDIO_READONLY_SYMBOLS


/////////////////////////////////////////////////////////////////////////////
//
// Icon
//

RESVIEWICON             ICON    DISCARDABLE     "RESVIEW.ICO"


/////////////////////////////////////////////////////////////////////////////
//
// Menu
//

RESVIEWMENU MENU DISCARDABLE
BEGIN
    POPUP "&Statistics"
    BEGIN
        MENUITEM "&USER Resources...",          IDM_USER
        MENUITEM "&GDI Resources...",           IDM_GDI
        MENUITEM "Global &Memory...",           IDM_GLOBAL
        MENUITEM "&Disk Space...",              IDM_DISK
    END
    POPUP "&Compact"
    BEGIN
        MENUITEM "Compact &Memory",             IDM_MEMORY
        MENUITEM "Free &Clipboard",             IDM_CLIPBOARD
    END
```

```
        POPUP "&Options"
        BEGIN
            MENUITEM "Set &Red Lines...",              IDM_REDLINES
            MENUITEM "Select &Disk...",                IDM_SETDISK
            MENUITEM "Set Update &Frequency...",       IDM_UPDATE
            POPUP "&Icon Shows:"
            BEGIN
                MENUITEM "&USER/GDI Resources",        IDM_ICONUSERGDI
                MENUITEM "&Global Memory",             IDM_ICONGLOBAL
                MENUITEM "&Disk Space",                IDM_ICONDISK
            END
            MENUITEM SEPARATOR
            MENUITEM "Always on &Top",                 IDM_ONTOP
        END
        POPUP "&Help"
        BEGIN
            MENUITEM "&Contents...\tF1",               IDM_HELPCONTENTS
            MENUITEM "&Search for Help On...",         IDM_HELPSEARCH
            MENUITEM "&How to Use Help...",            IDM_HELPHELP
            MENUITEM SEPARATOR
            MENUITEM "&About...",                      IDM_ABOUT
        END
END


/////////////////////////////////////////////////////////////////
// Accelerator
//

RESVIEWACCEL ACCELERATORS MOVEABLE PURE
BEGIN
    VK_F1,          IDM_HELPCONTENTS,        VIRTKEY
END


/////////////////////////////////////////////////////////////////
//
// Dialog
//

ABOUTDLG DIALOG DISCARDABLE  12, 28, 116, 100
STYLE DS_MODALFRAME | WS_POPUP | WS_VISIBLE | WS_CAPTION |
    WS_SYSMENU
```

```
CAPTION "About"
FONT 8, "MS Sans Serif"
BEGIN
    CTEXT           "Resource Viewer / Compactor",-1,0,10,116,8
    CTEXT           "by Michael J. Young",-1,0,28,116,8
    ICON            "ResViewIcon",-1,48,48,18,20
    DEFPUSHBUTTON   "OK",IDOK,36,80,40,14
END

MAINDLG DIALOG DISCARDABLE  14, 36, 162, 112
STYLE WS_MINIMIZEBOX | WS_POPUP | WS_VISIBLE | WS_CAPTION |
    WS_SYSMENU
CAPTION "Resource Viewer"
MENU ResViewMenu
FONT 8, "MS Sans Serif"
BEGIN
    CONTROL         "",IDC_USER,"Static",SS_BLACKFRAME,18,22,10,
                    54
    CTEXT           "USER Resources",-1,6,84,34,20
    CONTROL         "",IDC_GDI,"Static",SS_BLACKFRAME,54,22,10,
                    54
    CONTROL         "",IDC_GLOBAL,"Static",SS_BLACKFRAME,90,22,
                    10,54
    CONTROL         "",IDC_DISK,"Static",SS_BLACKFRAME,126,22,
                    10,54
    CTEXT           "GDI Resources",-1,44,84,34,20
    CTEXT           "Global Memory",-1,82,84,26,20
    CTEXT           "Disk Space C:",IDC_DISKT,120,84,24,28
    LTEXT           "Free",-1,144,10,18,12
    CTEXT           "",IDC_USERP,14,10,22,8
    CTEXT           "",IDC_GDIP,50,10,22,8
    CTEXT           "",IDC_GLOBALP,86,10,22,8
    CTEXT           "",IDC_DISKP,122,10,22,8
END

STATDLG DIALOG DISCARDABLE  6, 18, 128, 112
STYLE DS_MODALFRAME | WS_POPUP | WS_VISIBLE | WS_CAPTION |
    WS_SYSMENU
CAPTION "Statistics"
FONT 8, "MS Sans Serif"
BEGIN
```

```
        LTEXT             "Resource:",-1,8,12,38,8
        LTEXT             "USER Resources",IDC_RESOURCE,48,12,80,8
        LTEXT             "Free:",-1,8,30,20,8
        RTEXT             "999,999 KB",IDC_FREE,44,30,42,8
        RTEXT             "999,999 KB",IDC_USED,44,48,42,8
        RTEXT             "999,999 KB",IDC_TOTAL,44,70,42,8
        RTEXT             "100%",IDC_FREEP,100,30,20,8
        RTEXT             "100%",IDC_USEDP,100,48,20,8
        RTEXT             "100%",-1,100,70,20,8
        LTEXT             "Used:",-1,8,48,22,8
        LTEXT             "Total:",-1,8,70,20,8
        CONTROL           "",-1,"Static",SS_BLACKFRAME,48,62,74,2
        DEFPUSHBUTTON     "OK",IDOK,42,90,40,14
END


REDLINEDLG DIALOG DISCARDABLE  6, 18, 102, 106
STYLE DS_MODALFRAME | WS_POPUP | WS_VISIBLE | WS_CAPTION |
    WS_SYSMENU
CAPTION "Set Red Lines"
FONT 8, "MS Sans Serif"
BEGIN
        LTEXT             "USER Resources:",-1,4,10,60,8
        LTEXT             "GDI Resources:",-1,4,26,52,8
        LTEXT             "Global Memory:",-1,4,42,52,8
        LTEXT             "Disk Space:",-1,4,58,42,8
        EDITTEXT          IDC_USER,66,8,18,12,ES_AUTOHSCROLL
        EDITTEXT          IDC_GDI,66,24,18,12,ES_AUTOHSCROLL
        EDITTEXT          IDC_GLOBAL,66,40,18,12,ES_AUTOHSCROLL
        EDITTEXT          IDC_DISK,66,56,18,12,ES_AUTOHSCROLL
        LTEXT             "%",-1,90,10,12,8
        LTEXT             "%",-1,90,26,12,8
        LTEXT             "%",-1,90,42,12,8
        LTEXT             "%",-1,90,58,12,8
        PUSHBUTTON        "&Help",IDC_HELP,62,90,36,14
        DEFPUSHBUTTON     "OK",IDOK,4,74,36,14
        PUSHBUTTON        "Cancel",IDCANCEL,4,90,36,14
END


SETDISKDLG DIALOG DISCARDABLE  6, 18, 90, 86
STYLE DS_MODALFRAME | WS_POPUP | WS_VISIBLE | WS_CAPTION |
    WS_SYSMENU
```

```
CAPTION "Select Disk"
FONT 8, "MS Sans Serif"
BEGIN
    LISTBOX           IDC_DISK,6,20,38,64,LBS_SORT ¦ WS_VSCROLL ¦
                      WS_TABSTOP
    DEFPUSHBUTTON     "OK",IDOK,50,20,34,12
    LTEXT             "Disk Drive:",-1,6,6,38,8
    PUSHBUTTON        "Cancel",IDCANCEL,50,36,34,12
    PUSHBUTTON        "&Help",IDC_HELP,50,64,34,12
END

UPDATEDLG DIALOG DISCARDABLE  6, 18, 144, 54
STYLE DS_MODALFRAME ¦ WS_POPUP ¦ WS_VISIBLE ¦ WS_CAPTION ¦
    WS_SYSMENU
CAPTION "Set Update Frequency"
FONT 8, "MS Sans Serif"
BEGIN
    LTEXT             "&Check resources every",-1,8,10,76,8
    EDITTEXT          IDC_FREQ,88,8,16,12,ES_AUTOHSCROLL
    LTEXT             "seconds.",-1,108,10,30,8
    DEFPUSHBUTTON     "OK",IDOK,8,30,34,14
    PUSHBUTTON        "Cancel",IDCANCEL,46,30,34,14
    PUSHBUTTON        "&Help",IDC_HELP,102,30,34,14
END

#ifdef APSTUDIO_INVOKED
/////////////////////////////////////////////////////////////
//
// TEXTINCLUDE
//

1 TEXTINCLUDE DISCARDABLE
BEGIN
    "resource.h\0"
END

2 TEXTINCLUDE DISCARDABLE
BEGIN
    "#define APSTUDIO_HIDDEN_SYMBOLS\r\n"
    "#include ""windows.h""\r\n"
    "#undef APSTUDIO_HIDDEN_SYMBOLS\r\n"
```

```
    "\0"
END

3 TEXTINCLUDE DISCARDABLE
BEGIN
    "\r\n"
    "\0"
END

/////////////////////////////////////////////////////////////////
#endif    // APSTUDIO_INVOKED

#ifndef APSTUDIO_INVOKED
/////////////////////////////////////////////////////////////////
//
// Generated from the TEXTINCLUDE 3 resource.
//

/////////////////////////////////////////////////////////////////
#endif    // not APSTUDIO_INVOKED
```

The following sections explain the most important programming techniques and the general strategies used in the RESVIEW program. For more detailed information on specific portions of the program, see the comments in the source code.

Initializing

The CMainDialog class constructor (in MAINDLG.CPP of Listing 3.3) assigns initial values to several of the CMainDialog data members. The reason the constructor assigns 999 to the data members that hold the current resource percents (PercUser, and so on) is explained later, in the section "Measuring the Resources." The data members that are not set by the constructor are initialized in the main window initialization routine, On-InitDialog (also in MAINDLG.CPP).

OnInitDialog begins by obtaining the coordinates of the four bars that constitute the bar chart in the main window. Each of the rectangles that defines a bar was created using a black *Frame* control (a simple open frame, which is a type of *Picture* control) when the dialog box for the main window was designed in App Studio. The OnInitDialog function obtains the dimensions of these controls so that the program can later draw the colored zones and lines within the bars indicating the resource levels. The dimensions in screen units are obtained by calling the GetWindowRect API function; the screen units are then converted to client area units by calling the MapWindowPoints API function. The coordinates are stored within the RectDisk, RectGdi, RectGlobal, and RectUser data members of the main window object (MainDialog).

N O T E

You cannot use the coordinate values displayed by App Studio (or another dialog editor) for drawing within the frame controls, since these values are in *dialog units*. The size of a dialog unit depends upon the size of the font used to display text in the dialog box, which is not known until the dialog box is displayed at program run time (in other words, the dialog box and all of its controls are automatically scaled to match the actual size of the dialog box font). Accordingly, the RESVIEW program obtains the coordinates by calling GetWindowRect after the dialog box has been displayed.

OnInitDialog then assigns initial values to the CMainDialog data members that store program options; it attempts to read each value from the program's private initialization file, RESVIEW.INI, assigning a default value if a value has not been stored (see Chapter 2 for a discussion on saving and obtaining values from a private initialization file). Table 3.1 briefly describes each of the data members whose values are stored in the initialization file, and gives the default value for each member.

The default value assigned to the Disk data member (which stores the letter of the disk that is to be monitored) is the letter of the disk containing the Windows directory, which OnInitDialog obtains by calling the Get-WindowsDirectory API function.

If the initial value that is assigned to the OnTop data member is TRUE, On-InitDialog changes the style of the main window so that the window is

TABLE 3.1: The RESVIEW Option Values Stored in the Initialization File

CMainDialog DATA MEMBER	PURPOSE	DEFAULT VALUE
Disk	The letter of the disk drive that is monitored	The disk containing the Windows directory
IconRes	A code for the resource that is currently displayed when the window is minimized	IDM_ICONUSERGDI (USER/GDI system resources)
OnTop	A flag indicating whether the window is assigned the "always on top" style	0 (that is, the window will *not* always be on top)
RedDisk	The red-line percent for the disk-space resource (that is, the resource level that causes the program to issue a warning)	5
RedGdi	The red-line percent for the GDI resources	20
RedGlobal	The red-line percent for the global memory resources	15
RedUser	The red-line percent for the USER resources	20
TimeOut	The timeout value used for the timer (that is, the duration in milliseconds between WM_TIMER messages)	5000

always positioned on top of other windows, as explained in Chapter 2, in the section "Initializing."

The OnInitDialog function also obtains the total disk space on the monitored disk, as well as the total amount of global memory. As you will see, these values are used repeatedly throughout the program to calculate percents and display statistics. OnInitDialog calls the _dos_getdiskfree run-time library function to get the total disk space. The method it uses to get the total amount of global memory depends upon the current Windows operating mode.

To detect the Windows operating mode, OnInitDialog calls the GetWin-Flags API function. If Windows is running in 386 Enhanced mode, the total size of global memory is equal to the size of the virtual memory space managed by the Windows Virtual Memory Manager. It obtains this value by calling the MemManInfo API function (this is one of the functions provided in the TOOLHELP library, mentioned previously).

If, however, Windows is running in Standard mode, the total size of global memory is equal to the amount of physical memory—Conventional plus Extended—that is installed in the machine. To obtain the amount of Conventional memory, it calls the _bios_memsize run-time library function. To obtain the amount of Extended memory, it uses a short, assembly language routine to directly read the size of Extended memory that is stored in the machine's CMOS RAM (CMOS RAM is the nonvolatile memory that stores the machine configuration).

NOTE The assembly language routine that reads the CMOS RAM performs direct I/O to port addresses. Future versions of Windows may prohibit you from directly accessing ports from within an application (that is, from an .EXE file). However, you will be able to place the port I/O code within a dynamic-link library, which can be called by applications.

The OnInitDialog function then calls the SetTimer API function to create a *timer:*

```
SetTimer (mHDialog, 1, TimeOut, NULL);
```

Creating a timer causes Windows to begin sending a series of WM_TIMER messages to the window specified by the first parameter (which is assigned the main window handle). The interval in milliseconds between these messages—the *timeout*—is determined by the third parameter (which is assigned the `TimeOut` data member). As you will see in the next section, the routine that processes the timer messages serves to update the resource information that is displayed.

Before the program exits, the `OnDestroy` function calls the `KillTimer` API function to remove the timer. Also, as you will see later, if the user changes the timeout value through the Set Update Frequency... menu command, the program calls `KillTimer` to remove the current timer, and then calls `SetTimer` to create a new one.

After creating the timer, the `OnInitDialog` function calls `SendMessage` to manually send the first `WM_TIMER` message, so that the resource values will be calculated and the bar chart will be drawn immediately (otherwise, these actions would not occur until after the first timeout interval has elapsed and Windows sends the first timer message).

Measuring the Resources

The `WM_TIMER` messages are processed by the `OnTimer` function (in MAIN-DLG.CPP of Listing 3.3). `OnTimer` calculates and stores the current level of each resource, initiates redrawing of the bar chart if a resource level has changed, and warns the user if a resource has first gone below the red-line level.

For each resource, `OnTimer` first calculates the percent of the resource that is currently free. To obtain the free percents of USER and GDI resources, it calls the API function `GetFreeSystemResources`. To obtain the amount of free global memory (so that it can calculate the free percent), it calls the `GetFreeSpace` Windows API function. To obtain the amount of free disk space, it calls the `_dos_getdiskfree` run-time library function. Note that the temporary variable used to calculate the percents (`Percent`) is declared as an `unsigned long` to prevent arithmetic overflows.

TIP

As an alternative method for obtaining the free percents of system resources, you can call the `GetSystemHeapInfo` Windows API function, which is provided by the TOOLHELP library.

Next, if a resource has changed from its previous value (that is, from its initial value or the value calculated during processing of the previous timer message), the OnTimer function sets the flag Change to TRUE, and it performs the following operations:

1. It tests whether the free percent has just fallen below the red-line level for the resource; that is, it checks whether the *new* percent is equal to or less than the red-line percent *and* the *previous* percent is greater than the red-line value. This two-part test ensures that the warning is issued only when the resource *first* goes below the red-line level and is not reissued on each subsequent timer message. If both conditions are met, it assigns TRUE to the RedReached flag (which was initialized to FALSE).

NOTE

The stored free percents (PercUser, PercGdi, PercGlobal, and PercDisk) are initialized to 999 both in the CMainDialog class constructor and by the Set Red Lines dialog-box code (if the user changes a red-line value, as described later). Assigning 999 has two purposes. First, it forces OnTimer to test whether the resource has fallen below the newly established red-line level (the test is performed only if the stored percent differs from the newly calculated percent). Second, if a resource has fallen below its red-line level, OnTimer will always issue a warning (the warning is issued only if the stored percent is above the red-line level).

2. It stores the new free percent in the appropriate data member of the CMainDialog class, so that the value will be available for drawing the resource bar in the bar chart.

3. It calls the SetDlgItemText API function to update the percent printed above the resource bar.

4. It calls the `InvalidateRect` API function to invalidate the portion of the client area occupied by the resource bar, so that the bar can be redrawn when the next `WM_PAINT` message is sent.

Then, if one or more resources has changed (that is, the `Change` flag is `TRUE`), `OnTimer` calls the `UpdateWindow` API function to force Windows to send an immediate `WM_PAINT` message:

`UpdateWindow (mHDialog);`

(The handling of the `WM_PAINT` message is described in the next section.)

Finally, if one or more resources has fallen below the red-line level (that is, the `RedReached` flag is `TRUE`), `OnTimer` calls `MessageBeep` to sound the speaker and it calls `MessageBox` to display a warning message.

Drawing the Bar Chart

The bars for each resource are drawn or redrawn by the `OnPaint` function (in MAINDLG.CPP, Listing 3.3), which processes `WM_PAINT` messages. Windows sends a `WM_PAINT` message whenever the window needs painting or repainting.

`OnPaint` begins by calling the `BeginPaint` API function, and it calls the `EndPaint` API function immediately before exiting. These functions serve to notify Windows that the client area has been repainted, and also provide a device context handle, which is required for drawing within the client area. `OnPaint` uses standard Windows drawing functions to paint the colored areas of the bars and to draw the lines that indicate the levels of the resources.

`OnPaint` calls the `IsIconic` API function to determine whether the program window is its normal size or has been minimized. If the window is normal (that is, `IsIconic` returns `FALSE`), the function proceeds to paint the red and green areas, as well as the lines indicating the current free percents, within the frame controls used for the bars. Recall that the coordinates of these controls were obtained in the `OnInitDialog` function. The positions of the zones and lines are calculated based upon the values that were obtained by the `OnInitDialog` function and the most recent invocation of the `OnTimer` function.

If, however, the program window has been minimized (that is, IsIconic returns TRUE), OnPaint draws a single bar for the selected resource (that is, the one indicated by the value of the MainDialog.IconRes data member) within the minimized window area. Because the RESVIEW program does *not* call the MainDialog.SetIcon function (unlike the template program in Chapter 2), Windows does *not* automatically display an icon when the window is minimized. Rather, the program draws its own icon to allow the icon to display changing resource information.

NOTE Although Windows does not display an icon when the RESVIEW window is minimized, an icon was designed in App Studio and included in the program resources, as usual, so that the Windows Program Manager can display the icon if the RESVIEW program is added to a Program Manager group.

OnPaint obtains the dimensions of minimized window by calling the GetClientRect API function, so that it can assign the bar the correct size and center it within the minimized area. It then uses standard Windows drawing commands to draw the rectangle, paint the red and green areas, and draw the line.

Handling the Menu Commands

When the user chooses a menu command, control passes to the OnCommand member function of CMainDialog (defined in MAINDLG.CPP, Listing 3.3). Some of the menu commands are processed immediately, and some are processed by displaying modal dialog boxes. CMainDialog::OnCommand displays each dialog box by declaring an instance of the dialog box class, and then calling the Create member function. The program header file (RESVIEW.H, Listing 3.1) defines a class—derived from the CMDialog class—for each of these modal dialog boxes. The MODALDLG.CPP source file (Listing 3.4) defines a DialogProc member function for each dialog box class to handle the messages sent to the dialog box.

NOTE See Chapter 2 for a general discussion on using the CMDialog general class to manage modal dialog boxes. Chapter 2 also explains how the Help menu commands are processed.

The Statistics Menu Commands

Each of the commands on the Statistics menu displays information on a specific resource. The CMainDialog::OnCommand function handles these commands using a common routine, which is contained in the branch of the switch statement that processes the menu identifiers IDM_DISK, IDM_GDI, IDM_GLOBAL, and IDM_USER. This routine does the following:

1. It declares an instance of the CStatDialog class named StatDialog.

2. It assigns a value to the CStatDialog data member ResourceType, which tells the dialog box code which command was chosen and therefore which resource it should display (the value it assigns is the same as the identifier for the menu command).

3. It displays the Statistics dialog box by calling the CStatDialog member function Create.

When the dialog box is displayed, the WM_INITDIALOG routine within the CStatDialog::DialogProc function (in MODALDLG.CPP of Listing 3.4) displays statistics on the resource that is indicated by the value of the ResourceType data member. The statistics include the amount and percent of the resource that is free and the amount and percent that is used, as shown in Figure 3.2. These values are calculated from the current values of MainDialog data members.

The user can also activate the Statistics dialog box by clicking within one of the bars in the main window. See the section "Reading the Mouse," near the end of the chapter, for a description of the code that supports this feature.

The Compact Menu Commands

The Compact menu contains two commands: Compact Memory and Free Clipboard.

The routine in `CMainDialog::OnCommand` that processes the Compact Memory command (the `IDM_MEMORY` branch of the `switch` statement) calls the `GlobalCompact` API function:

```
GlobalCompact (0xffffffffL);
```

`GlobalCompact` compacts global memory and frees discardable memory segments in an attempt to create a free, contiguous block of memory that has the size specified by the parameter it is passed (it does *not* allocate the block). `OnCommand` passes the maximum parameter value so that the greatest amount of compaction is performed. According to the API documentation, this function is useful primarily when the Windows virtual memory manager is inactive—that is, when Windows is run in Standard mode, or in Enhanced mode with virtual memory disabled.

`OnCommand` processes the Free Clipboard command using the following steps (in the `IDM_CLIPBOARD` branch of the `switch` statement):

1. It calls the `OpenClipboard` API function to open the Clipboard.

2. It calls the `CountClipboardFormats` API function to determine whether the Clipboard contains data (this function returns the number of data formats that are currently stored in the Clipboard; a nonzero return value, therefore, indicates that data is present).

3. If data is present, it displays a message box asking the user to confirm that the data should be released.

4. If the user clicks the Yes button, it erases the Clipboard data by calling the `EmptyClipboard` API function.

5. It calls the `CloseClipboard` API function to close the Clipboard.

The Options Menu Commands

The Options menu contains four commands: Set Red Lines..., Select Disk..., Set Update Frequency..., and Always on Top. It also contains one submenu labeled Icon Shows:.

Set Red Lines In response to the Set Red Lines... command, the CMain-Dialog::OnCommand function (the IDM_REDLINES branch of the switch statement) displays the Set Red Lines modal dialog box, which is managed by the CRedLinesDialog class. If the user selects the OK button in the dialog box, the CRedLinesDialog::DialogProc function (in MO-DALDLG.CPP of Listing 3.4) assigns the new red-line values to the appropriate MainDialog data members, and posts a WM_TIMER message to force the OnTimer function both to test whether any resource has gone below its new red-line level and to initiate redrawing of the dialog box. Before posting this message, however, it sets the percent values (Main-Dialog.PercDisk, and so on) to 999, for the reasons that were explained in the section "Measuring the Resources."

Select Disk When the user chooses the Select Disk... command, CMain-Dialog::OnCommand (the IDM_SETDISK branch) displays the Select Disk dialog box, which is managed by the CSetDiskDialog class. When this dialog box is created, the initialization routine in the CSetDiskDialog::Dialog-Proc function (in MODALDLG.CPP) first calls the DlgDirList API function to fill the list box with the names of the disk drives installed in the machine,

```
DlgDirList
    (mHDialog,
    Buffer,
    IDC_DISK,
    0,
    DDL_DRIVES);
```

and it then sends the list box the LB_SELECTSTRING message to select the letter of the drive that is currently being monitored (which is stored in the MainDialog.Disk data member). If the user clicks the OK button, DialogProc stores the newly selected letter in MainDialog.Disk, updates the label under the disk space bar, and then calls the _dos_getdiskfree run-time function to obtain the total disk space on the newly selected drive.

Set Update Frequency To process the Set Update Frequency... command, the CMainDialog::OnCommand function (the IDM_UPDATE branch) displays the Set Update Frequency dialog box, which is managed by the CUpdateDialog class. If the user clicks the OK button in this dialog box, the CUpdateDialog::DialogProc function (also in MODALDLG.CPP) tests to make sure that the value the user has entered is between 1 and 65 seconds; 65 is the largest whole number of seconds that can be used, because the timeout is specified by assigning the number of milliseconds to an unsigned int parameter, which has a maximum value of 65,535.

Next, if the user has entered a new timeout value, DialogProc calls the KillTimer API function to destroy the old timer and then calls SetTimer to create a new timer using the new timeout value.

Icon Shows When the user chooses one of the three options on the Icon Shows: submenu, the CMainDialog::OnCommand function (the branch that processes the IDM_DISK, IDM_GLOBAL, and IDM_USERGDI menu identifiers) simply assigns the appropriate code to the MainDialog.IconRes data member (the code equals the identifier of the corresponding menu command). As explained previously (in the section "Drawing the Bar Chart"), the OnPaint function uses this code to determine which resource it must display when the program window is minimized.

Always on Top When the user chooses the Always on Top menu option, CMainDialog::OnCommand (the IDM_ONTOP branch) toggles the value of the MainDialog::OnTop data member and then calls the SetWindowPos API function to adjust the window style according to the new value of OnTop. The technique was explained in Chapter 2, in the section "Initializing."

Other Techniques

This section discusses several additional programming techniques used in the RESVIEW program.

Changing the Window Text

The text that is assigned to the RESVIEW program window depends upon whether the window is displayed in its normal size or is minimized. If the window has its normal size, the text is set to the name of the program so that this name will appear in the title bar, following the usual custom. However, if the window is minimized, the text is set to a short description of the resource that is displayed within the minimized area, to serve as a label for the bar depicting the resource level.

Whenever the window is minimized or restored, it receives a `WM_SIZE` message, which is processed by the `CMainDialog::OnSize` function (in MAIN-DLG.CPP). If the window has been minimized, the `SizeType` parameter passed to `OnSize` (which is derived from the `WParam` parameter passed to `DialogProc`) equals `SIZE_MINIMIZED`, and `OnSize` sets the window text to the resource description. If the window has been restored, the `SizeType` parameter equals `SIZE_RESTORED`, and `OnSize` sets the window text to the program title.

Reading the Mouse

If the user clicks the left mouse button while the pointer is within one of the bars in the main window, the RESVIEW program displays the Statistics dialog box containing information on the associated resource. To read mouse input, the `CMainDialog::OnLButtonDown` function (in MAIN-DLG.CPP) processes `WM_LBUTTONDOWN` messages, which are sent whenever the user presses the left mouse button. To determine whether the pointer is within one of the rectangles, `OnLButtonDown` calls the `PtInRect` API function, once for each bar, passing it both the `RECT` structure containing the dimensions of the bar (obtained by the `OnInitDialog` function) and a `POINT` structure containing the current coordinates of the pointer (obtained from the parameters passed with the message). `PtInRect` returns `TRUE` if the coordinates contained in the `POINT` structure are within the rectangle specified by the `RECT` structure.

If the pointer is found to be within one of the rectangles, `OnLButtonDown` calls the `SendMessage` API function to send the main window a `WM_COMMAND` message bearing the identifier of the appropriate command on the Statistics menu. The `OnCommand` function then processes this message just as if the user had selected the menu command. The following code—for the USER resources—illustrates these steps:

```
if (PtInRect (&RectUser, Point))
   SendMessage (mHDialog, WM_COMMAND, IDM_USER, OL);
```

Enhancing the Resource Viewer

This section describes how you might enhance the Resource Viewer by displaying the memory usage of each running program.

The Resource Viewer displays the total amount of memory that is currently used, but it does not show how much memory has been consumed by each running program. It might be useful to know the current global memory usage on a program-by-program basis. This information would give you a picture of the memory efficiency of each application, and, further, would help you decide which programs to terminate if you needed to generate additional free memory.

To provide this information, you could display a list box containing the name of each running program, together with the program's memory consumption. You could obtain this information by directly examining the Windows global heap using the `GlobalFirst` and `GlobalNext` API functions (provided by the TOOLHELP library). These functions allow you to obtain information on each item in the global heap, which contains the memory allocated for each program; this information includes the size of each global memory object, the type of the object, and the module handle of the object's owner.

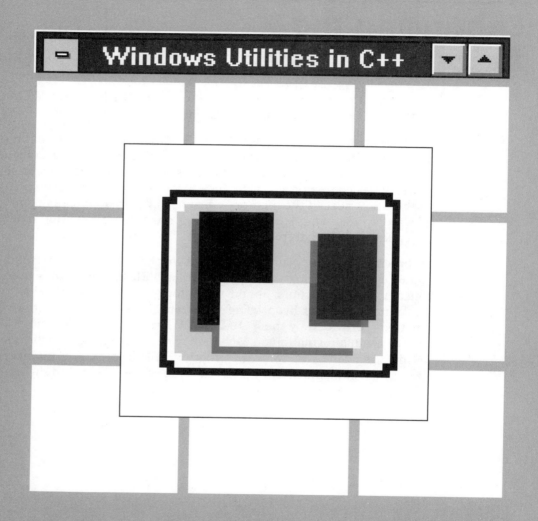

CHAPTER

4

Setup Saver

WHEN running programs using the Windows 3.1 Program Manager or File Manager, you cannot start more than one program at a time, nor can you specify the sizes or positions of the windows belonging to these programs. The Setup Saver presented in this chapter allows you to save and restore setups consisting of entire groups of programs. When you restore a setup, the Setup Saver automatically runs all of the programs and assigns each program window its original size and position. Thus, with a single command, you can quickly establish a complete Windows environment for doing a particular type of work. As you become accustomed to the Setup Saver, you might find yourself using it to start programs more often than you use the Windows Program Manager.

You can also use the Setup Saver to automatically save the entire set of applications you are running when you quit Windows and then restore these programs when you restart Windows. For each program stored in a setup, you can specify a set of parameters to be passed to the program when it is run, as well as a working directory that is activated when the program is run.

The source code for the Setup Saver illustrates a variety of methods for obtaining information on all of the Windows programs that are currently running, including the name of each executable file as well as the size and position of each main program window. The code also shows how to terminate or run other programs from within a Windows program, and how to control the size and position of the main windows belonging to these programs.

How to Use the Setup Saver

In this section, you will learn how to perform the following tasks with the Setup Saver:

- Saving a setup
- Editing a setup to specify parameters or a working directory for one or more of the programs in the setup
- Restoring a setup
- Automatically saving the state of your programs when you quit Windows, and restoring these programs when you restart Windows
- Setting options for the Setup Saver program

NOTE By using the Setup Saver in conjunction with the Task Scheduler presented in the next chapter, you can automatically restore setups at prespecified times. You can also run a Windows Recorder macro after a setup is restored in order to fully automate a task involving one or more programs. See Chapter 5 for information on using these two programs together.

Saving a Setup

To save a setup, perform the following steps:

1. Run all of the Windows programs that you want to include in the setup. Arrange the program windows so that each one has the size and position you want it to have whenever you restore the setup. Also, make sure that overlapping windows are stacked in the

desired order; when the Setup Saver restores the windows, it re-establishes the original stacking order.

NOTE

DOS sessions are *not* saved within a setup; the Setup Saver works only with Windows applications. You can, however, run one or more DOS programs when you save a setup; they will simply be ignored.

2. If the Setup Saver is not already running, run it now. The main program window will appear, as shown in Figure 4.1.

3. Enter a name for the new setup into the Setup Name: text box (at the top of the list). The name can consist of up to 16 characters

FIGURE 4.1

The Setup Saver main window

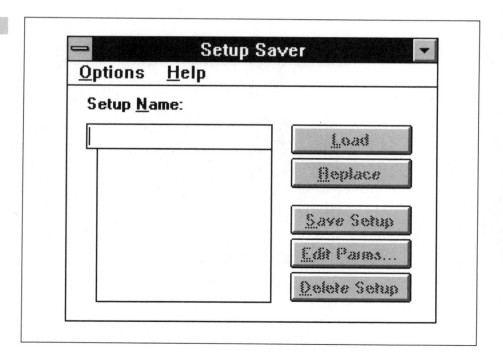

and can include spaces (the program ignores the case of the letters). If you choose the name of a setup you have already defined, the program will ask if you want to redefine the existing setup.

NOTE   In general, you should not give a setup the name "AutoSave." This name is reserved for a setup that is automatically saved when you exit Windows, as described later in the chapter, in the section "Preserving the Desktop When You Quit and Restart Windows."

4. Click the Save Setup button. The new setup will be added to the list box.

You can create up to 24 different setups (plus an AutoSave setup, as described later). All setups that you define are saved in the Setup Saver's initialization file (SETSAVE.INI) and will be available whenever you run the program. If you want to eliminate a setup, select it and click the Delete Setup button.

Editing the Setup

When you click the Save Setup button, the Setup Saver creates a setup that stores the full file path for each running Windows program, as well as the size and position of each program's main window. If you wish, you can then edit the setup in order to specify command-line parameters or a working directory for one or more of the programs in the setup.

If you specify command-line parameters for a program, Windows will pass the parameters to the program when you restore the setup. For example, if the program is a word processor, you might specify the name of a document to open as well as one or more switches that affect the program's behavior.

If you specify a working directory for a program, Windows will switch to that directory immediately before running the program. This directory will then become the program's current directory.

To edit a setup, perform the following steps:

1. Type the name of the setup you want to edit into the Setup Name: text box, or simply select the setup name in the list box (it will then be copied to the text box).

2. Click the Edit Parms... (short for "Parameters") button, and the program will open the Edit Parms dialog box, which is shown in Figure 4.2. Within this dialog box, the Applications: list box will display the name of each program belonging to the setup.

3. Select the name of the program you want to edit. The dialog box displays the following information for the selected program: the program window status (normal, zoomed, or icon), the position of the window (that is, the horizontal and vertical screen coordinates of the upper-left window corner), and the dimensions of the window (the width followed by the height).

FIGURE 4.2

The Edit Parms
dialog box

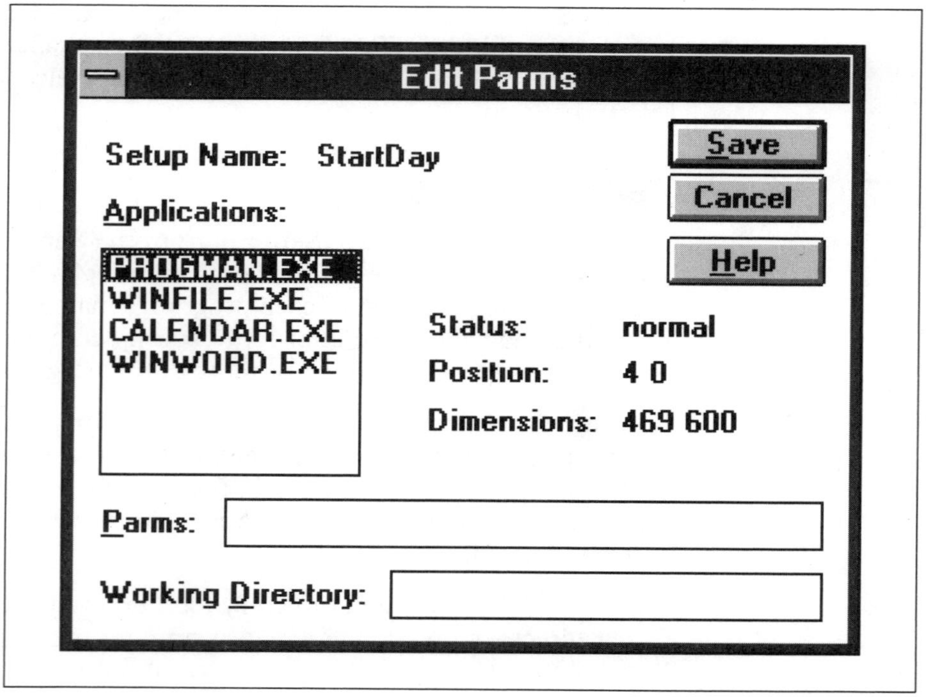

4. Enter into the Parms: text box any parameters you want passed to the program when it is run. They will be passed exactly as you type them.

5. Enter into the Working Directory: text box the *full path* specification (including the drive) of the directory you want to be the current directory when the program is run.

6. Click the Save button to store the parameters and working directory (or any changes you have made to these items). Figure 4.3 illustrates the Edit Parms dialog box after parameters and a working directory have been specified.

7. Repeat steps 3 through 6 for any other programs within the setup that you want to edit.

8. When you are done editing the setup, click the Close button (which is labeled Cancel if you have not yet saved any changes).

FIGURE 4.3

The Edit Parms dialog box specifying parameters and a working directory for an application (CALENDAR.EXE) in a setup named StartDay

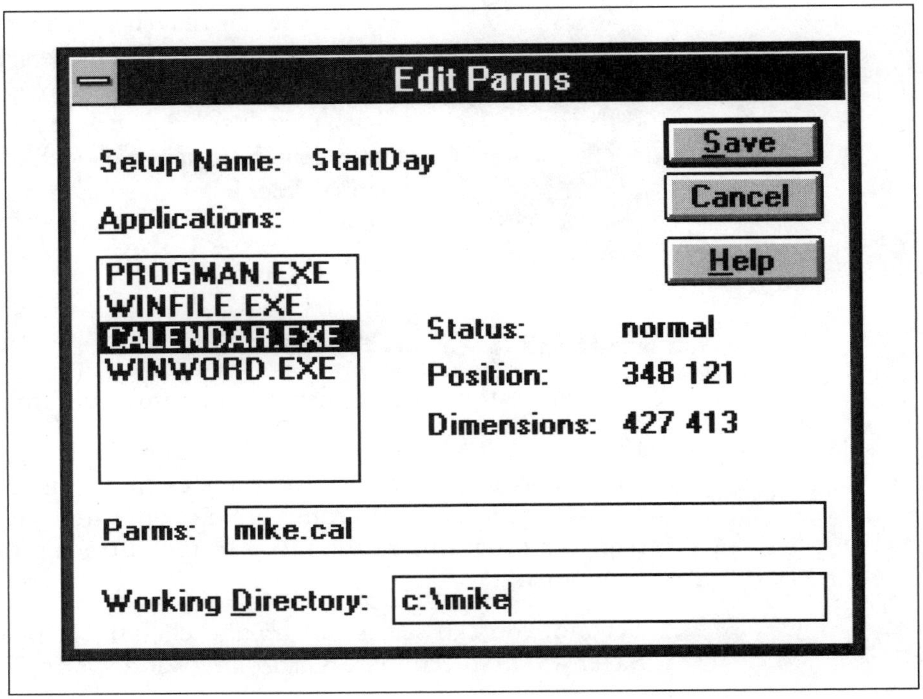

Edit Parms

Setup Name: StartDay

Applications:

Save
Cancel
Help

PROGMAN.EXE
WINFILE.EXE
CALENDAR.EXE
WINWORD.EXE

Status: normal
Position: 348 121
Dimensions: 427 413

Parms: mike.cal

Working Directory: c:\mike

The programs listed in the Applications: list box are listed in the order in which they are run (thus, if the windows overlap, the first program will be the bottom-most and the last window will be the top-most). If you specify a working directory for a program, the Setup Saver will use this same directory for all subsequent programs it runs, until it encounters a program for which a different directory is specified. Thus, for example, if you want all programs to have the *same* working directory, you need specify the directory only for the first application in the list.

NOTE

You can delete one or more programs from a setup by directly editing the program initialization file, SETSAVE.INI, which is stored in your Windows directory. To delete a program, erase the line containing the description of the program. After you have deleted one or more lines from a section that defines a particular setup, you must make sure that the entries for the remaining setup programs are labeled using consecutive numbers; that is, they must be labeled as *win1*, *win2*, *win3*, and so on. You can also directly edit any of the other setup information; the format of the information will be described later in the chapter, in the section "Saving a Setup."

Restoring a Setup

You can restore a setup, using one of three different methods.

First, you can select a setup and click the Load button. The Setup Saver will simply load all of the programs contained in the setup, and any programs that are already running will continue to run. This method thus *adds* the programs in the setup to the current set of Windows or DOS programs.

Second, you can select a setup and click the Replace button. The Setup Saver will first terminate all running Windows applications, except for the

Program Manager (or an alternative Windows shell program if you have installed one). It will then load the programs contained in the setup. This method thus *replaces* the current set of programs with the programs in the setup. Note, however, that the Replace option will *not* terminate a DOS session.

NOTE

If you click the Replace button, one or more of the current programs may prompt you before terminating (for example, a program may prompt you if it has unsaved data). If you wish to stop the Setup Saver from terminating additional programs at this time, you can click the Cancel button in the Replace dialog box (which the Setup Saver displays while it is terminating Windows programs); no more programs will be terminated and no programs will be loaded.

Third, you can cause the Setup Saver to load a particular setup by passing the name of a setup on the command line when running the program. This has the same effect as running the Setup Saver, selecting the setup, and then clicking the Load button. For example, the following command line would run the Setup Saver and load the setup named StartDay:

```
SETSAVE StartDay
```

If desired, you can define a Program Manager item to run the Setup Saver, specifying the name of a setup on the command line. This would allow you to load an entire group of programs by simply clicking on a single Program Manager icon (or to load a single program and assign its window the desired position and size). Figure 4.4 illustrates the Program Item Properties dialog box of the Program Manager, in which a program item is being defined to load a setup named StartDay (note that this figure does not show the complete command line, since the text in the Command Line: box has scrolled).

FIGURE 4.4

Defining a Program
Manager item to run a
setup

> **NOTE**
>
> If you run the Setup Saver when an instance of the program is already running, the original instance will be activated and will load the setup specified on the command line (if any). The second instance will then exit (since Setup Saver allows you to run only a single program instance). Thus, you can always use the command line method to load a setup, even if the Setup Saver is already running.

Preserving the Desktop When You Quit and Restart Windows

You can use the Setup Saver to automatically save the state of the Windows programs that are running when you exit Windows, and then to automatically restore these programs the next time you start Windows. Use the following procedure:

- Enable the Auto Save option on the Setup Saver Options menu.

- Add a program item to the Program Manager StartUp group; placing a program item in this group causes Windows to automatically run the program when Windows is first started. This item should run the Setup Saver, and pass the name AutoStart as a parameter, as shown in Figure 4.5.

- Make sure that the Setup Saver is running whenever you quit Windows (it need not be the active program, and it can be minimized).

This procedure will have the following result: Whenever you quit Windows, the Setup Saver will automatically save the current set of programs in a setup named AutoSave. The next time you start Windows, the Setup Saver will run and will load this setup, restoring the Windows desktop.

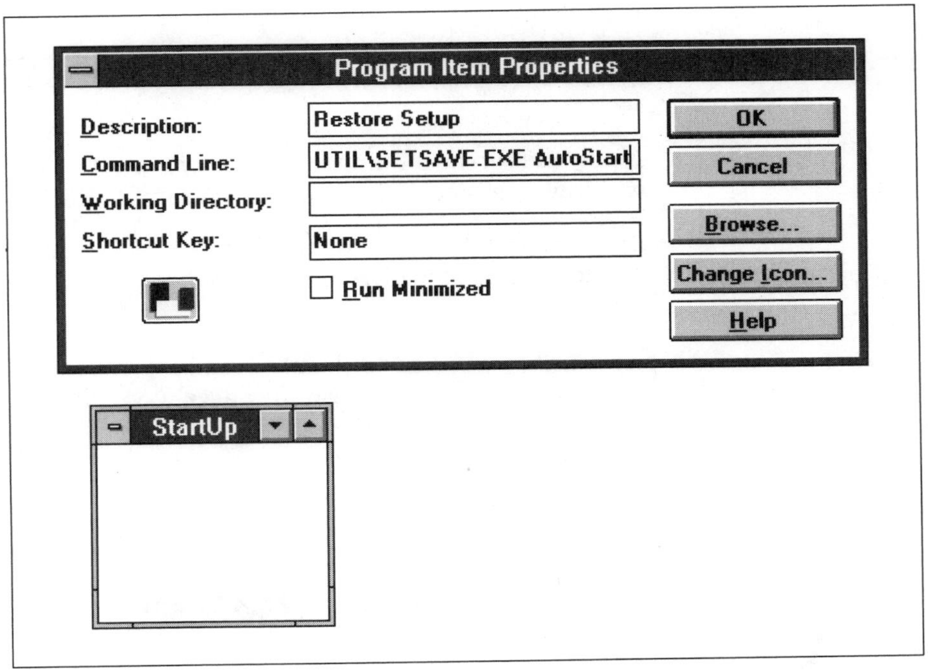

FIGURE 4.5

Defining a Program Manager item to restore the previous set of programs when Windows is started

NOTE

Unless you want to load one or more programs *in addition to* those that were running when you quit Windows, you should *not* have any other icons in the Program Manager StartUp group, nor should you specify any other programs in RUN= or LOAD= statements in the WIN.INI file.

Setting Options

The Options menu allows you to enable or disable three different options: Auto Save, Minimize on Use, and Always on Top.

If you enable the Auto Save option, whenever you end the Windows session, the Setup Saver will automatically save the current set of Windows programs within a setup named AutoSave, as explained in the previous section.

If you enable the Minimize on Use option, the Setup Saver will reduce its window to an icon immediately after it restores a setup.

If you select the Always on Top menu option, the Setup Saver main window or icon will remain visible, even if an overlapping window is activated.

You might want to enable both the Minimize on Use and the Always on Top options so that the Setup Saver icon will always be visible on your screen, ready for quickly loading a setup.

How the Setup Saver Works

The source code for the Setup Saver program, SETSAVE, is contained in Listings 4.1 through 4.6, and the program icon is shown in Figure 4.6.

FIGURE 4.6

The SETSAVE
program icon

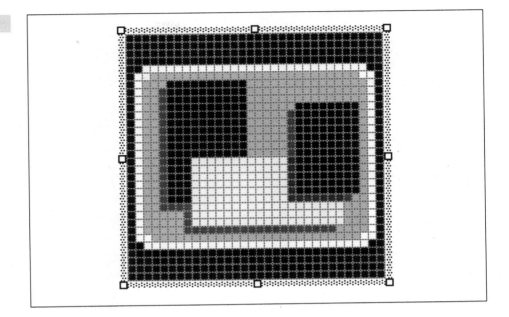

Listing 4.1 is the program header file (SETSAVE.H), which is included
in the C++ source files. Listing 4.2 (SETSAVE.CPP) contains the C++
source code for WinMain and declarations for global objects. Listing 4.3
(DIALOG.CPP) defines the member functions belonging to the main
window class (CMainDialog) as well as the member functions belonging
to the other classes that manage modal and modeless dialog boxes.

Listing 4.4 (SETSAVE.DEF) is the module definition file, and Listings 4.5 and 4.6 (RESOURCE.H and SETSAVE.RC) are the program
resource files generated by the Microsoft App Studio.

Listing 4.1

```
/////////////////////////////////////////////////////////////////
//                                                             //
// SETSAVE.H:  Header file for the SETSAVE program.            //
//                                                             //
/////////////////////////////////////////////////////////////////

#include "..\wclasses\wclasses.h"
```

```
#include "resource.h"

// constant for help topic:
#define HELPEDITDLG 100

////////////////////////////////////////////////////////////////////
// main dialog box class definition:                              //
////////////////////////////////////////////////////////////////////

class CMainDialog : public CMLDialog
{
    int AutoSave;
    HBRUSH HBrushWorkSpace;
    int MinOnUse;
    int OnTop;

    virtual BOOL DialogProc (UINT Msg, WPARAM WParam,
                             LPARAM LParam);

    BOOL AllClosed ();
    HWND GetShellHandle (char *ShellName);
    HWND GetWindowHandle (HINSTANCE HInstance);
    BOOL IsShell (char *ModuleFileName);
    BOOL OnCommand (int IDItem, HWND HWndCtl, WORD NotifyCode);
    BOOL OnCtlColor (HDC HDCChild, HWND HWndChild, int CtlType);
    BOOL OnDestroy ();
    BOOL OnInitDialog (HWND HWndFocus, LPARAM Data);
    BOOL OnQueryEndSession ();
    BOOL OnSysColorChange ();
    void WrapUp ();

public:
    CMainDialog ();
    void CloseApp (HWND HWnd);
    int GetSecIdx (char *SetupName, int *IdxSection);

};


////////////////////////////////////////////////////////////////////
// 'Replace' cancel modeless dialog box class definition:      //
////////////////////////////////////////////////////////////////////
```

```
class CMessageDialog : public CMLDialog
{
    virtual BOOL DialogProc (UINT Msg, WPARAM WParam,
                             LPARAM LParam);

public:
    BOOL QuitReplace;

};

////////////////////////////////////////////////////////////////////
// 'Edit Parms' modal dialog box class definition:                  //
////////////////////////////////////////////////////////////////////

class CEditDialog : public CMDialog
{
    virtual BOOL DialogProc (UINT Msg, WPARAM WParam,
                             LPARAM LParam);

    void ReplaceField (char *Position, char *NewString);
};
```

Listing 4.2

```
////////////////////////////////////////////////////////////////////
//                                                                  //
// SETSAVE.CPP:  Global object declarations and program entry       //
//               point for the SETSAVE program.                     //
//                                                                  //
////////////////////////////////////////////////////////////////////

#include "setsave.h"

////////////////////////////////////////////////////////////////////
// global object declarations:                                      //
////////////////////////////////////////////////////////////////////

CApplication App;
CMainDialog MainDialog;
```

SETUP SAVER

```
///////////////////////////////////////////////////////////
// program entry function:                                //
///////////////////////////////////////////////////////////

int PASCAL WinMain
   (HINSTANCE HInstCurrent,
   HINSTANCE HInstPrevious,
   LPSTR CmdLine,
   int CmdShow)
   {
   MSG Msg;

   if (HInstPrevious)
      {
      HWND HWndPopup;
      int Result;

      GetInstanceData
         (HInstPrevious,
         (BYTE *)&MainDialog.mHDialog,
         sizeof (HWND));
      ShowWindow (MainDialog.mHDialog, SW_SHOWNORMAL);
      HWndPopup = GetLastActivePopup (MainDialog.mHDialog);
      BringWindowToTop (MainDialog.mHDialog);
      BringWindowToTop (HWndPopup);

      // if command line contains the name of a setup,
      // cause previous instance to load the setup:

      if (CmdLine [0] == '\0')
         return (FALSE);  // empty command line

      // try to find a setup that matches command line:
      Result = (int)SendDlgItemMessage
         (MainDialog.mHDialog,
         IDC_COMBO,
         CB_FINDSTRINGEXACT,
         -1,
         (LPARAM)CmdLine);
      if (Result == CB_ERR)
         return (FALSE);  // no matching setup found
```

```
// setup found; place setup name in combo box edit control:
SendDlgItemMessage
    (MainDialog.mHDialog,
    IDC_COMBO,
    WM_SETTEXT,
    0,
    (LPARAM)(LPCSTR)CmdLine);

// enable buttons, as if user had entered the setup:
EnableWindow (GetDlgItem (MainDialog.mHDialog, IDC_SAVE),
              TRUE);
EnableWindow (GetDlgItem (MainDialog.mHDialog, IDC_LOAD),
              TRUE);
EnableWindow (GetDlgItem (MainDialog.mHDialog,
              IDC_REPLACE), TRUE);
EnableWindow (GetDlgItem (MainDialog.mHDialog, IDC_EDIT),
              TRUE);
EnableWindow (GetDlgItem (MainDialog.mHDialog, IDC_DELETE),
              TRUE);

// cause previous instance to load setup:
PostMessage (MainDialog.mHDialog, WM_COMMAND, IDC_LOAD,
              0L);
return (FALSE);
}

App.Initialize (HInstCurrent, HInstPrevious, CmdLine,
              CmdShow);

if (!App.LoadAccel ("SetSaveAccel"))
    return (FALSE);

if (!MainDialog.SetIcon ("SetSaveIcon"))
    return (FALSE);

if (!MainDialog.Create ("MainDlg"))
    return (FALSE);

while (GetMessage (&Msg, NULL, NULL, NULL))
    if (!TranslateAccelerator (MainDialog.mHDialog,
```

```
                                    App.mHAccelTable,
                                    &Msg))
            if (!IsDialogMessage (MainDialog.mHDialog, &Msg))
                {
                TranslateMessage (&Msg);
                DispatchMessage (&Msg);
                }

        return (Msg.wParam);
        }
```

Listing 4.3

```
///////////////////////////////////////////////////////////////////
//                                                                 //
// DIALOG.CPP:  Dialog class member functions for the              //
//              SETSAVE program.                                    //
//                                                                 //
///////////////////////////////////////////////////////////////////

#include "setsave.h"
#include <ctype.h>
#include <direct.h>
#include <stdio.h>
#include <stdlib.h>
#include <string.h>

#define MAXSETUPS  25   // max number of setups
#define MAXWINDOWS 99   // max number of apps per setup
#define PARMLIMIT  64   // max length of app parms
#define SIZENAME   17   // size of buffer to hold setup name

// constants returned by CMainDialog::GetSecIdx function:
#define GS_FOUND    0
#define GS_NOTFOUND 1
#define GS_NOROOM   2


extern CApplication App;
static char Buffer [_MAX_PATH + _MAX_PATH + PARMLIMIT + 64];
extern CMainDialog MainDialog;
CMessageDialog MessageDialog;
```

```
//////////////////////////////////////////////////////////////
// CMainDialog member functions:                             //
//////////////////////////////////////////////////////////////

CMainDialog::CMainDialog ()
   {
   HBrushWorkSpace = 0;
   }

BOOL CMainDialog::DialogProc (UINT Msg, WPARAM WParam,
                              LPARAM LParam)
   {
   switch (Msg)
      {
      case WM_CLOSE:
         Destroy ();
         return (TRUE);

      case WM_COMMAND:
         return OnCommand ((int)WParam, (HWND)LOWORD (LParam),
                           HIWORD (LParam));

      case WM_CTLCOLOR:
         return OnCtlColor ((HDC)WParam, (HWND)LOWORD (LParam),
                            (int)HIWORD (LParam));

      case WM_DESTROY:
         return OnDestroy ();

      case WM_ENDSESSION:  // sent when Windows session is ended
         if (WParam)
            WrapUp ();
         return (TRUE);

      case WM_INITDIALOG:
         return OnInitDialog ((HWND)WParam, LParam);

      case WM_QUERYENDSESSION:  // sent BEFORE Windows session
                                // is ended
         return OnQueryEndSession ();
```

```
      case WM_SYSCOLORCHANGE:
         return OnSysColorChange ();

      default:
         return (FALSE);
      }
   }

BOOL CMainDialog::AllClosed ()
// returns TRUE if all applications have been terminated except
// the Windows shell or a DOS program
   {
   HWND HWnd;
   char ModuleFileName [_MAX_PATH + 1];

   // cycle through all top-level windows:
   HWnd = GetWindow (mHDialog, GW_HWNDFIRST);
   while (HWnd != NULL)
      {
      // test that window does not belong to SETSAVE and that it
      // is visible:
      if (HWnd != mHDialog && HWnd != MessageDialog.mHDialog &&
         IsWindowVisible (HWnd))
         {
         // get the file path of the application that has created
         // the window:
         GetModuleFileName
            ((HINSTANCE)GetWindowWord (HWnd, GWW_HINSTANCE),
            ModuleFileName,
            sizeof (ModuleFileName));

         // if the application is NOT the Windows shell and NOT
         // a DOS session (a .MOD file), return FALSE,
         // indicating that a Windows app is still running:
         if (!IsShell (ModuleFileName) &&
            strstr (ModuleFileName ,".MOD") == NULL)
            return (FALSE);
         }
      HWnd = GetNextWindow (HWnd, GW_HWNDNEXT);
      }
```

```
    return (TRUE);
    }


void CMainDialog::CloseApp (HWND HWnd)
// closes the application associated with the top-level window
// 'HWnd', unless the window is not visible, or it is created
// by the current app, the Windows shell, or a DOS session
    {
    char ModuleFileName [_MAX_PATH + 1];

    if (!IsWindow (HWnd) || HWnd == mHDialog ||
        !IsWindowVisible (HWnd))
        return;

    // get the file path of the application that has created
    // the window:
    GetModuleFileName
        ((HINSTANCE)GetWindowWord (HWnd, GWW_HINSTANCE),
        ModuleFileName,
        sizeof (ModuleFileName));

    // post close message if the application is NOT the Windows
    // shell and NOT a DOS session:
    if (!IsShell (ModuleFileName) &&
        strstr (ModuleFileName ,".MOD") == NULL)
        PostMessage (HWnd, WM_CLOSE, 0, 0L);
    }


BOOL CALLBACK _export EnumWindowsProc (HWND HWnd, LPARAM LParam)
// calling EnumWindows causes Windows to call this function
// once for each top-level window
    {
    MainDialog.CloseApp (HWnd);  // try to close the app
    return (TRUE);  // return TRUE to continue enumerating windows
    }


int CMainDialog::GetSecIdx (char *SetupName, int *IdxSection)
// returns one of the following values:
//
// GS_FOUND if 'SetupName' is found in the INI file; *IdxSection
//    is assigned index of the INI section containing name
```

```
//
// GS_NOTFOUND if 'SetupName' is NOT found in INI file;
//    *IdxSection is assigned the index of the first free section
//    in INI file
//
// GS_NOROOM if 'SetupName' not found and no INI section is free
   {
   char Buf [SIZENAME];
   int Length;
   char SectionName [8];
   int SectionNumber;

   *IdxSection = 0;

   // the last INI section is reserved for the 'AutoSave' setup;
   // if 'SetupName' equals 'AutoSave', test whether an
   // 'AutoSave' setup has been stored:
   if (stricmp (SetupName, "AutoSave") == 0)
      {
      *IdxSection = MAXSETUPS;  // index of last section

      // derive section name and try to get name from section:
      sprintf (SectionName, "setup%d", MAXSETUPS);
      Length = GetPrivateProfileString
         (SectionName,
         "name",
         "",
         Buf,
         sizeof (Buf),
         "SETSAVE.INI");
      if (Length == 0)
         return (GS_NOTFOUND);  // no 'AutoSave' setup
      else
         return (GS_FOUND);     // 'AutoSave' setup present
      }

   // test the nonreserved INI sections:
   for (SectionNumber = 1; SectionNumber < MAXSETUPS;
      ++SectionNumber)
      {
      sprintf (SectionName, "setup%d", SectionNumber);
```

```
    Length = GetPrivateProfileString
       (SectionName,
       "name",
       "",
       Buf,
       sizeof (Buf),
       "SETSAVE.INI");

    if (Length == 0 && *IdxSection == 0)
       // first free section; save index:
       *IdxSection = SectionNumber;
    else if (stricmp (Buf, SetupName) == 0)
       {
       // section contains matching name; return index:
       *IdxSection = SectionNumber;
       return (GS_FOUND);
       }
    }
  if (*IdxSection == 0)
     return (GS_NOROOM);     // no free or matching section found
  else
     return (GS_NOTFOUND);  // free nonmatching section found
  }

HWND CMainDialog::GetShellHandle (char *ShellName)
// returns the handle of the top-level window belonging to
// the shell program (usually, PROGMAN.EXE);
// 'ShellName' must contain the full path name of
// the shell's executable file
  {
  HWND HWnd;
  char ModuleFileName [_MAX_PATH + 1];

  // cycle through all top-level windows:
  HWnd = GetWindow (mHDialog, GW_HWNDFIRST);
  while (HWnd != NULL)
     {
     // get the file path of the application that has created
     // the window:
     GetModuleFileName
        ((HINSTANCE)GetWindowWord (HWnd, GWW_HINSTANCE),
```

```
            ModuleFileName,
            sizeof (ModuleFileName));

        // if the application is the shell, AND the window is not
        // an owned window, AND the window is visible,
        // return the handle:
        if (stricmp (ModuleFileName, ShellName) == 0 &&
            !GetWindow (HWnd, GW_OWNER) &&
            IsWindowVisible (HWnd))
            return (HWnd);

        HWnd = GetNextWindow (HWnd, GW_HWNDNEXT);
        }
    return (NULL);  // handle not found
    }


HWND CMainDialog::GetWindowHandle (HINSTANCE HInstance)
// returns the handle of the top-level, nonowned, visible window
// created by the 'HInstance' program instance
    {
    HWND HWnd;

    HWnd = GetWindow (mHDialog, GW_HWNDFIRST);
    while (HWnd != NULL)
        {
        if ((HINSTANCE)GetWindowWord (HWnd, GWW_HINSTANCE) ==
            HInstance && !GetWindow (HWnd, GW_OWNER) &&
            IsWindowVisible (HWnd))
            return (HWnd);

        HWnd = GetNextWindow (HWnd, GW_HWNDNEXT);
        }
    return (NULL);
    }


BOOL CMainDialog::IsShell (char *ModuleFileName)
// returns TRUE if the file path in 'ModuleFileName' contains the
// name of the Windows shell program (usually PROGMAN.EXE)
    {
    char ShellName [13];
```

```
    // get the name of the shell program the user has installed:
    GetPrivateProfileString
        ("boot",
        "shell",
        "",
        ShellName,
        sizeof (ShellName),
        "SYSTEM.INI");

    strupr (ModuleFileName);    // convert both names to uppercase
    strupr (ShellName);

    return (BOOL)strstr (ModuleFileName, ShellName);
    }

BOOL CMainDialog::OnCommand (int IDItem, HWND HWndCtl,
                            WORD NotifyCode)
    {
    char Char;
    UINT CmdShow;
    int Count = 0;
    HINSTANCE HInstance;
    HWND HWnd;
    int Idx = 0;
    char EntryName [6];
    int Length;
    char ModuleFileName [_MAX_PATH + 1];
    MSG Msg;
    char *PChar;
    RECT Rect;
    int Result;
    char SectionName [8];
    char SetupName [SIZENAME];
    char *WorkDir;

    switch (IDItem)
        {
        case IDC_COMBO:
            if (NotifyCode == CBN_EDITCHANGE)
                {
                // user has changed text in edit control of combo box
```

```
               // get text from edit control:
               GetDlgItemText (mHDialog, IDC_COMBO, SetupName,
                              SIZENAME);
               // enable Save button if edit control contains text:
               EnableWindow
                  (GetDlgItem (mHDialog, IDC_SAVE),
                  SetupName [0] != '\0');

               // try to find edit-control text in list box:
               Result = (int)SendDlgItemMessage
                  (mHDialog,
                  IDC_COMBO,
                  CB_FINDSTRINGEXACT,
                  -1,
                  (LPARAM)(LPCSTR)SetupName);

               // if Result != CB_ERR, text is found, meaning that
               // the text control contains the name of an existing
               // setup; therefore, enable the other buttons:

               EnableWindow (GetDlgItem (mHDialog, IDC_LOAD),
                              Result != CB_ERR);
               EnableWindow (GetDlgItem (mHDialog, IDC_REPLACE),
                              Result != CB_ERR);
               EnableWindow (GetDlgItem (mHDialog, IDC_EDIT),
                              Result != CB_ERR);
               EnableWindow (GetDlgItem (mHDialog, IDC_DELETE),
                              Result != CB_ERR);
               }

           else if (NotifyCode == CBN_SELCHANGE)
               {
               // user has selected a new item in list box; the text
               // for the item is automatically copied to the edit
               // control; therefore, edit control contains the name
               // of an existing setup and all buttons should be
               // enabled:

               EnableWindow
                  (GetDlgItem (mHDialog, IDC_SAVE), TRUE);
```

```
        EnableWindow
           (GetDlgItem (mHDialog, IDC_LOAD), TRUE);
        EnableWindow
           (GetDlgItem (mHDialog, IDC_REPLACE), TRUE);
        EnableWindow
           (GetDlgItem (mHDialog, IDC_EDIT), TRUE);
        EnableWindow
           (GetDlgItem (mHDialog, IDC_DELETE), TRUE);
        }
     return (TRUE);

case IDC_DELETE:  // user clicked Delete button
     // get text in edit control of combo box:
     GetDlgItemText (mHDialog, IDC_COMBO, SetupName,
                     SIZENAME);

     // verify that user wants to delete the setup:
     sprintf (Buffer,"Delete setup '%s'?", SetupName);
     Result = MessageBox
        (mHDialog,
        Buffer,
        "Delete Setup",
        MB_YESNO | MB_ICONQUESTION);
     if (Result != IDYES)
        return (TRUE);

     // remove the string from the list box of combo box:
     Result = (int)SendDlgItemMessage
        (mHDialog,
        IDC_COMBO,
        CB_FINDSTRINGEXACT,
        -1,
        (LPARAM)(LPCSTR)SetupName);
     SendDlgItemMessage
        (mHDialog,
        IDC_COMBO,
        CB_DELETESTRING,
        Result,
        OL);

     // obtain the name of the INI file section containing
```

```
                  // the setup that is to be deleted:
                  GetSecIdx (SetupName, &Idx);
                  sprintf (SectionName, "setup%d", Idx);

                  // delete the entire INI section:
                  WritePrivateProfileString (SectionName, NULL, NULL,
                                             "SETSAVE.INI");

                  // delete the setup name from the edit control and
                  // disable all buttons:
                  SetDlgItemText (mHDialog, IDC_COMBO, "");
                  EnableWindow
                     (GetDlgItem (mHDialog, IDC_SAVE), FALSE);
                  EnableWindow
                     (GetDlgItem (mHDialog, IDC_LOAD), FALSE);
                  EnableWindow
                     (GetDlgItem (mHDialog, IDC_REPLACE), FALSE);
                  EnableWindow
                     (GetDlgItem (mHDialog, IDC_EDIT), FALSE);
                  EnableWindow
                     (GetDlgItem (mHDialog, IDC_DELETE), FALSE);

                  // give focus to the edit control (don't leave focus
                  // with a disabled button):
                  SetFocus (GetDlgItem (mHDialog, IDC_COMBO));

                  return (TRUE);

            case IDC_EDIT:  // user clicked Edit Parms... button
               {
               // display Edit Parms dialog box:
               CEditDialog EditDialog;
               EditDialog.Create ("EditDlg", mHDialog);
               return (TRUE);
               }

            case IDC_LOAD:      // user clicked Load or Replace button
            case IDC_REPLACE:

               // if user clicked Replace button, terminate all running
               // Windows applications, except the Windows shell:
```

```
if (IDItem == IDC_REPLACE)
  {
  // calling EnumWindows forces Windows to call
  // EnumWindowsProc once for each top-level window;
  // EnumWindowsProc terminates the app (if it is not
  // the shell):
  EnumWindows (EnumWindowsProc, OL);

  // display the modeless dialog box w/ Cancel button:
  MessageDialog.Create ("MessageDlg", mHDialog);
  MessageDialog.QuitReplace = FALSE;

  // disable the main window:
  EnableWindow (mHDialog, FALSE);

  // process messages while waiting for all apps to
  // terminate or for the user to click Cancel button
  // in modeless dialog box:
  while (!AllClosed () && !MessageDialog.QuitReplace)
     {
     while (PeekMessage (&Msg, NULL, NULL, NULL,
                         PM_REMOVE))
       {
       if (!IsDialogMessage (MessageDialog.mHDialog,
                             &Msg)
           && !IsDialogMessage (mHDialog, &Msg))
          {
          TranslateMessage (&Msg);
          DispatchMessage (&Msg);
          }
       }
     }
  // reenable the main window:
  EnableWindow (mHDialog, TRUE);

  // remove the modeless dialog box:
  MessageDialog.Destroy ();

  // exit if user cancelled replace operation:
  if (MessageDialog.QuitReplace)
     return (TRUE);
```

```
    }

// now load the setup:

// get setup name and derive the INI section name:
GetDlgItemText (mHDialog, IDC_COMBO, SetupName,
                SIZENAME);
GetSecIdx (SetupName, &Idx);
sprintf (SectionName, "setup%d", Idx);

// cycle through all applications listed within the
// INI section for the setup:
Idx = 0;
for (;;)
    {
    // load the application description into 'Buffer':
    sprintf (EntryName, "win%d", ++Idx);
    Length = GetPrivateProfileString
        (SectionName,
        EntryName,
        "",
        Buffer,
        sizeof (Buffer),
        "SETSAVE.INI");
    if (Length <= 0)
        break;

    // process the description:

    // place NULL after the app name:
    PChar = strchr (Buffer, '¦');
    *PChar = '\0';

    // if app is the shell, assign its handle to HWnd;
    // otherwise, set HWnd to NULL:
    if (IsShell (Buffer))
        {
        HWnd = GetShellHandle (Buffer);
        if (HWnd == NULL)
            continue;
        }
```

```
else
   HWnd = NULL;

// replace NULL with blank and place NULL after
// the command line:
*PChar = ' ';
PChar = strchr (PChar, '¦');
*PChar = '\0';

// make PChar point to the character that encodes the
// window state, and store value that will be passed
// to ShowWindow:
++PChar;
switch (*PChar)
   {
   case 'n':
      CmdShow = SW_SHOWNORMAL;
      break;
   case 'z':
      CmdShow = SW_SHOWMAXIMIZED;
      break;
   case 'i':
      CmdShow = SW_SHOWMINIMIZED;
      break;
   }

// now point PChar to working directory:
PChar += 2;
if (*PChar != '¦')  // working directory is specified
   {
   WorkDir = PChar;

   // add NULL at end of working directory:
   PChar = strchr (PChar, '¦');
   *PChar = '\0';

   // if working directory contains drive spec,
   // change to that drive:
   if (isalpha (*WorkDir) && *(WorkDir+1) == ':')
      _chdrive (toupper (*WorkDir) - 64);
```

```
                     // change directory:
                     chdir (WorkDir);
                     }

             if (HWnd == NULL) // HWnd is NULL if program is NOT
                               // the shell
                 {
                 // execute the app:
                 HInstance = (HINSTANCE)WinExec (Buffer, CmdShow);
                 // HInstance < 32 indicates an error:
                 if ((UINT)HInstance < 32)
                    continue;

                 // get the handle of the app's top-level window:
                 HWnd = GetWindowHandle (HInstance);
                 if (HWnd == NULL)
                    continue;
                 }

             // display the window as normal, maximized, or
             // minimized:
             ShowWindow (HWnd, CmdShow);

             // if window is normal, assign it the specified size:
             if (CmdShow == SW_SHOWNORMAL)
                 {
                 int Left, Top, Width, Height;

                 ++PChar;
                 sscanf (PChar, "%d%d%d%d", &Left, &Top, &Width,
                         &Height);
                 MoveWindow (HWnd, Left, Top, Width, Height, TRUE);
                 }
             }

         if (MinOnUse)
             // Minimize on Use option is enabled;
             // therefore minimize SETSAVE window:
             ShowWindow (mHDialog, SW_MINIMIZE);

         if (IsWindow (HWnd))
```

```
          // place window of last app on top:
          BringWindowToTop (HWnd);

      return (TRUE);

  case IDC_SAVE:   // user clicked Save button

      // get name of setup to define:
      GetDlgItemText (mHDialog, IDC_COMBO, SetupName,
                      SIZENAME);

      // obtain the index of the INI file section for
      // the setup:
      switch (GetSecIdx (SetupName, &Idx))
          {
          case GS_FOUND: // setup already exists
              // if setup not 'AutoSave', warn user ('AutoSave'
              // is automatically redefined):
              if (stricmp (SetupName, "AutoSave") != 0)
                  {
                  sprintf (Buffer, "Setup '%s' already exists.\n"
                          "Do you want to redefine it?",
                          SetupName);
                  Result = MessageBox
                      (mHDialog,
                      Buffer,
                      "Save Setup",
                      MB_YESNO | MB_ICONQUESTION);
                  if (Result != IDYES)
                      return (TRUE);
                  }
              break;

          case GS_NOTFOUND:  // setup is new
              // add new setup name to list box:
              SendDlgItemMessage
                  (mHDialog,
                  IDC_COMBO,
                  CB_ADDSTRING,
                  0,
                  (LPARAM)(LPSTR)SetupName);
```

```
              break;

          case GS_NOROOM:  // cannot accommodate new setup
              MessageBox
                  (mHDialog,
                   "Cannot add another setup.\n"
                   "Delete or redefine an existing setup.",
                   "Save Setup",
                   MB_ICONEXCLAMATION | MB_OK);
              return (TRUE);
          }

      // derive name of INI file section name for setup:
      sprintf (SectionName, "setup%d", Idx);

      // if INI section already exists, this will erase it:
      WritePrivateProfileString (SectionName, NULL, NULL,
                                 "SETSAVE.INI");

      // add setup name to INI file:
      WritePrivateProfileString (SectionName, "name",
                                 SetupName, "SETSAVE.INI");

      // cycle through all top-level windows, starting with
      // the bottom window in the stacking order:
      HWnd = GetWindow (mHDialog, GW_HWNDLAST);
      while (HWnd != NULL)
          {
          // test that window is NOT the SETSAVE window, that
          // it is visible, that it is NOT owned, and that
          // maximum number of windows has not been exceeded:
          if (HWnd != mHDialog && IsWindowVisible (HWnd) &&
              !GetWindow (HWnd, GW_OWNER))
              {
              if (Count >= MAXWINDOWS)
                  break;

              // get the file path of the app that has
              // created the window:
              GetModuleFileName
                  ((HINSTANCE)GetWindowWord (HWnd,GWW_HINSTANCE),
```

```
      ModuleFileName,
      sizeof (ModuleFileName));
   strupr (ModuleFileName);  // convert to upper-case

   // obtain state of window:
   Rect.left=Rect.top=Rect.right=Rect.bottom=0;
   if (IsIconic (HWnd))
      Char = 'i';
   else if (IsZoomed (HWnd))
      Char = 'z';
   else
      {
      Char = 'n';
      // because window is normal, obtain its
      // dimensions:
      GetWindowRect (HWnd, &Rect);
      }

   // store complete app description in Buffer:
   sprintf (Buffer, "%s||%c||%d %d %d %d",
            ModuleFileName,
            Char,
            Rect.left,
            Rect.top,
            Rect.right - Rect.left,
            Rect.bottom - Rect.top);

   // if app is not a DOS session, save app
   // description in INI file:
   if (strstr (ModuleFileName, ".MOD") == NULL)
      {
      sprintf (EntryName,"win%d", ++Count);
      WritePrivateProfileString
         (SectionName,
         EntryName,
         Buffer,
         "SETSAVE.INI");
      }
   }
HWnd = GetNextWindow (HWnd, GW_HWNDPREV);
}
```

```
                        // enable all the buttons, since the edit control
                        // contains the name of a (new) setup:
                        EnableWindow (GetDlgItem (mHDialog, IDC_LOAD), TRUE);
                        EnableWindow (GetDlgItem (mHDialog, IDC_REPLACE), TRUE);
                        EnableWindow (GetDlgItem (mHDialog, IDC_EDIT), TRUE);
                        EnableWindow (GetDlgItem (mHDialog, IDC_DELETE), TRUE);

                        return (TRUE);

                   case IDM_ABOUT:
                        {
                        CMDialog MDialog;
                        MDialog.Create ("AboutDlg", mHDialog);
                        return (TRUE);
                        }

                   case IDM_AUTO:   // user chose Auto Save command on Options
                                    // menu
                        AutoSave = !AutoSave;
                        CheckMenuItem (GetMenu (mHDialog), IDM_AUTO,
                                    AutoSave ? MF_CHECKED : MF_UNCHECKED);
                        return (FALSE);

                   case IDM_HELPCONTENTS:
                        WinHelp (mHDialog, "SETSAVE.HLP", HELP_CONTENTS, OL);
                        return (TRUE);

                   case IDM_HELPHELP:
                        WinHelp (mHDialog, "SETSAVE.HLP", HELP_HELPONHELP, OL);
                        return (TRUE);

                   case IDM_HELPSEARCH:
                        WinHelp (mHDialog, "SETSAVE.HLP", HELP_PARTIALKEY,
                                (DWORD)(LPCSTR)"");
                        return (TRUE);

                   case IDM_MINIMIZE:   // user chose Minimize on Use command
                                        // on Options menu
                        MinOnUse = !MinOnUse;
                        CheckMenuItem (GetMenu (mHDialog), IDM_MINIMIZE,
```

```
                            MinOnUse ? MF_CHECKED : MF_UNCHECKED);
          return (FALSE);

      case IDM_ONTOP:    // user chose Always on Top command on
                         // Options menu
          OnTop = !OnTop;
          CheckMenuItem (GetMenu (mHDialog), IDM_ONTOP,
                         OnTop ? MF_CHECKED : MF_UNCHECKED);
          SetWindowPos (mHDialog,
                        OnTop ? HWND_TOPMOST : HWND_NOTOPMOST,
                        0, 0, 0, 0, SWP_NOMOVE ¦ SWP_NOSIZE);
          return (TRUE);


      default:
          return (FALSE);


    }
  }


BOOL CMainDialog::OnCtlColor (HDC HDCChild, HWND HWndChild,
                             int CtlType)

  {
  COLORREF WorkSpaceColor;


  switch (CtlType)
      {
      case CTLCOLOR_BTN:
      case CTLCOLOR_STATIC:
          WorkSpaceColor = GetSysColor (COLOR_APPWORKSPACE);
          if (GetRValue (WorkSpaceColor) * 2 +
              GetGValue (WorkSpaceColor) * 5 +
              GetBValue (WorkSpaceColor) > 1020)
            SetTextColor (HDCChild, RGB (0, 0, 0));
          else
            SetTextColor (HDCChild, RGB (255, 255, 255));
          SetBkMode (HDCChild, TRANSPARENT);
          return ((BOOL)HBrushWorkSpace);

      case CTLCOLOR_DLG:
          return ((BOOL)HBrushWorkSpace);
```

```
            default:
                return (FALSE);
            }
    }


BOOL CMainDialog::OnDestroy ()
    {
    WrapUp ();
    if (HBrushWorkSpace != 0)
        DeleteObject (HBrushWorkSpace);
    WinHelp (mHDialog, "SETSAVE.HLP", HELP_QUIT, OL);
    PostQuitMessage (0);
    return (TRUE);
    }


BOOL CMainDialog::OnInitDialog (HWND HWndFocus, LPARAM Data)
    {
    int Result;
    char SectionName [8];
    int SectionNumber;
    char SetupName [SIZENAME];

    // cycle through all possible sections in INI file:
    for (SectionNumber = 1; SectionNumber <= MAXSETUPS;
         ++SectionNumber)
        {
        // try to obtain setup name from section:
        sprintf (SectionName, "setup%d", SectionNumber);
        Result = GetPrivateProfileString
            (SectionName,
            "name",
            "",
            SetupName,
            sizeof (SetupName),
            "SETSAVE.INI");
        if (Result <= 0)
            // section does not exist, try next possible section:
            continue;

        // add setup name to combo box list:
        SendDlgItemMessage
```

```
      (mHDialog,
      IDC_COMBO,
      CB_ADDSTRING,
      0,
      (LPARAM)(LPSTR)SetupName);

   // if the SETSAVE command line contains the name of the
   // setup, cause program to load the setup:
   if (_fstricmp (SetupName, App.mCmdLine) == 0)
      {
      SetDlgItemText (mHDialog, IDC_COMBO, SetupName);
      EnableWindow (GetDlgItem (mHDialog, IDC_SAVE), TRUE);
      EnableWindow (GetDlgItem (mHDialog, IDC_LOAD), TRUE);
      EnableWindow (GetDlgItem (mHDialog, IDC_REPLACE), TRUE);
      EnableWindow (GetDlgItem (mHDialog, IDC_EDIT), TRUE);
      EnableWindow (GetDlgItem (mHDialog, IDC_DELETE), TRUE);
      PostMessage (mHDialog, WM_COMMAND, IDC_LOAD, 0L);
      }
   }

// limit size of setup name that user can enter:
SendDlgItemMessage
   (mHDialog,
   IDC_COMBO,
   CB_LIMITTEXT,
   SIZENAME - 1,
   0);

// read option values from INI file:

AutoSave = (int)GetPrivateProfileInt
   ("options",
   "autosave",
   0,
   "SETSAVE.INI");
if (AutoSave)
   CheckMenuItem (GetMenu (mHDialog), IDM_AUTO, MF_CHECKED);

MinOnUse = (int)GetPrivateProfileInt
   ("options",
   "minonuse",
```

```
                1,
                "SETSAVE.INI");
         if (MinOnUse)
            CheckMenuItem (GetMenu (mHDialog), IDM_MINIMIZE,
                           MF_CHECKED);

         OnTop = (int)GetPrivateProfileInt
            ("options",
             "ontop",
             1,
             "SETSAVE.INI");
         if (OnTop)
            {
            CheckMenuItem (GetMenu (mHDialog), IDM_ONTOP, MF_CHECKED);
            SetWindowPos (mHDialog, HWND_TOPMOST, 0, 0, 0, 0,
                          SWP_NOMOVE | SWP_NOSIZE);
            }

         HBrushWorkSpace = CreateSolidBrush
            (GetSysColor (COLOR_APPWORKSPACE));

         return (TRUE);
         }

BOOL CMainDialog::OnQueryEndSession ()
         {
         // this message is sent to all top-level windows BEFORE
         // the Windows session ends; if the Auto Save feature is
         // enabled, force program to save the current set of
         // apps under the setup name 'AutoSave':
         if (AutoSave)
            {
            SetDlgItemText (mHDialog, IDC_COMBO, "AutoSave");
            SendMessage (mHDialog, WM_COMMAND, IDC_SAVE, OL);
            EnableWindow (GetDlgItem (mHDialog, IDC_SAVE), TRUE);
            }
         return (FALSE);
         }

BOOL CMainDialog::OnSysColorChange ()
         {
```

```
        if (HBrushWorkSpace != 0)
            DeleteObject (HBrushWorkSpace);
        HBrushWorkSpace =
            CreateSolidBrush (GetSysColor (COLOR_APPWORKSPACE));
        return (TRUE);
        }


void CMainDialog::WrapUp ()
    {
    WritePrivateProfileString
        ("options",
         "autosave",
          AutoSave ? "1" : "0",
         "SETSAVE.INI");

    WritePrivateProfileString
        ("options",
         "minonuse",
          MinOnUse ? "1" : "0",
         "SETSAVE.INI");

    WritePrivateProfileString
        ("options",
         "ontop",
          OnTop ? "1" : "0",
         "SETSAVE.INI");
    }


/////////////////////////////////////////////////////////////////
// CEditDialog member functions:                                //
/////////////////////////////////////////////////////////////////

BOOL CEditDialog::DialogProc (UINT Msg, WPARAM WParam,
                               LPARAM LParam)
    {
    static BOOL Dirty;
    static char EntryName [6];
    int Idx;
    int Length;
    char Parms [PARMLIMIT + 1];
    char *PChar;
```

```c
char *PString;
int Result;
static char SectionName [8];
char SetupName [SIZENAME];
char *SimpleName;
char WorkDir [_MAX_PATH + 1];

switch (Msg)
   {
   case WM_COMMAND:
      switch (WParam)
         {
         case IDCANCEL:
         case IDC_CLOSE:

            // if IDC_CLOSE button is labeled "Close" and
            // user has changed data for an app, ask whether
            // data should be saved:
            GetDlgItemText (mHDialog, IDC_CLOSE, Buffer,
                            sizeof (Buffer));
            if (stricmp (Buffer, "&Close") == 0 && Dirty)
               {
               Result = MessageBox
                  (mHDialog,
                   "Do you want to save changes for selected "
                   "application?",
                   "Edit Parms",
                   MB_YESNO | MB_ICONQUESTION);
               if (Result == IDYES)
                  // save the app's data:
                  SendMessage (mHDialog, WM_COMMAND,
                               IDC_SAVE, OL);
               }

            EndDialog (mHDialog, 0);
            return (TRUE);

         case IDC_HELP:
            WinHelp (MainDialog.mHDialog, "SETSAVE.HLP",
                     HELP_CONTEXT, HELPEDITDLG);
            return (TRUE);
```

```
case IDC_LIST:
   if (HIWORD (LParam) == LBN_SELCHANGE)
       {
       // user has selected a new app in list box

       if (Dirty)
           {
           // data for previously selected app has been
           // changed
           Result = MessageBox
               (mHDialog,
               "Do you want to save changes for "
               "previous application?",
               "Edit Parms",
               MB_YESNO | MB_ICONQUESTION);
           if (Result == IDYES)
               // save the app's data:
               SendMessage (mHDialog, WM_COMMAND,
                           IDC_SAVE, OL);
           }

       // get index of newly selected app:
       Idx = (int)SendDlgItemMessage
               (mHDialog,
               IDC_LIST,
               LB_GETCURSEL, O,
               OL) + 1;

       // derive name of INI entry for app:
       sprintf (EntryName, "win%d", Idx);

       // get data for app from INI file:
       Length = GetPrivateProfileString
           (SectionName,
           EntryName,
           "",
           Buffer,
           sizeof (Buffer),
           "SETSAVE.INI");
       if (Length == 0)
```

```
                              return (TRUE);

              // display app parms in IDC_PARMS edit control:
              PChar = strchr (Buffer, '¦') + 1;
              PString = PChar;
              PChar = strchr (PChar, '¦');
              *PChar = '\0';
              SetDlgItemText (mHDialog, IDC_PARMS, PString);

              // display app status:
              ++PChar;
              PString = PChar;
              ++PChar;
              *PChar = '\0';
              switch (*PString)
                 {
                 case 'n':
                    SetDlgItemText (mHDialog, IDC_STATUS,
                                    "normal");
                    break;
                 case 'z':
                    SetDlgItemText (mHDialog, IDC_STATUS,
                                    "zoomed");
                    break;
                 case 'i':
                    SetDlgItemText (mHDialog, IDC_STATUS,
                                    "icon");
                    break;
                 }

              // display app working directory:
              ++PChar;
              PString = PChar;
              PChar = strchr (PChar, '¦');
              *PChar = '\0';
              SetDlgItemText (mHDialog, IDC_WORKDIR,
                              PString);

              // display position of app window:
              ++PChar;
              PString = PChar;
```

```
            PChar = strchr (PChar, ' ');
            PChar = strchr (PChar + 1, ' ');
            *PChar = '\0';
            SetDlgItemText (mHDialog, IDC_POS, PString);

            // display dimensions of app window:
            ++PChar;
            PString = PChar;
            SetDlgItemText (mHDialog, IDC_DIMS, PString);

            Dirty = FALSE; // set flag for changed data
            }

        return (FALSE);

    case IDC_PARMS:
    case IDC_WORKDIR:
        if (HIWORD (LParam) == EN_CHANGE)
            // user has changed data for app; set flag:
            Dirty = TRUE;

        return (TRUE);

    case IDC_SAVE:  // user clicked Save button
        // get existing data for selected app from INI:
        Length = GetPrivateProfileString
            (SectionName,
            EntryName,
            "",
            Buffer,
            sizeof (Buffer),
            "SETSAVE.INI");
        if (Length == 0)
            return (TRUE);

        // update parms:
        PChar = strchr (Buffer, '¦') + 1;
        GetDlgItemText (mHDialog, IDC_PARMS, Parms,
                        PARMLIMIT);
        ReplaceField (PChar, Parms);
```

```
        // update working directory:
        PChar = strchr (PChar, '|') + 1;
        PChar = strchr (PChar, '|') + 1;
        GetDlgItemText (mHDialog, IDC_WORKDIR, WorkDir,
                        _MAX_PATH);
        ReplaceField (PChar, WorkDir);

        // write the app data back to INI file:
        WritePrivateProfileString (SectionName, EntryName,
                                   Buffer, "SETSAVE.INI");

        // reset flag indicating changed data:
        Dirty = FALSE;

        // once data has been permanently saved, button
        // should be labeled 'Close' rather than 'Cancel':
        SetDlgItemText (mHDialog, IDC_CLOSE, "&Close");

        return (TRUE);

    default:
        return (FALSE);
    }

case WM_INITDIALOG:
    SendDlgItemMessage (mHDialog, IDC_PARMS, EM_LIMITTEXT,
                        (WPARAM)PARMLIMIT, OL);
    SendDlgItemMessage (mHDialog, IDC_WORKDIR, EM_LIMITTEXT,
                        (WPARAM)_MAX_PATH, OL);

    // display name of setup in dialog box:
    GetDlgItemText (MainDialog.mHDialog, IDC_COMBO,
                    SetupName, SIZENAME);
    SetDlgItemText (mHDialog, IDC_NAME, SetupName);

    // derive name of INI section for the setup:
    MainDialog.GetSecIdx (SetupName, &Idx);
    sprintf (SectionName, "setup%d", Idx);

    // cycle through all INI entries within the section:
    Idx = 0;
```

```
for (;;)
   {
   // get app data from the entry:
   sprintf (EntryName, "win%d", ++Idx);
   Length = GetPrivateProfileString
      (SectionName,
      EntryName,
      "",
      Buffer,
      sizeof (Buffer),
      "SETSAVE.INI");
   if (Length <= 0)
      // no more entries within section:
      break;

   // isolate the simple file name from the app data:
   SimpleName = strchr (Buffer, '¦');
   *SimpleName = '\0';
   while(SimpleName > Buffer && *(SimpleName-1) != '\\')
      --SimpleName;

   // add the simple name to the list box:
   SendDlgItemMessage (mHDialog, IDC_LIST, LB_ADDSTRING,
                  0, (LPARAM)(LPCSTR)SimpleName);

   }

// select the first app within the list box:
SendDlgItemMessage (mHDialog, IDC_LIST, LB_SETCURSEL, 0,
                  0L);
Dirty = FALSE; // set flag indicating changed app data

// send message to notify dialog box that an app has
// been selected:
SendMessage (mHDialog, WM_COMMAND, (WPARAM)IDC_LIST,
            MAKELPARAM (GetDlgItem (mHDialog,IDC_LIST),
            LBN_SELCHANGE));

return (TRUE);

default:
   if (Msg == mHelpMessage)
```

```
                  {
                  SendMessage (mHDialog, WM_COMMAND, IDC_HELP, OL);
                  return (TRUE);
                  }
             else
                  return (FALSE);
        }
    }

void CEditDialog::ReplaceField (char *Position, char *NewString)
// this function replaces a field (delimited with '¦' characters)
// within an application description; 'Position' points to the
// first character within the field, and 'NewString' contains the
// new characters to be written to the field
    {
    int Length;
    char *PChar;

    PChar = strchr (Position, '¦');
    Length = strlen (PChar) + 1;
    memmove (Position, PChar, Length);

    memmove (Position + strlen (NewString), Position,
             strlen (Position) + 1);

    memmove (Position, NewString, strlen (NewString));
    }


/////////////////////////////////////////////////////////////////
// CMessageDialog member function:                              //
/////////////////////////////////////////////////////////////////

BOOL CMessageDialog::DialogProc (UINT Msg, WPARAM WParam,
                                 LPARAM LParam)
    {
    switch (Msg)
        {
        case WM_COMMAND:
            // user has clicked the Cancel button; therefore set
            // the 'QuitReplace' flag so that the replace process
            // will be terminated:
```

```
        QuitReplace = TRUE;
        return (TRUE);

    case WM_INITDIALOG:
        return (TRUE);

    default:
        return (FALSE);
    }
}
```

Listing 4.4

```
;;;;;;;;;;;;;;;;;;;;;;;;;;;;;;;;;;;;;;;;;;;;;;;;;;;;;;;;;;;;;;;;;;
;                                                                ;
; SETSAVE.DEF:  Module-definition file for the SETSAVE program. ;
;                                                                ;
;;;;;;;;;;;;;;;;;;;;;;;;;;;;;;;;;;;;;;;;;;;;;;;;;;;;;;;;;;;;;;;;;;

NAME SETSAVE

DESCRIPTION  'Windows Setup Saver'

EXETYPE WINDOWS

CODE PRELOAD MOVEABLE DISCARDABLE

DATA PRELOAD MOVEABLE MULTIPLE

HEAPSIZE 1024

STACKSIZE 10240
```

Listing 4.5

```
////////////////////////////////////////////////////////////////
//                                                            //
// RESOURCE.H:  Constant definitions for the SETSAVE program  //
//              resources (generated by Microsoft App Studio). //
//                                                            //
////////////////////////////////////////////////////////////////
```

```
//{{NO_DEPENDENCIES}}
// App Studio generated include file.
// Used by SETSAVE.RC
//
#define IDC_DELETE                      101
#define IDC_LOAD                        102
#define IDC_SAVE                        103
#define IDC_EDIT                        104
#define IDC_COMBO                       106
#define IDC_REPLACE                     107
#define IDC_NAME                        108
#define IDC_LIST                        109
#define IDC_HELP                        110
#define IDC_PARMS                       111
#define IDC_STATUS                      112
#define IDC_DIMS                        113
#define IDC_POS                         114
#define IDC_CLOSE                       115
#define IDC_WORKDIR                     116
#define IDM_ABOUT                       1000
#define IDM_AUTO                        1001
#define IDM_HELPCONTENTS                1002
#define IDM_HELPHELP                    1003
#define IDM_HELPSEARCH                  1004
#define IDM_MINIMIZE                    1005
#define IDM_ONTOP                       1006

// Next default values for new objects
//
#ifdef APSTUDIO_INVOKED
#ifndef APSTUDIO_READONLY_SYMBOLS

#define _APS_NEXT_RESOURCE_VALUE        101
#define _APS_NEXT_COMMAND_VALUE         101
#define _APS_NEXT_CONTROL_VALUE         1000
#define _APS_NEXT_SYMED_VALUE           101
#endif
#endif
```

Listing 4.6

```
///////////////////////////////////////////////////////////////
//                                                             //
// SETSAVE.RC:  Resource-definition file for the SETSAVE       //
//              program (generated by Microsoft App Studio).   //
//                                                             //
///////////////////////////////////////////////////////////////

//Microsoft App Studio generated resource script.
//
#include "resource.h"

#define APSTUDIO_READONLY_SYMBOLS
///////////////////////////////////////////////////////////////
//
// Generated from the TEXTINCLUDE 2 resource.
//
#define APSTUDIO_HIDDEN_SYMBOLS
#include "windows.h"
#undef APSTUDIO_HIDDEN_SYMBOLS


///////////////////////////////////////////////////////////////
#undef APSTUDIO_READONLY_SYMBOLS


///////////////////////////////////////////////////////////////
//
// Icon
//

SETSAVEICON             ICON    DISCARDABLE     "SETSAVE.ICO"


///////////////////////////////////////////////////////////////
//
// Menu
//

SETSAVEMENU MENU DISCARDABLE
BEGIN
    POPUP "&Options"
    BEGIN
```

```
            MENUITEM "&Auto Save",                  IDM_AUTO
            MENUITEM "&Minimize on Use",            IDM_MINIMIZE
            MENUITEM "Always on &Top",              IDM_ONTOP
        END
        POPUP "&Help"
        BEGIN
            MENUITEM "&Contents...\tF1",            IDM_HELPCONTENTS
            MENUITEM "&Search for Help On...",      IDM_HELPSEARCH
            MENUITEM "&How to Use Help...",         IDM_HELPHELP
            MENUITEM SEPARATOR
            MENUITEM "&About...",                   IDM_ABOUT
        END
END


/////////////////////////////////////////////////////////////////
//
// Accelerator
//

SETSAVEACCEL ACCELERATORS MOVEABLE PURE
BEGIN
    VK_F1,          IDM_HELPCONTENTS,       VIRTKEY
END


/////////////////////////////////////////////////////////////////
//
// Dialog
//

ABOUTDLG DIALOG DISCARDABLE  12, 24, 106, 96
STYLE DS_MODALFRAME | WS_POPUP | WS_VISIBLE | WS_CAPTION |
    WS_SYSMENU
CAPTION "About"
FONT 8, "MS Sans Serif"
BEGIN
    CTEXT           "Windows Setup Saver",-1,0,10,106,12
    PUSHBUTTON      "OK",IDOK,32,74,40,14
    ICON            "SetSaveIcon",-1,42,42,18,20
    CTEXT           "by Michael J. Young",-1,0,28,106,8
END
```

```
MAINDLG DIALOG DISCARDABLE  16, 40, 158, 112
STYLE WS_MINIMIZEBOX ¦ WS_POPUP ¦ WS_VISIBLE ¦ WS_CAPTION ¦
   WS_SYSMENU
CAPTION "Setup Saver"
MENU SetSaveMenu
FONT 8, "MS Sans Serif"
BEGIN
    LTEXT           "Setup &Name:",-1,8,4,60,8
    COMBOBOX        IDC_COMBO,8,18,80,86,CBS_SIMPLE ¦ CBS_SORT ¦
                    WS_VSCROLL ¦ WS_TABSTOP
    PUSHBUTTON      "&Load",IDC_LOAD,96,18,52,14,WS_DISABLED
    PUSHBUTTON      "&Replace",IDC_REPLACE,96,34,52,14,
                    WS_DISABLED
    PUSHBUTTON      "&Save Setup",IDC_SAVE,96,56,52,14,
                    WS_DISABLED
    PUSHBUTTON      "&Edit Parms...",IDC_EDIT,96,72,52,14,
                    WS_DISABLED
    PUSHBUTTON      "&Delete Setup",IDC_DELETE,96,88,52,14,
                    WS_DISABLED
END

MESSAGEDLG DIALOG DISCARDABLE  34, 50, 106, 56
STYLE WS_POPUP ¦ WS_VISIBLE ¦ WS_CAPTION ¦ WS_SYSMENU
CAPTION "Replace"
FONT 8, "MS Sans Serif"
BEGIN
    PUSHBUTTON      "Cancel",IDCANCEL,32,18,40,14
END

EDITDLG DIALOG DISCARDABLE  10, 22, 176, 136
STYLE DS_MODALFRAME ¦ WS_POPUP ¦ WS_VISIBLE ¦ WS_CAPTION ¦
   WS_SYSMENU
CAPTION "Edit Parms"
FONT 8, "MS Sans Serif"
BEGIN
    LTEXT           "&Applications:",IDC_REPLACE,6,24,46,8
    LISTBOX         IDC_LIST,6,38,58,66,WS_VSCROLL ¦ WS_TABSTOP
    LTEXT           "&Parms:",-1,6,102,24,8
    EDITTEXT        IDC_PARMS,34,100,136,12,ES_AUTOHSCROLL
    LTEXT           "Working &Directory:",-1,6,120,64,8
    EDITTEXT        IDC_WORKDIR,72,118,98,12,ES_AUTOHSCROLL
```

```
        DEFPUSHBUTTON    "&Save",IDC_SAVE,134,4,36,12
        PUSHBUTTON       "Cancel",IDC_CLOSE,134,18,36,12
        LTEXT            "Setup Name:",-1,6,10,44,8
        LTEXT            "1234567890123456",IDC_NAME,54,10,76,8
        LTEXT            "Status:",-1,80,52,26,8
        LTEXT            "Position:",-1,80,64,42,8
        LTEXT            "Dimensions:",-1,80,76,52,8
        LTEXT            "n",IDC_STATUS,124,52,52,8
        LTEXT            "1024, 1139",IDC_POS,124,64,52,8
        LTEXT            "1024, 1139",IDC_DIMS,124,76,52,8
        PUSHBUTTON       "&Help",IDC_HELP,134,34,36,12
END


#ifdef APSTUDIO_INVOKED
/////////////////////////////////////////////////////////////////////
//
// TEXTINCLUDE
//

1 TEXTINCLUDE DISCARDABLE
BEGIN
    "resource.h\0"
END

2 TEXTINCLUDE DISCARDABLE
BEGIN
    "#define APSTUDIO_HIDDEN_SYMBOLS\r\n"
    "#include ""windows.h""\r\n"
    "#undef APSTUDIO_HIDDEN_SYMBOLS\r\n"
    "\0"
END

3 TEXTINCLUDE DISCARDABLE
BEGIN
    "\r\n"
    "\0"
END

/////////////////////////////////////////////////////////////////////
#endif    // APSTUDIO_INVOKED
```

```
#ifndef APSTUDIO_INVOKED
/////////////////////////////////////////////////////////////
//
// Generated from the TEXTINCLUDE 3 resource.
//


/////////////////////////////////////////////////////////////
#endif    // not APSTUDIO_INVOKED
```

The following sections explain the highlights of the source code. For more detailed information on specific functions, see the comments in the source code.

Initializing

As usual, if an instance of the program is already running, the WinMain function (in SETSAVE.CPP of Listing 4.2) activates the previous instance and exits. Before exiting, however, it tests whether the program command line contains a valid setup name. It does this by sending a CB_FINDSTRING message to the combo box belonging to the previous instance, to determine whether the list in the combo box contains a setup name that matches the contents of the command line. If a match is found, WinMain performs a series of actions to force the previous program instance to load the setup. These actions simulate the events that normally occur when the user enters or selects a setup name and clicks the Load button, and are as follows:

1. It sends a WM_SETTEXT message to the Setup Name: combo box belonging to the previous instance in order to place the name of the setup within the text box.

2. It enables the buttons belonging to the previous instance (when the text box contains a valid setup name, all buttons are normally enabled).

3. It posts a WM_COMMAND message bearing the identifier of the Load button (IDC_LOAD) to the main window of the previous instance. This is the message that is normally sent when the user clicks the Load button.

When the main window is created, the CMainDialog::OnInitDialog function (in DIALOG.CPP of Listing 4.3) begins by reading through the setups stored in the program initialization file, SETSAVE.INI. The description of each setup is stored within a separate section; these sections are labeled [setup1], [setup2], and so on (there may be gaps in the numbering because of deleted setups). OnInitDialog reads the name of each setup (which is stored in the "name" entry within the setup's section) and inserts this name into the combo box list. If it encounters a setup name that matches the contents of the program command line, OnInitDialog causes the program to load this setup, using the same basic technique that is employed by the WinMain function (the three steps that were just described).

NOTE

The SETSAVE program does *not* store the setup information within memory as program data. Rather, whenever it needs to obtain setup information, it reads it from the initialization file. Also, whenever the setup information is changed, SETSAVE immediately updates the initialization file.

Saving a Setup

When the user enters a setup name into the Setup Name: text box and clicks the Save Setup button, control passes to the routine that processes the IDC_SAVE identifier within the CMainDialog::OnCommand function (in DIALOG.CPP of Listing 4.3). This routine must obtain the state of all Windows applications that are currently running, and then must save this information in a setup description within the initialization file. Specifically, to be able to restore the setup, SETSAVE must save the following minimum information for each Windows program:

- The full path name of the program's executable file
- The state of the program's main window; that is, whether the window is maximized, minimized, or is of a normal size
- The dimensions of the program's main window, if it is neither maximized nor minimized

To obtain this information, OnCommand begins by calling the API functions GetWindow (once) and then GetNextWindow (repeatedly) to obtain the handle of each top-level window currently maintained by the system (a *top-level* window is one that is not a child of another window). OnCommand, however, does not want the handle of every top-level window; rather, it wants only the handle of each *main* window belonging to a program other than SETSAVE itself. Consequently, it *ignores* any of the following handles returned by GetWindow or GetNextWindow:

- The handle of the SETSAVE program window; that is, the handle that equals mHDialog
- A handle of an invisible window; the visibility of the window is determined by calling the IsWindowVisible API function; (some applications, such as Microsoft Excel 4.0, create an invisible top-level window in addition to the main program window)
- A handle of a window that is owned by another window (and is therefore not a main program window); to determine whether a window is owned by another window, OnCommand calls the Get-Window API function, passing the window's handle together with the flag GW_OWNER:

  GetWindow (HWnd, GW_OWNER)

If GetWindow returns a non-NULL value, the window has an owner window and it is therefore ignored. Ignoring such owned windows prevents SET-SAVE from treating an icon label as if it were a main program window (an icon label is actually a separate, top-level window that is owned by another window).

NOTE

OnCommand passes GetWindow the flag GW_HWND-LAST and passes GetNextWindow the flag GW_HWNDPREV. These flags cause Windows to enumerate windows, beginning with the bottom window in the stacking order and proceeding toward the top; OnCommand saves the windows in this order. When SETSAVE restores the setup, it loads the programs in the same order, thereby restoring the original window stacking order.

If a window handle returned by GetWindow or GetNextWindow does not fit into any of the three categories above, OnCommand assumes that it is the handle of a main window belonging to a program other than SETSAVE. It then proceeds to call the API function GetModuleFileName to obtain the full file path of the program that created the window, as follows:

```
GetModuleFileName
    ((HINSTANCE)GetWindowWord (HWnd,GWW_HINSTANCE),
    ModuleFileName,
    sizeof (ModuleFileName));
```

The first parameter passed to GetModuleFileName is the instance handle of the program that created the window, which is obtained by passing the window handle to the GetWindowWord function. Note that if the path obtained from GetModuleFileName contains the file extension .MOD rather than .EXE, the window has been created by a DOS session rather than a Windows program, and therefore OnCommand does *not* save the program information in the setup.

Next, OnCommand determines the state of the program window. If the IsIconic API function returns TRUE, the window is minimized; if the IsZoomed API function returns TRUE, it is maximized. If neither function returns TRUE, the window has a normal size; in this case, OnCommand calls the API function GetWindowRect to obtain the window dimensions.

Finally, OnCommand formats the setup information and stores it within the initialization file. All of the information for a given setup is stored within a single section of the initialization file (as mentioned, these sections are labeled [setup1], [setup2], and so on). The section begins with a "name" entry containing the name of the setup, followed by an entry that describes each program in the setup (these entries are labeled *win1, win2,* and so on). Each entry that describes a program has the following format:

program path | parameters | window state | working directory | position and size

Note that the information is divided into fields separated using ' | ' characters. The *window state* field contains a *z* if the window is maximized (*zoomed*), an *i* if the window is minimized (*iconized*), or an *n* if the window is *normal*. The *position and size* field contains four numbers, separated with space characters; the first two numbers are the screen coordinates of the upper-left corner of the window, and the second two numbers are the width and height of the window.

The *parameters* field contains the parameters that are passed to the program when it is run, and the *working directory* field contains the file directory that is made current when the program is run. OnCommand leaves these fields empty. These two fields are maintained by the member functions of the CEditDialog class, which manages the dialog box that is activated when the user clicks the Edit Parms... button. If the user specifies parameters or a working directory for a particular application, the CEdit-Dialog::DialogProc function (in DIALOG.CPP) inserts the specified text into the appropriate field of the program description.

The following is an example of a complete setup description within the initialization file:

```
[setup1]
name=StartDay
win1=C:\WINDOWS\PROGMAN.EXE||n||4 0 469 600
win2=C:\WINDOWS\WINFILE.EXE||n||125 0 671 600
win3=C:\WINDOWS\CALENDAR.EXE|mike.cal|n|c:\mike|348 121 427 413
win4=C:\WINWORD\WINWORD.EXE|todo.doc|n|c:\mike|4 0 708 575
```

Note, finally, that before OnCommand begins writing information for a new setup to the initialization file, it calls WritePrivateProfileString to erase any existing section for a setup having the same name (such a section would exist if the user is *redefining* an existing setup). The section is erased by passing NULL as the second and third parameters, as follows:

```
WritePrivateProfileString (SectionName, NULL, NULL,
                           "SETSAVE.INI");
```

This is the same technique that the program uses to remove a setup description from the initialization file when the user clicks the Delete Setup button to remove a setup.

Automatic Setup Saving on Windows Exit

If the user has enabled the Auto Save option on the Options menu, when the Windows session ends, the SETSAVE program automatically saves the state of all currently running Windows programs within a setup named AutoSave.

When the user chooses to end the Windows session, Windows sends the WM_QUERYENDSESSION message to all applications. If all applications return TRUE after processing this message, Windows terminates; if, however, any application returns FALSE, Windows does *not* terminate. If Windows is going to terminate, it then sends a WM_ENDSESSION message to all applications, with the wParam parameter set to TRUE (as you have seen, in response to the WM_ENDSESSION message, the utilities in this book save the program option information in the initialization file).

SETSAVE creates the AutoSave setup in response to the WM_QUERYEND-SESSION message rather than the WM_ENDSESSION message. If it were to wait until it receives a WM_ENDSESSION message, some of the Windows programs may have already terminated, and it would not be able to save information on these programs.

The WM_QUERYENDSESSION message is processed by the CMainDialog::On-QueryEndSession function (in DIALOG.CPP of Listing 4.3). If the Auto Save option is enabled, this function first calls the SetDlgItemText API function to write the name AutoSave to the Setup Name text box, and then causes the program to save the current set of programs under this name by sending the main window a WM_COMMAND message bearing the identifier IDC_SAVE (this is the same message that is sent when the user clicks the Save Setup button).

N O T E

Unlike the other message-handling functions in SETSAVE, `OnQueryEndSession` returns FALSE. The Win-dows dialog box code therefore assumes that the mes-sage has *not* been handled and it performs the default message processing. The default processing returns TRUE to Windows, which allows the Windows session to be ended. (If `OnQueryEndSession` returned TRUE, the Windows dialog code would assume that the message had been handled and would return FALSE to Windows; Windows termination would thus be halted.)

Restoring a Setup

When the user selects a setup and clicks either the Load or the Replace button, control passes to a common routine within the `CMainDialog::On-Command` function (specifically, to the branch of this function that proc-esses the `IDC_LOAD` and `IDC_REPLACE` identifiers). If the user has clicked the Replace button, `OnCommand` must first terminate all other Windows ap-plications except the Windows Program Manager (or alternative shell program). For either button, `OnCommand` must then load all of the pro-grams contained in the setup.

Terminating the Current Programs

To terminate Windows applications in response to the Replace button, `OnCommand` begins by calling the API function `EnumWindows` to obtain the handle of each top-level window:

```
EnumWindows (EnumWindowsProc, OL);
```

`EnumWindows` causes Windows to call the `EnumWindowsProc` function once for each top-level window, passing this function the window handle. `EnumWindowsProc` is defined as follows within DIALOG.CPP:

```
BOOL CALLBACK _export EnumWindowsProc (HWND HWnd, LPARAM LParam)
    {
```

```
MainDialog.CloseApp (HWnd);
return (TRUE);
}
```

EnumWindowsProc (which is not a member function of the CMainDialog class) calls the CMainDialog::CloseApp function (also defined within DIALOG.CPP) to close the application associated with the window handle that it is passed, if appropriate.

When CloseApp receives the window handle, it calls the API function Get-ModuleFileName to obtain the file path of the program that created the window. It ignores the window if any of the following conditions is true:

- The handle is not a valid window handle; that is, the IsWindow API function returns FALSE.

- The window is the SETSAVE main window; that is, the handle equals mHDialog.

- The window is not visible; that is, the IsVisible API function returns FALSE.

- The program is the Windows shell (that is, it is the Windows Program Manager or alternative shell program). To test whether the program is the shell, CloseApp passes the program path name to the function IsShell, which is also defined in DIALOG.CPP. Is-Shell obtains the name of the current Windows shell by calling the GetPrivateProfileString API function to read the "shell" entry from the "[boot]" section of the SYSTEM.INI file.

- The program name has the file extension .MOD rather than .EXE, indicating that the window is associated with a DOS session rather than a Windows program.

If the window does *not* fit into any of these five categories, CloseApp assumes that it is a main window belonging to a Windows application other than the Windows shell or SETSAVE itself. In this case, it proceeds to terminate the program by posting a WM_CLOSE message to the program's main window:

```
PostMessage (HWnd, WM_CLOSE, 0, OL);
```

WM_CLOSE is the message that a main window normally receives when the user chooses the Close command from the program's system menu.

When a Windows program processes this message, it typically destroys its main window and terminates; before doing so, however, it has the opportunity to save data and perform any other required final tasks.

NOTE When closing applications, SETSAVE uses `Enum-Windows` rather than `GetWindow` and `GetNext-Window` (which other parts of the program use to enumerate windows). Using `GetWindow` and `GetNextWindow` is not reliable if the routine that calls these functions performs some action—such as terminating applications—that af-fects the list of windows that are present.

After calling `EnumWindows` to cause the applications to be closed, the `On-Command` function waits until all applications have actually terminated. Running the new programs before all of the current programs have terminated could cause problems, especially if one of the new programs is the same as one of the current programs.

To pause until all applications have ended, `OnCommand` repeatedly calls the function `AllClosed`, which returns `TRUE` when all Windows applications (except SETSAVE and the Windows shell) have ended. `AllClosed`, defined in DIALOG.CPP (Listing 4.3), uses the `GetWindow` and `GetNextWindow` functions to cycle through all top-level windows in search of running Windows applications.

While waiting for the applications to end, `OnCommand` displays a modeless dialog box, which is managed by the `CMessageDialog` class. This dialog box, titled Replace, contains a Cancel button. If the user clicks this button, the dialog procedure for this dialog box sets the `CMessage-Dialog::QuitReplace` flag to `TRUE`. If `OnCommand` discovers that this flag is `TRUE`, it stops terminating programs and returns without loading the setup.

N O T E

While the modeless dialog box is displayed, the main window is disabled so that the user cannot attempt to issue a program command while applications are being terminated.

On each pass of the loop, after OnCommand calls AllClosed and checks the QuitReplace flag, it calls the PeekMessage API function to obtain any pending messages and then dispatches these messages. There are two important reasons for processing messages at this time:

- Processing messages yields control to other Windows programs, thus allowing the programs that are being terminated to process both their WM_CLOSE messages and other messages that need to be handled when the applications terminate.

- Processing messages allows the modeless dialog box to respond if the user clicks the Cancel button to end the operation.

Running the New Programs

After all of the current Windows applications have been terminated (if the user clicked the Replace button), OnCommand proceeds to load the applications defined in the selected setup. To obtain the information needed to load each application, OnCommand reads the description for that application contained within the section of the initialization file that defines the selected setup (the format of an application description was given previously, in the section "Saving a Setup").

If the program specified in a description is the Windows shell (that is, IsShell returns TRUE), OnCommand calls the function CMainDialog::GetShellHandle (defined within DIALOG.CPP) to obtain the handle of the shell's main window. GetShellHandle cycles through all top-level windows until it finds a visible window created by the shell program. The shell must be handled specially because, unlike the other programs in the setup, it is *not* executed (rather, OnCommand only adjusts the size and position of its window).

Next, OnCommand calls the _chdrive and chdir run-time functions to change to the working directory, if any is specified.

If the program is *not* the shell, it then calls the WinExec API function to run the application, passing any parameters that are specified as well as a code for the initial window state (normal, maximized, or minimized). WinExec returns the instance handle of the program that it runs. On-Command passes this handle to the function CMainDialog::GetWindow-Handle (defined in DIALOG.CPP), which returns the handle of the program's main window. GetWindowHandle cycles through all top-level windows until it finds one that has a matching instance handle.

Whether or not the program is the shell, once OnCommand has the handle of the program's main window, it performs the following two actions:

1. It calls the ShowWindow API function to set the state of the window (normal, maximized, or minimized). Although a code for the window state was passed to WinExec (unless the program is the shell), a program may choose to ignore this code; explicitly calling Show-Window ensures that the window has the desired state.

2. If the window is normal, it calls the MoveWindow API function to assign the window the specified position and size.

Maintaining the Buttons

At any time during the course of the program, a button is enabled only if it represents a command that is currently valid; specifically:

- If the Setup Name box contains the name of an existing setup, all buttons are enabled.

- If the Setup Name box contains text that is *not* the name of an existing setup, only the Save Setup button is enabled.

- If the Setup Name box is empty, all buttons are disabled.

Enabling and disabling buttons in this way makes it clear to the user which commands can be performed at a given time, and also eliminates the need for the routine that processes a specific button to check whether the text box currently contains an appropriate entry. The code that maintains the enabled status of the buttons is spread throughout the OnCommand function of DIALOG.CPP (Listing 4.3) and is thoroughly commented.

Enhancing the Setup Saver

The following items suggest several ways in which you might enhance the Setup Saver:

- *Allow the user to include DOS programs in a setup.* Unfortunately, the GetModuleFileName function that SETSAVE uses to obtain the file name of each application does *not* report the name of the executable file for a DOS session (rather, it returns the name of a system file with the .MOD extension that is used to manage the session). To get around this limitation, you could have the user manually enter the path of the executable file or .PIF file for each DOS program in a setup. Entering this information could be done through the Edit Parms dialog box. A DOS program can be run using the WinExec API function, in the same manner as running a Windows application.

- *Provide an option for each program in a setup* that would assign the program's window the "always on top" style, so that the window could be made to appear on top of overlapping windows even when it is inactive. The user could enable this option through a check box in the Edit Parms dialog box. To assign this style, you could call the SetWindowPos API function after running the program and obtaining the program's main window handle, as explained in Chapter 2 (in the section "Initializing").

- *Provide a command line flag or a menu option* that would cause the Setup Saver to exit immediately after it loads a setup.

- Currently, when the user passes the name of a setup on the command line, the Setup Saver always *loads* the setup (that is, it runs the programs without first terminating the current programs, as if the user had clicked the Load button). You could *provide a command-line flag* (such as /r) that would cause the Setup Saver to *replace* the current programs with the setup specified on the command line (as if the user had clicked the Replace button).

- *Permit the user to delete a program belonging to a setup* by clicking a button in the Edit Parms dialog box.

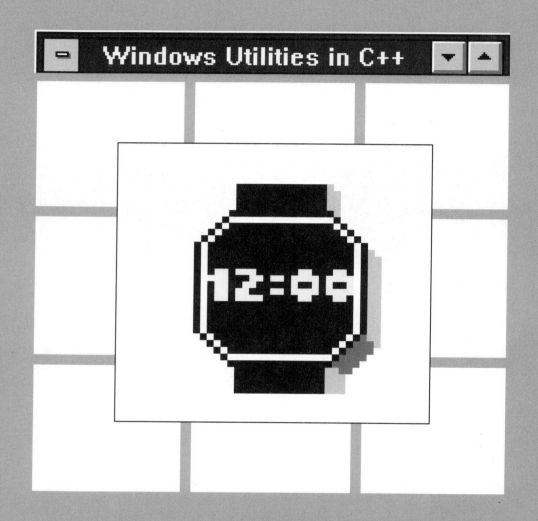

CHAPTER

5

Task Scheduler

THE Task Scheduler presented in this chapter automatically runs Windows or DOS programs at prespecified times. You can define up to 25 different tasks. For each task, you can specify the name of a program and the time that the program is to be run. You can also specify a Windows Recorder macro that is run immediately after the program is loaded so that you can fully automate a complex series of keyboard or mouse actions (you can also simply run a macro without loading a program).

You might, for example, use the Task Scheduler to automatically start a word processor and print a series of documents at a time when the computer is not busy. You might use it to run reports after business hours. You might use it to load a communications program, connect to an online service, and download information at a time when rates are low.

You can also use the Task Scheduler to run the Setup Saver (presented in the previous chapter) and load an entire set of Windows applications, so that you can automate a task that requires more than one program. You can schedule a task to run once, or you can have it repeated at regular intervals; for example, you could define a task to automatically perform a daily file backup. The Task Scheduler also allows you to run a task immediately by clicking a button.

The Task Scheduler program uses a C++ class to encapsulate all of the information for a task as well as a function for executing the task. The code also shows how to obtain, store, manipulate, and compare time values, using the time functions provided by the C++ run-time library.

How to Use the Task Scheduler

The first step in using the Task Scheduler is to define one or more tasks. In this section, you will learn how to define a task, and how to edit a task if you later want to change any of the task information. You will also learn how to run a task manually at any time, and how to set program options.

Defining a Task

When you first run the Task Scheduler, the program window will appear as shown in Figure 5.1. To define a task, click the New... button. The program will then display the Task dialog box, which is shown in Figure 5.2.

First, enter a name for the task into the Name: text box. The name can consist of up to 16 characters and can include spaces (the program ignores the case of the letters). If you enter the name of an existing task, the program will ask you to choose a new name.

FIGURE 5.2

The Task dialog
box before defining
a new task

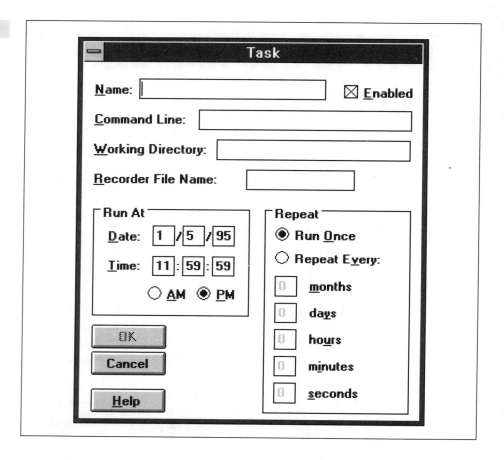

The Enabled option (to the right of the task name) is initially selected. If
you turn this option off, the task will be stored but will *not* be run at its
specified time (you can later enable the task; also, you can run a disabled
task by clicking the Run Now button, as described later).

Next, if you want the Task Scheduler to load a program when the task is
run, enter the command line for the program into the Command Line:
text box. The command line must include the name of the executable program file, followed by any parameters you want passed to the program.
The executable file can be for a Windows or DOS application, and can

have the .EXE, .COM, .BAT, or .PIF extension (you need not include the extension unless it is necessary to distinguish between different executable files). You must include the full path name for the program file if this file is not in a directory specified by your PATH environment variable (or in the directory you enter into the Working Directory: text box, if any).

If you want the Task Scheduler to switch to a particular directory before running the task, enter the *full path specification* of this directory into the Working Directory: text box. This directory will be the current one when the Task Scheduler runs the program or macro assigned to the task. You might, for example, specify the directory that contains the data files that the program uses.

If you want the Task Scheduler to play a macro that you have defined using the Windows Recorder program, enter the name of the Recorder file that contains this macro into the Recorder File Name: text box. If the file has the .REC extension (the usual extension for a Recorder file), you do not need to include the extension.

The Recorder File Name: text box allows you to enter only 12 characters; therefore, you will probably not be able to specify the complete directory path. Rather, you should enter the simple file name and store the file either within the Windows directory or within the directory specified in the Working Directory: text box (if any).

If you specify a Recorder file, the Task Scheduler will run the *first (or only) macro contained in the file*. Therefore, you must store each macro that you want to use with the Task Scheduler within a separate file; and if any file contains more than one macro, make sure that the one you want the Task Scheduler to run is the first one in the list. (One of the program enhancements suggested at the end of the chapter is to permit running a *specific* macro within a Recorder file.)

If you have specified a program in the Command Line: text box, the Task Scheduler will run the macro immediately after loading the program.

NOTE

When defining a task you *must* specify either a program or a macro, or both.

Next, specify the exact time at which the task is to be run by entering the date and time into the Run At box (the initial time displayed in this box is one second before midnight on the current day). You can enter a year value in the range from 70 through 99 (representing the years 1970 through 1999); you can also enter a value in the range from 0 through 35 (representing the years 2000 through 2035).

If you choose the Run Once option in the Repeat box (selected by default), the Task Scheduler will run the task only once, at the specified time. Note that after the task is run, it will *not* be deleted; rather, it will merely be disabled. You can later revive the task by editing the task information (as explained later), checking the Enabled option, and updating the time in the Run At box.

If you choose the Repeat Every: option in the Repeat box, the task will be run first at the time specified in the Run At box; it will then be rerun at regular intervals. You specify the amount of time between each repetition by entering the desired values into the boxes below the Repeat Every: button. For example, if you specify the time 12 noon on some date within the Run At box, choose the Repeat Every: option, and enter 1 into the "hours" box, the task will be run at 12 noon, 1:00 p.m., 2:00 p.m., 3:00 p.m., and so on. If you enter 1 into the "hours" box and 30 into the "minutes" box, the task will be run at 12 noon, 1:30 p.m., 3:00 p.m., 4:30 p.m., and so on.

The value you enter into the "months" box refers to calendar months, rather than a specific number of days. If, therefore, you specify January 1 in the Run At box, and enter 1 into the "months" box, the task will be run on January 1 and then on the first of each subsequent month.

When you click the OK button, the task you defined will be added to the Tasks: list box in the main program window. The Task Scheduler will then run the task at the specified time. The Task Scheduler must, of course, be running when the task is due to be run; it need not, however, be the active program, and the Task Scheduler window can be reduced to an icon.

NOTE

The Task Scheduler may run a task *after* the specified time. It runs a task the first time it checks the clock and discovers that the task is due. If, for example, it checks the clock every 15 seconds, the task may be run up to 15 seconds late. A task might also be started late if you are running a full-screen DOS session in Exclusive mode, which blocks the timer messages that cause the Task Scheduler to check the clock. Additionally, if you terminate the Task Scheduler and later restart it, it will run all tasks that are currently due, possibly quite a while after the scheduled run times. Later in the chapter, you will see how to set the frequency at which the Task Scheduler checks the system clock.

If you want to have several tasks run in sequence, just assign each subsequent task a slightly later run time. Tasks are always executed in the order of their run times, even if more than one task is due when the Task Scheduler reads the clock. You can also run a group of programs by having the Task Scheduler run the Setup Saver, as described in the next section.

You can use the technique discussed in this section to define up to 25 different tasks. If you want to delete a task, select the task in the Tasks: list box and click the Delete button. When you terminate the Task Scheduler, the information on all currently defined tasks is stored in the program's initialization file (SCHEDULE.INI) and is retrieved from this file when the program is run again.

Using the Task Scheduler with the Setup Saver

You can have the Task Scheduler run an entire set of programs at a specified time by using the Setup Saver program, which was presented in the previous chapter. When you are defining the task, simply enter into the Command Line: box the Setup Saver file name (SETSAVE.EXE, including the full path description of this file, if necessary), followed by the name of the setup you want to run. For example, entering the following text into the Command Line: box would load the setup named RunReports:

```
C:\CUTIL\SETSAVE.EXE RunReports
```

You can also create a Recorder macro that sends keystrokes or mouse commands to one or more of the programs in the setup, in order to fully automate a complex job. When defining the task, enter the name of the file containing this macro into the Recorder File Name: text box. (An added advantage of using the Setup Saver to run programs is that the program windows will have known positions and sizes, making it easier to automate a job with a macro, especially a macro that includes mouse actions.)

Editing a Task

If you want to change the information for a task that you have already defined, select the task in the Tasks: list box and click the Edit... button. The Setup Saver will display the Task dialog box (the same dialog box used to define a new task), which will contain the current task information. You can then change any of the task information—as described in the previous section—and click the OK button.

NOTE For a repeated task, the time you see in the Run At box may not be the time you originally entered. Whenever a repeated task is run, the program updates the run time to the *next* time the task will be run.

Running a Task Manually

You can immediately run any defined task (whether or not it is enabled) by selecting the task in the Tasks: list box and clicking the Run Now button.

The Run Now button allows you to test a task that you have just defined or edited. You might also want to define a task and run it, using the Run

Now button as an alternative to running a program through the Windows Program or File Manager. The advantage of using the Task Scheduler is that you can have a Recorder macro run automatically after the program is launched.

Setting Options

You can specify how frequently the Task Scheduler checks the system clock by choosing the Set Frequency... command on the Options menu. The program will display a dialog box; you can then enter a value between 1 and 65. This value specifies the number of seconds that elapse between the times the program checks the clock. Entering a small value makes the timing of tasks more accurate; entering a large value reduces the program overhead.

If you enable the Always on Top option on the Options menu, the program window will always be displayed on top of overlapping windows, even when the window is not active.

How the Task Scheduler Works

The source files for the Task Scheduler program, SCHEDULE, are provided in Listings 5.1 through 5.7, and the program icon is shown in Figure 5.3. Listing 5.1 (SCHEDULE.H) is the main header file, which is included in all of the C++ source files. Listing 5.2 (SCHEDULE.CPP) contains the C++ source code for the WinMain function and declarations for global objects. Listing 5.3 (DIALOG.CPP) defines the member functions belonging to the classes that manage dialog boxes (including the main program window). Listing 5.4 (TASK.CPP) defines the member functions of the CTask class; each task is managed by an instance of this class. Listing 5.5 (SCHEDULE.DEF) is the module-definition file, and Listings 5.6 and 5.7 (RESOURCE.H and SCHEDULE.RC) are the resource files generated by Microsoft App Studio.

FIGURE 5.3

The SCHEDULE program icon, as it appears in the Microsoft App Studio icon editor

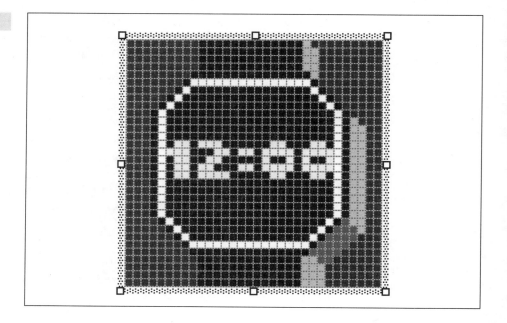

Listing 5.1

```
///////////////////////////////////////////////////////////////
//                                                             //
// SCHEDULE.H:  Header file for the SCHEDULE program.          //
//                                                             //
///////////////////////////////////////////////////////////////

#include "..\wclasses\wclasses.h"
#include "resource.h"
#include <time.h>

#define MAXTASKS 25  // max number of tasks that can be defined
#define SIZENAME 17  // size of buffer to hold task name

// constants for help topics:
#define HELPFREQDLG 100
#define HELPTASKDLG 101
```

```
////////////////////////////////////////////////////////////
// Definition of class for managing each task:             //
////////////////////////////////////////////////////////////

class CTask
{
public:
    CTask ();
    ~CTask ();
    void Execute (BOOL RunNow);

    char *Command;
    int DayRep;
    char *Directory;
    BOOL Enabled;
    int HourRep;
    int MinuteRep;
    int MonthRep;
    char Name [SIZENAME];
    char RecFile [13];
    BOOL Repeat;
    time_t RunTime;
    int SecondRep;

};

////////////////////////////////////////////////////////////
// main dialog box class definition:                       //
////////////////////////////////////////////////////////////

class CMainDialog : public CMLDialog
{
    HBRUSH HBrushWorkSpace;
    int OnTop;
    CTask *PTaskTable [MAXTASKS];

    virtual BOOL DialogProc (UINT Msg, WPARAM WParam,
                             LPARAM LParam);
    BOOL OnCommand (int IDItem, HWND HWndCtl, WORD NotifyCode);
    BOOL OnCtlColor (HDC HDCChild, HWND HWndChild, int CtlType);
    BOOL OnDestroy ();
```

```
   BOOL OnInitDialog (HWND HWndFocus, LPARAM Data);
   BOOL OnSysColorChange ();
   BOOL OnTimer ();
   void WrapUp ();

public:
   CMainDialog ();
   BOOL TaskNameExists (char *TaskName);
   UINT TimeOut;

};


///////////////////////////////////////////////////////////////
// 'Set Frequency' dialog box class definition:               //
///////////////////////////////////////////////////////////////

class CFrequencyDialog : public CMDialog
{
   virtual BOOL DialogProc (UINT Msg, WPARAM WParam,
                            LPARAM LParam);
};


///////////////////////////////////////////////////////////////
// Modal dialog box class definition for 'New' and 'Edit' cmds://
///////////////////////////////////////////////////////////////

class CTaskDialog : public CMDialog
{
   virtual BOOL DialogProc (UINT Msg, WPARAM WParam,
                            LPARAM LParam);

public:
   CTask *PTask;

   CTaskDialog ();

};
```

Listing 5.2

```cpp
////////////////////////////////////////////////////////////
//                                                          //
// SCHEDULE.CPP:  Global object declarations and program entry //
//                point for the SCHEDULE program.           //
//                                                          //
////////////////////////////////////////////////////////////

#include "schedule.h"


////////////////////////////////////////////////////////////
// global object declarations:                             //
////////////////////////////////////////////////////////////

CApplication App;
CMainDialog MainDialog;


////////////////////////////////////////////////////////////
// program entry function:                                 //
////////////////////////////////////////////////////////////

int PASCAL WinMain
    (HINSTANCE HInstCurrent,
    HINSTANCE HInstPrevious,
    LPSTR CmdLine,
    int CmdShow)
    {
    MSG Msg;

    if (HInstPrevious)
        {
        HWND HWndPopup;

        GetInstanceData
            (HInstPrevious,
            (BYTE *)&MainDialog.mHDialog,
            sizeof (HWND));
        ShowWindow (MainDialog.mHDialog, SW_SHOWNORMAL);
        HWndPopup = GetLastActivePopup (MainDialog.mHDialog);
        BringWindowToTop (MainDialog.mHDialog);
```

```
      BringWindowToTop (HWndPopup);
      return (FALSE);
      }

  App.Initialize (HInstCurrent, HInstPrevious, CmdLine,
                  CmdShow);

  if (!App.LoadAccel ("ScheduleAccel"))
      return (FALSE);

  if (!MainDialog.SetIcon ("ScheduleIcon"))
      return (FALSE);

  if (!MainDialog.Create ("MainDlg"))
      return (FALSE);

  while (GetMessage (&Msg, NULL, NULL, NULL))
      if (!TranslateAccelerator (MainDialog.mHDialog,
                                 App.mHAccelTable,
                                 &Msg))
          if (!IsDialogMessage (MainDialog.mHDialog, &Msg))
            {
            TranslateMessage (&Msg);
            DispatchMessage (&Msg);
            }

  return (Msg.wParam);
  }
```

Listing 5.3

```
/////////////////////////////////////////////////////////////
//                                                         //
// DIALOG.CPP:  Dialog class member functions for the      //
//              SCHEDULE program.                          //
//                                                         //
/////////////////////////////////////////////////////////////

#include "schedule.h"
#include <stdio.h>
#include <stdlib.h>
```

```c
#include <string.h>

extern CApplication App;
extern CMainDialog MainDialog;

////////////////////////////////////////////////////////////////
// CMainDialog member functions:                              //
////////////////////////////////////////////////////////////////

CMainDialog::CMainDialog ()
   {
   // initialize PTaskTable to all 0's:
   memset (PTaskTable, 0, sizeof (PTaskTable));
   HBrushWorkSpace = 0;
   }

BOOL CMainDialog::DialogProc (UINT Msg, WPARAM WParam,
                              LPARAM LParam)
   {
   switch (Msg)
      {
      case WM_CLOSE:
         Destroy ();
         return (TRUE);

      case WM_COMMAND:
         return OnCommand ((int)WParam, (HWND)LOWORD (LParam),
                           HIWORD (LParam));

      case WM_CTLCOLOR:
         return OnCtlColor ((HDC)WParam, (HWND)LOWORD (LParam),
                            (int)HIWORD (LParam));

      case WM_DESTROY:
         return OnDestroy ();

      case WM_ENDSESSION:
         if (WParam)
            WrapUp ();
         return (TRUE);
```

```
        case WM_INITDIALOG:
            return OnInitDialog ((HWND)WParam, LParam);

        case WM_SYSCOLORCHANGE:
            return OnSysColorChange ();

        case WM_TIMER:
            return OnTimer ();

        default:
            return (FALSE);
        }
    }

BOOL CMainDialog::OnCommand (int IDItem, HWND HWndCtl,
                            WORD NotifyCode)
    {
    char Buffer [64];
    int Idx;
    int LBIdx;
    int Result;
    char TaskName [SIZENAME];

    switch (IDItem)
        {
        case IDC_DELETE:  // user clicked Delete button

            // get name of selected task:
            Idx = (int)SendDlgItemMessage (mHDialog, IDC_LISTBOX,
                                        LB_GETCURSEL, 0, OL);
            SendDlgItemMessage
                (mHDialog,
                 IDC_LISTBOX,
                 LB_GETTEXT,
                 (WPARAM)Idx,
                 (LPARAM)(LPCSTR)TaskName);

            // get user to confirm deletion of task:
            sprintf (Buffer, "Delete task '%s'?", TaskName);
            Result = MessageBox
                (mHDialog,
```

```
    Buffer,
    "Task Scheduler",
    MB_ICONQUESTION | MB_YESNO);
if (Result != IDYES)
    return (TRUE);

// remove task name from list box:
SendDlgItemMessage
    (mHDialog,
    IDC_LISTBOX,
    LB_DELETESTRING,
    (WPARAM)Idx,
    OL);

// if all tasks have been deleted, disable buttons;
// otherwise, select first task in list box:
if (SendDlgItemMessage (mHDialog, IDC_LISTBOX,
                        LB_GETCOUNT, O, OL) == 0)
    {
    EnableWindow (GetDlgItem (mHDialog, IDC_EDIT),
                FALSE);
    EnableWindow (GetDlgItem (mHDialog, IDC_DELETE),
                FALSE);
    EnableWindow (GetDlgItem (mHDialog, IDC_RUN),
                FALSE);
    }
else
    SendDlgItemMessage
        (mHDialog,
        IDC_LISTBOX,
        LB_SETCURSEL,
        O,
        OL);

// look for task in PTaskTable:
for (Idx = O; Idx < MAXTASKS; ++Idx)
    if (PTaskTable [Idx] != O &&
        stricmp (PTaskTable [Idx]->Name, TaskName) == 0)
        break;

// if task found, delete task object and set
```

```
            // PTaskTable entry to O:
            if (Idx < MAXTASKS)
               {
               delete PTaskTable [Idx];
               PTaskTable [Idx] = 0;
               }

            return (TRUE);

         case IDC_EDIT:  // user clicked Edit button
            {
            CTaskDialog TaskDialog;  // Task dialog box object

            // get name of selected task; store in Buffer:
            LBIdx = (int)SendDlgItemMessage (mHDialog, IDC_LISTBOX,
                                          LB_GETCURSEL, 0, OL);
            SendDlgItemMessage
               (mHDialog,
               IDC_LISTBOX,
               LB_GETTEXT,
               (WPARAM)LBIdx,
               (LPARAM)(LPCSTR)Buffer);

            // look for index of the task in PTaskTable:
            for (Idx = 0; Idx < MAXTASKS; ++Idx)
               if (PTaskTable [Idx] != 0 &&
                  stricmp (PTaskTable [Idx]->Name, Buffer) == 0)
                  break;

            if (Idx < MAXTASKS)  // task is found
               {
               // remove task name from list box; after the dialog
               // box is displayed, the task name (possibly a
               // DIFFERENT name) will be put back into the list;
               // these steps are done in case user changes task
               // name:
               SendDlgItemMessage
                  (mHDialog,
                  IDC_LISTBOX,
                  LB_DELETESTRING,
                  (WPARAM)LBIdx,
```

```
        0L);

        // store pointer to task object in CTaskDialog data
        // member PTask, so that dialog box procedure has
        // access to the task:
        TaskDialog.PTask = PTaskTable [Idx];

        // temporarily remove timer while dialog box is
        // displayed so that timer routine does not attempt
        // to run a task while a task is being edited:
        KillTimer (mHDialog, 1);
        TaskDialog.Create ("TaskDlg", mHDialog);
        SetTimer (mHDialog, 1, TimeOut, NULL);

        // put task name back into list box:
        SendDlgItemMessage
            (mHDialog,
            IDC_LISTBOX,
            LB_SETCURSEL,
            (WPARAM)SendDlgItemMessage (mHDialog, IDC_LISTBOX,
              LB_ADDSTRING, 0,
              (LPARAM)(LPCSTR)PTaskTable [Idx]->Name),
            0L);
        }

    return (TRUE);
    }

case IDC_NEW:  // user clicked New button
    {
    CTaskDialog TaskDialog;  // Task dialog box object

    // look for a free entry in PTaskTable:
    for (Idx = 0; Idx < MAXTASKS; ++Idx)
        if (PTaskTable [Idx] == 0)
            break;

    if (Idx == MAXTASKS)  // no free entry found
        {
        sprintf (Buffer,"Cannot define more than %d tasks.",
                MAXTASKS);
```

```
MessageBox
   (mHDialog,
   Buffer,
   "Task Scheduler",
   MB_OK | MB_ICONEXCLAMATION);
return (TRUE);
}

// create CTask object for new task:
PTaskTable [Idx] = new CTask;
if (PTaskTable [Idx] == 0)
   {
   MessageBox
      (mHDialog,
      "Insufficient memory to define new task.",
      "Task Scheduler",
      MB_OK | MB_ICONEXCLAMATION);
   return (TRUE);
   }

// store pointer to task object in CTaskDialog data
// member:
TaskDialog.PTask = PTaskTable [Idx];

// suspend timer and display Task dialog box:
KillTimer (mHDialog, 1);
Result = TaskDialog.Create ("TaskDlg", mHDialog);
SetTimer (mHDialog, 1, TimeOut, NULL);

if (Result == IDCANCEL)  // user clicked Cancel button
   {                     // in Task dialog box
   // delete the new task object and set PTaskTable
   // entry back to 0:
   delete PTaskTable [Idx];
   PTaskTable [Idx] = 0;
   return (TRUE);
   }

// add name of new task to list box, and select it:
SendDlgItemMessage
   (mHDialog,
```

```
        IDC_LISTBOX,
        LB_SETCURSEL,
        (WPARAM)SendDlgItemMessage (mHDialog, IDC_LISTBOX,
           LB_ADDSTRING, 0,
           (LPARAM)(LPCSTR)PTaskTable [Idx]->Name),
        OL);

    // enable buttons because list box contains at least
    // one task:
    EnableWindow (GetDlgItem (mHDialog, IDC_EDIT), TRUE);
    EnableWindow (GetDlgItem (mHDialog, IDC_DELETE), TRUE);
    EnableWindow (GetDlgItem (mHDialog, IDC_RUN), TRUE);

    return (TRUE);
    }

case IDC_RUN:  // user clicked Run Now button

    // get name of selected task from list box:
    Idx = (int)SendDlgItemMessage (mHDialog, IDC_LISTBOX,
                             LB_GETCURSEL, 0, OL);
    SendDlgItemMessage
       (mHDialog,
        IDC_LISTBOX,
        LB_GETTEXT,
        (WPARAM)Idx,
        (LPARAM)(LPCSTR)TaskName);

    // look for task in PTaskTable:
    for (Idx = 0; Idx < MAXTASKS; ++Idx)
       if (PTaskTable [Idx] != 0 &&
            stricmp (PTaskTable [Idx]->Name, TaskName) == 0)
          {
          // task is found; run it:
          PTaskTable [Idx]->Execute (TRUE);
          break;
          }

    return (TRUE);

case IDM_ABOUT:
```

```
      {
      CMDialog MDialog;
      MDialog.Create ("AboutDlg", mHDialog);
      return (TRUE);
      }

case IDM_FREQUENCY:   // user chose Set Frequency command on
                      // options menu
      {
      // display the Set Frequency dialog box:
      CFrequencyDialog FrequencyDialog;
      FrequencyDialog.Create ("FrequencyDlg", mHDialog);
      return (TRUE);
      }

case IDM_HELPCONTENTS:
   WinHelp (mHDialog, "SCHEDULE.HLP", HELP_CONTENTS, OL);
   return (TRUE);

case IDM_HELPHELP:
   WinHelp (mHDialog, "SCHEDULE.HLP", HELP_HELPONHELP, OL);
   return (TRUE);

case IDM_HELPSEARCH:
   WinHelp (mHDialog, "SCHEDULE.HLP", HELP_PARTIALKEY,
            (DWORD)(LPCSTR)"");
   return (TRUE);

case IDM_ONTOP:
   OnTop = !OnTop;
   CheckMenuItem (GetMenu (mHDialog), IDM_ONTOP,
                  OnTop ? MF_CHECKED : MF_UNCHECKED);
   SetWindowPos (mHDialog,
                 OnTop ? HWND_TOPMOST : HWND_NOTOPMOST,
                 0, 0, 0, 0, SWP_NOMOVE | SWP_NOSIZE);
   return (FALSE);

default:
   return (FALSE);

}
```

```
        }

BOOL CMainDialog::OnCtlColor (HDC HDCChild, HWND HWndChild,
                             int CtlType)
    {
    COLORREF WorkSpaceColor;
    switch (CtlType)
        {
        case CTLCOLOR_BTN:
        case CTLCOLOR_STATIC:
            WorkSpaceColor = GetSysColor (COLOR_APPWORKSPACE);
            if (GetRValue (WorkSpaceColor) * 2 +
                GetGValue (WorkSpaceColor) * 5 +
                GetBValue (WorkSpaceColor) > 1020)
                SetTextColor (HDCChild, RGB (0, 0, 0));
            else
                SetTextColor (HDCChild, RGB (255, 255, 255));
            SetBkMode (HDCChild, TRANSPARENT);
            return ((BOOL)HBrushWorkSpace);

        case CTLCOLOR_DLG:
            return ((BOOL)HBrushWorkSpace);

        default:
            return (FALSE);
        }
    }-
}

BOOL CMainDialog::OnDestroy ()
    {
    WrapUp ();
    if (HBrushWorkSpace != 0)
        DeleteObject (HBrushWorkSpace);
    KillTimer (mHDialog, 1);
    WinHelp (mHDialog, "SCHEDULE.HLP", HELP_QUIT, OL);
    PostQuitMessage (0);
    return (TRUE);
    }

BOOL CMainDialog::OnInitDialog (HWND HWndFocus, LPARAM Data)
```

```
{
char Buffer [512];
int Idx;
int Length;
int Result;
char SectionName [8];
char TaskName [SIZENAME];

// 'daylight' is predefined by the run-time library, and is
// declared in TIME.H; setting it to O tells the C++ time
// functions not to convert for daylight savings time; this
// setting is necessary so that a program run time can be set
// for ANY time of the year, without worrying about daylight
// savings times:
daylight = 0;

// read program options from initialization file:

OnTop = (int)GetPrivateProfileInt
   ("options",
   "ontop",
   0,
   "SCHEDULE.INI");
if (OnTop)
   {
   CheckMenuItem (GetMenu (mHDialog), IDM_ONTOP, MF_CHECKED);
   SetWindowPos (mHDialog, HWND_TOPMOST, 0, 0, 0, 0,
                 SWP_NOMOVE | SWP_NOSIZE);
   }

TimeOut = GetPrivateProfileInt
   ("options",
   "timeout",
   10000,
   "SCHEDULE.INI");

// read description of each task that the user has defined
// from initialization file and store it in a CTask object:
for (Idx = 0; Idx < MAXTASKS; ++Idx)
   {
   // attempt to read a section for another task:
```

```
sprintf (SectionName, "task%d", Idx);
Length = GetPrivateProfileString
   (SectionName,
   "name",
   "",
   TaskName,
   sizeof (TaskName),
   "SCHEDULE.INI");
if (Length == 0)   // no more tasks
   break;

// put task name in list box:
SendDlgItemMessage (mHDialog, IDC_LISTBOX, LB_ADDSTRING,
                    0, (LPARAM)(LPCSTR)TaskName);

// create a CTask object for the new task, and store its
// address in the next PTaskTable entry:
PTaskTable [Idx] = new CTask;
if (PTaskTable [Idx] == 0)
   {
   MessageBox
      (mHDialog,
      "Insufficient memory to store tasks.",
      "Task Scheduler",
      MB_OK ¦ MB_ICONEXCLAMATION);
   Destroy ();
   return (TRUE);
   }

// store the task information in the data members of the
// new CTask object:

// store name:
strcpy (PTaskTable [Idx]->Name, TaskName);

// store enabled status:
PTaskTable [Idx]->Enabled = GetPrivateProfileInt
   (SectionName,
   "enabled",
   0,
   "SCHEDULE.INI");
```

```
// store the task run time (can't use GetPrivateProfileInt
// because RunTime is a long):
GetPrivateProfileString
   (SectionName,
   "runtime",
   "",
   Buffer,
   sizeof (Buffer),
   "SCHEDULE.INI");
sscanf (Buffer, "%lu", &PTaskTable [Idx]->RunTime);

// store command line:

// get command-line text:
Length = GetPrivateProfileString
   (SectionName,
   "command",
   "",
   Buffer,
   sizeof (Buffer),
   "SCHEDULE.INI");

// first delete previous buffer (allocated when CTask
// is created):
delete [] PTaskTable [Idx]->Command;

// allocate new buffer to hold command line:
PTaskTable [Idx]->Command = new char [Length + 1];
if (PTaskTable [Idx]->Command == 0)
   {
   MessageBox
      (mHDialog,
      "Insufficient memory to store tasks.",
      "Task Scheduler",
      MB_OK | MB_ICONEXCLAMATION);
   Destroy ();
   return (TRUE);
   }
// copy command-line text into new buffer:
strcpy (PTaskTable [Idx]->Command, Buffer);
```

```cpp
// store working directory:
Length = GetPrivateProfileString
    (SectionName,
    "directory",
    "",
    Buffer,
    sizeof (Buffer),
    "SCHEDULE.INI");
delete [] PTaskTable [Idx]->Directory;
PTaskTable [Idx]->Directory = new char [Length + 1];
if (PTaskTable [Idx]->Directory == 0)
    {
    MessageBox
        (mHDialog,
        "Insufficient memory to store tasks.",
        "Task Scheduler",
        MB_OK | MB_ICONEXCLAMATION);
    Destroy ();
    return (TRUE);
    }
strcpy (PTaskTable [Idx]->Directory, Buffer);

// store name of Recorder file:
GetPrivateProfileString
    (SectionName,
    "recfile",
    "",
    PTaskTable [Idx]->RecFile,
    13,
    "SCHEDULE.INI");

// store flag indicating whether task is repeated:
PTaskTable [Idx]->Repeat = GetPrivateProfileInt
    (SectionName,
    "repeat",
    0,
    "SCHEDULE.INI");

// store the time values indicating the delay between
// repetitions of the task:
```

```
PTaskTable [Idx]->MonthRep = GetPrivateProfileInt
   (SectionName,
   "monthrep",
   0,
   "SCHEDULE.INI");

PTaskTable [Idx]->DayRep = GetPrivateProfileInt
   (SectionName,
   "dayrep",
   0,
   "SCHEDULE.INI");

PTaskTable [Idx]->HourRep = GetPrivateProfileInt
   (SectionName,
   "hourrep",
   0,
   "SCHEDULE.INI");

PTaskTable [Idx]->MinuteRep = GetPrivateProfileInt
   (SectionName,
   "minuterep",
   0,
   "SCHEDULE.INI");

PTaskTable [Idx]->SecondRep = GetPrivateProfileInt
   (SectionName,
   "secondrep",
   0,
   "SCHEDULE.INI");

} // end for

// if list box contains at least 1 task name, select first
// name in list; otherwise, disable buttons:
if (SendDlgItemMessage (mHDialog, IDC_LISTBOX, LB_GETCOUNT,
                        0, OL))
   SendDlgItemMessage
      (mHDialog,
      IDC_LISTBOX,
      LB_SETCURSEL,
```

```
          0,
          0L);
    else
        {
        EnableWindow (GetDlgItem (mHDialog, IDC_EDIT), FALSE);
        EnableWindow (GetDlgItem (mHDialog, IDC_DELETE), FALSE);
        EnableWindow (GetDlgItem (mHDialog, IDC_RUN), FALSE);
        }

    HBrushWorkSpace = CreateSolidBrush
        (GetSysColor (COLOR_APPWORKSPACE));

    // create the timer:
    Result = SetTimer (mHDialog, 1, TimeOut, NULL);
    if (!Result)
        {
        MessageBox
            (mHDialog,
            "Could not create timer!",
            "Task Scheduler",
            MB_ICONEXCLAMATION | MB_OK);
        Destroy ();
        }

    return (TRUE);
    }

BOOL CMainDialog::OnSysColorChange ()
    {
    if (HBrushWorkSpace != 0)
        DeleteObject (HBrushWorkSpace);
    HBrushWorkSpace =
        CreateSolidBrush (GetSysColor (COLOR_APPWORKSPACE));
    return (TRUE);
    }

BOOL CMainDialog::OnTimer ()
    {
    time_t CurrentTime;
    int Idx;
    int NextTask = -1;
```

```
            time_t NextTime = 0xffffffffL;

            // first obtain the current time:
            CurrentTime = time (0);

            // look for all tasks that are enabled and due to be run;
            // store (in NextTask) the index of the due task that has the
            // EARLIEST run time:
            for (Idx = 0; Idx < MAXTASKS; ++Idx)
               if (PTaskTable [Idx] &&
                   PTaskTable [Idx]->Enabled &&
                   (unsigned long)PTaskTable [Idx]->RunTime <=
                   (unsigned long)CurrentTime &&
                   (unsigned long)PTaskTable [Idx]->RunTime <
                   (unsigned long)NextTime)
                  {
                  NextTask = Idx;
                  NextTime = PTaskTable [Idx]->RunTime;
                  }

            // if a task was found, run it:
            if (NextTask != -1)
               PTaskTable [NextTask]->Execute (FALSE);

            return (TRUE);
            }

        BOOL CMainDialog::TaskNameExists (char *TaskName)
        // returns TRUE if PTaskTable contains a task that has the name
        // TaskName (case of letters is ignored)
            {
            int Idx;

            for (Idx = 0; Idx < MAXTASKS; ++Idx)
               if (PTaskTable [Idx] != 0 &&
                   stricmp (PTaskTable [Idx]->Name, TaskName) == 0)
                  return (TRUE);

            return (FALSE);

            }
```

```
void CMainDialog::WrapUp ()
    {
    char Buffer [16];
    int Idx;
    int IdxIni = 0;
    char SectionName [8];

    WritePrivateProfileString
        ("options",
         "ontop",
         OnTop ? "1" : "0",
         "SCHEDULE.INI");

    sprintf (Buffer, "%d", TimeOut);
    WritePrivateProfileString
        ("options",
         "timeout",
         Buffer,
         "SCHEDULE.INI");

    // create a new INI file section to store the information for
    // each task that is currently defined:
    for (Idx = 0; Idx < MAXTASKS; ++Idx)
        {
        sprintf (SectionName, "task%d", Idx);

        // delete the previous section having the same name
        // (if any):
        WritePrivateProfileString
            (SectionName,
             NULL,
             NULL,
             "SCHEDULE.INI");

        if (PTaskTable [Idx] == 0)  // PTaskTable entry not used
            continue;

        // now write the task information to the new section:

        sprintf (SectionName, "task%d", IdxIni++);
```

```
WritePrivateProfileString
   (SectionName,
   "name",
   PTaskTable [Idx]->Name,
   "SCHEDULE.INI");

WritePrivateProfileString
   (SectionName,
   "enabled",
   PTaskTable [Idx]->Enabled ? "1" : "0",
   "SCHEDULE.INI");

sprintf (Buffer, "%lu", PTaskTable [Idx]->RunTime);
WritePrivateProfileString
   (SectionName,
   "runtime",
   Buffer,
   "SCHEDULE.INI");

WritePrivateProfileString
   (SectionName,
   "command",
   PTaskTable [Idx]->Command,
   "SCHEDULE.INI");

WritePrivateProfileString
   (SectionName,
   "directory",
   PTaskTable [Idx]->Directory,
   "SCHEDULE.INI");

WritePrivateProfileString
   (SectionName,
   "recfile",
   PTaskTable [Idx]->RecFile,
   "SCHEDULE.INI");

WritePrivateProfileString
   (SectionName,
   "repeat",
```

```
        PTaskTable [Idx]->Repeat ? "1" : "0",
        "SCHEDULE.INI");

    sprintf (Buffer, "%d", PTaskTable [Idx]->MonthRep);
    WritePrivateProfileString
        (SectionName,
        "monthrep",
        Buffer,
        "SCHEDULE.INI");

    sprintf (Buffer, "%d", PTaskTable [Idx]->DayRep);
    WritePrivateProfileString
        (SectionName,
        "dayrep",
        Buffer,
        "SCHEDULE.INI");

    sprintf (Buffer, "%d", PTaskTable [Idx]->HourRep);
    WritePrivateProfileString
        (SectionName,
        "hourrep",
        Buffer,
        "SCHEDULE.INI");

    sprintf (Buffer, "%d", PTaskTable [Idx]->MinuteRep);
    WritePrivateProfileString
        (SectionName,
        "minuterep",
        Buffer,
        "SCHEDULE.INI");

    sprintf (Buffer, "%d", PTaskTable [Idx]->SecondRep);
    WritePrivateProfileString
        (SectionName,
        "secondrep",
        Buffer,
        "SCHEDULE.INI");

    } // end for
}
```

```
////////////////////////////////////////////////////////////
// CFrequencyDialog member function:                        //
////////////////////////////////////////////////////////////

BOOL CFrequencyDialog::DialogProc (UINT Msg, WPARAM WParam,
                                   LPARAM LParam)
   {
   char Buffer [3];
   int Result;

   switch (Msg)
      {
      case WM_COMMAND:
         switch (WParam)
            {
            case IDCANCEL:
               EndDialog (mHDialog, O);
               return (TRUE);

            case IDC_HELP:
               WinHelp (MainDialog.mHDialog, "SCHEDULE.HLP",
                        HELP_CONTEXT, HELPFREQDLG);
               return (TRUE);

            case IDOK:
               // obtain timeout value from edit control,
               // convert to an integer, and test that it is
               // within valid range:
               GetDlgItemText (mHDialog, IDC_FREQ, Buffer,
                               sizeof (Buffer));
               Result = atoi (Buffer);
               if (Result < 1 || Result > 65)
                  {
                  MessageBox
                     (mHDialog,
                     "Must enter a value between 1 and 65.",
                     "Set Frequency",
                     MB_ICONEXCLAMATION | MB_OK);
                  SetFocus (GetDlgItem (mHDialog, IDC_FREQ));
                  return (TRUE);
                  }
```

```
                    // exit immediately if the user has not entered
                    // a new timeout value:
                    if (MainDialog.TimeOut == (unsigned)Result * 1000)
                        {
                        EndDialog (mHDialog, 0);
                        return (TRUE);
                        }

                    // convert value to milliseconds and store:
                    MainDialog.TimeOut = (unsigned)Result * 1000;

                    // remove old timer and create a new one:
                    KillTimer (MainDialog.mHDialog, 1);

                    Result = SetTimer (MainDialog.mHDialog, 1,
                                       MainDialog.TimeOut, NULL);
                    if (!Result)
                        {
                        MessageBox
                            (mHDialog,
                            "Could not create new timer!",
                            "Set Frequency",
                            MB_ICONEXCLAMATION | MB_OK);
                        MainDialog.Destroy ();
                        }

                    EndDialog (mHDialog, 0);
                    return (TRUE);

                default:
                    return (TRUE);
                }

        case WM_INITDIALOG:
            // limit edit control text to 2 digits:
            SendDlgItemMessage (mHDialog, IDC_FREQ, EM_LIMITTEXT,
                                2, 0L);

            // convert current timeout value to seconds and
            // display in edit control:
```

```
                   sprintf (Buffer, "%d", MainDialog.TimeOut / 1000);
                   SetDlgItemText (mHDialog, IDC_FREQ, Buffer);

                   return (TRUE);

              default:
                 if (Msg == mHelpMessage)
                    {
                    SendMessage (mHDialog, WM_COMMAND, IDC_HELP, OL);
                    return (TRUE);
                    }
                 else
                    return (FALSE);


          }
      }


//////////////////////////////////////////////////////////////////
// CTaskDialog member functions:                                 //
//////////////////////////////////////////////////////////////////

CTaskDialog::CTaskDialog ()
    {
    PTask = 0;
    }

BOOL CTaskDialog::DialogProc (UINT Msg, WPARAM WParam,
                              LPARAM LParam)
    {
    int Hour;
    int Length;
    BOOL Repeat;
    static struct tm TM;

    switch (Msg)
        {
        case WM_INITDIALOG:
           SendDlgItemMessage (mHDialog, IDC_NAME, EM_LIMITTEXT,
                               SIZENAME - 1, OL);
           SendDlgItemMessage (mHDialog, IDC_COMMAND, EM_LIMITTEXT,
                               511, OL);
```

```
SendDlgItemMessage (mHDialog, IDC_DIRECTORY,
                    EM_LIMITTEXT, 511, OL);
SendDlgItemMessage (mHDialog, IDC_RECFILE, EM_LIMITTEXT,
                    12, OL);
SendDlgItemMessage (mHDialog, IDC_MONTH, EM_LIMITTEXT,
                    2, OL);
SendDlgItemMessage (mHDialog, IDC_DAY, EM_LIMITTEXT, 2,
                    OL);
SendDlgItemMessage (mHDialog, IDC_YEAR, EM_LIMITTEXT,
                    2, OL);
SendDlgItemMessage (mHDialog, IDC_HOURS, EM_LIMITTEXT,
                    2, OL);
SendDlgItemMessage (mHDialog, IDC_MINUTES, EM_LIMITTEXT,
                    2, OL);
SendDlgItemMessage (mHDialog, IDC_SECONDS, EM_LIMITTEXT,
                    2, OL);
SendDlgItemMessage (mHDialog, IDC_MONTHREP,
                    EM_LIMITTEXT, 2, OL);
SendDlgItemMessage (mHDialog, IDC_DAYREP, EM_LIMITTEXT,
                    2, OL);
SendDlgItemMessage (mHDialog, IDC_HOURREP, EM_LIMITTEXT,
                    2, OL);
SendDlgItemMessage (mHDialog, IDC_MINUTEREP,
                    EM_LIMITTEXT, 2, OL);
SendDlgItemMessage (mHDialog, IDC_SECONDREP,
                    EM_LIMITTEXT, 2, OL);

// display the task information contained in the CTask
// object pointed to by CTaskDialog::PTask:

SetDlgItemText (mHDialog, IDC_NAME, PTask->Name);
CheckDlgButton (mHDialog, IDC_ENABLED, PTask->Enabled);
SetDlgItemText (mHDialog, IDC_COMMAND, PTask->Command);
SetDlgItemText (mHDialog, IDC_DIRECTORY,
                PTask->Directory);
SetDlgItemText (mHDialog, IDC_RECFILE, PTask->RecFile);

// display the date:

// convert CTask::RunTime from seconds value (time_t) to
// month, day, year, etc. (struct tm):
```

```
TM = *localtime (&PTask->RunTime);

SetDlgItemInt (mHDialog, IDC_MONTH, TM.tm_mon + 1,
               TRUE);
SetDlgItemInt (mHDialog, IDC_DAY, TM.tm_mday, TRUE);
SetDlgItemInt (mHDialog, IDC_YEAR,
               TM.tm_year % 100,
               TRUE);
// convert 24 hour time to 12 hour, AM/PM time:
if (TM.tm_hour == 0)
   Hour = 12;
else if (TM.tm_hour >= 1 && TM.tm_hour <= 12)
   Hour = TM.tm_hour;
else
   Hour = TM.tm_hour - 12;
SetDlgItemInt (mHDialog, IDC_HOURS, Hour, TRUE);

SetDlgItemInt (mHDialog, IDC_MINUTES, TM.tm_min, TRUE);
SetDlgItemInt (mHDialog, IDC_SECONDS, TM.tm_sec, TRUE);

CheckDlgButton (mHDialog,
                TM.tm_hour < 12 ? IDC_AM : IDC_PM,
                1);
// enable OK button only if task name is not empty:
EnableWindow
   (GetDlgItem (mHDialog, IDOK),
   (BOOL)PTask->Name [0]);

CheckDlgButton (mHDialog,
                PTask->Repeat ? IDC_REPEAT : IDC_ONCE,
                1);
SetDlgItemInt (mHDialog, IDC_MONTHREP, PTask->MonthRep,
               TRUE);
SetDlgItemInt (mHDialog, IDC_DAYREP, PTask->DayRep,
               TRUE);
SetDlgItemInt (mHDialog, IDC_HOURREP, PTask->HourRep,
               TRUE);
SetDlgItemInt (mHDialog, IDC_MINUTEREP,
               PTask->MinuteRep, TRUE);
SetDlgItemInt (mHDialog, IDC_SECONDREP,
               PTask->SecondRep, TRUE);
```

```
                    // send message so that the IDC_ONCE routine enables
                    // the text boxes in the Repeat group only if the
                    // Repeat Every radio button is checked:
                    SendMessage (mHDialog, WM_COMMAND, IDC_ONCE,
                                MAKELPARAM (O, BN_CLICKED));

                    return (TRUE);

            case WM_COMMAND:
                switch (WParam)
                    {
                    case IDCANCEL:
                        EndDialog (mHDialog, IDCANCEL);
                        return (TRUE);

                    case IDC_COMMAND:
                    case IDC_NAME:
                    case IDC_RECFILE:
                        if (HIWORD (LParam) == EN_CHANGE)
                            {
                            // user has changed text in Name, Command
                            // Line, or Recorder File Name edit
                            // control; enable OK button only if
                            // Name control and either Command Line
                            // or Recorder File Name control contains
                            // text:
                            EnableWindow
                                (GetDlgItem (mHDialog, IDOK),
                                GetWindowTextLength (GetDlgItem (mHDialog,
                                                IDC_NAME)) &&
                                (GetWindowTextLength (GetDlgItem (mHDialog,
                                                IDC_COMMAND)) ||
                                GetWindowTextLength (GetDlgItem (mHDialog,
                                                IDC_RECFILE))));
                            return (TRUE);
                            }
                        else
                            return (FALSE);

                    case IDC_HELP:
```

```
            WinHelp (MainDialog.mHDialog, "SCHEDULE.HLP",
                    HELP_CONTEXT, HELPTASKDLG);
            return (TRUE);

        case IDOK:
            {
            // this local block contains variables and code
            // for validating the data the user has entered:

            int DayRep;
            // number of days in each month for regular and
            // leap years:
            static int DayTable[2][12] =
                {
                {31,28,31,30,31,30,31,31,30,31,30,31},
                {31,29,31,30,31,30,31,31,30,31,30,31}
                };
            int HourRep;
            BOOL Leap;
            char Message [128];
            int MinuteRep;
            int MonthRep;
            int SecondRep;
            char TaskName [SIZENAME];
            int Value;

            // make sure that user has not entered a new name
            // into the Name box that matches the name of an
            // existing task:
            GetDlgItemText (mHDialog, IDC_NAME, TaskName,
                            SIZENAME);
            if (stricmp (PTask->Name, TaskName) != 0 &&
                MainDialog.TaskNameExists (TaskName))
                {
                sprintf (Message, "Task '%s' already exists. "
                        "Choose another name.", TaskName);
                MessageBox
                    (mHDialog,
                    Message,
                    "Task Scheduler",
                    MB_OK | MB_ICONEXCLAMATION);
```

```
      SetFocus (GetDlgItem (mHDialog, IDC_NAME));
      return (TRUE);
      }

// validate month:
Value = GetDlgItemInt (mHDialog, IDC_MONTH, 0,
                      TRUE);
if (Value < 1 || Value > 12)
   {
   MessageBox
      (mHDialog,
      "Month must be a value between 1 and 12.",
      "Task Scheduler",
      MB_OK | MB_ICONEXCLAMATION);
   SetFocus (GetDlgItem (mHDialog, IDC_MONTH));
   return (TRUE);
   }
TM.tm_mon = Value - 1;

// validate year:
Value = GetDlgItemInt (mHDialog, IDC_YEAR, 0,
                      TRUE);
if (Value < 0 ||
    Value > 35 && Value < 70)
   {
   MessageBox
      (mHDialog,
      "Year must between between 70 and 99 OR "
      "between 0 and 35.",
      "Task Scheduler",
      MB_OK | MB_ICONEXCLAMATION);
   SetFocus (GetDlgItem (mHDialog, IDC_YEAR));
   return (TRUE);
   }
// convert year to the number of years since 1900:
TM.tm_year = Value < 70 ? Value + 100 : Value;

// set flag for leap year:
Leap = Value % 4 == 0;

// validate day:
```

```
Value = GetDlgItemInt (mHDialog, IDC_DAY, 0,
                       TRUE);
if (Value < 1 ||
    Value > DayTable [Leap][TM.tm_mon])
   {
   MessageBox
      (mHDialog,
      "Invalid day of month.",
      "Task Scheduler",
      MB_OK | MB_ICONEXCLAMATION);
   SetFocus (GetDlgItem (mHDialog, IDC_DAY));
   return (TRUE);
   }
TM.tm_mday = Value;

// validate hour:
Value = GetDlgItemInt (mHDialog, IDC_HOURS, 0,
                       TRUE);
if (Value < 1 || Value > 12)
   {
   MessageBox
      (mHDialog,
      "Hour must be between 1 and 12.",
      "Task Scheduler",
      MB_OK | MB_ICONEXCLAMATION);
   SetFocus (GetDlgItem (mHDialog, IDC_HOURS));
   return (TRUE);
   }
if (IsDlgButtonChecked (mHDialog, IDC_AM))
   TM.tm_hour = Value == 12 ? 0 : Value;
else
   TM.tm_hour = Value == 12 ? 12 : Value + 12;

// validate minutes:
Value = GetDlgItemInt (mHDialog, IDC_MINUTES, 0,
                       TRUE);
if (Value < 0 || Value > 59)
   {
   MessageBox
      (mHDialog,
      "Minutes must be between 0 and 59.",
```

```
         "Task Scheduler",
         MB_OK | MB_ICONEXCLAMATION);
      SetFocus (GetDlgItem (mHDialog, IDC_MINUTES));
      return (TRUE);
      }
TM.tm_min = Value;

// validate seconds:
Value = GetDlgItemInt (mHDialog, IDC_SECONDS, 0,
                       TRUE);
if (Value < 0 || Value > 59)
   {
   MessageBox
      (mHDialog,
       "Seconds must be between 0 and 59.",
       "Task Scheduler",
       MB_OK | MB_ICONEXCLAMATION);
   SetFocus (GetDlgItem (mHDialog, IDC_SECONDS));
   return (TRUE);
   }
TM.tm_sec = Value;

// validate the time values that specify the delay
// between repetitions of the task:

MonthRep = GetDlgItemInt (mHDialog, IDC_MONTHREP,
                          0, TRUE);
DayRep = GetDlgItemInt (mHDialog, IDC_DAYREP, 0,
                        TRUE);
HourRep = GetDlgItemInt (mHDialog, IDC_HOURREP,
                         0, TRUE);
MinuteRep = GetDlgItemInt (mHDialog,
                           IDC_MINUTEREP, 0,
                           TRUE);
SecondRep = GetDlgItemInt (mHDialog,
                           IDC_SECONDREP, 0,TRUE);

if (MonthRep < 0 || DayRep < 0 || HourRep < 0 ||
    MinuteRep < 0 || SecondRep < 0)
   {
   MessageBox
```

```
            (mHDialog,
            "Repeat duration values must be between 0 "
            "and 99.",
            "Task Scheduler",
            MB_OK | MB_ICONEXCLAMATION);
          SetFocus (GetDlgItem (mHDialog, IDC_MONTHREP));
          return (TRUE);
          }

      // store the repetition delay values:
      PTask->MonthRep = MonthRep;
      PTask->DayRep = DayRep;
      PTask->HourRep = HourRep;
      PTask->MinuteRep = MinuteRep;
      PTask->SecondRep = SecondRep;

      // store the task name:
      strcpy (PTask->Name, TaskName);

      // convert run time (struct tm) to seconds value
      // (time_t) and store:
      PTask->RunTime = mktime (&TM);

      }  // end data validation block

      // store the data from the remaining dialog box
      // controls in data members of task object:

      PTask->Enabled = IsDlgButtonChecked
          (mHDialog, IDC_ENABLED) ? TRUE : FALSE;

      delete [] (PTask->Command);
      Length = GetWindowTextLength
          (GetDlgItem (mHDialog, IDC_COMMAND));
      PTask->Command = new char [Length + 1];
      if (PTask->Command == 0)
          {
          MessageBox
              (mHDialog,
              "Insufficient memory to store task.",
              "Task Scheduler",
```

```
            MB_OK | MB_ICONEXCLAMATION);
        EndDialog (mHDialog, IDCANCEL);
        return (TRUE);
        }
    if (Length == 0)
        PTask->Command [0] = '\0';
    else
        GetDlgItemText (mHDialog, IDC_COMMAND,
                        PTask->Command, Length + 1);

    delete [] (PTask->Directory);
    Length = GetWindowTextLength
        (GetDlgItem (mHDialog, IDC_DIRECTORY));
    PTask->Directory = new char [Length + 1];
    if (PTask->Directory == 0)
        {
        MessageBox
            (mHDialog,
            "Insufficient memory to store task.",
            "Task Scheduler",
            MB_OK | MB_ICONEXCLAMATION);
        EndDialog (mHDialog, IDCANCEL);
        return (TRUE);
        }
    if (Length == 0)
        PTask->Directory [0] = '\0';
    else
        GetDlgItemText (mHDialog, IDC_DIRECTORY,
                        PTask->Directory, Length + 1);

    GetDlgItemText (mHDialog, IDC_RECFILE,
                    PTask->RecFile, 13);

    PTask->Repeat = IsDlgButtonChecked
        (mHDialog, IDC_REPEAT);

    EndDialog (mHDialog, IDOK);
    return (TRUE);

case IDC_ONCE:
case IDC_REPEAT:
```

```
            if (HIWORD (LParam) == BN_CLICKED)
                {
                // user has clicked either the Run Once or the
                // Repeat Every radio button; enable the edit
                // controls within the Repeat group only if the
                // Repeat Every button is checked:

                Repeat = IsDlgButtonChecked
                    (mHDialog, IDC_REPEAT);

                EnableWindow
                    (GetDlgItem (mHDialog, IDC_MONTHREP),
                    Repeat);
                EnableWindow
                    (GetDlgItem (mHDialog, IDC_DAYREP),
                    Repeat);
                EnableWindow
                    (GetDlgItem (mHDialog, IDC_HOURREP),
                    Repeat);
                EnableWindow
                    (GetDlgItem (mHDialog, IDC_MINUTEREP),
                    Repeat);
                EnableWindow
                    (GetDlgItem (mHDialog, IDC_SECONDREP),
                    Repeat);

                return (TRUE);
                }
            else
                return (TRUE);

        default:
            return (FALSE);
        }

    default:
        if (Msg == mHelpMessage)
            {
            SendMessage (mHDialog, WM_COMMAND, IDC_HELP, OL);
            return (TRUE);
            }
```

```
        else
            return (FALSE);
        }
    }
```

Listing 5.4

```cpp
//////////////////////////////////////////////////////////////////
//                                                              //
// TASK.CPP:  CTask member functions for the SCHEDULE program. //
//                                                              //
//////////////////////////////////////////////////////////////////

#include "schedule.h"
#include <ctype.h>
#include <direct.h>
#include <stdio.h>
#include <time.h>

CTask::CTask ()
    {
    struct tm TM;

    Command = new char [1];
    *Command = '\0';
    DayRep = 0;
    Directory = new char [1];
    *Directory = '\0';
    Enabled = TRUE;
    HourRep = 0;
    MinuteRep = 0;
    MonthRep = 0;
    Name [0] = '\0';
    RecFile [0] = '\0';
    Repeat = FALSE;

    RunTime = time (0);
    TM = *localtime (&RunTime);
    TM.tm_hour = 23;
    TM.tm_min = TM.tm_sec = 59;
    RunTime = mktime (&TM);
```

```
   SecondRep = 0;
   }

CTask::~CTask ()
   {
   if (Command)
      delete [] Command;
   if (Directory)
      delete [] Directory;
   }

void CTask::Execute (BOOL RunNow)
   {
   char Buffer [32];
   time_t CurrentTime;
   HWND HWndRecorder;
   struct tm TM;

   // if working directory specifies drive, change to that drive:
   if (isalpha (Directory [0]) && Directory [1] == ':')
      _chdrive (toupper (Directory [0]) - 64);

   // if working directory is specified, change to it:
   if (Directory [0])
      chdir (Directory);

   // if command line is specified, run it:
   if (Command [0])
      WinExec (Command, SW_SHOWNORMAL);

   // if Windows Recorder file is specified, run macro:
   if (RecFile [0])
      {
      // run the Recorder, passing the name of the macro file:
      sprintf (Buffer, "RECORDER %s", RecFile);
      WinExec (Buffer, SW_SHOWNORMAL);

      // obtain the handle of the Recorder main window by
      // passing the name of the class to FindWindow:
      HWndRecorder = FindWindow ("Recorder", 0);
```

```
        // if handle supplied, post a WM_COMMAND message with ID of
        // Run command on Macro menu; causes Recorder to run the
        // selected macro (that is, the first macro in list):
        if (HWndRecorder)
            PostMessage (HWndRecorder, WM_COMMAND, 0x0011, OL);
        }


if (RunNow)
    // task is being run in response to the Run Now button
    return;

// task is being run through the timer routine

if (Repeat &&
    MonthRep + DayRep + HourRep + MinuteRep + SecondRep != 0)
    {
    // user chose the 'Repeat Every' option to repeat task,
    // and entered a nonzero duration between repetitions;
    // therefore, update task's run time by repeatedly
    // adding the specified duration until the new run time
    // is later than the current time:

    CurrentTime = time (0);
    do
        {
        TM = *localtime (&RunTime);
        TM.tm_mon += MonthRep;
        TM.tm_mday += DayRep;
        TM.tm_hour += HourRep;
        TM.tm_min += MinuteRep;
        TM.tm_sec += SecondRep;
        RunTime = mktime (&TM);
        }
    while ((unsigned long)RunTime <=
            (unsigned long)CurrentTime);
    }
else
```

```
        // user chose the 'Run Once' option; therefore, disable
        // task so that it is not run with each subsequent timer
        // message!:
        Enabled = FALSE;
    }
```

Listing 5.5

```
;;;;;;;;;;;;;;;;;;;;;;;;;;;;;;;;;;;;;;;;;;;;;;;;;;;;;;;;;;;;;;;;;;;;;;
;                                                                   ;
; SCHEDULE.DEF:  Module-definition file for the SCHEDULE            ;
;                program.                                           ;
;                                                                   ;
;;;;;;;;;;;;;;;;;;;;;;;;;;;;;;;;;;;;;;;;;;;;;;;;;;;;;;;;;;;;;;;;;;;;;;

NAME SCHEDULE

DESCRIPTION  'Windows Task Scheduler'

EXETYPE WINDOWS

CODE PRELOAD MOVEABLE DISCARDABLE

DATA PRELOAD MOVEABLE MULTIPLE

HEAPSIZE 1024

STACKSIZE 10240
```

Listing 5.6

```
//////////////////////////////////////////////////////////////////
//                                                                //
// RESOURCE.H:  Constant definitions for the SCHEDULE program     //
//              resources (generated by Microsoft App Studio).    //
//                                                                //
//////////////////////////////////////////////////////////////////

//{{NO_DEPENDENCIES}}
// App Studio generated include file.
// Used by SCHEDULE.RC
```

```
//
#define IDC_DELETE                    101
#define IDC_NAME                      102
#define IDC_ENABLED                   103
#define IDC_EDIT                      104
#define IDC_LISTBOX                   105
#define IDC_NEW                       106
#define IDC_RUN                       107
#define IDC_MONTH                     108
#define IDC_DAY                       109
#define IDC_YEAR                      110
#define IDC_COMMAND                   111
#define IDC_AM                        112
#define IDC_PM                        113
#define IDC_HELP                      114
#define IDC_DIRECTORY                 115
#define IDC_HOURS                     116
#define IDC_RECFILE                   117
#define IDC_MINUTES                   118
#define IDC_SECONDS                   119
#define IDC_FREQ                      120
#define IDC_ONCE                      121
#define IDC_REPEAT                    122
#define IDC_MONTHREP                  123
#define IDC_DAYREP                    124
#define IDC_HOURREP                   125
#define IDC_MINUTEREP                 126
#define IDC_SECONDREP                 127
#define IDM_ABOUT                     1000
#define IDM_FREQUENCY                 1001
#define IDM_HELPCONTENTS              1002
#define IDM_HELPHELP                  1003
#define IDM_HELPSEARCH                1004
#define IDM_ONTOP                     1005

// Next default values for new objects
//
#ifdef APSTUDIO_INVOKED
#ifndef APSTUDIO_READONLY_SYMBOLS

#define _APS_NEXT_RESOURCE_VALUE      101
```

```
#define _APS_NEXT_COMMAND_VALUE         101
#define _APS_NEXT_CONTROL_VALUE         1000
#define _APS_NEXT_SYMED_VALUE           101
#endif
#endif
```

Listing 5.7

```
/////////////////////////////////////////////////////////////////
//                                                             //
// SCHEDULE.RC:  Resource-definition file for the SCHEDULE     //
//               program (generated by Microsoft App Studio).  //
//                                                             //
/////////////////////////////////////////////////////////////////

//Microsoft App Studio generated resource script.
//
#include "resource.h"

#define APSTUDIO_READONLY_SYMBOLS
/////////////////////////////////////////////////////////////////
//
// Generated from the TEXTINCLUDE 2 resource.
//
#define APSTUDIO_HIDDEN_SYMBOLS
#include "windows.h"
#undef APSTUDIO_HIDDEN_SYMBOLS


/////////////////////////////////////////////////////////////////
#undef APSTUDIO_READONLY_SYMBOLS


/////////////////////////////////////////////////////////////////
//
// Icon
//

SCHEDULEICON            ICON    DISCARDABLE     "SCHEDULE.ICO"


/////////////////////////////////////////////////////////////////
//
// Menu
```

```
//

SCHEDULEMENU MENU DISCARDABLE
BEGIN
    POPUP "&Options"
    BEGIN
        MENUITEM "Set &Frequency...",           IDM_FREQUENCY
        MENUITEM "Always on &Top",              IDM_ONTOP
    END
    POPUP "&Help"
    BEGIN
        MENUITEM "&Contents...\tF1",            IDM_HELPCONTENTS
        MENUITEM "&Search for Help On...",      IDM_HELPSEARCH
        MENUITEM "&How to Use Help...",         IDM_HELPHELP
        MENUITEM SEPARATOR
        MENUITEM "&About...",                   IDM_ABOUT
    END
END


/////////////////////////////////////////////////////////////////
//
// Accelerator
//

SCHEDULEACCEL ACCELERATORS MOVEABLE PURE
BEGIN
    VK_F1,          IDM_HELPCONTENTS,       VIRTKEY
END


/////////////////////////////////////////////////////////////////
//
// Dialog
//

ABOUTDLG DIALOG DISCARDABLE  12, 24, 106, 96
STYLE DS_MODALFRAME ¦ WS_POPUP ¦ WS_VISIBLE ¦ WS_CAPTION ¦
   WS_SYSMENU
CAPTION "About"
FONT 8, "MS Sans Serif"
BEGIN
    CTEXT           "Windows Task Scheduler",-1,0,10,106,12
```

```
        PUSHBUTTON      "OK",IDOK,32,74,40,14
        ICON            "ScheduleIcon",-1,42,42,18,20
        CTEXT           "by Michael J. Young",-1,0,28,106,8
END


MAINDLG DIALOG DISCARDABLE  18, 42, 136, 106
STYLE WS_MINIMIZEBOX | WS_POPUP | WS_VISIBLE | WS_CAPTION |
    WS_SYSMENU
CAPTION "Task Scheduler"
MENU ScheduleMenu
FONT 8, "MS Sans Serif"
BEGIN
        LTEXT           "&Tasks:",-1,6,4,26,8
        LISTBOX         IDC_LISTBOX,8,16,66,82,LBS_SORT |
                        WS_VSCROLL | WS_TABSTOP
        PUSHBUTTON      "&New...",IDC_NEW,84,16,44,14
        PUSHBUTTON      "&Edit...",IDC_EDIT,84,40,44,14
        PUSHBUTTON      "&Delete",IDC_DELETE,84,58,44,14
        PUSHBUTTON      "&Run Now",IDC_RUN,84,82,44,14
END


TASKDLG DIALOG DISCARDABLE  6, 18, 182, 214
STYLE DS_MODALFRAME | WS_POPUP | WS_VISIBLE | WS_CAPTION |
    WS_SYSMENU
CAPTION "Task"
FONT 8, "MS Sans Serif"
BEGIN
        LTEXT           "/",-1,50,100,8,8
        LTEXT           "/",-1,66,100,8,8
        CTEXT           ":",-1,50,118,4,8
        CTEXT           ":",-1,66,118,4,8
        LTEXT           "&Name:",-1,6,12,24,8
        EDITTEXT        IDC_NAME,30,10,100,12,ES_AUTOHSCROLL
        CONTROL         "&Enabled",IDC_ENABLED,"Button",
                        BS_AUTOCHECKBOX | WS_TABSTOP,140,12,40,10
        LTEXT           "&Command Line:",-1,6,30,50,8
        EDITTEXT        IDC_COMMAND,62,28,114,12,ES_AUTOHSCROLL
        LTEXT           "&Working Directory:",-1,6,48,62,8
        EDITTEXT        IDC_DIRECTORY,72,46,104,12,ES_AUTOHSCROLL
        LTEXT           "&Recorder File Name:",-1,6,66,80,8
        EDITTEXT        IDC_RECFILE,88,64,58,12,ES_AUTOHSCROLL
```

```
        LTEXT               "&Date:",-1,14,100,20,8
        EDITTEXT            IDC_MONTH,38,98,12,12,ES_AUTOHSCROLL |
                            WS_GROUP
        EDITTEXT            IDC_DAY,54,98,12,12,ES_AUTOHSCROLL
        EDITTEXT            IDC_YEAR,70,98,12,12,ES_AUTOHSCROLL
        LTEXT               "&Time:",-1,14,118,20,8
        EDITTEXT            IDC_HOURS,38,116,12,12,ES_AUTOHSCROLL |
                            WS_GROUP
        EDITTEXT            IDC_MINUTES,54,116,12,12,ES_AUTOHSCROLL
        EDITTEXT            IDC_SECONDS,70,116,12,12,ES_AUTOHSCROLL
        CONTROL             "&AM",IDC_AM,"Button",BS_AUTORADIOBUTTON |
                            WS_GROUP | WS_TABSTOP,36,134,24,10
        CONTROL             "&PM",IDC_PM,"Button",BS_AUTORADIOBUTTON,62,
                            134,24,10
        PUSHBUTTON          "OK",IDOK,6,158,40,14,WS_GROUP
        PUSHBUTTON          "Cancel",IDCANCEL,6,174,40,14
        PUSHBUTTON          "&Help",IDC_HELP,6,196,40,14
        CONTROL             "Run &Once",IDC_ONCE,"Button",
                            BS_AUTORADIOBUTTON | WS_GROUP | WS_TABSTOP,
                            104,98,46,10
        CONTROL             "Repeat E&very:",IDC_REPEAT,"Button",
                            BS_AUTORADIOBUTTON,104,112,60,10
        LTEXT               "&months",-1,122,130,30,8
        EDITTEXT            IDC_MONTHREP,104,128,12,12,ES_AUTOHSCROLL
        LTEXT               "da&ys",-1,122,146,30,8,NOT WS_GROUP
        EDITTEXT            IDC_DAYREP,104,144,12,12,ES_AUTOHSCROLL
        LTEXT               "ho&urs",-1,122,162,30,8,NOT WS_GROUP
        EDITTEXT            IDC_HOURREP,104,160,12,12,ES_AUTOHSCROLL
        LTEXT               "m&inutes",-1,122,178,30,8,NOT WS_GROUP
        EDITTEXT            IDC_MINUTEREP,104,176,12,12,ES_AUTOHSCROLL
        LTEXT               "&seconds",-1,122,194,30,8,NOT WS_GROUP
        EDITTEXT            IDC_SECONDREP,104,192,12,12,ES_AUTOHSCROLL
        GROUPBOX            "Run At",-1,6,84,84,68
        GROUPBOX            "Repeat",-1,98,84,78,126,WS_GROUP
END

FREQUENCYDLG DIALOG DISCARDABLE  6, 18, 116, 64
STYLE DS_MODALFRAME | WS_POPUP | WS_VISIBLE | WS_CAPTION |
    WS_SYSMENU
CAPTION "Set Frequency"
FONT 8, "MS Sans Serif"
```

```
BEGIN
    LTEXT               "&Check time every",-1,6,8,60,8
    EDITTEXT            IDC_FREQ,68,6,12,12,ES_AUTOHSCROLL
    LTEXT               "seconds.",-1,84,8,28,8
    PUSHBUTTON          "OK",IDOK,8,28,36,14
    PUSHBUTTON          "Cancel",IDCANCEL,8,44,36,14
    PUSHBUTTON          "&Help",IDC_HELP,74,44,36,14
END


#ifdef APSTUDIO_INVOKED
/////////////////////////////////////////////////////////////////////////
//
// TEXTINCLUDE
//

1 TEXTINCLUDE DISCARDABLE
BEGIN
    "resource.h\0"
END

2 TEXTINCLUDE DISCARDABLE
BEGIN
    "#define APSTUDIO_HIDDEN_SYMBOLS\r\n"
    "#include ""windows.h""\r\n"
    "#undef APSTUDIO_HIDDEN_SYMBOLS\r\n"
    "\0"
END

3 TEXTINCLUDE DISCARDABLE
BEGIN
    "\r\n"
    "\0"
END


/////////////////////////////////////////////////////////////////////////
#endif      // APSTUDIO_INVOKED

#ifndef APSTUDIO_INVOKED
/////////////////////////////////////////////////////////////////////////
//
// Generated from the TEXTINCLUDE 3 resource.
```

```
//

////////////////////////////////////////////////////////////////////
#endif    // not APSTUDIO_INVOKED
```

Storing Task Information

Each task stored by the SCHEDULE program is managed by an object belonging to the CTask class. This class is defined in SCHEDULE.H (Listing 5.1) and its member functions are implemented in TASK.CPP (Listing 5.4). The data members of a CTask object store complete information on a task, including the name of the task, the command line, the run time, and so on. Table 5.1 lists each of these data members and briefly describes the information it stores. CTask also provides a member function, Execute, that runs the task (this function is described later, in the section "Running the Tasks").

TABLE 5.1: The CTask Data Members

CTask DATA MEMBER	INFORMATION STORED
Command	Pointer to a string containing the task command line (a program name, possibly followed by parameters)
DayRep	Number of days between iterations of a repeated task
Directory	Pointer to a string containing the working directory that is switched to when the task is run
Enabled	Flag indicating whether the task is enabled (that is, whether it will be run when due)
HourRep	Number of hours between iterations of a repeated task
MinuteRep	Number of minutes between iterations of a repeated task
MonthRep	Number of calendar months between iterations of a repeated task
Name	String containing the name of the task
RecFile	String containing the name of a Recorder macro file

TABLE 5.1: The CTask Data Members (continued)

CTask DATA MEMBER	INFORMATION STORED
Repeat	Flag indicating whether the task is to be repeated at regular intervals
RunTime	Time at which the task is to be run, stored as the number of seconds from a base time (as a time_t type variable)
SecondRep	Number of seconds between iterations of a repeated task

Initializing and Destroying CTask Objects

Whenever the program creates a CTask object, the class constructor assigns the data members their initial default values (the constructor and destructor are implemented in TASK.CPP of Listing 5.4).

Because the information that they store can vary greatly in length, the Command and Directory data members are *pointers* to character arrays rather than fixed-length character arrays. When the program obtains the information that one of these data members stores, it uses the new operator to allocate a buffer of appropriate length and assigns the buffer address to the data member. The constructor initializes each of these data members by allocating a one-byte buffer using new, writing a NULL character to the buffer, and assigning the buffer address to the data member. Whenever the program assigns the address of a new buffer to either Command or Directory, it first uses the delete operator to delete the old buffer. When the program destroys a CTask object, the class destructor also uses delete to free the buffers pointed to by Command and Directory.

The CTask constructor assigns an initial time value to the RunTime data member, which stores the time at which the task is to be run. RunTime, which is of type time_t (defined in the standard header file TIME.H), stores the time as the number of seconds that have elapsed from a base time (for both Microsoft Visual C++ and Borland C++ the base time is midnight, January 1, 1970).

The initial time that the CTask constructor assigns to RunTime is one second before midnight on the current day (the choice of this default time was arbitrary). To obtain the initial time, the constructor performs the following four steps:

1. It calls the C++ run-time function time to obtain the current time as a time_t value (the number of seconds from a base time) and assigns this value to RunTime:

```
RunTime = time (0);
```

2. It calls the run-time function localtime to convert the time_t value to the time expressed as the year, month, day, hours, minutes, and seconds; these time values are assigned to the fields of a tm structure (tm is also defined in TIME.H):

```
struct tm TM;
.
.
.
TM = *localtime (&RunTime);
```

3. It adjusts the number of hours, minutes, and seconds stored in the tm structure so that the time is one second before midnight:

```
TM.tm_hour = 23;
TM.tm_min = TM.tm_sec = 59;
```

4. It calls the mktime run-time function to convert the tm time back to the equivalent time_t time, assigning the result to the RunTime data member:

```
RunTime = mktime (&TM);
```

The advantage of storing the task run time as a time_t type is that the time can be easily saved—both within the program and within the initialization file—as a single integer value. Also, the timer routine (which is explained later) can compare a task's run time with the current time (obtained by calling the `time` run-time function), using a single, fast integer comparison.

However, the Task dialog box (managed by the `CTaskDialog` function) obtains the time from the user as a year, month, day, hour, minute, and second value. When the dialog box is first displayed, the `WM_INITDIALOG` branch of the `CTaskDialog::DialogProc` function (in DIALOG.CPP of Listing 5.3) calls the `localtime` run-time function to convert the time currently stored in `RunTime` to a year, month, day, hour, minute, and second time stored in a `tm` structure; it then displays these values within the appropriate text boxes. If the user clicks the OK button to dismiss the dialog box, `DialogProc` then calls the `mktime` run-time function to convert the year, month, day, hour, minute, and second values that the user entered back to a `time_t` value, assigning the result to `RunTime`.

When `DialogProc` checks the validity of the date the user has entered, it makes sure that the year falls within the range of 70 through 99 (representing 1970 through 1999) *or* 0 to 35 (representing 2000 through 2035), because the run-time library functions can handle dates only from 1970 through approximately 2035. Specifically, the functions can handle dates from January 1, 1970, through February 5, 2036 (for Microsoft), or January 19, 2038 (for Borland).

NOTE

When you pass a `tm` structure to `mktime`, you normally need to set the `tm_isdst` field to indicate whether the specified time represents a daylight savings time. However, to simplify the coding and use of the program, SCHEDULE assigns 0 to the predefined run-time library variable `daylight`. Assigning `daylight` 0 prevents the run-time library functions from adjusting for daylight savings time (such adjustments are necessary only for applications that require absolute, GMT or Universal Coordinated Time, time values).

Using CTask Objects

This section describes how the CTask class is used by the other parts of the program to store task information and run tasks.

The main window class, CMainDialog, stores a list of pointers to each task object, using the data member PTaskTable, which is defined as follows in SCHEDULE.H (Listing 5.1):

```
CTask *PTaskTable [MAXTASKS];
```

The CMainDialog constructor (in DIALOG.CPP of Listing 5.3) calls the run-time function memset to initialize each member of this array to 0 (a 0 value indicates that a member is free to hold a new task):

```
memset (PTaskTable, 0, sizeof (PTaskTable));
```

Whenever the user clicks the New... button, the CMainDialog::OnCommand function (also in DIALOG.CPP) uses the C++ new operator to create a new CTask object to manage the new task, and it assigns the address of this object to the first free element of PTaskTable:

```
PTaskTable [Idx] = new CTask;
```

(Idx contains the index of the first free element.) Creating the new CTask object triggers the CTask constructor, which initializes the data members as described in the previous section.

Also in response to the New... button, OnCommand declares an instance of the CTaskDialog class to manage the Task dialog box, which allows the user to enter the information for the new task:

```
CTaskDialog TaskDialog;
```

Before calling TaskDialog::Create to display the dialog box, however, OnCommand assigns the address of the new task object to the TaskDialog data member PTask:

```
TaskDialog.PTask = PTaskTable [Idx];
```

The CTaskDialog code uses the PTask member to access the task object, so that it can display the current task information and then assign the new values that the user enters to the appropriate data members of this object.

If the user clicks the Cancel button in the Task dialog box, the Create function returns IDCANCEL. In this case, OnCommand deletes the CTask object that it created for the new task, and sets the PTaskTable element back to 0 to indicate that it is free:

```
if (Result == IDCANCEL)
    {
    delete PTaskTable [Idx];
    PTaskTable [Idx] = 0;
    return (TRUE);
    }
```

Deleting the object triggers the CTask destructor, which deletes the buffers containing the command line and working directory, as explained in the previous section. Note that the routine that processes the Delete button also uses the delete operator to delete a task (in this case, the task that the user selected).

If the user selects a task and clicks the Edit... button, the OnCommand function again declares a CTaskDialog object, TaskDialog, and calls Create to display the Task dialog box. However, rather than creating a new CTask object before displaying the dialog box, it assigns the address of the existing object that contains the selected task to the TaskDialog.PTask data member.

Note, finally, that when the main window is first displayed, the OnInit-Dialog function (in DIALOG.CPP) reads the description of each task stored in the initialization file, and creates a new CTask object to store the information for each task. (Unlike the SETSAVE program of Chapter 4, SCHEDULE reads and stores all information from the initialization file, and does not write the updated information back to the file until the program terminates.)

Running the Tasks

The CTask class provides a member function, Execute, that runs the task stored in a CTask object. SCHEDULE calls Execute both from the timer routine and from the routine that processes the Run Now button.

When each timer message is sent to the SCHEDULE main window, the CMainDialog::OnTimer function (in DIALOG.CPP) receives control. OnTimer first calls the time run-time function to obtain the current time. It then cycles through all of the members of PTaskTable, looking for a task that is enabled and that has a run time equal to or prior to the current time. If it finds more than one such task, it runs the task that has the *earliest* run time (this is to make sure that tasks are executed in the order of their run times; the next later due task will be run on the following timer message). The task is executed by calling the Execute function belonging to the task's object, assigning FALSE to the RunNow parameter to indicate that Execute is being called in response to a timer message.

N O T E   See Chapter 3 (which presents the Resource Viewer) for information on creating and responding to a Windows timer.

When the user selects a task and clicks the Run Now button, the routine that handles the IDC_RUN identifier in CMainDialog::OnCommand (in DIA-LOG.CPP) calls the Execute function belonging to the selected task's object, assigning TRUE to the RunNow parameter to indicate that the function is being called in response to the Run Now button.

The Execute function is defined in TASK.CPP of Listing 5.4. When it receives control, it performs the following steps:

1. If the object's Directory data member (the working directory) specifies a drive, Execute changes to that drive.

2. If Directory is not empty, Execute assumes that it contains a directory specification, and attempts to switch to that directory.

3. If Command is not empty, Execute assumes that it contains a command line and attempts to execute the command by passing it to the WinExec API function.

4. If RecFile is not empty, Execute assumes that it contains the name of a Recorder macro file. In this case, it first calls WinExec to run the Recorder program (RECORDER.EXE), passing it the name of the macro file so that Recorder will open the file as soon as it begins running. Next, Execute calls the FindWindow API function to obtain the handle of Recorder's main window (it passes FindWindow the name of the window's class, which is "Recorder"). Finally, it posts a WM_COMMAND message to the main Recorder

window, assigning the identifier of the Run command on the Recorder's Macro menu to the wParam message parameter. This call generates the same message that the Recorder receives when the user chooses the Run command; it causes the Recorder to play the selected macro (when the Recorder first begins running, the first—or only—macro in the file is selected).

5. If the RunNow parameter is TRUE, indicating that Execute was called in response to the Run Now button, the Execute function returns immediately; otherwise, it continues with the following steps.

6. If the task is to be repeated, Execute updates the task's run time by adding to it the specified duration between repetitions. Execute adds the duration value repeatedly, if necessary, until the new run time is later than the current time (to prevent running the task more than once if one or more repetitions of the task have been missed).

7. If the task is *not* to be repeated, Execute disables it by setting the Enabled data member to FALSE (so that the task is not rerun on each subsequent timer message!).

TIP

Both the class name for the Recorder's main window and the identifier of the Run menu command were obtained using the Microsoft Spy program (included with the Windows 3.1 Software Development Kit).

Enhancing the Task Scheduler

The following is a list of suggestions for enhancing the Task Scheduler:

- *Allow the user to specify* any *macro within a Recorder macro file* (rather than automatically running the *first* macro in the list of macros in the file). To do this, you could use the following undocumented Recorder feature: In addition to specifying a macro file on the Recorder command line, you can use the –H flag to specify a particular macro within this file; after the Recorder loads the file, it automatically runs the designated macro. The –H flag is followed by a description of the *shortcut key* used to run the macro (yes, the user must assign a shortcut key to each macro that is to be run from the Task Scheduler). When specifying the shortcut key, you can use the following special symbols to indicate shift keys:

KEY	SYMBOL
Alt	%
Ctrl	^
Shift	+

For example, the following command line runs the Recorder and causes it to load the recorder file JOB1.REC and to run the macro that has the shortcut key Ctrl+F10:

```
RECORDER -H ^F10 JOB1
```

- *Permit the user to run a task* by including the task name on the Task Scheduler command line. This feature would allow the user to run a task by clicking a Program Manager icon (and, if the icon is located in the StartUp group, the task could be made to run automatically when Windows starts). If the user runs a second instance of the program and passes a task name, the second instance should activate the first instance, cause the first instance to run the specified task, and then exit. You can use the same techniques that are employed by the Setup Saver program, presented in Chapter 4.

- *Allow the user to define a task that would simply display a message* (and maybe beep) at the scheduled time. When defining the task, the user could designate it as an announcement (perhaps by checking an "Announcement Only" check box) and enter the message text (rather than entering a command line or macro file).

- *Provide a Browse command* within the Task dialog box, which would help the user locate the desired program by displaying a dialog box that lists the executable files within any directory. This command could work just like the Browse command provided by the

Windows Program Manager when you define a program item. To display the dialog box, you could call the GetOpenFileName API function (which displays a predefined dialog box for opening files).

- If a previously defined task is past due when the user first runs the Task Scheduler, *have the program display a dialog box asking whether the task should be run* (currently the program automatically runs any past-due task). If the user chooses not to run the task, the program should disable it.

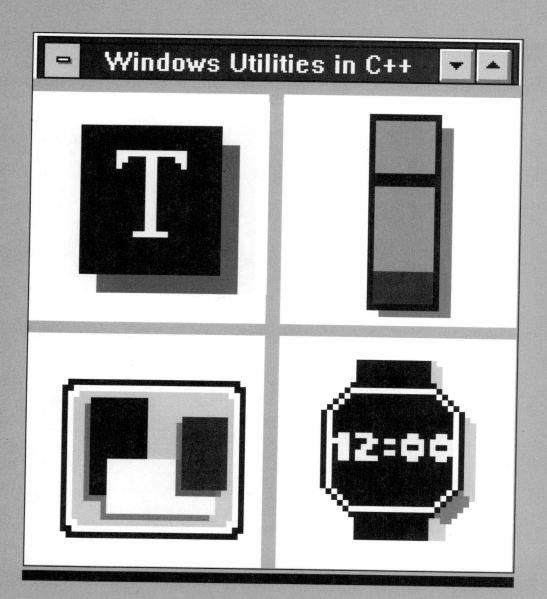

Screen Saver

THIS chapter presents a screen saver titled "Sliding Tiles," which turns your Windows screen into an animated sliding-tile puzzle. You can add this program to your collection of standard Windows screen savers that are selected through the Control Panel; you can also use the program source code as a template for creating your own custom screen savers.

The source code illustrates a simple method for creating a screen saver using either Microsoft C++ or Borland C++; it does *not* use the complicated screen saver library provided with the Microsoft Windows Software Development Kit (which is not included with Borland C++).

How to Use the Screen Saver

When you install the utilities from the companion disk, the Install program copies the screen saver program (SLIDER.SCR), together with its help file (SLIDER.HLP), directly to your Windows directory. You can then begin using this screen saver by performing the following steps:

1. Run the Windows Control Panel program.

2. Choose the Desktop icon; the Control Panel will then display the Desktop dialog box.

3. Select the Sliding Tiles screen saver in the Name: list box (within the Screen Saver area).

4. Enter the desired delay (the number of minutes of idle time before the screen saver is activated) into the Delay: text box. An example of a completed Desktop dialog box is shown in Figure 6.1.

5. Click the OK button.

When the screen saver is activated after the designated idle period, it divides your Windows screen into a set of rectangles, one of which is blank. It then begins randomly sliding the rectangles into the blank space, in the

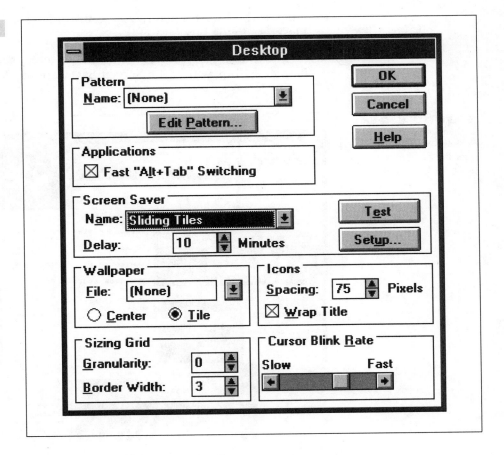

FIGURE 6.1

An example of a completed Desktop dialog box

same way that the tiles are moved in the traditional sliding-tile puzzle (recall the hand-held puzzle containing a blank space and 15 numbered tiles, which you arrange in order by repeatedly sliding tiles into the blank space). The result is that your screen graphics are kept moving, preventing burn-in and providing an amusing visual effect. An example screen is shown in Figure 6.2.

You can adjust the screen saver settings, using the following technique:

1. Run the Windows Control Panel program.

2. Choose the Desktop icon; the Control Panel will then display the Desktop dialog box.

3. If the Sliding Tile screen saver is not selected, select it now (in the Name: list box within the Screen Saver area).

FIGURE 6.2

A Windows screen after the Screen Saver has been activated

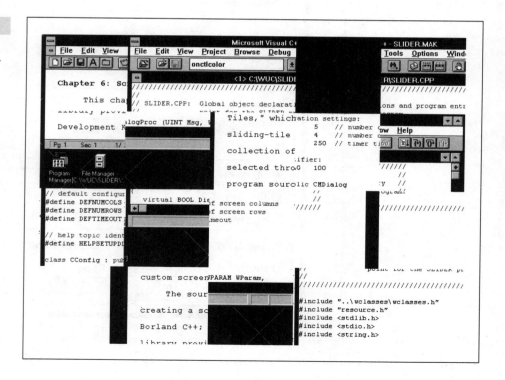

4. Click the Setup... button within the Screen Saver area. The screen saver program will now display the Sliding Tiles Setup dialog box, shown in Figure 6.3.

5. To control the number of sliding rectangles that are created, choose the desired number of rows and columns.

6. To control how rapidly the rectangles are moved, enter a value into the Pause Between Slides: text box to specify the time in milliseconds between tile movements.

7. If you want to restore the default setting values, click the Restore Defaults button.

8. Click OK.

After closing the Sliding Tiles Setup dialog box, you can test your new settings by clicking the Test button in the Desktop dialog box.

FIGURE 6.3

The Sliding Tiles Setup dialog box, with the default settings

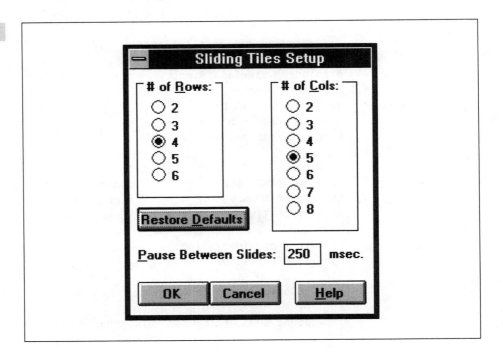

How the Screen Saver Works

The source code for the screen saver program, SLIDER, is given in Listings 6.1 through 6.4 (the program does not have an icon). Listing 6.1 (SLIDER.CPP) is the C++ source code. Listing 6.2 (SLIDER.DEF) is the module-definition file. Listings 6.3 and 6.4 (RESOURCE.H and SLIDER.RC) are the resource files produced by Microsoft App Studio.

Listing 6.1

```
////////////////////////////////////////////////////////////////////////
//                                                                      //
// SLIDER.CPP:  Global object declarations and program entry            //
//              point for the SLIDER program.                           //
//                                                                      //
////////////////////////////////////////////////////////////////////////

#include "..\wclasses\wclasses.h"
#include "resource.h"
#include <stdlib.h>
#include <stdio.h>
#include <string.h>

// default configuration settings:
#define DEFNUMCOLS      5     // number of screen columns
#define DEFNUMROWS      4     // number of screen rows
#define DEFTIMEOUT      250   // timer timeout

// help topic identifier:
#define HELPSETUPDLG    100

class CConfig : public CMDialog
{
    virtual BOOL DialogProc (UINT Msg, WPARAM WParam,
                                LPARAM LParam);
public:
```

```
    int NumCols;
    int NumRows;
    int Timeout;

    void Read ();
    void Write ();
};

CApplication App;
CConfig Config;
int DeltaX;
int DeltaY;
BOOL DestroyWindowCalled = FALSE;
int EmptyCol;
int EmptyRow;
RECT RectTable [6][8];

LRESULT CALLBACK _export WindowProc (HWND HWnd, UINT Msg,
                                     WPARAM WParam,
                                     LPARAM LParam);


///////////////////////////////////////////////////////////////
// program entry function:                                    //
///////////////////////////////////////////////////////////////

int PASCAL WinMain
    (HINSTANCE HInstCurrent,
    HINSTANCE HInstPrevious,
    LPSTR CmdLine,
    int CmdShow)
    {
    HWND HWnd;
    MSG Msg;
    WNDCLASS WndClass;

    App.Initialize (HInstCurrent, HInstPrevious, CmdLine,
                    CmdShow);

    // read configuration option values from initialization file:
    Config.Read ();
```

```
// look for '/s' flag in command line:
if (!_fstrstr (CmdLine, "/s") && !_fstrstr (CmdLine, "-s"))
    {
    // '/s' flag is NOT present; therefore display the
    // configuration dialog box rather than activating
    // the screen saver:

    Config.Create ("ConfigDlg", GetActiveWindow ());

    // write the new option values back to the initialization
    // file:
    Config.Write ();
    return (0);
    }
// '/s' flag is present; proceed to display screen saver

// register the class for the main window:
memset (&WndClass, 0, sizeof (WNDCLASS));
WndClass.style = CS_SAVEBITS;
WndClass.lpfnWndProc = WindowProc;
WndClass.hInstance = App.mHInstCurrent;
WndClass.lpszClassName = "SliderClass";
RegisterClass (&WndClass);

// create the main window:
HWnd = CreateWindowEx
    (WS_EX_TOPMOST,
    "SliderClass",
    0,
    WS_VISIBLE | WS_POPUP,
    0,
    0,
    GetSystemMetrics (SM_CXSCREEN),
    GetSystemMetrics (SM_CYSCREEN),
    HWND_DESKTOP,
    0,
    App.mHInstCurrent,
    0);
if (HWnd == 0)
    return (FALSE);
```

```
    // process messages:
    while (GetMessage (&Msg, NULL, NULL, NULL))
       DispatchMessage (&Msg);

    return (Msg.wParam);
    }

////////////////////////////////////////////////////////////////
// main window procedure:                                       //
////////////////////////////////////////////////////////////////

LRESULT CALLBACK _export WindowProc (HWND HWnd, UINT Msg,
                                     WPARAM WParam,
                                     LPARAM LParam)
   {
   static BOOL FirstMessage = TRUE;

   switch (Msg)
      {
      case WM_CLOSE:
         // set flag so that WM_NCACTIVATE branch (which gets
         // control thru call to DestroyWindow) doesn't post
         // a WM_CLOSE message, causing an infinite recursion:
         DestroyWindowCalled = TRUE;

         DestroyWindow (HWnd);
         return (0);

      case WM_CREATE:
         {
         int Col;
         RECT Rect;
         int Result;
         int Row;
         int X;
         int Y;

         // obtain width (DeltaX) and height (DeltaY) of one
         // of the sliding screen rectangles:
         GetClientRect (HWnd, &Rect);
         DeltaX = Rect.right / Config.NumCols;
```

```
DeltaY = Rect.bottom / Config.NumRows;

// assign the coordinates of the screen rectangles to
// the elements of the RectTable array:
Y = 0;
for (Row = 0; Row < Config.NumRows; ++Row)
   {
   X = 0;
   for (Col = 0; Col < Config.NumCols; ++Col)
      {
      RectTable [Row][Col].left = X;
      RectTable [Row][Col].top = Y;

      if (Col == Config.NumCols - 1)
         RectTable [Row][Col].right = Rect.right;
      else
         RectTable [Row][Col].right = X + DeltaX;
      if (Row == Config.NumRows - 1)
         RectTable [Row][Col].bottom = Rect.bottom;
      else
         RectTable [Row][Col].bottom = Y + DeltaY;

      X += DeltaX;
      }
   Y += DeltaY;
   }

// set first empty rectangle to the lower-right square:
EmptyRow = Config.NumRows - 1;
EmptyCol = Config.NumCols - 1;

// create the Windows timer:
Result = SetTimer (HWnd, 1, Config.Timeout, NULL);
if (!Result)
   {
   MessageBox
      (HWnd,
      "Could not create timer!",
      "Sliding Tiles",
      MB_ICONEXCLAMATION | MB_OK);
   return (-1);
```

```
            }

        return (0);
        }

case WM_DESTROY:
    KillTimer (HWnd, 1);
    PostQuitMessage (0);
    return (0);

case WM_KEYDOWN:
case WM_SYSKEYDOWN:
case WM_LBUTTONDOWN:
case WM_MBUTTONDOWN:
case WM_RBUTTONDOWN:
    // user pressed a key or mouse button; therefore,
    // terminate the screen saver:

    PostMessage (HWnd, WM_CLOSE, 0, OL);
    return (0);

case WM_MOUSEMOVE:
    if (FirstMessage)
        // ignore the first WM_MOUSEMOVE message, which is
        // sent automatically even if the user did not move
        // the mouse:
        FirstMessage = FALSE;
    else
        // receiving a second WM_MOUSEMOVE message means that
        // the user moved the mouse after the screen
        // saver was activated; therefore, terminate the
        // screen saver:
        PostMessage (HWnd, WM_CLOSE, 0, OL);
    return (0);

case WM_NCACTIVATE:
case WM_ACTIVATE:
case WM_ACTIVATEAPP:

    if (!WParam && !DestroyWindowCalled)
        // WParam is FALSE, meaning that the window is
```

```
                    // losing its active status for some reason; also,
                    // DestroyWindowCalled is FALSE, meaning that the
                    // program has not already called DestroyWindow;
                    // therefore, terminate the screen saver:
                    PostMessage (HWnd, WM_CLOSE, 0, OL);

            return DefWindowProc (HWnd, Msg, WParam, LParam);

        case WM_SETCURSOR:
            // remove the mouse cursor:
            SetCursor (0);
            return (0);

        case WM_SYSCOMMAND:
            if (WParam == SC_SCREENSAVE || WParam == SC_CLOSE)
                // return FALSE to prevent system from restarting
                // the screen saver or closing the window:
                return (0);
            else
                return DefWindowProc (HWnd, Msg, WParam, LParam);

        case WM_TIMER:
            {
            HBRUSH HBrush;
            HDC HDc;
            int NewCol = EmptyCol;
            int NewRow = EmptyRow;

            // determine new position of blank rectangle by getting
            // a random number in range 1-4; if number is 1, move
            // blank rectangle up; if number is 2, move it right; if
            // number is 3, move it down; if number is 4, move it
            // left; if blank rectangle cannot be moved in selected
            // direction, move it in opposite direction:
            switch (rand () % 4 + 1)
                {
                case 1:  // up
                    // if blank rectangle is already on the top row,
                    // move it down; otherwise, move it up:
                    if (EmptyRow == 0)
                        NewRow = EmptyRow + 1;
```

```
      else
         NewRow = EmptyRow - 1;
      break;

   case 2:   // right
      // if blank rectangle is already in right column,
      // move it left; otherwise, move it right:
      if (EmptyCol == Config.NumCols - 1)
         NewCol = EmptyCol - 1;
      else
         NewCol = EmptyCol + 1;
      break;

   case 3:   // down
      if (EmptyRow == Config.NumRows - 1)
         NewRow = EmptyRow - 1;
      else
         NewRow = EmptyRow + 1;
      break;

   case 4:   // left
      if (EmptyCol == 0)
         NewCol = EmptyCol + 1;
      else
         NewCol = EmptyCol - 1;
      break;
   }

// obtain device context for client area of window:
HDc = GetDC (HWnd);

// transfer screen graphics from new position of blank
// rectangle to old position of blank rectangle:
BitBlt
   (HDc,
   RectTable [EmptyRow][EmptyCol].left,
   RectTable [EmptyRow][EmptyCol].top,
   DeltaX,
   DeltaY,
   HDc,
   RectTable [NewRow][NewCol].left,
```

```
                              RectTable [NewRow][NewCol].top,
                              SRCCOPY);

                // update position of blank rectangle:
                EmptyRow = NewRow;
                EmptyCol = NewCol;

                // paint new position of blank rectangle black:
                HBrush = (HBRUSH)GetStockObject (BLACK_BRUSH);
                FillRect (HDc, &RectTable [EmptyRow][EmptyCol], HBrush);

                ReleaseDC (HWnd, HDc);

                return (0);
                }

         default:
            return DefWindowProc (HWnd, Msg, WParam, LParam);
         }
     }


//////////////////////////////////////////////////////////////////////
// configuration class member functions:                            //
//////////////////////////////////////////////////////////////////////

BOOL CConfig::DialogProc (UINT Msg, WPARAM WParam,
                          LPARAM LParam)
    {
    int HoldTimeout;
    int ID;

    switch (Msg)
        {
        case WM_COMMAND:
            switch (WParam)
                {
                case IDCANCEL:
                    WinHelp (mHDialog, "SLIDER.HLP", HELP_QUIT, OL);
                    EndDialog (mHDialog, 0);
                    return (TRUE);
```

```
case IDC_DEFAULTS:
   // user clicked Restore Defaults button; therefore
   // display all default option settings:

   // calculate ID of radio button for default
   // number of rows and check button:
   ID = IDC_2ROW + DEFNUMROWS - 2;
   CheckRadioButton (mHDialog, IDC_2ROW, IDC_6ROW,
                     ID);

   // calculate ID of radio button for default
   // number of columns and check button:
   ID = IDC_2COL + DEFNUMCOLS - 2;
   CheckRadioButton (mHDialog, IDC_2COL, IDC_8COL,
                     ID);

   // display default timeout:
   SetDlgItemInt (mHDialog, IDC_TIMEOUT,
                  DEFTIMEOUT, 1);
   return (TRUE);

case IDC_HELP:
   WinHelp (mHDialog, "SLIDER.HLP",
            HELP_CONTEXT, HELPSETUPDLG);
   return (TRUE);

case IDOK:
   // obtain and validate timeout value:
   HoldTimeout = GetDlgItemInt
      (mHDialog,
      IDC_TIMEOUT,
      0,
      TRUE);
   if (HoldTimeout < 1)
      {
      MessageBox
         (mHDialog,
         "Pause must be an integer greater than 0.",
         "Sliding Tiles Setup",
         MB_OK | MB_ICONEXCLAMATION);
      SetFocus (GetDlgItem (mHDialog, IDC_TIMEOUT));
```

```
                        return (TRUE);
                        }

                Timeout = HoldTimeout;

                // determine which radio button in '# of Rows'
                // group is checked and set 'NumRows' accordingly:
                for (ID = IDC_2ROW; ID <= IDC_6ROW; ++ID)
                    if (IsDlgButtonChecked (mHDialog, ID))
                        {
                        NumRows = ID - IDC_2ROW + 2;
                        break;
                        }

                // determine which radio button in '# of Cols'
                // group is checked and set 'NumCols' accordingly:
                for (ID = IDC_2COL; ID <= IDC_8COL; ++ID)
                    if (IsDlgButtonChecked (mHDialog, ID))
                        {
                        NumCols = ID - IDC_2COL + 2;
                        break;
                        }

                WinHelp (mHDialog, "SLIDER.HLP", HELP_QUIT, OL);
                EndDialog (mHDialog, O);
                return (TRUE);

            default:
                return (TRUE);
            }

    case WM_INITDIALOG:
        // display current values:

        ID = IDC_2ROW + NumRows - 2;
        CheckDlgButton (mHDialog, ID, 1);

        ID = IDC_2COL + NumCols - 2;
        CheckDlgButton (mHDialog, ID, 1);

        SetDlgItemInt (mHDialog, IDC_TIMEOUT, Timeout, TRUE);
```

```
            SendDlgItemMessage (mHDialog, IDC_TIMEOUT, EM_LIMITTEXT,
                               4, OL);
            return (TRUE);

         default:
            if (Msg == mHelpMessage)
               {
               SendMessage (mHDialog, WM_COMMAND, IDC_HELP, OL);
               return (TRUE);
               }
            else
               return (FALSE);
         }
      }

void CConfig::Read ()
// reads the values of all option data members from the
// initialization file:
   {
   NumCols = GetPrivateProfileInt
      ("Screen Saver.Sliding Tiles",
      "numcols",
      DEFNUMCOLS,
      "CONTROL.INI");

   NumRows = GetPrivateProfileInt
      ("Screen Saver.Sliding Tiles",
      "numrows",
      DEFNUMROWS,
      "CONTROL.INI");

   Timeout = GetPrivateProfileInt
      ("Screen Saver.Sliding Tiles",
      "timeout",
      DEFTIMEOUT,
      "CONTROL.INI");
   }

void CConfig::Write ()
// writes the values of all option data members to the
```

```
// initialization file
   {
   char Buffer [8];

   sprintf (Buffer, "%d", NumCols);
   WritePrivateProfileString
      ("Screen Saver.Sliding Tiles",
      "numcols",
      Buffer,
      "CONTROL.INI");

   sprintf (Buffer, "%d", NumRows);
   WritePrivateProfileString
      ("Screen Saver.Sliding Tiles",
      "numrows",
      Buffer,
      "CONTROL.INI");

   sprintf (Buffer, "%d", Timeout);
   WritePrivateProfileString
      ("Screen Saver.Sliding Tiles",
      "timeout",
      Buffer,
      "CONTROL.INI");
   }
```

Listing 6.2

```
;;;;;;;;;;;;;;;;;;;;;;;;;;;;;;;;;;;;;;;;;;;;;;;;;;;;;;;;;;;;;;;;;;;;;
;                                                                 ;
; SLIDER.DEF:  Module-definition file for the SETSAVE program.    ;
;                                                                 ;
;;;;;;;;;;;;;;;;;;;;;;;;;;;;;;;;;;;;;;;;;;;;;;;;;;;;;;;;;;;;;;;;;;;;;

NAME SLIDER

; the following description tells the Windows Control Panel that
; the program is a screen saver, and that its title is "Sliding
; Tiles" (the title appears when the user chooses the screen
; saver in the Control Panel):
DESCRIPTION  'SCRNSAVE : Sliding Tiles'
```

```
EXETYPE WINDOWS

CODE PRELOAD MOVEABLE DISCARDABLE

DATA PRELOAD MOVEABLE MULTIPLE

HEAPSIZE 1024

STACKSIZE 10240
```

Listing 6.3

```
///////////////////////////////////////////////////////////////
//                                                             //
// RESOURCE.H:  Constant definitions for the SLIDER program    //
//              resources (generated by Microsoft App Studio). //
//                                                             //
///////////////////////////////////////////////////////////////

//{{NO_DEPENDENCIES}}
// App Studio generated include file.
// Used by SLIDER.RC
//
#define IDC_TEMP                    101
#define IDC_2ROW                    102
#define IDC_3ROW                    103
#define IDC_4ROW                    104
#define IDC_5ROW                    105
#define IDC_6ROW                    106
#define IDC_TIMEOUT                 107
#define IDC_2COL                    108
#define IDC_3COL                    109
#define IDC_4COL                    110
#define IDC_5COL                    111
#define IDC_6COL                    112
#define IDC_7COL                    113
#define IDC_8COL                    114
#define IDC_DEFAULTS                116
#define IDC_HELP                    117
```

```
// Next default values for new objects
//
#ifdef APSTUDIO_INVOKED
#ifndef APSTUDIO_READONLY_SYMBOLS

#define _APS_NEXT_RESOURCE_VALUE        101
#define _APS_NEXT_COMMAND_VALUE         101
#define _APS_NEXT_CONTROL_VALUE         1000
#define _APS_NEXT_SYMED_VALUE           101
#endif
#endif
```

Listing 6.4

```
////////////////////////////////////////////////////////////////////
//                                                                  //
// SLIDER.RC:  Resource-definition file for the SLIDER              //
//             program (generated by Microsoft App Studio).         //
//                                                                  //
////////////////////////////////////////////////////////////////////

//Microsoft App Studio generated resource script.
//
#include "resource.h"

#define APSTUDIO_READONLY_SYMBOLS
/////////////////////////////////////////////////////////////////////
//
// Generated from the TEXTINCLUDE 2 resource.
//
#define APSTUDIO_HIDDEN_SYMBOLS
#include "windows.h"
#undef APSTUDIO_HIDDEN_SYMBOLS


/////////////////////////////////////////////////////////////////////
#undef APSTUDIO_READONLY_SYMBOLS


/////////////////////////////////////////////////////////////////////
//
// Dialog
//
```

```
CONFIGDLG DIALOG DISCARDABLE  8, 20, 130, 146
STYLE DS_MODALFRAME | WS_POPUP | WS_VISIBLE | WS_CAPTION |
    WS_SYSMENU
CAPTION "Sliding Tiles Setup"
FONT 8, "MS Sans Serif"
BEGIN
    GROUPBOX        "# of &Rows:",-1,4,4,46,72,WS_GROUP
    CONTROL         "2",IDC_2ROW,"Button",BS_AUTORADIOBUTTON |
                    WS_GROUP | WS_TABSTOP,12,18,20,10
    CONTROL         "3",IDC_3ROW,"Button",BS_AUTORADIOBUTTON,12,
                    28,20,10
    CONTROL         "4",IDC_4ROW,"Button",BS_AUTORADIOBUTTON,12,
                    38,20,10
    CONTROL         "5",IDC_5ROW,"Button",BS_AUTORADIOBUTTON,12,
                    48,20,10
    CONTROL         "6",IDC_6ROW,"Button",BS_AUTORADIOBUTTON,12,
                    58,20,10
    GROUPBOX        "# of &Cols:",-1,76,4,46,92,WS_GROUP
    CONTROL         "2",IDC_2COL,"Button",BS_AUTORADIOBUTTON |
                    WS_GROUP | WS_TABSTOP,84,18,20,10
    CONTROL         "3",IDC_3COL,"Button",BS_AUTORADIOBUTTON,84,
                    28,20,10
    CONTROL         "4",IDC_4COL,"Button",BS_AUTORADIOBUTTON,84,
                    38,20,10
    CONTROL         "5",IDC_5COL,"Button",BS_AUTORADIOBUTTON,84,
                    48,20,10
    CONTROL         "6",IDC_6COL,"Button",BS_AUTORADIOBUTTON,84,
                    58,20,10
    CONTROL         "7",IDC_7COL,"Button",BS_AUTORADIOBUTTON,84,
                    68,20,10
    CONTROL         "8",IDC_8COL,"Button",BS_AUTORADIOBUTTON,84,
                    78,20,10
    EDITTEXT        IDC_TIMEOUT,82,104,20,12,ES_AUTOHSCROLL |
                    WS_GROUP
    PUSHBUTTON      "Restore &Defaults",IDC_DEFAULTS,4,82,60,14,
                    WS_GROUP
    DEFPUSHBUTTON   "OK",IDOK,4,126,38,14
    PUSHBUTTON      "Cancel",IDCANCEL,42,126,38,14
    PUSHBUTTON      "&Help",IDC_HELP,88,126,38,14
    LTEXT           "&Pause Between Slides:",-1,4,106,78,8
```

```
    LTEXT            "msec.",-1,106,106,20,8
END

#ifdef APSTUDIO_INVOKED
/////////////////////////////////////////////////////////////////
//
// TEXTINCLUDE
//

1 TEXTINCLUDE DISCARDABLE
BEGIN
    "resource.h\0"
END

2 TEXTINCLUDE DISCARDABLE
BEGIN
    "#define APSTUDIO_HIDDEN_SYMBOLS\r\n"
    "#include ""windows.h""\r\n"
    "#undef APSTUDIO_HIDDEN_SYMBOLS\r\n"
    "\0"
END

3 TEXTINCLUDE DISCARDABLE
BEGIN
    "\r\n"
    "\0"
END


/////////////////////////////////////////////////////////////////
#endif    // APSTUDIO_INVOKED

#ifndef APSTUDIO_INVOKED
/////////////////////////////////////////////////////////////////
//
// Generated from the TEXTINCLUDE 3 resource.
//


/////////////////////////////////////////////////////////////////
#endif    // not APSTUDIO_INVOKED
```

The Basics

Writing a screen saver is easy under Windows 3.1. A screen saver program no longer has to monitor other programs in order to detect when the computer has been idle for the specified time; rather, the system handles this task for it. The following are the minimum requirements for writing a standard Windows 3.1 screen saver program that can be installed and run through the Windows Control Panel:

- Write and build the screen saver as a standard Windows executable program.

- The DESCRIPTION statement in the resource-definition file for the program must conform to the format,

```
DESCRIPTION 'SCRNSAVE: title'
```

  where *title* is the title of the screen saver. This description tells the Control Panel that the executable file is a screen saver, and supplies the title that the Control Panel displays in the combo box that lists all available screen savers. The DESCRIPTION statement for the SLIDER program is as follows:

```
DESCRIPTION 'SCRNSAVE : Sliding Tiles'
```

- Name the executable file, using the .SCR extension (rather than .EXE), and copy it to the Windows directory (you should also copy the program help file, if any, to the Windows directory). The Control Panel program will then list the title of your screen saver in the Desktop dialog box, along with the titles of all other valid screen savers that it finds in the Windows directory. The user can now select your screen saver as the current Windows screen saver and can specify the desired delay before it is activated.

- If Windows has been idle for the specified time (or the user clicks the Test button in the Desktop dialog box), the system runs the selected screen saver program, passing it the /s or –s command-line flag. When your screen saver program begins running and receives this flag, it should generate its screen-saving display. When the user presses any key or moves the mouse, the program should destroy its window and exit. The way that the SLIDER program performs these steps is described in the next section.

- If the user selects your screen saver and clicks the Setup... button in the Desktop dialog box, the Control Panel runs the screen saver program, passing it the /c or -c command-line flag (alternatively, the Control Panel may pass *no* command line flags when the user clicks Setup...). If your program receives this flag, it should display a setup dialog box *rather than* generating the screen-saving display. The setup dialog should allow the user to modify any settings that can be adjusted (if there are no settings that the user can modify, the program should display a message box indicating that fact). The way that the SLIDER program performs this task is described later, in the section "Displaying the Setup Dialog Box."

- Normally, the screen saver saves all changeable settings in a private section of the CONTROL.INI initialization file, so that they can be read whenever the program is run. This section must be labeled using the following format:

```
[Screen Saver.title]
```

where *title* is the title of the screen saver. The SLIDER program saves its option settings in a section of CONTROL.INI labeled as follows:

```
[Screen Saver.Sliding Tiles]
```

Displaying the Screen Saver

When the SLIDER program starts running, the WinMain function (in SLIDER.CPP of Listing 6.1) checks the command line to see whether the /s or -s flag is present. If this flag is present, WinMain proceeds to activate the screen saver display. To generate this display, it creates a borderless window that fills the entire Windows screen. When it creates this window, it does *not* assign a brush to the window class. Consequently, the window is not automatically erased when it is first displayed; rather, it acquires the existing screen graphics. A timer routine then manipulates the graphics to generate the sliding tile effect.

WinMain creates the main window by calling the RegisterClass and CreateWindowEx API functions, rather than by using the CMLDialog class, so that it can easily assign the window the required styles.

When it calls RegisterClass to create the window class, it specifies the class style CS_SAVEBITS. This style causes Windows to save the graphics underlying the window and then restore the graphics when the window is removed. When the screen saver exits, therefore, it can simply destroy its window without having to restore the original screen contents. WinMain also assigns 0 as the background brush handle, so that the client area of the window is not erased.

When WinMain calls CreateWindowEx to create the window, it specifies the extended window style WS_EX_TOPMOST; this style causes the window to be displayed on top of any other window, even a window that has also been assigned the WS_EX_TOPMOST style (if another window with the WS_EX_TOP-MOST style were activated, it would appear on top of the SLIDER window; however, the SLIDER program always terminates before another window becomes active). The call to CreateWindowEx also specifies the WS_VISIBLE style to make the window visible, and the WS_POPUP style to allow the window to be displayed without a title bar. Because no other styles are included (such as WS_BORDER or WS_CAPTION), the window has no visible features other than the client area itself. The CreateWindowEx call assigns the window the dimensions of the entire Windows screen, which are obtained by calling the API function GetSystemMetrics.

When the window is first created, the system sends it a WM_CREATE message (this message is equivalent to the WM_INITDIALOG message sent to a dialog box). The routine that handles this message in the WindowProc function first calculates the size of each of the "sliding" rectangles that partition the Windows screen. It then assigns the dimensions of each rectangle to an element of the RectTable array. RectTable is later used to move graphics from one rectangle to another, and to color the blank rectangle. The variables that keep track of the position of the blank rectangle, EmptyRow and EmptyCol, are initially assigned the indices of the rectangle in the lower-right corner of the screen.

Next, the WM_CREATE routine creates a Windows timer. Note that the number and dimensions of the rectangles, as well as the timeout period for the timer, depend upon program options that the user can adjust. These options are stored in an instance of the CConfig class, which is described later (in the section "Displaying the Setup Dialog Box").

Before the mouse cursor is displayed in the window, the window receives a WM_SETCURSOR message. In response to this message, WindowProc passes

0 to the SetCursor API function to *remove* the cursor, so that no mouse cursor will be visible while the screen saver is active:

```
SetCursor (0);
```

With each timer message that is sent to the window, the WM_TIMER routine in WindowProc "slides" a rectangle into the position of the blank rectangle. To do this, it performs the following steps:

1. The blank rectangle is surrounded by up to four adjoining rectangles. The routine chooses one of these rectangles randomly by calling the rand run-time library function to obtain a random number in the range from 1 through 4. If the random number is 1, it chooses the rectangle above; if it is 2, it chooses the one to the right; if it is 3, it chooses the one below; and if it is 4, it chooses the one to the left. If there is no rectangle in the chosen direction, it chooses the one in the opposite direction.

2. It uses the BitBlt API function to transfer the graphics from the chosen rectangle into the blank rectangle.

3. Once the graphics have been moved, the chosen rectangle becomes the new blank rectangle. Accordingly, the routine then calls FillRect to color this rectangle black, and it assigns the indices of the blank rectangle to EmptyRow and EmptyCol.

Terminating the Program

The SLIDER program destroys its window and terminates if the user presses a key or mouse button, if the user moves the mouse, or if the program window loses its active status for any reason (for example, if another program automatically displays a message box). In response to any of these events, the WindowProc function posts a WM_CLOSE message to the program window. As customary, the WM_CLOSE routine then calls the DestroyWindow API function to destroy the window and cause the application to terminate.

Specifically, WindowProc posts a WM_CLOSE message in response to any of the following messages, which indicate that the user pressed a key or mouse button:

```
WM_KEYDOWN
WM_SYSKEYDOWN
```

```
WM_LBUTTONDOWN
WM_MBUTTONDOWN
WM_RBUTTONDOWN
```

WindowProc ignores the *first* WM_MOUSEMOVE message, which the system sends when the mouse cursor is first positioned within the window. However, it posts a WM_CLOSE message in response to a *second* WM_MOUSEMOVE message, which indicates that the user has moved the mouse after the screen saver was activated.

Finally, if it receives any of the following messages with the WParam parameter set to FALSE, the window is losing its active status for some reason:

```
WM_NCACTIVATE
WM_ACTIVATE
WM_ACTIVATEAPP
```

If it receives such a message, it posts a WM_CLOSE message, but *only* if it has not already posted a WM_CLOSE message and therefore already called DestroyWindow (calling DestroyWindow is one of the actions that can cause these messages to be sent; if the program called DestroyWindow again, an infinite recursion would result).

Displaying the Setup Dialog Box

If the command line does *not* contain the /s or –s flag when the program is run, WinMain displays a dialog box that allows the user to change the program options, rather than activating the screen saver.

The SLIDER program defines a class, CConfig, and declares a global instance of this class, Config, to manage the program option settings. The CConfig object stores the number of rows and columns in the NumRows and NumCols public data members, and it stores the timer duration in the Timeout public data member.

CConfig provides a member function, Read, which reads the option settings from the program's section of the CONTROL.INI initialization file, and assigns the values to the CConfig data members. WinMain always calls this function (whether or not the /s or -s flag is present) to initialize the Config object.

Because CConfig is derived from the CMDialog class, it can be used to display a modal dialog box. To display the Sliding Tiles Setup dialog box (which was designed using App Studio and was assigned the identifier "ConfigDlg"), WinMain calls the CConfig member function Create. The dialog box displays the current settings of the three program options and allows the user to enter new values. After calling Create, WinMain calls the CConfig::Write function, which writes the new option settings back to the initialization file. WinMain then exits.

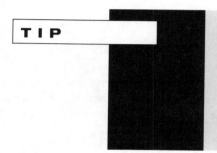

TIP

When WinMain calls CConfig::Create to display the setup dialog box, the program has no window handle to pass. To obtain a window handle, it calls the GetActiveWindow API function to get the handle of the Desktop dialog box (displayed by the Control Panel). As a result, the dialog box is positioned a fixed distance from the Desktop dialog box.

Enhancing the Screen Saver

The following are some ways that you might enhance the screen saver program presented in this chapter:

- Rather than always using the existing contents of the screen, you could *allow the user to choose one of a variety of bitmaps to be used as the screen saver background.* The following is a brief description of one method for displaying such a bitmap: First, use App Studio (or other resource editor) to design a new bitmap or import an existing bitmap into the program resources. Then, when the program is running, call the `LoadBitmap` API function to obtain a handle to the bitmap, call the `CreateCompatibleDC` API function to create a memory device context for accessing the bitmap, call the `Select-Object` API function to select the bitmap into the memory device context, and call the `StretchBlt` API function to copy the bitmap from the memory device context to the client area of the window and to change the dimensions of the bitmap—if necessary—so that it fills the entire screen. These steps could be performed in response to a `WM_PAINT` message (the screen saver window should receive only one such message, when the window is first created). Once the bitmap is displayed, the program could employ the same method that it currently uses to move the rectangular areas.

- *Provide a* play mode *for the user who is not always anxious to begin working again!* The following is an example of how this might work: If the user presses the P key while the screen saver is displayed, rather than exiting, the program enters the play mode. In play mode, the user attempts to rearrange the screen rectangles in the correct, original order. To make a move, the user clicks one of the rectangles adjoining the empty space, causing that rectangle to move into the empty area. (In other words, the rectangles are moved in the same way as the tiles in the traditional sliding-tile puzzle.) At any time, the user can end the game and remove the screen saver by hitting another key.

- *Require the user to enter a password before the screen saver is removed.* All of the standard screen savers provided with Windows 3.1 use the *same* password. (That is, once the user has specified a password with one of these screen savers, all of the other screen savers begin using this same password. The password is stored—in encrypted format—within the [ScreenSaver] section of the CONTROL.INI file.) If you want your screen saver to use this same password, you must develop your program with the Microsoft Screen Saver Library (included with Visual C++ but not Borland C++). See the *Programmer's Reference, Volume 1* SDK manual and the BOUNCER Microsoft example program for instructions on using the Screen Saver Library. If, however, your screen uses its own independent password, you do not need to use the Screen Saver Library.

PART THREE

Personal Information Utilities

This part of the book presents a collection of personal information utilities. These utilities can be used together as an integrated set, or they can be used individually or with other Windows programs. Chapter 7 presents an Address Manager, which allows you to store and quickly retrieve names, addresses, telephone numbers, and free-form information for your friends, family members, and business contacts. Chapter 8 provides an Envelope and Label Printer, designed to quickly print envelopes or labels on any printer that is supported by Windows; this program permanently stores the return address, font, and format to be used for printing envelopes and labels. Chapter 9 offers a Phone Dialer, which dials phone numbers automatically, using your modem, and will automatically redial phone numbers to help you get through busy phone lines.

When you use the Envelope and Label Printer, you can enter the recipient's address manually, or you can use an address that you have copied into the Windows Clipboard from another program. Similarly, when you run the Phone Dialer, you can either enter a number manually or use a number in the Clipboard. Alternatively, once you have retrieved a record in the Address Manager, you can simply click a button to automatically run the Envelope and Label Printer and print an envelope or label, using the displayed address. Likewise, you can click a different button in the Address Manager to run the Phone Dialer and dial the selected phone number.

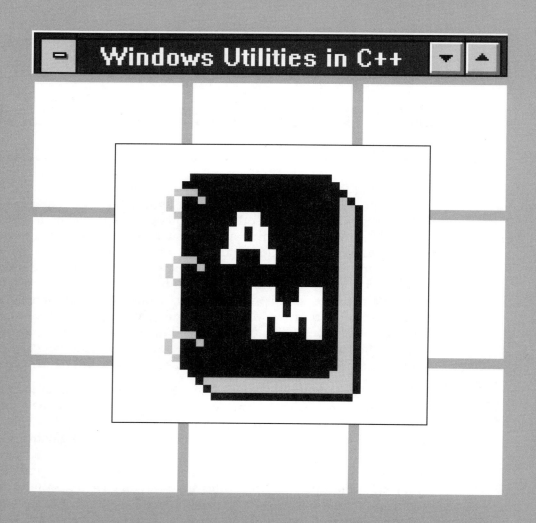

CHAPTER

7

Address Manager

THE address Manager stores a set of address records. Each record contains a name, company, address, a set of phone numbers, as well as unlimited free-form information. You can retrieve records using a variety of techniques: You can browse through records in sorted order (arranged by name), you can search for records matching a specific name, or you can search for records containing a specified text string. Once you have retrieved a record, you can copy either the name and address or a selected phone number to the Windows Clipboard, so that you can use the information in another program. Also, you can print an envelope or label, using the displayed address, or—if you have a modem—you can automatically dial a selected phone number.

The following are among the important programming techniques illustrated by the source code for the Address Manager program: storing and accessing variable-length file records in sorted order; implementing standard New, Open..., Save, and Save As... file commands; displaying Open and Save As common dialog boxes; searching for text within a file; transferring text using the Windows Clipboard; and using flags to prevent data loss.

How to Use the Address Manager

In this section, you will learn how to enter new address records into the Address Manager; how to manage disk files for storing address records; how to retrieve specific records from a file; and how to perform various operations on address records, such as printing envelopes or labels, dialing numbers, and copying addresses or numbers to the Clipboard.

Creating Address Records

When the Address Manager first begins running, it automatically creates a new, blank address record, and the program window appears as shown in Figure 7.1. (If, however, you specify a file name on the Address Manager command line—as discussed later in the chapter—the program will display the first record in the file rather than creating a new record.) To add data to the fields of this record, enter the desired information into the text boxes. To move from box to box, use the mouse or the Tab and Shift+Tab keystrokes.

To create an additional new address record, choose the New command on the Record menu. This command will clear the text boxes, allowing you to enter the desired information into the fields of the new record. In this way, you can create as many records as you wish.

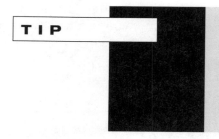

T I P

If you are entering a record for a company that does not include a person's name, you might want to enter the company name into the Name: box and leave the Company: box empty. The record will then be sorted by the company name and will be easier to retrieve.

The Name:, Company:, City:, State:, and Zip: text boxes allow you to enter only a single line and a limited amount of text (the number of characters you can enter depends upon the specific text box). Pressing the Enter key in one of these boxes has no effect. The Street Address: text box allows you to enter one or two lines (press Enter to start the second line), up to a maximum of 80 characters.

T I P

When entering text into any of the text boxes, you can perform cut, copy, and paste operations, using the standard Windows keystrokes.

You can type an almost unlimited number of lines and characters into the Notes or Phone Numbers text box, and you can scroll through the text you have entered, using the arrow keys. You can type any sort of free-form information into the Notes box. When entering text into the Phone Numbers box, however, you should observe the following guidelines:

- Enter no more than one phone number on a line. (As you will see later, the Dial and Copy Telephone commands extract only a single number from a given line.)

- You can include any of the following separator characters *within* the phone number: (,), -, or /. However, do not insert more than one separator between any two digits.

- You can include * and # characters within the phone number to generate various phone commands.

- You can also embed one or more comma characters (,) within the phone number. When the number is dialed (using the Dial command), each comma creates a pause in the dialing operation (by default, the pause is two seconds, but most modems allow you to program the duration).

- You can enter additional text on a line containing a phone number or on a separate line. (The Dial and Copy Telephone commands ignore the additional text.)

- Do *not*, however, enter a digit, *, #, or comma within the text preceding the phone number on a given line. For example, the following line is erroneous: phone #1: 627-7291. (The Dial and Copy Telephone commands extract the *first* sequence of valid phone number characters found on the line.)

Figure 7.2 illustrates a Phone Numbers box with several correctly entered numbers.

FIGURE 7.2

A Phone Numbers text box with several correctly entered phone numbers

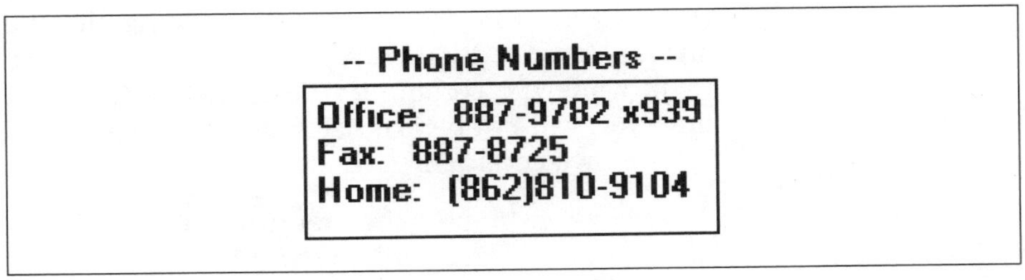

```
-- Phone Numbers --
Office:  887-9782 x939
Fax:  887-8725
Home:  (862)810-9104
```

TIP

You can include within a phone number any additional characters required to complete the call, such as a voice-mail extension. For example, the following number would dial a main phone number, pause for eight seconds, and then dial a voice mail extension: 983/387-3876,,,,325. As explained in Chapter 9, the Phone Dialer also allows you to store a general-purpose prefix and a general-purpose suffix that you can use when dialing phone numbers.

If you want to remove a record that you have entered, choose the Delete command on the Record menu to erase the currently displayed record.

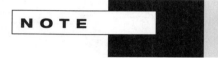

NOTE

For more information on specifying phone numbers that are dialed with a modem, see Chapter 9.

Managing Files

When the Address Manager begins running, it opens a new, empty file (unless you specify the name of an existing file on the program command line, as described later). You can add as many records to this file as you wish, using the techniques described in the previous section. The file, however, will not have a name and it will not be saved on disk until you issue a save command.

To save a new file for the first time, choose either the Save command or the Save As... command on the File menu (the result will be the same for either command). The program will display the standard Save As dialog box; in this dialog box, choose the desired directory and file name for saving the file; if you omit the period and extension portion of the file name, the program will automatically use the default extension, .ADM. When you are done, click OK; the file will be saved on disk, and the file name will appear in the window's title bar, replacing the initial description, "(Untitled)".

If you subsequently change the contents of the file, you can save the latest version by choosing either the Save command to save the file under its current name, or the Save As... command to save the file under a new name (if you use the Save As... command to save the file under a new name, the disk file generated during the previous save operation is left intact).

You can create a new, empty file at any time by choosing the New command on the File menu. When the program opens a new file, it automatically generates a new, blank record. To open an existing file that you saved previously, choose the Open... command on the File menu, and use the Open dialog box to specify the directory and name of the file (if you omit the period and extension, the program will attempt to open a file with the default .ADM extension). When the program opens an existing file, it initially displays the first record in this file.

Because you can open only one file at a time, the New and Open... commands *replace* the file that is currently open. If the current file contains unsaved data, the program will warn you and you will have an opportunity to save your data (the program will also warn you if you attempt to quit the program or terminate Windows before saving data).

Also, you can have the program open an existing file when it is first run by including the name of the file on the command line. For example, you can create a Program Manager item for running the Address Manager and opening a specific file by including the name of this file in the Command Line: text box when defining the new item. Figure 7.3 shows

FIGURE 7.3

Creating a Program Manager item that runs the Address Manager and opens the file CONTACTS.ADM

Program Item Properties

Description:	Contact Addresses
Command Line:	address.exe contacts.adm
Working Directory:	c:\sales
Shortcut Key:	None

☐ Run Minimized

OK   Cancel   Browse...   Change Icon...   Help

the Program Manager's Program Item Properties dialog box for creating an item that runs the Address Manager and opens the file CONTACTS.ADM.

Retrieving Address Records

Once you have added a collection of address records to an Address Manager file, you can retrieve specific records using various methods. First, you can browse through the records in sorted order by choosing the Previous and Next commands on the Record menu, or by simply clicking the "<< Previous" and "Next >>" buttons. The records are sorted in alphabetical order by the contents of the Name field (that is, the text entered into the Name: text box). To view the first record in the file, choose the First command on the Record menu. In sorting the records, the case of characters is ignored.

NOTE   If a new, blank record is currently displayed, choosing the Previous or Next command retrieves the *first* record in the file.

Second, you can search for a record containing specific text by choosing the Find... command on the Record menu, or by clicking the Find... button. The Find dialog box will appear, as shown in Figure 7.4. If you enter text into the Name: box, the program will search for records that contain the specified text within the Name field. When performing the search, the Address Manager always ignores the case of letters. For example, entering "jones" into the Name: box would match records with the following Name fields:

```
Jones, Davey
JONES
David T. Jones
```

If you enter text into the Any Text: box, the program will search for records that contain the specified text within *any* field of the record (including the Name, Phone Numbers, and Notes fields). If you enter text

FIGURE 7.4

The Find dialog box

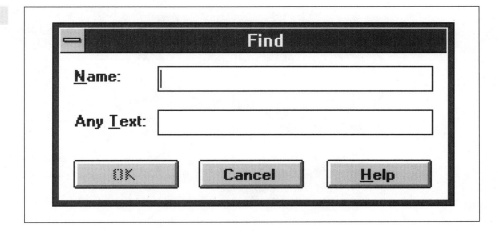

into *both* the Name: *and* the Any Text: boxes, the program will search for only those records that contain the Name: text in the Name field *and* contain the Any Text: text within any field (entering text into both boxes thus narrows the search criteria).

TIP

Searching for text within only the Name fields is faster than searching for text within all of the fields. Therefore, if you know that the specified text is contained within the Name field of the desired record, be sure to enter it into the Name: box rather than the Any Text: box.

The Find command begins searching the record that immediately follows the currently displayed record, and proceeds through the records in sorted order until it finds a match or until all records have been searched (after searching the last record, it goes to the first record). After finding a record, you can search for the *next* record that matches the search text by choosing the Find Next command on the Record menu, by clicking the Find Next button, or by pressing F3 (if you choose the Find Next command *before* choosing the Find command, the Find dialog box will be displayed so that you can specify search text). For example, if you wanted to view all records with San Francisco addresses, you could choose the Find command, enter "San Francisco" into the Any Text: box, and then, after the first matching record is displayed, choose the Find Again command to view each additional matching record.

Working with Address Records

Once you have retrieved a specific address record and it is displayed in the Address Manager window, you can perform the following operations with the record:

- You can print an envelope or mailing label, using the displayed address.
- You can copy the address to the Clipboard.
- You can dial a phone number shown in the Phone Numbers box.
- You can copy a phone number to the Clipboard.
- You can delete the record.

Printing an Envelope or Mailing Label

To print an envelope or mailing label, using the address that is currently displayed in the Address Manager window, choose the Print Env/Label command on the Record menu or simply click the Print E/L button. In response, the Address Manager will copy the address to the Clipboard, run the Envelope and Label Printer utility (if it is not already running), and cause this utility to print an envelope or label using the text in the Clipboard. (The Envelope and Label Printer is presented in Chapter 8.)

The type of object printed (an envelope or label), as well as the format used to print the object, depends upon the most recent settings that you have entered into the Envelope and Label Printer. For information on making these settings, see Chapter 8.

TIP

When you issue the Print Env/Label command, the program does not pause for you to change the type or format of the object printed. Therefore, if you need to change one or more settings, be sure to run the Envelope and Label Printer and make any desired changes *before* issuing the Print Env/Label command in the Address Manager.

Copying the Address to the Clipboard

You can also have the Address Manager copy the currently displayed address to the Clipboard by choosing the Copy Address command on the Edit menu or by clicking the Copy Addr button. When the address is copied to the Clipboard, it is formatted in the way that an address is normally printed, so that you can paste the address directly into another program. Figure 7.5 shows a record within the Address Manager, together with the text that would be copied to the Clipboard by the Copy Address command.

FIGURE 7.5

An Address Manager record and the text that would be copied to the Clipboard by the Copy Address command

As an example, if you are using a word processor to write a letter to a person whose address is stored in the Address Manager, you could retrieve the record, issue the Copy Address command, and then paste the formatted address directly into the word processor document.

Dialing a Phone Number

If you have a Hayes-compatible modem attached to your computer, you can automatically dial a phone number that is stored in an address record, using the following two steps:

1. Place the insertion point anywhere on the line within the Phone Numbers text box that contains the number you want to dial. (Alternatively, you can select all or part of the line.)

2. Choose the Dial command on the Record menu, or click the Dial button.

The Address Manager will copy the phone number to the Clipboard, run the Phone Dialer utility (if it is not already running), and cause this utility to dial the number. (The Phone Dialer is presented in Chapter 9.) The number will be dialed, using the most recent dialing and modem settings that you entered into the Phone Dialer. For information on making these settings, see Chapter 9.

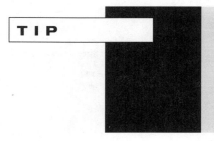

TIP

When you issue the Dial command, the program does not pause for you to change the dialing or modem settings. Therefore, if you need to change one or more settings, be sure to run the Phone Dialer and make any desired changes *before* issuing the Dial command in the Address Manager.

Copying a Phone Number to the Clipboard

You can also copy a phone number to the Clipboard, using the following two steps:

1. Place the insertion point anywhere on the line within the Phone Numbers text box that contains the number you want to copy. (Alternatively, you can select all or part of the line.)

2. Choose the Copy Telephone command on the Edit menu, or click the Copy Tel button.

The Address Manager will extract the phone number from the indicated line and will copy it to the Clipboard, ignoring any additional text contained in the line.

Deleting the Record

Finally, you can delete the record that is currently displayed by choosing the Delete command on the Record menu. Be sure that you have retrieved the appropriate record before issuing this command, because the command is carried out immediately *without requesting verification*.

Setting the Always on Top Option

The Options menu has only a single item: Always on Top. As in the other programs, if you enable this option, the program window will always be displayed on top of overlapping windows, even when the window is inactive or minimized.

How the Address Manager Works

Listings 7.1 through 7.7 are the source code for the Address Manager Program, and Figure 7.6 shows the program icon. Listing 7.1 is the program header file (ADDRESS.H), which contains all of the class definitions and is included in each of the C++ source files. Listing 7.2 (ADDRESS.CPP) contains the C++ source code for WinMain and declarations for the global objects. Listing 7.3 (DIALOG.CPP) defines the member functions belonging to the main window class (CMainDialog) as well as the class that manages the Find modal dialog box (CFindDialog). Listing 7.4 (DOCUMENT.CPP) defines the member functions of the class that stores and retrieves the document data (CDocument).

Listing 7.5 (ADDRESS.DEF) is the module-definition file, and Listings 7.6 and 7.7 (RESOURCE.H and ADDRESS.RC) are the program resource files generated by the Microsoft App Studio.

FIGURE 7.6

The ADDRESS
program icon

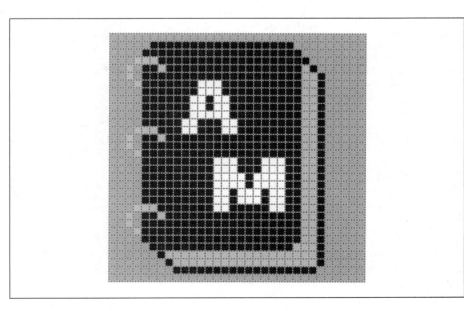

Listing 7.1

```
///////////////////////////////////////////////////////////
//                                                         //
// ADDRESS.H:  Header file for the ADDRESS program.        //
//                                                         //
///////////////////////////////////////////////////////////

#include "..\wclasses\wclasses.h"
#include "resource.h"

// constant for help topic:
#define HELPFINDDLG 100


///////////////////////////////////////////////////////////
// main dialog box class definition:                       //
///////////////////////////////////////////////////////////

class CMainDialog : public CMLDialog
{
    HBRUSH HBrushWorkSpace;
    BOOL Modified;
    int OnTop;

    virtual BOOL DialogProc (UINT Msg, WPARAM WParam,
                             LPARAM LParam);
    BOOL IsPhoneDigit (char Ch);
    BOOL IsPhoneSep (char Ch);
    BOOL OnCommand (int IDItem, HWND HWndCtl, WORD NotifyCode);
    BOOL OnCtlColor (HDC HDCChild, HWND HWndChild, int CtlType);
    BOOL OnDestroy ();
    BOOL OnInitDialog (HWND HWndFocus, LPARAM Data);
    BOOL OnSysColorChange ();
    BOOL QuerySave ();
    void RightTrim (char *String, int Length);
    BOOL SaveAs ();
    void WrapUp ();

public:
    CMainDialog ();
};
```

```
///////////////////////////////////////////////////////////
// Document management class definition:                   //
///////////////////////////////////////////////////////////

struct TagRecord
    {
    long OffNextRec;
    long OffPrevRec;
    char Name [41];
    char Company [41];
    char Address [81];
    char City [27];
    char State [3];
    char Zip [11];
    };

class CDocument
{
    HFILE HTempFile;
    BOOL NewRecord;
    char *Notes;
    long OffCurrentRec;
    long OffFirstRec;
    char *Phones;
    OFSTRUCT TempFileStruct;

    void ReadRecord (long Offset);
    void ShowRecord ();
public:
    BOOL Modified;
    OFSTRUCT PermFileStruct;
    TagRecord Record;

    CDocument ();

    void Dump ();
    void FileNew ();
    BOOL FileOpen (char _far *FileName);
    void FileSave (char *FileName);
    void RecDelete ();
```

```
    BOOL RecFind ();
    void RecFirst ();
    void RecNew ();
    void RecNext ();
    void RecPrevious ();
    void RecSave ();
    void WrapUp ();
};

////////////////////////////////////////////////////////////////////
// 'Find' modal dialog box class definition:                        //
////////////////////////////////////////////////////////////////////

class CFindDialog : public CMDialog
{
    virtual BOOL DialogProc (UINT Msg, WPARAM WParam,
                             LPARAM LParam);
public:
    char Name [41];
    char AnyText [41];

    CFindDialog ();
};
```

Listing 7.2

```
////////////////////////////////////////////////////////////////////
//                                                                  //
// ADDRESS.CPP:  Global object declarations and program entry       //
//               point for the ADDRESS program.                     //
//                                                                  //
////////////////////////////////////////////////////////////////////

#include "address.h"

////////////////////////////////////////////////////////////////////
// global object declarations:                                      //
////////////////////////////////////////////////////////////////////

CApplication App;
CDocument Document;
```

```
CFindDialog FindDialog;
CMainDialog MainDialog;

//////////////////////////////////////////////////////////////////
// program entry function:                                        //
//////////////////////////////////////////////////////////////////

int PASCAL WinMain
   (HINSTANCE HInstCurrent,
   HINSTANCE HInstPrevious,
   LPSTR CmdLine,
   int CmdShow)
   {
   MSG Msg;

   if (HInstPrevious)
      {
      HWND HWndPopup;

      GetInstanceData
         (HInstPrevious,
         (BYTE *)&MainDialog.mHDialog,
         sizeof (HWND));
      ShowWindow (MainDialog.mHDialog, SW_SHOWNORMAL);
      HWndPopup = GetLastActivePopup (MainDialog.mHDialog);
      BringWindowToTop (MainDialog.mHDialog);
      BringWindowToTop (HWndPopup);
      return (FALSE);
      }

   App.Initialize (HInstCurrent, HInstPrevious, CmdLine,
                   CmdShow);

   if (!App.LoadAccel ("AddressAccel"))
      return (FALSE);

   if (!MainDialog.SetIcon ("AddressIcon"))
      return (FALSE);

   if (!MainDialog.Create ("MainDlg"))
      return (FALSE);
```

```
    while (GetMessage (&Msg, NULL, NULL, NULL))
        if (!TranslateAccelerator (MainDialog.mHDialog,
                                   App.mHAccelTable,
                                   &Msg))
            if (!IsDialogMessage (MainDialog.mHDialog, &Msg))
                {
                TranslateMessage (&Msg);
                DispatchMessage (&Msg);
                }

    return (Msg.wParam);
    }
```

Listing 7.3

```
//////////////////////////////////////////////////////////////////
//                                                                //
// DIALOG.CPP:  Dialog class member functions for the            //
//              ADDRESS program.                                  //
//                                                                //
//////////////////////////////////////////////////////////////////

#include "address.h"
#include <commdlg.h>
#include <ctype.h>
#include <stdio.h>
#include <string.h>

#define SIZENUMBER 64  // buffer size to hold phone number

extern CApplication App;
extern CDocument Document;
extern CFindDialog FindDialog;
extern CMainDialog MainDialog;

//////////////////////////////////////////////////////////////////
// CMainDialog member functions:                                  //
//////////////////////////////////////////////////////////////////
```

```
CMainDialog::CMainDialog ()
   {
   HBrushWorkSpace = 0;
   }

BOOL CMainDialog::DialogProc (UINT Msg, WPARAM WParam,
                              LPARAM LParam)
   {
   switch (Msg)
      {
      case WM_CLOSE:
         if (QuerySave ())   // test for unsaved data before
            Destroy ();      // destroying window
         return (TRUE);

      case WM_COMMAND:
         return OnCommand ((int)WParam, (HWND)LOWORD (LParam),
                           HIWORD (LParam));

      case WM_CTLCOLOR:
         return OnCtlColor ((HDC)WParam, (HWND)LOWORD (LParam),
                            (int)HIWORD (LParam));

      case WM_DESTROY:
         return OnDestroy ();

      case WM_ENDSESSION:
         if (WParam)
            WrapUp ();
         return (TRUE);

      case WM_INITDIALOG:
         return OnInitDialog ((HWND)WParam, LParam);

      case WM_QUERYENDSESSION:  // check for unsaved data before
         return (!QuerySave ());  // allowing Windows to quit

      case WM_SYSCOLORCHANGE:
         return OnSysColorChange ();
```

```
        default:
           return (FALSE);
        }
    }


BOOL CMainDialog::IsPhoneDigit (char Ch)
// returns TRUE if Ch is a character that can be sent to the
// modem as part of a phone number, and FALSE otherwise
    {
    if (isdigit (Ch) || Ch == ',' || Ch == '*' || Ch == '#')
       return (TRUE);
    else
       return (FALSE);
    }


BOOL CMainDialog::IsPhoneSep (char Ch)
// returns TRUE if Ch is a valid separator character that can be
// inserted within a phone number, and FALSE otherwise
    {
    if (Ch == '(' || Ch == ')' || Ch == '-' || Ch == '/')
       return (TRUE);
    else
       return (FALSE);
    }


BOOL CMainDialog::OnCommand (int IDItem, HWND HWndCtl,
                            WORD NotifyCode)

    {
    if (NotifyCode == EN_CHANGE)   // set flag if contents of an
       Modified = TRUE;            // edit control have changed

    switch (IDItem)
        {
        case IDM_ABOUT:   // Help/About menu command
           {
           CMDialog MDialog;
           MDialog.Create ("AboutDlg", mHDialog);
           return (TRUE);
           }

        case IDM_COPYADDRESS:   // Edit/Copy Address menu command
```

```
case IDM_COPYPHONE:      // Edit/Copy Telephone menu command
   {
   if (Modified)  // save record if edit control contents
      {              // have changed
      Document.RecSave ();
      Modified = FALSE;
      }
   HGLOBAL HGlobalMem;
   LPSTR PGlobalMem;

   if (IDItem == IDM_COPYADDRESS)  // Edit/Copy Address
      {
      // allocate a block of global memory large enough
      // to contain the formatted address:
      HGlobalMem = GlobalAlloc
         (GMEM_MOVEABLE,
         sizeof (Document.Record.Name) + 2 +
         sizeof (Document.Record.Company) + 2 +
         sizeof (Document.Record.Address) + 2 +
         sizeof (Document.Record.City) + 2 +
         sizeof (Document.Record.State) + 2 +
         sizeof (Document.Record.Zip) + 2);
      if (HGlobalMem == 0)  // allocation error
         return (TRUE);
      // lock memory block and obtain a pointer to it:
      PGlobalMem = (LPSTR)GlobalLock (HGlobalMem);
      // remove trailing blanks from 'City' field:
      RightTrim (Document.Record.City,
               strlen (Document.Record.City));
      // format the address:
      wsprintf
         (PGlobalMem, "%s%s%s%s%s%s%s, %s  %s\r\n",
         (LPSTR)Document.Record.Name,
         (LPSTR)(Document.Record.Name [0] ? "\r\n" : ""),
         (LPSTR)Document.Record.Company,
         (LPSTR)(Document.Record.Company[0] ? "\r\n" : ""),
         (LPSTR)Document.Record.Address,
         (LPSTR)(Document.Record.Address[0] ? "\r\n" : ""),
         (LPSTR)Document.Record.City,
         (LPSTR)Document.Record.State,
         (LPSTR)Document.Record.Zip);
```

```
    }
else  // IDM_COPYPHONE:  Edit/Copy Phone menu command
    {
    int IdxLine;
    int IdxStart;
    char *LineBuf;
    int LineLength;

    // get the text of the selected line within the
    // IDC_PHONES edit control (that is, the line that
    // contains the caret or the beginning of the
    // selection); store text in LineBuf:
    IdxStart = LOWORD (SendDlgItemMessage
        (mHDialog, IDC_PHONES, EM_GETSEL, O, OL));
    IdxLine =(int)SendDlgItemMessage (mHDialog,
        IDC_PHONES, EM_LINEFROMCHAR, (WPARAM)IdxStart,
        OL);
    LineLength = (int)SendDlgItemMessage (mHDialog,
        IDC_PHONES, EM_LINELENGTH, (WPARAM)IdxStart, OL);
    LineBuf = new char [LineLength + 1];
    *(WORD *)LineBuf = LineLength;
    SendDlgItemMessage (mHDialog, IDC_PHONES, EM_GETLINE,
        (WPARAM)IdxLine, (LPARAM)(LPSTR)LineBuf);
    LineBuf [LineLength] = '\0';

    // allocate and lock a block of global memory large
    // enough to hold a phone number:
    HGlobalMem = GlobalAlloc (GMEM_MOVEABLE, SIZENUMBER);
    if (HGlobalMem == O)
        return (TRUE);
    PGlobalMem = (LPSTR)GlobalLock (HGlobalMem);

    // extract the phone number from the text from the
    // edit control (LineBuffer) and copy the number to
    // the global memory block (PGlobalMem); the phone
    // number is considered to be the first sequence of
    // characters beginning with a valid phone digit
    // (a number, comma, '*', or '#'), and consisting of
    // valid phone digits or single occurrences of
    // separator characters ('-', '/', '(', or ')'):
```

```
// move to first valid phone digit:
int LIdx = 0;
while (LineBuf [LIdx] &&
   !IsPhoneDigit (LineBuf [LIdx]))
   ++LIdx;

// back up to include a preceding '(' character:
if (LIdx > 0 && LineBuf [LIdx-1] == '(')
   --LIdx;

// scan thru remainder of phone number:
BOOL PrevSeparator = FALSE;
int GIdx = 0;
while (LineBuf [LIdx] && GIdx < SIZENUMBER-1)
   {
   if (IsPhoneDigit (LineBuf [LIdx])) // copy a valid
      {                              // phone digit
      PGlobalMem [GIdx++] =  LineBuf [LIdx];
      PrevSeparator = FALSE;          // reset flag
      }
   else if (IsPhoneSep (LineBuf [LIdx]))
      {                    // copy a valid separator
      if (PrevSeparator)  // unless there are 2
         break;           // contiguous separators
      PrevSeparator = TRUE;
      PGlobalMem [GIdx++] = LineBuf [LIdx];
      }
   else       // quit scanning on first character
      break;  // that is neither a valid phone digit
   ++LIdx;    // nor a separator
   }
PGlobalMem [GIdx] = '\0';

delete [] LineBuf;
}

// routine for both Edit/Copy Address and
// Edit/Copy Telephone commands:

// unlock global memory block: ·
GlobalUnlock (HGlobalMem);
```

```
    // open the Clipboard:
    if (!OpenClipboard (mHDialog))
        {
        GlobalFree (HGlobalMem);
        return (TRUE);
        }
    EmptyClipboard (); // remove current Clipboard contents:
    // place the global memory block in the Clipboard:
    SetClipboardData (CF_TEXT, HGlobalMem);
    CloseClipboard ();  // close the Clipboard
    return (TRUE);
    }

case IDM_DELETE:  // Record/Delete menu command
    Document.RecDelete ();  // delete the current record
    // place caret in IDC_NAME edit control:
    SetFocus (GetDlgItem (mHDialog, IDC_NAME));
    Modified = FALSE;  // edit controls contain no modified
    return (TRUE);     // data

case IDM_DIAL:  // Record/Dial menu command
    {
    HWND HWnd;
    UINT Result;

    // if DIAL.EXE is already running, FindWindow
    // will return the handle to its main window:
    HWnd = FindWindow (0, "Phone Dialer");
    if (HWnd == 0)  // DIAL.EXE is not running
        {
        // run it:
        Result = WinExec ("..\\DIAL\\DIAL.EXE",
            SW_SHOWNORMAL);
        if (Result < 32)  // error occurred
            {
            MessageBox
                (mHDialog,
                "Cannot find DIAL.EXE.\n"
                "Make sure the directory containing this file "
                "is in your PATH statement.",
                "Address Manager",
```

```
                    MB_ICONEXCLAMATION | MB_OK);
             return (TRUE);
             }
          // now get handle to DIAL.EXE's main window:
          HWnd = FindWindow (0, "Phone Dialer");
          }
       // copy current address to Clipboard:
       OnCommand (IDM_COPYPHONE, 0, 0L);

       // check 'From Clipboard' radio button in DIAL:
       CheckDlgButton (HWnd, 104 /*IDC_CLIPBOARD*/, 1);
       CheckDlgButton (HWnd, 105 /*IDC_ENTERED*/, 0);

       // cause DIAL to dial the number in the Clipboard:
       PostMessage (HWnd, WM_COMMAND, 1008 /*IDM_DIAL*/, 0L);
       return (TRUE);
       }

   case IDM_DUMP:     // user pressed Ctrl+Shift+D accelerator;
      if (Modified)   // save record if edit control contents
         {            // have changed
         Document.RecSave ();
         Modified = FALSE;
         }
      Document.Dump ();   // display contents of file for
      return (TRUE);      // debugging

   case IDM_EXIT:  // File/Exit menu command
      SendMessage (mHDialog, WM_CLOSE, 0, 0L);
      return (TRUE);

   case IDM_FIND:      // Record/Find menu command
   case IDM_FINDNEXT:  // Record/Find Next or F3 command
      // display Find dialog box if user chose Record/Find
      // menu command, OR user chose Record/Find Next (or F3)
      // and no previous search string was entered:
      if (IDItem == IDM_FIND ||
         !FindDialog.Name [0] && !FindDialog.AnyText [0])
         {
         int Result = FindDialog.Create ("FindDlg", mHDialog);
         if (Result != IDOK)
```

```
        return (TRUE);
      }
  if (Modified)  // save record if edit control contents
     Document.RecSave ();   // have changed
  // search for record matching search string(s) contained
  // in 'Name' or 'AnyText' members of FindDialog object:
  if (!Document.RecFind ())
     {
     MessageBox (mHDialog, "Record not found.",
        "Address Manager", MB_ICONINFORMATION | MB_OK);
     return (TRUE);
     }
  // place caret in IDC_NAME edit control:
  SetFocus (GetDlgItem (mHDialog, IDC_NAME));
  Modified = FALSE; // new record has been read into
                    // edit controls
  return (TRUE);

case IDM_FIRST:  // Record/First menu command
   if (Modified)
      Document.RecSave ();
   // display the FIRST record in file (records are
   // sorted by the 'Name' field):
   Document.RecFirst ();
   SetFocus (GetDlgItem (mHDialog, IDC_NAME));
   Modified = FALSE;
   return (TRUE);

case IDM_HELPCONTENTS: // Help/Contents menu command
   WinHelp (mHDialog, "ADDRESS.HLP", HELP_CONTENTS, OL);
   return (TRUE);

case IDM_HELPHELP:  // Help/How to Use Help menu command
   WinHelp (mHDialog, "ADDRESS.HLP", HELP_HELPONHELP, OL);
   return (TRUE);

case IDM_HELPSEARCH:  // Help/Search for Help On menu
                      // command
   WinHelp (mHDialog, "ADDRESS.HLP", HELP_PARTIALKEY,
         (DWORD)(LPCSTR)"");
   return (TRUE);
```

```
case IDM_NEW:  // File/New menu command
   if (!QuerySave ())  // test for unsaved data before
      return (TRUE);   // discarding current file
   SetWindowText (mHDialog,
      "Address Manager - (Untitled)");
   Document.FileNew ();  // create a new file
   Document.RecNew ();   // create a new record
   SetFocus (GetDlgItem (mHDialog, IDC_NAME));
   Modified = FALSE;
   return (TRUE);

case IDM_NEXT:  // Record/Next menu command
   if (Modified)
      Document.RecSave ();
   Document.RecNext ();  // display next record in sorted
                         // order
   SetFocus (GetDlgItem (mHDialog, IDC_NAME));
   Modified = FALSE;
   return (TRUE);

case IDM_ONTOP: // Options/Always menu command
   OnTop = !OnTop;
   CheckMenuItem (GetMenu (mHDialog), IDM_ONTOP,
                  OnTop ? MF_CHECKED : MF_UNCHECKED);
   SetWindowPos (mHDialog,
                 OnTop ? HWND_TOPMOST : HWND_NOTOPMOST,
                 0, 0, 0, 0, SWP_NOMOVE | SWP_NOSIZE);
   return (TRUE);

case IDM_OPEN:  // File/Open menu command
   {
   // display the Open common Windows dialog box:

   OPENFILENAME OFName;
   char FileName [128] = "";
   char FileTitle [13] = "";
   char Filter [] = "Address Manager Files *.adm ";
   char WindowTitle [40];
```

```
        if (!QuerySave ())
           return (TRUE);

        // Filter specifies the default file extension to
        // be displayed in the Open dialog box:
        Filter [21] = Filter [27] = '\0';

        // assign values to OFName to control behavior of
        // Open dialog box:
        memset (&OFName, 0, sizeof (OPENFILENAME));
        OFName.lStructSize = sizeof (OPENFILENAME);
        OFName.hwndOwner = mHDialog; // owner of dialog box
        OFName.lpstrFilter = Filter;
        OFName.lpstrFile = FileName; // holds the full file name
        OFName.nMaxFile = sizeof (FileName); // chosen by user;
        OFName.lpstrFileTitle = FileTitle;  // holds the short
        OFName.nMaxFileTitle = sizeof (FileTitle); // file name;
        // don't display "Read Only" check box; user must
        // choose an existing file:
        OFName.Flags = OFN_HIDEREADONLY | OFN_FILEMUSTEXIST;
        OFName.lpstrDefExt = "adm";  // default file extension
                                     // to append if user does
                                     // not specify extension
        // display the dialog box:
        if (!GetOpenFileName (&OFName))
           return (TRUE);  // user canceled the open operation

        // attempt to open and display the file:
        if (Document.FileOpen (FileName))
           { // successful
           sprintf (WindowTitle,
              "Address Manager - %s", FileTitle);
           SetWindowText (mHDialog, WindowTitle);
           SetFocus (GetDlgItem (mHDialog, IDC_NAME));
           Modified = FALSE;
           }
        return (TRUE);
        }

case IDM_PREVIOUS:  // Record/Previous menu command
   if (Modified)
```

```
            Document.RecSave ();
        Document.RecPrevious ();
        SetFocus (GetDlgItem (mHDialog, IDC_NAME));
        Modified = FALSE;
        return (TRUE);

    case IDM_PRINTENVELOPE:    // Record/Print Envelope menu
        {                      // command
        HWND HWnd;
        UINT Result;

        // if ENVELOPE.EXE is already running, FindWindow
        // will return handle to its main window:
        HWnd = FindWindow (0, "Envelope & Label Printer");
        if (HWnd == 0)  // ENVELOPE.EXE is not running
            {
            // run it:
            Result = WinExec ("..\\ENVELOPE\\ENVELOPE.EXE",
                SW_SHOWNORMAL);
            if (Result < 32)  // error occurred
                {
                MessageBox
                    (mHDialog,
                    "Cannot find ENVELOPE.EXE.\n"
                    "Make sure the directory containing this file "
                    "is in your PATH statement.",
                    "Address Manager",
                    MB_ICONEXCLAMATION | MB_OK);
                return (TRUE);
                }
            // now get handle to ENVELOPE.EXE's main window:
            HWnd = FindWindow (0, "Envelope & Label Printer");
            SetActiveWindow (mHDialog); // reactivate ADDRESS.EXE
            }
        // copy current address to Clipboard:
        OnCommand (IDM_COPYADDRESS, 0, OL);

        // check 'From Clipboard' radio button and uncheck
        // 'Entered Here:' button in ENVELOPE:
        CheckDlgButton (HWnd, 104 /*IDC_CLIPBOARD*/, 1);
        CheckDlgButton (HWnd, 105 /*IDC_ENTERED*/, 0);
```

```
                // cause ENVELOPE to print the address from Clipboard:
                PostMessage (HWnd, WM_COMMAND, 1009 /*IDM_PRINT*/, OL);
                return (TRUE);
                }

        case IDM_RECNEW:   // Record/New menu command
            if (Modified)
                Document.RecSave ();
            Document.RecNew ();   // create a new, empty record
            SetFocus (GetDlgItem (mHDialog, IDC_NAME));
            Modified = FALSE;
            return (TRUE);

        case IDM_SAVE:   // File/Save menu command
            if (Document.PermFileStruct.szPathName [0])
                {                           // file has been saved
                if (Modified)               // previously
                    {
                    Document.RecSave ();
                    Modified = FALSE;
                    }
                Document.FileSave (0);   // save file using previous
                }                        // file name;
            else             // file has NOT been saved previously;
                SaveAs ();   // save file under a new file name
            return (TRUE);

        case IDM_SAVEAS:   // File/Save As menu command
            SaveAs ();   // save file under a new file name
            return (TRUE);

        default:
            return (FALSE);
        }
    }

BOOL CMainDialog::OnCtlColor (HDC HDCChild, HWND HWndChild,
                                int CtlType)

    {
    COLORREF WorkSpaceColor;
```

```
    switch (CtlType)
        {
        case CTLCOLOR_BTN:
        case CTLCOLOR_STATIC:
            WorkSpaceColor = GetSysColor (COLOR_APPWORKSPACE);
            if (GetRValue (WorkSpaceColor) * 2 +
                GetGValue (WorkSpaceColor) * 5 +
                GetBValue (WorkSpaceColor) > 1020)
                SetTextColor (HDCChild, RGB (0, 0, 0));
            else
                SetTextColor (HDCChild, RGB (255, 255, 255));
            SetBkMode (HDCChild, TRANSPARENT);
            return ((BOOL)HBrushWorkSpace);

        case CTLCOLOR_DLG:
            return ((BOOL)HBrushWorkSpace);

        default:
            return (FALSE);
        }
}

BOOL CMainDialog::OnDestroy ()
    {
    WrapUp ();
    if (HBrushWorkSpace != 0)
        DeleteObject (HBrushWorkSpace);
    WinHelp (mHDialog, "ADDRESS.HLP", HELP_QUIT, OL);
    PostQuitMessage (0);
    return (TRUE);
    }

BOOL CMainDialog::OnInitDialog (HWND HWndFocus, LPARAM Data)
    {
    OnTop = (int)GetPrivateProfileInt
        ("options",
        "ontop",
        0,
        "ADDRESS.INI");
    if (OnTop)
```

```
   {
   CheckMenuItem (GetMenu (mHDialog), IDM_ONTOP, MF_CHECKED);
   SetWindowPos (mHDialog, HWND_TOPMOST, 0, 0, 0, 0,
                 SWP_NOMOVE | SWP_NOSIZE);
   }
HBrushWorkSpace = CreateSolidBrush
   (GetSysColor (COLOR_APPWORKSPACE));

// limit length of text that can be entered into the edit
// controls:
SendDlgItemMessage (mHDialog, IDC_NAME, EM_LIMITTEXT,
   (WPARAM)sizeof (Document.Record.Name) - 1, OL);
SendDlgItemMessage (mHDialog, IDC_COMPANY, EM_LIMITTEXT,
   (WPARAM)sizeof (Document.Record.Company) - 1, OL);
SendDlgItemMessage (mHDialog, IDC_ADDRESS, EM_LIMITTEXT,
   (WPARAM)sizeof (Document.Record.Address) - 1, OL);
SendDlgItemMessage (mHDialog, IDC_CITY, EM_LIMITTEXT,
   (WPARAM)sizeof (Document.Record.City) - 1, OL);
SendDlgItemMessage (mHDialog, IDC_STATE, EM_LIMITTEXT,
   (WPARAM)sizeof (Document.Record.State) - 1, OL);
SendDlgItemMessage (mHDialog, IDC_ZIP, EM_LIMITTEXT,
   (WPARAM)sizeof (Document.Record.Zip) - 1, OL);

if (App.mCmdLine [0])   // command line contains a parameter
    {
    // attempt to open file using command-line parameter as
    // the file name:
    if (Document.FileOpen (App.mCmdLine))
       { // successful
       char WindowTitle [40];
       // display the simple file name (without path) in
       // title bar:
       strcpy (WindowTitle, "Address Manager - ");
       GetFileTitle (Document.PermFileStruct.szPathName,
          WindowTitle+18, 13);
       SetWindowText (mHDialog, WindowTitle);
       Modified = FALSE;
       return (TRUE);
       }
    }
// either no command line parameter was entered, or parameter
```

```
      // was not a valid file name; therefore, establish a new file
      // and a new record:
      Document.FileNew ();
      Document.RecNew ();
      SetWindowText (mHDialog, "Address Manager - (Untitled)");
      Modified = FALSE;
      return (TRUE);
      }

BOOL CMainDialog::OnSysColorChange ()
   {
   if (HBrushWorkSpace != 0)
      DeleteObject (HBrushWorkSpace);
   HBrushWorkSpace =
      CreateSolidBrush (GetSysColor (COLOR_APPWORKSPACE));
   return (TRUE);
   }

BOOL CMainDialog::QuerySave ()
// if document contains unsaved data, allows user to save it;
// returns FALSE if user clicked Cancel button, or TRUE otherwise
   {
   if (Modified)  // first save any modified data contained in
      {           // the edit controls
      Document.RecSave ();
      Modified = FALSE;
      }
   if (!Document.Modified)
      return (TRUE);  // document does not contain modified data

   // document contains changes; therefore, ask user if it should
   // be saved:
   int Result = MessageBox
      (mHDialog,
      "File is modified.\nDo you want to save your changes?",
      "Address Manager",
      MB_ICONQUESTION | MB_YESNOCANCEL);
   switch (Result)
      {
      case IDYES:  // user clicked Yes button; save document:
         if (Document.PermFileStruct.szPathName [0])
```

```
                  {
                  Document.FileSave (0);
                  return (TRUE);
                  }
              else                       // note that if user clicks
                  return (SaveAs ());  // Cancel button in Save As
                                       // dialog, QuerySave returns
                                       // FALSE, stopping current
                                       // operation
          case IDNO:  // user clicked No button; don't save file
              return (TRUE);

          case IDCANCEL:  // user clicked Cancel button; return
          default:        // FALSE to stop current operation
              return (FALSE);
          }
      }

void CMainDialog::RightTrim (char *String, int Length)
// removes all trailing blank characters from
// 'String'; the parameter 'Length' must give the length of
// 'String', NOT including a NULL termination
    {char *ChPt;  // points to characters in the string

    if (Length < 1)  // must be at least 1 character
        return;
    ChPt = String + Length - 1; // points to last character of
                                // string;
    // scan backwards in string until first nonblank, non-NULL
    // character:
    while (ChPt > String && (*ChPt == '\0' || *ChPt == ' '))
        --ChPt;

    if (*ChPt == '\0' || *ChPt == ' ') // string all blank or NULL
        *ChPt = '\0';  // place NULL at first position

    else if (ChPt < String + Length - 1) // string contains non-
        *(++ChPt) = '\0';    // blank, non-NULL character(s); place
    }                        // a NULL after last character
```

```
BOOL CMainDialog::SaveAs ()
// saves the current file under a new file name; returns FALSE
// if user clicks Cancel button in Save As dialog box, and TRUE
// otherwise
    {
    // display the Save As common Windows dialog box:

    OPENFILENAME OFName;
    char FileName [128];
    char FileTitle [13];
    char Filter [] = "Address Manager Files *.adm ";
    char WindowTitle [40];

    // copy current file name to FileName so that it is initially
    // displayed in Save As dialog box:
    memcpy (FileName, Document.PermFileStruct.szPathName,
        sizeof (FileName));
    // Filter specifies default extension of files displayed in
    // Save As dialog box:
    Filter [21] = Filter [27] = '\0';

    // assign fields of OFName to control behavior of dialog box:
    memset (&OFName, O, sizeof (OPENFILENAME));
    OFName.lStructSize = sizeof (OPENFILENAME);
    OFName.hwndOwner = mHDialog;
    OFName.lpstrFilter = Filter;
    OFName.lpstrFile = FileName;  // receives full file name
    OFName.nMaxFile = sizeof (FileName);  // entered by user;
    OFName.lpstrFileTitle = FileTitle;  // receives short file
    OFName.nMaxFileTitle = sizeof (FileTitle);  // name;
    // warn user if file already exists; do not display Read Only
    // check box:
    OFName.Flags = OFN_OVERWRITEPROMPT | OFN_HIDEREADONLY;
    OFName.lpstrDefExt = "adm";  // default extension added if
                                 // user enters no extension
    // display the dialog box:
    if (!GetSaveFileName (&OFName))
        return (FALSE);  // user clicked Cancel button

    sprintf (WindowTitle, "Address Manager - %s", FileTitle);
    SetWindowText (mHDialog, WindowTitle);
```

```
   if (Modified)           // first save any modified data
      {                    // from edit controls
      Document.RecSave ();
      Modified = FALSE;
      }
   Document.FileSave (FileName);  // now save the file under
   return (TRUE);                 // the newly specified name
   }

void CMainDialog::WrapUp ()
   {
   // let document class perform required final tasks:
   Document.WrapUp ();

   WritePrivateProfileString
      ("options",
       "ontop",
        OnTop ? "1" : "0",
       "ADDRESS.INI");
   }


/////////////////////////////////////////////////////////////////
// CFindDialog member functions:                               //
/////////////////////////////////////////////////////////////////

CFindDialog::CFindDialog ()
   {
   Name [0] = '\0';    // initialize search text to empty strings
   AnyText [0] = '\0';
   }

BOOL CFindDialog::DialogProc (UINT Msg, WPARAM WParam,
                              LPARAM LParam)

   {
   switch (Msg)
      {
      case WM_COMMAND:
         switch (WParam)
            {
            case IDCANCEL:
```

```
                    EndDialog (mHDialog, IDCANCEL);
                    return (TRUE);

                case IDC_ANYTEXT:
                case IDC_NAME:
                    if (HIWORD (LParam) == EN_CHANGE)
                    // user changed text in an edit control; enable
                    // OK button ONLY if at least 1 of the 2 edit
                    // controls contains text:
                        EnableWindow
                           (GetDlgItem (mHDialog, IDOK),
                            SendDlgItemMessage (mHDialog, IDC_NAME,
                                WM_GETTEXTLENGTH, 0, OL) ||
                            SendDlgItemMessage (mHDialog, IDC_ANYTEXT,
                                WM_GETTEXTLENGTH, 0, OL));
                    return (TRUE);

                case IDC_HELP:
                    WinHelp (MainDialog.mHDialog, "ADDRESS.HLP",
                             HELP_CONTEXT, HELPFINDDLG);
                    return (TRUE);

                case IDOK:
                    // get the search text from the edit controls into
                    // the CFindDialog data members:
                    GetDlgItemText (mHDialog, IDC_NAME, Name,
                        sizeof (Name));
                    GetDlgItemText (mHDialog, IDC_ANYTEXT, AnyText,
                        sizeof (AnyText));
                    EndDialog (mHDialog, IDOK);
                    return (TRUE);

                default:
                    return (TRUE);
                }

        case WM_INITDIALOG:
            {
            SendDlgItemMessage (mHDialog, IDC_NAME, EM_LIMITTEXT,
                               (WPARAM)sizeof (Name) - 1, OL);
            SendDlgItemMessage (mHDialog, IDC_ANYTEXT, EM_LIMITTEXT,
```

```
                                (WPARAM)sizeof (AnyText) - 1, OL);
        SetDlgItemText (mHDialog, IDC_NAME, Name);
        SetDlgItemText (mHDialog, IDC_ANYTEXT, AnyText);

        // disable the OK button if the data members contain
        // no search text:
        if (!Name [0] && !AnyText [0])
            EnableWindow (GetDlgItem (mHDialog, IDOK), FALSE);
        return (TRUE);
        }

    default:
        if (Msg == mHelpMessage)
            {
            SendMessage (mHDialog, WM_COMMAND, IDC_HELP, OL);
            return (TRUE);
            }
        else
            return (FALSE);
    }
  }
```

Listing 7.4

```
//////////////////////////////////////////////////////////////////
//                                                              //
// DOCUMENT.CPP:  Document class member functions for the       //
//               ADDRESS program.                               //
//                                                              //
//////////////////////////////////////////////////////////////////

#include "address.h"
#include <fcntl.h>
#include <io.h>
#include <memory.h>
#include <stdlib.h>
#include <stdio.h>
#include <string.h>

extern CFindDialog FindDialog;
```

```
extern CMainDialog MainDialog;

CDocument::CDocument ()
    {
    // cause all files to be opened in binary mode:
    _fmode = O_BINARY;
    HTempFile = 0;
    }

void CDocument::Dump ()
// displays the current values of CDocument data members, and
// the current contents of the temporary file; to be used as a
// debugging aid; values are displayed in the debugging window
    {
    char Buffer [640];
    char DebugString [64];
    int Size;
    TagRecord TempRecord;

    // display CDocument data members:
    sprintf (DebugString, "NewRecord = %s\n",
        NewRecord ? "TRUE" : "FALSE");
    OutputDebugString (DebugString);
    sprintf (DebugString, "OffFirstRec = %Ld\n", OffFirstRec);
    OutputDebugString (DebugString);
    sprintf (DebugString, "OffCurrentRec = %Ld\n", OffCurrentRec);
    OutputDebugString (DebugString);
    sprintf (DebugString, "Record.OffNextRec = %Ld\n",
        Record.OffNextRec);
    OutputDebugString (DebugString);
    sprintf (DebugString, "Record.OffPrevRec = %Ld\n",
        Record.OffPrevRec);
    OutputDebugString (DebugString);
    OutputDebugString ("\n");

    // move file pointer to beginning of temporary file:
    lseek (HTempFile, OL, SEEK_SET);

    // read and display all records in the file:
    for (;;)
        {
```

```
sprintf (DebugString, "OFFSET: %Ld\n", tell (HTempFile));
OutputDebugString (DebugString);

// quit when end-of-file is reached:
if (read (HTempFile, &TempRecord,
    sizeof (TempRecord)) < sizeof (TempRecord))
    return;

sprintf (DebugString, "OffNextRec = %Ld\n",
    TempRecord.OffNextRec);
OutputDebugString (DebugString);
sprintf (DebugString, "OffPrevRec = %Ld\n",
    TempRecord.OffPrevRec);
OutputDebugString (DebugString);
sprintf (DebugString, "Name: %s \n", TempRecord.Name);
OutputDebugString (DebugString);
sprintf (DebugString, "Company: %s \n",
    TempRecord.Company);
OutputDebugString (DebugString);
sprintf (DebugString, "Address: %s \n",
    TempRecord.Address);
OutputDebugString (DebugString);
sprintf (DebugString, "City: %s \n", TempRecord.City);
OutputDebugString (DebugString);
sprintf (DebugString, "State: %s \n", TempRecord.State);
OutputDebugString (DebugString);
sprintf (DebugString, "Zip: %s \n", TempRecord.Zip);
OutputDebugString (DebugString);

read (HTempFile, &Size, sizeof (Size));
sprintf (DebugString, "PHONES: %d\n", Size);
OutputDebugString (DebugString);

read (HTempFile, Buffer, Size);
OutputDebugString (Buffer); OutputDebugString ("\n");

read (HTempFile, &Size, sizeof (Size));
sprintf (DebugString, "NOTES: %d\n", Size);
OutputDebugString (DebugString);

read (HTempFile, Buffer, Size);
```

```
         OutputDebugString (Buffer);
         OutputDebugString ("\n######\n");
         }
      }

void CDocument::FileNew ()
// opens a new, empty file
   {
   // if a previous temporary file exists, delete it:
   if (HTempFile != 0)
      OpenFile (TempFileStruct.szPathName, &TempFileStruct,
               OF_DELETE);

   // construct a unique file name for the temporary file:
   char TempFileName [13] = "amXXXXXX";
   mktemp (TempFileName);

   // create and open the temporary file:
   memset (&TempFileStruct, 0, sizeof (TempFileStruct));
   HTempFile = OpenFile
      (TempFileName,
      &TempFileStruct,
      OF_CREATE ¦ OF_READWRITE); // open for reading & writing

   OffFirstRec = -1;   // -1 indicates file is empty
   Modified = FALSE;
   PermFileStruct.szPathName [0] = '\0';   // NULL value indicates
   }                      // that file has not yet been assigned a name

BOOL CDocument::FileOpen (char _far *FileName)
// opens the file whose path name is contained in 'FileName';
// returns TRUE if successful, or FALSE if an error occurs
   {
   char Buffer [512];
   int BytesRead;

   // open the permanent file for reading:
   memset (&PermFileStruct, 0, sizeof (PermFileStruct));
   HFILE HPermFile = OpenFile
      (FileName,
      &PermFileStruct,
```

```
        OF_READ);
if (HPermFile == HFILE_ERROR)   // open failure
    {
    wsprintf (Buffer, "Cannot open file %s.", FileName);
    MessageBox
        (MainDialog.mHDialog,
        Buffer,
        "Address Manager",
        MB_OK | MB_ICONEXCLAMATION);
    return (FALSE);
    }

// if a previous temporary file exists, delete it:
if (HTempFile != 0)
    OpenFile (TempFileStruct.szPathName, &TempFileStruct,
            OF_DELETE);

// construct a unique file name for the temporary file:
char TempFileName [13] = "amXXXXXX";
mktemp (TempFileName);

// create and open the temporary file:
memset (&TempFileStruct, 0, sizeof (TempFileStruct));
HTempFile = OpenFile
    (TempFileName,
    &TempFileStruct,
    OF_CREATE | OF_READWRITE);

// copy the contents of the permanent file into the temporary
// file:
do
    {
    BytesRead = read (HPermFile, Buffer, sizeof (Buffer));
    write (HTempFile, Buffer, BytesRead);
    }
while (BytesRead == sizeof (Buffer));

_lclose (HPermFile);  // close the permanent file

if (tell (HTempFile) > 0)  // file has at least 1 record;
    {                      // therefore, read and display
```

```
        OffFirstRec = 0;           // the first record
        ReadRecord (0);
        }
    else
        {                          // file is empty; therefore,
        OffFirstRec = -1;          // create a new record
        RecNew ();
        }
    Modified = FALSE;

    return (TRUE);
    }


void CDocument::FileSave (char *FileName)
// saves the current document (contained in the temporary file)
// in a permanent file having the name 'FileName'; if 'FileName'
// is NULL, the file is assigned the same name that was used
// for the previous save operation
    {
    HFILE HPermFile;
    long OffsetSource;
    long OffsetPrevTarget;
    int SizeNotes;
    int SizePhones;
    TagRecord TempRecord;

    if (FileName == 0)
    // no new name is specified; therefore, reopen the permanent
    // file under its previous name (contained in
    // PermFileStruct.szPathName):
        HPermFile = OpenFile (0, &PermFileStruct, OF_CREATE |
            OF_REOPEN | OF_WRITE);
    else  // a new name is specified; therefore create a permanent
        {  // file having the new name
        memset (&PermFileStruct, 0, sizeof (PermFileStruct));
        HPermFile = OpenFile (FileName, &PermFileStruct, OF_CREATE
            | OF_WRITE);
        }

    // copy the data from the temporary file to the newly opened
    // permanent file:
```

```
    OffsetPrevTarget = -1;
    OffsetSource = OffFirstRec;
    while (OffsetSource != -1)
        {
        // read the next record (in sorted order) from the
        // temporary file:
        lseek (HTempFile, OffsetSource, SEEK_SET);
        read (HTempFile, &TempRecord, sizeof (TempRecord));
        read (HTempFile, &SizePhones, sizeof (SizePhones));
        Phones = new char [SizePhones];
        read (HTempFile, Phones, SizePhones);
        read (HTempFile, &SizeNotes, sizeof (SizeNotes));
        Notes = new char [SizeNotes];
        read (HTempFile, Notes, SizeNotes);

        // move offset to next record:
        OffsetSource = TempRecord.OffNextRec;

        // adjust the offsets and write the record to the
        // permanent file:
        TempRecord.OffPrevRec = OffsetPrevTarget;
        OffsetPrevTarget = tell (HPermFile);
        if (TempRecord.OffNextRec != -1)
            TempRecord.OffNextRec = OffsetPrevTarget +
                sizeof (TempRecord) + sizeof (int) + SizePhones +
                sizeof (int) + SizeNotes;
        write (HPermFile, &TempRecord, sizeof (TempRecord));
        write (HPermFile, &SizePhones, sizeof (SizePhones));
        write (HPermFile, Phones, SizePhones);
        write (HPermFile, &SizeNotes, sizeof (SizeNotes));
        write (HPermFile, Notes, SizeNotes);

        delete [] Phones;
        delete [] Notes;
        }
    _lclose (HPermFile);  // close the permanent file
    Modified = FALSE;
    }

void CDocument::ReadRecord (long Offset)
```

```
// reads and displays the record from the temporary file at
// offset 'Offset'
   {
   NewRecord = FALSE;
   OffCurrentRec = Offset;

   lseek (HTempFile, OffCurrentRec, SEEK_SET);
   read (HTempFile, &Record, sizeof (Record));

   int Size;
   read (HTempFile, &Size, sizeof (Size));
   Phones = new char [Size];
   read (HTempFile, Phones, Size);
   read (HTempFile, &Size, sizeof (Size));
   Notes = new char [Size];
   read (HTempFile, Notes, Size);

   ShowRecord ();   // copies the record data to the edit controls

   delete [] Phones;
   delete [] Notes;
   }

void CDocument::RecDelete ()
// deletes the record presently displayed by the program (the
// "current record")
   {
   if (NewRecord) // record is new
      {
      // if file contains at least 1 record, read it in;
      // otherwise, create another new record:
      if (OffFirstRec != -1)
         ReadRecord (OffFirstRec);
      else
         RecNew ();
      }
   else            // record already exists
      {
      // because record has been saved to the temporary file,
      // it must be unlinked from the list to delete it:
      if (Record.OffPrevRec != -1)
```

```
        {
        lseek (HTempFile, Record.OffPrevRec, SEEK_SET);
        write (HTempFile, &Record.OffNextRec,
            sizeof (Record.OffNextRec));
        }
    if (Record.OffNextRec != -1)
        {
        lseek (HTempFile, Record.OffNextRec + sizeof (long),
            SEEK_SET);
        write (HTempFile, &Record.OffPrevRec,
            sizeof (Record.OffPrevRec));
        }
    // adjust 'OffFirstRec' if deleting first record in list:
    if (OffCurrentRec == OffFirstRec)
        OffFirstRec = Record.OffNextRec;

    // if another record exists, read it in; otherwise, create
    // a new record:
    if (Record.OffPrevRec != -1)      // previous record exists
        ReadRecord (Record.OffPrevRec);
    else if (Record.OffNextRec != -1) // next record exists
        ReadRecord (Record.OffNextRec);
    else                              // no other records in
        RecNew ();                    // file; create new one
    Modified = TRUE;
    }
    }


BOOL CDocument::RecFind ()
// searches for the record that matches the search string(s)
// contained in the CFindDialog data members; returns TRUE if
// record found, and FALSE otherwise
    {
    long Offset;
    TagRecord TempRecord;

    // convert search strings to uppercase because the search
    // is to be case-insensitive and 'strstr' is case-sensitive:
    strupr (FindDialog.Name);
    strupr (FindDialog.AnyText);
```

```
// if the current record is a new, empty record, search
// beginning with the first record in the list and ending
// with the last record in the list; if the current record
// is an existing record stored in the temporary file, search
// beginning with the NEXT record in the list and ending with
// the current record (wrapping around the end of the list):
if (NewRecord)
   {
   if (OffFirstRec != -1)
      Offset = OffFirstRec;
   else
      return (FALSE);   // no records to search
   }
else
   Offset = Record.OffNextRec;
for (;;)  // go through linked list of records
   {
   if (Offset == -1)         // at end of list;
      Offset = OffFirstRec;  // wrap to beginning

   // read next record
   lseek (HTempFile, Offset, SEEK_SET);
   read (HTempFile, &TempRecord, sizeof (TempRecord));

   // if 'Name' search string is found in the 'Name' field,
   // proceed to look for the 'AnyText' search string
   // within any field; if both strings are found, read the
   // record and return TRUE; note that an empty search string
   // (second parameter to strstr) causes strstr to return
   // TRUE:
   if (strstr (strupr (TempRecord.Name), FindDialog.Name))
      {  // first quickly search fixed-length data:
      if (strstr (TempRecord.Name, FindDialog.AnyText) ||
         strstr (strupr (TempRecord.Company),
            FindDialog.AnyText) ||
         strstr (strupr (TempRecord.Address),
            FindDialog.AnyText) ||
         strstr (strupr (TempRecord.City),
            FindDialog.AnyText) ||
         strstr (strupr (TempRecord.State),
```

```
      FindDialog.AnyText) ||
    strstr (strupr (TempRecord.Zip),
      FindDialog.AnyText))
    {
    ReadRecord (Offset);
    return (TRUE);
    }

// AnyText not found in fixed-length data; therefore,
// proceed with slower search of variable-length data:
int Size;
read (HTempFile, &Size, sizeof (Size));
Phones = new char [Size];
read (HTempFile, Phones, Size);
read (HTempFile, &Size, sizeof (Size));
Notes = new char [Size];
read (HTempFile, Notes, Size);

int Result = strstr (strupr (Phones),
    FindDialog.AnyText) || strstr (strupr (Notes),
    FindDialog.AnyText);
delete [] Phones;
delete [] Notes;
if (Result)
    {
    ReadRecord (Offset);
    return (TRUE);
    }
}

if (NewRecord)  // with an empty new record, quit with the
    {           // last record in list
    if (TempRecord.OffNextRec == -1)
      return (FALSE);
    }
else            // with an existing record, quit when the
    {           // current record has been searched
    if (Offset == OffCurrentRec)
      return (FALSE);
    }
Offset = TempRecord.OffNextRec;
```

```
      }
   }

void CDocument::RecFirst ()
// reads first record in linked list (if any)
   {
   if (OffFirstRec != -1)
      ReadRecord (OffFirstRec);
   }

void CDocument::RecNew ()
// creates a new, empty record
   {
   NewRecord = TRUE;  // set flag indicating new record

   // blank all fields:
   Record.Name [0] = '\0';
   Record.Company [0] = '\0';
   Record.Address [0] = '\0';
   Record.City [0] = '\0';
   Record.State [0] = '\0';
   Record.Zip [0] = '\0';
   Phones = "";
   Notes = "";

   ShowRecord ();  // display blank fields in edit controls
   }

void CDocument::RecNext ()
// displays the next record in the linked list; if the current
// record is a blank, new record, displays the first record in
// the list
   {
   if (NewRecord)  // a blank, new record
      {
      if (OffFirstRec != -1)
         ReadRecord (OffFirstRec);
      }
   else            // an existing record
      {
      if (Record.OffNextRec != -1)
```

```
            ReadRecord (Record.OffNextRec);
        }
    }


void CDocument::RecPrevious ()
// displays the previous record in the linked list; if the
// current record is a blank, new record, displays the first
// record in the list
    {
    if (NewRecord)  // a blank, new record
        {
        if (OffFirstRec != -1)
            ReadRecord (OffFirstRec);
        }
    else            // an existing record
        {
        if (Record.OffPrevRec != -1)
            ReadRecord (Record.OffPrevRec);
        }
    }


void CDocument::RecSave ()
// saves the current record within the temporary file; record
// is inserted into its proper sorted position within the linked
// list maintained in the file
    {
    // if record to be saved is an existing record, unlink
    // the previous version of record from the list (thereby
    // deleting it):
    if (!NewRecord)
        {
        if (OffCurrentRec == OffFirstRec)     // adjust OffFirstRec
            OffFirstRec = Record.OffNextRec;  // if deleting first
                                              // record
        if (Record.OffPrevRec != -1)  // if previous record exists,
            {                         // adjust its 'next' offset
            lseek (HTempFile, Record.OffPrevRec, SEEK_SET);
            write (HTempFile, &Record.OffNextRec,
                sizeof (Record.OffNextRec));
            }
        if (Record.OffNextRec != -1)  // if next record exists,
```

```
                         {                              // adjust its 'previous' off.
            lseek (HTempFile, Record.OffNextRec + sizeof (long),
                SEEK_SET);
            write (HTempFile, &Record.OffPrevRec,
                sizeof (Record.OffPrevRec));
            }
        }
    // get file offset of record to be saved (at end):
    OffCurrentRec = lseek (HTempFile, 0L, SEEK_END);

    // find position of record to be saved in linked list:

    // get the name (or new name) of the record to be saved:
    char NewName [sizeof (Record.Name)];
    GetDlgItemText (MainDialog.mHDialog, IDC_NAME, NewName,
        sizeof (NewName));
    long Offset = OffFirstRec;
    for (;;)  // scan through linked list
        {
        // no records in file:
        if (Offset == -1)
            {
            // adjust current record:
            Record.OffPrevRec = -1;
            Record.OffNextRec = -1;
            break;
            }

        // read next record in list:
        lseek (HTempFile, Offset, SEEK_SET);
        read (HTempFile, &Record, sizeof (Record));

        // found record that immediately FOLLOWS the
        // new record:
        if (stricmp (NewName, Record.Name) < 0)
            {
            // adjust previous record, if any:
            if (Record.OffPrevRec != -1)
                {
                lseek (HTempFile, Record.OffPrevRec, SEEK_SET);
                write (HTempFile, &OffCurrentRec,
```

```
            sizeof (OffCurrentRec));
        }
    // adjust following record:
    lseek (HTempFile, Offset + sizeof (long), SEEK_SET);
    write (HTempFile, &OffCurrentRec,
        sizeof (OffCurrentRec));

    // adjust current record:
    Record.OffNextRec = Offset;
    break;
    }

  // record goes at END of list:
  if (Record.OffNextRec == -1)
      {
      // adjust previous record:
      lseek (HTempFile, Offset, SEEK_SET);
      write (HTempFile, &OffCurrentRec,
          sizeof (OffCurrentRec));

      // adjust current record:
      Record.OffPrevRec = Offset;
      break;
      }

  // record goes AFTER record at Offset, and more
  // records are in list; go on to next record:
  Offset = Record.OffNextRec;
  }

// adjust OffFirstRec if record is at beginning of list:
if (Record.OffPrevRec == -1)
   OffFirstRec = OffCurrentRec;

// get text from controls and write record to file:
GetDlgItemText (MainDialog.mHDialog, IDC_NAME, Record.Name,
   sizeof (Record.Name));
GetDlgItemText (MainDialog.mHDialog, IDC_COMPANY,
   Record.Company, sizeof (Record.Company));
GetDlgItemText (MainDialog.mHDialog, IDC_ADDRESS,
   Record.Address, sizeof (Record.Address));
```

```
GetDlgItemText (MainDialog.mHDialog, IDC_CITY, Record.City,
   sizeof (Record.City));
GetDlgItemText (MainDialog.mHDialog, IDC_STATE, Record.State,
   sizeof (Record.State));
GetDlgItemText (MainDialog.mHDialog, IDC_ZIP, Record.Zip,
   sizeof (Record.Zip));
lseek (HTempFile, OffCurrentRec, SEEK_SET);
write (HTempFile, &Record, sizeof (Record));

// get IDC_PHONES text and write to file:
int Size = (int)SendDlgItemMessage (MainDialog.mHDialog,
   IDC_PHONES, WM_GETTEXTLENGTH, O, OL) + 1;
write (HTempFile, &Size, sizeof (Size));
Phones = new char [Size];
GetDlgItemText (MainDialog.mHDialog, IDC_PHONES, Phones,
   Size);
write (HTempFile, Phones, Size);
delete [] Phones;

// get IDC_NOTES text and write to file:
Size = (int)SendDlgItemMessage (MainDialog.mHDialog,
   IDC_NOTES, WM_GETTEXTLENGTH, O, OL) + 1;
write (HTempFile, &Size, sizeof (Size));
Notes = new char [Size];
GetDlgItemText (MainDialog.mHDialog, IDC_NOTES, Notes, Size);
write (HTempFile, Notes, Size);
delete [] Notes;

NewRecord = FALSE;  // set flags
Modified = TRUE;
}

void CDocument::ShowRecord ()
// displays current values of record fields in the text controls
{
SetDlgItemText (MainDialog.mHDialog, IDC_NAME, Record.Name);
SetDlgItemText (MainDialog.mHDialog, IDC_COMPANY,
   Record.Company);
SetDlgItemText (MainDialog.mHDialog, IDC_ADDRESS,
   Record.Address);
SetDlgItemText (MainDialog.mHDialog, IDC_CITY, Record.City);
```

```
    SetDlgItemText (MainDialog.mHDialog, IDC_STATE, Record.State);
    SetDlgItemText (MainDialog.mHDialog, IDC_ZIP, Record.Zip);

    SetDlgItemText (MainDialog.mHDialog, IDC_PHONES, Phones);
    SetDlgItemText (MainDialog.mHDialog, IDC_NOTES, Notes);
    }

void CDocument::WrapUp ()
// to be called before program exits
    {
    // delete temporary file before program terminates:
    if (HTempFile != O)
       OpenFile (TempFileStruct.szPathName, &TempFileStruct,
                 OF_DELETE);
    }
```

Listing 7.5

```
;;;;;;;;;;;;;;;;;;;;;;;;;;;;;;;;;;;;;;;;;;;;;;;;;;;;;;;;;;;;;;;;;;;;;;
;                                                                    ;
; ADDRESS.DEF:  Module-definition file for the ADDRESS               ;
;               program.                                             ;
;                                                                    ;
;;;;;;;;;;;;;;;;;;;;;;;;;;;;;;;;;;;;;;;;;;;;;;;;;;;;;;;;;;;;;;;;;;;;;;


NAME ADDRESS

DESCRIPTION  'Address Manager'

EXETYPE WINDOWS

CODE PRELOAD MOVEABLE DISCARDABLE

DATA PRELOAD MOVEABLE MULTIPLE

HEAPSIZE 1024

STACKSIZE 10240
```

Listing 7.6

```
/////////////////////////////////////////////////////////////
//                                                           //
// RESOURCE.H:  Constant definitions for the ADDRESS program //
//              resources (generated by Microsoft App Studio). //
//                                                           //
/////////////////////////////////////////////////////////////

//{{NO_DEPENDENCIES}}
// App Studio generated include file.
// Used by ADDRESS.RC
//
#define IDC_HELP                        100
#define IDC_TEXT                        101
#define IDC_NAME                        102
#define IDC_COMPANY                     103
#define IDC_ADDRESS                     104
#define IDC_NOTES                       106
#define IDC_ANYTEXT                     115
#define IDC_CITY                        116
#define IDC_STATE                       117
#define IDC_ZIP                         118
#define IDC_PHONES                      119
#define IDM_ABOUT                       1000
#define IDM_HELPHELP                    1001
#define IDM_HELPSEARCH                  1002
#define IDM_HELPCONTENTS                1003
#define IDM_ONTOP                       1005
#define IDM_NEW                         1007
#define IDM_OPEN                        1008
#define IDM_SAVE                        1009
#define IDM_SAVEAS                      1010
#define IDM_EXIT                        1011
#define IDM_COPYADDRESS                 1012
#define IDM_COPYPHONE                   1013
#define IDM_RECNEW                      1014
#define IDM_DELETE                      1015
#define IDM_PREVIOUS                    1016
#define IDM_NEXT                        1017
#define IDM_FIND                        1018
```

```
#define IDM_DIAL                        1019
#define IDM_PRINTENVELOPE               1020
#define IDM_FIRST                       1022
#define IDM_FINDNEXT                    1023
#define IDM_DUMP                        1024
#define IDC_STATIC                      -1

// Next default values for new objects
//
#ifdef APSTUDIO_INVOKED
#ifndef APSTUDIO_READONLY_SYMBOLS

#define _APS_NEXT_RESOURCE_VALUE        103
#define _APS_NEXT_COMMAND_VALUE         1025
#define _APS_NEXT_CONTROL_VALUE         121
#define _APS_NEXT_SYMED_VALUE           101
#endif
#endif
```

Listing 7.7

```
/////////////////////////////////////////////////////////////////
//                                                             //
// ADDRESS.RC:  Resource-definition file for the ADDRESS        //
//              program (generated by Microsoft App Studio).    //
//                                                             //
/////////////////////////////////////////////////////////////////

//Microsoft App Studio generated resource script.
//
#include "resource.h"

#define APSTUDIO_READONLY_SYMBOLS
/////////////////////////////////////////////////////////////////
//
// Generated from the TEXTINCLUDE 2 resource.
//
#include "windows.h"


/////////////////////////////////////////////////////////////////
#undef APSTUDIO_READONLY_SYMBOLS
```

```
//////////////////////////////////////////////////////////////
//
// Accelerator
//

ADDRESSACCEL ACCELERATORS DISCARDABLE
BEGIN
    "D",               IDM_DUMP,               VIRTKEY,SHIFT,
                                               CONTROL, NOINVERT
    VK_F1,             IDM_HELPCONTENTS,       VIRTKEY,NOINVERT
    VK_F3,             IDM_FINDNEXT,           VIRTKEY,NOINVERT
END


//////////////////////////////////////////////////////////////
//
// Dialog
//

MAINDLG DIALOG DISCARDABLE  0, 0, 177, 185
STYLE WS_MINIMIZEBOX | WS_POPUP | WS_VISIBLE | WS_CAPTION |
    WS_SYSMENU
CAPTION "Address Manager"
MENU AddressMenu
FONT 8, "MS Sans Serif"
BEGIN
    LTEXT              "Name:",IDC_STATIC,6,37,21,9
    EDITTEXT           IDC_NAME,42,36,126,12,ES_AUTOHSCROLL
    LTEXT              "Company:",IDC_STATIC,6,56,30,9
    EDITTEXT           IDC_COMPANY,42,55,126,12,ES_AUTOHSCROLL
    LTEXT              "Street",IDC_STATIC,6,74,23,9
    LTEXT              "Address:",IDC_STATIC,6,83,29,9
    EDITTEXT           IDC_ADDRESS,42,73,126,21,ES_MULTILINE |
                       ES_AUTOHSCROLL | 0x1000
    LTEXT              "City:",IDC_STATIC,6,102,20,9
    EDITTEXT           IDC_CITY,42,100,85,12,ES_AUTOHSCROLL
    LTEXT              "State:",IDC_STATIC,131,102,19,9
    EDITTEXT           IDC_STATE,152,100,16,12,ES_AUTOHSCROLL
    LTEXT              "Zip:",IDC_STATIC,7,119,15,9
```

```
    EDITTEXT        IDC_ZIP,42,118,46,12,ES_AUTOHSCROLL
    CTEXT           "-- Phone Numbers --",IDC_STATIC,10,135,76,9
    EDITTEXT        IDC_PHONES,8,144,80,33,ES_MULTILINE |
                    ES_AUTOVSCROLL | ES_AUTOHSCROLL | 0x1000
    CTEXT           "-- Notes --",IDC_STATIC,96,117,70,7
    EDITTEXT        IDC_NOTES,94,126,74,51,ES_MULTILINE |
                    ES_AUTOVSCROLL | ES_AUTOHSCROLL | 0x1000
    PUSHBUTTON      "<< &Previous",IDM_PREVIOUS,0,0,45,15,
                    NOT WS_TABSTOP
    PUSHBUTTON      "&Next >>",IDM_NEXT,44,0,45,15,NOT WS_TABSTOP
    PUSHBUTTON      "F&ind...",IDM_FIND,88,0,45,15,NOT WS_TABSTOP
    PUSHBUTTON      "Find Ne&xt",IDM_FINDNEXT,132,0,45,15,
                    NOT WS_TABSTOP
    PUSHBUTTON      "Prin&t E/L",IDM_PRINTENVELOPE,0,14,45,15,
                    NOT WS_TABSTOP
    PUSHBUTTON      "&Dial",IDM_DIAL,44,14,45,15,NOT WS_TABSTOP
    PUSHBUTTON      "Copy &Addr",IDM_COPYADDRESS,88,14,45,15,
                    NOT WS_TABSTOP
    PUSHBUTTON      "Copy Te&l",IDM_COPYPHONE,132,14,45,15,
                    NOT WS_TABSTOP
END

DEMODLG DIALOG DISCARDABLE  12, 24, 105, 87
STYLE DS_MODALFRAME | WS_POPUP | WS_VISIBLE | WS_CAPTION |
    WS_SYSMENU
CAPTION "Dialog"
FONT 8, "MS Sans Serif"
BEGIN
    DEFPUSHBUTTON   "OK",IDOK,7,50,39,14
    PUSHBUTTON      "Cancel",IDCANCEL,7,67,39,14
    CTEXT           "Modal Dialog Box Demo",-1,0,10,105,12
    PUSHBUTTON      "&Help",IDC_HELP,59,67,39,14
    CTEXT           "Static",IDC_TEXT,0,26,105,11
END

ABOUTDLG DIALOG DISCARDABLE  12, 24, 116, 100
STYLE DS_MODALFRAME | WS_POPUP | WS_VISIBLE | WS_CAPTION |
    WS_SYSMENU
CAPTION "About"
FONT 8, "MS Sans Serif"
BEGIN
```

```
    CTEXT           "Windows Address Manager",-1,0,10,116,8
    CTEXT           "by Michael J. Young",-1,0,28,116,8
    ICON            "AddressIcon",-1,48,48,18,20
    DEFPUSHBUTTON   "OK",IDOK,36,80,40,14
END


FINDDLG DIALOG DISCARDABLE  12, 24, 167, 71
STYLE DS_MODALFRAME | WS_POPUP | WS_VISIBLE | WS_CAPTION |
    WS_SYSMENU
CAPTION "Find"
FONT 8, "MS Sans Serif"
BEGIN
    LTEXT           "&Name:",IDC_STATIC,6,7,23,9
    EDITTEXT        IDC_NAME,42,6,118,12,ES_AUTOHSCROLL
    LTEXT           "Any &Text:",IDC_STATIC,7,28,32,9
    EDITTEXT        IDC_ANYTEXT,42,27,118,12,ES_AUTOHSCROLL
    DEFPUSHBUTTON   "OK",IDOK,6,51,45,14,NOT WS_TABSTOP
    PUSHBUTTON      "Cancel",IDCANCEL,60,51,45,14,NOT WS_TABSTOP
    PUSHBUTTON      "&Help",IDC_HELP,115,51,45,14,NOT WS_TABSTOP
END


#ifdef APSTUDIO_INVOKED
/////////////////////////////////////////////////////////////////
//
// TEXTINCLUDE
//

1 TEXTINCLUDE DISCARDABLE
BEGIN
    "resource.h\0"
END

2 TEXTINCLUDE DISCARDABLE
BEGIN
    "#include ""windows.h""\r\n"
    "\0"
END

3 TEXTINCLUDE DISCARDABLE
```

```
BEGIN
    "\r\n"
    "\0"
END


////////////////////////////////////////////////////////////////
#endif    // APSTUDIO_INVOKED


////////////////////////////////////////////////////////////////
//
// Icon
//

ADDRESSICON            ICON    DISCARDABLE    "ADDRESS.ICO"

////////////////////////////////////////////////////////////////
//
// Menu
//

ADDRESSMENU MENU DISCARDABLE
BEGIN
    POPUP "&File"
    BEGIN
        MENUITEM "&New",                        IDM_NEW
        MENUITEM "&Open...",                    IDM_OPEN
        MENUITEM "&Save",                       IDM_SAVE
        MENUITEM "Save &As...",                 IDM_SAVEAS
        MENUITEM SEPARATOR
        MENUITEM "E&xit",                       IDM_EXIT
    END
    POPUP "&Edit"
    BEGIN
        MENUITEM "Copy &Address",               IDM_COPYADDRESS
        MENUITEM "Copy Te&lephone",             IDM_COPYPHONE
    END
    POPUP "&Record"
```

```
        BEGIN
            MENUITEM "&Previous",                 IDM_PREVIOUS
            MENUITEM "&Next",                     IDM_NEXT
            MENUITEM "&First",                    IDM_FIRST
            MENUITEM SEPARATOR
            MENUITEM "F&ind...",                  IDM_FIND
            MENUITEM "Find Ne&xt\tF3",            IDM_FINDNEXT
            MENUITEM SEPARATOR
            MENUITEM "N&ew",                      IDM_RECNEW
            MENUITEM SEPARATOR
            MENUITEM "De&lete",                   IDM_DELETE
            MENUITEM SEPARATOR
            MENUITEM "Prin&t Env/Label",          IDM_PRINTENVELOPE
            MENUITEM "&Dial",                     IDM_DIAL
        END
        POPUP "&Options"
        BEGIN
            MENUITEM "Always on &Top",            IDM_ONTOP
        END
        POPUP "&Help"
        BEGIN
            MENUITEM "&Contents...\tF1",          IDM_HELPCONTENTS
            MENUITEM "&Search for Help On...",    IDM_HELPSEARCH
            MENUITEM "&How to Use Help...",       IDM_HELPHELP
            MENUITEM SEPARATOR
            MENUITEM "&About...",                 IDM_ABOUT
        END
END


#ifndef APSTUDIO_INVOKED
/////////////////////////////////////////////////////////////////
//
// Generated from the TEXTINCLUDE 3 resource.
//


/////////////////////////////////////////////////////////////////
#endif    // not APSTUDIO_INVOKED
```

The Division of Labor

The primary duties in managing documents are divided between the CMain-Dialog class (defined in DIALOG.CPP of Listing 7.3) and the CDocument class (defined in DOCUMENT.CPP of Listing 7.4).

CMainDialog manages the user interface to the document. That is, it displays the main dialog box, which contains controls for displaying and editing the document data, and it responds to the commands from the menu, buttons, and keyboard, which allow the user to access and modify the document. This class also displays the dialog boxes that are required to carry out various commands, such as the Open... or Find... command. To perform the actual operations on the document files or on the records contained within a document, CMainDialog calls public member functions of the CDocument class.

CDocument manages the storage and retrieval of the document data. It provides one set of public member functions for opening, creating, and saving documents (FileOpen, FileNew, and FileSave), and another set of public member functions for creating, retrieving, and saving individual records contained in the open document (RecNew, RecFirst, RecSave, and others). In the following sections, you will see how the CMainDialog and CDocument classes work together to implement the program commands.

Managing Files

Under the Windows file I/O model, a program does not save the document data to the permanent disk file until the user explicitly issues a save command (Save or Save As... on the File menu). In the meantime, it must store all modified data in memory or in a temporary file. (This model is in contrast to many database programs written for MS-DOS, which automatically write new or modified records to the permanent disk file.)

To support this model, the Address Manager uses a temporary file to store the document data, as follows:

- When the program starts, or when the user chooses the New command on the File menu, the program creates a new temporary file. All records that the user enters are stored within this file.

- When the user chooses the Open... command on the File menu, the program opens the selected permanent file, creates a new temporary file, copies the contents of the permanent file to the temporary file, and then closes the permanent file. All additions, deletions, and changes are then made to the temporary file.

- When the user chooses the Save or Save As... command on the File menu, the program copies the current contents of the temporary file to the specified permanent file (overwriting the previous contents of the permanent file if it already exists).

Before the program exits, or before the program creates a new temporary file in response to the New or Open... command on the File menu, it deletes the current temporary file.

The following sections briefly discuss the implementation of each of the File menu commands.

The New Command

In response to the New command on the File menu, the IDM_NEW branch of the CMainDialog::OnCommand function (in DIALOG.CPP of Listing 7.3) first calls CDocument::FileNew to create a new, empty document, and then it calls CDocument::RecNew to create and display a new record so that the user can immediately begin entering data into the first record to be added to the document (both of these functions are defined in DOCUMENT.CPP of Listing 7.4; RecNew will be discussed later in the chapter).

To construct a unique file name for the temporary file, FileNew calls the C++ run-time library function mktemp. To create and open the temporary file, it calls the Windows API function OpenFile:

```
HTempFile = OpenFile
   (TempFileName,
   &TempFileStruct,
   OF_CREATE | OF_READWRITE);
```

OpenFile writes the full path name of the file to the szPathName field of the OFSTRUCT structure it is passed as the second parameter (TempFileStruct). As a result, the program can later find and delete the file even if the current directory has changed. In fact, to delete the file, the program can simply call OpenFile again, passing it the full path name, the original OFStruct that was passed when opening the file, and the OF_DELETE flag, as follows:

```
OpenFile (TempFileStruct.szPathName, &TempFileStruct,
        OF_DELETE);
```

Because the program opens only one document at a time, the CDocument code deletes the existing temporary file before opening a new one (as you will see later, the user is first given an opportunity to save any changes). Also, the CDocument::WrapUp function deletes the temporary file immediately before the program exits (CDocument::WrapUp is called by the CMainDialog::WrapUp function, which receives control whenever the program is about to be terminated).

Note that if the user does not specify a valid file name on the ADDRESS command line, the CMainDialog::OnInitDialog function calls FileNew and RecNew to automatically create a new document when the program first starts running.

The Open... Command

When the user chooses the Open... command on the File menu, the IDM_OPEN branch of CMainDialog::OnCommand begins by displaying the Open common dialog box, shown in Figure 7.7, which allows the user to

FIGURE 7.7

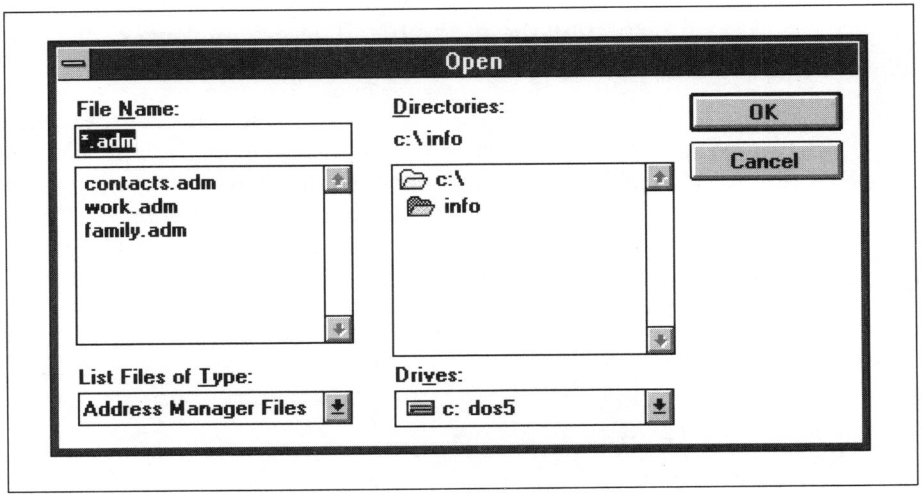

The Open dialog box displayed by the Address Manager program

select the name and directory of the file to be opened. The Open dialog box is displayed by filling in the fields of an OPENFILENAME structure and then passing the address of this structure to the Windows API function GetOpenFileName. The values assigned to the structure affect both the behavior of the dialog box and the initial information that it displays. The GetOpenFileName function handles all of the details of displaying and managing the dialog box.

When the user closes the Open dialog box, control returns from the call to GetOpenFileName, and the fields of the OPENFILENAME structure contain the values that the user selected in the dialog box; most importantly, the lpstrFile field points to the full path name of the selected file and the lpstrFileTitle field points to the file title (that is, the simple file name without the drive or directory specification). OnCommand displays the file title in the window's title bar, and it passes the full path name to the CDocument::FileOpen function, which opens the file.

FileOpen calls the Windows API function OpenFile to open the file for reading:

```
HFILE HPermFile = OpenFile
    (FileName,
    &PermFileStruct,
    OF_READ);
```

OpenFile assigns information on the opened file to the OFSTRUCT structure that is passed as the third parameter (PermFileStruct), including the full path name of the file. The program uses this information to reopen the file when the user later saves the document.

Next, FileOpen deletes the previous temporary file (if any) and creates a new temporary file. It then copies the entire contents of the permanent file to the temporary file and closes the permanent file. Finally, if the file contains at least one record, it calls CDocument::ReadRecord to read and display that record, or, if the file is empty, it calls CDocument::RecNew to create a new, blank record.

Note that if the user specifies a valid file name on the ADDRESS command line, the CMainDialog::OnInitDialog function calls FileOpen to open the document when the program first starts running.

The Save and Save As... Commands

The IDM_SAVE branch of CMainDialog::OnCommand (which processes the Save command) and the IDM_SAVEAS branch (which processes the Save As... command) both call the CDocument::FileSave function to save the current contents of the document to a permanent disk file. The IDM_SAVE routine passes 0 to FileSave to cause this function to save the document under the *same* file name that was used by the previous call to FileSave. The IDM_SAVEAS routine first displays the Save As common dialog box (by calling the GetSaveFileName Windows API function), and then passes the path name of the file that the user selected to FileSave to cause this function to save the file under the selected name.

If FileSave receives a 0 parameter, it opens the permanent disk file using the information that was stored in the OFSTRUCT structure, PermFileStruct, by the previous call to OpenFile (hence, the first parameter, which normally specifies the file name, is set to 0):

```
HPermFile = OpenFile (0, &PermFileStruct, OF_CREATE |
   OF_REOPEN | OF_WRITE);
```

The OF_REOPEN flag causes OpenFile to use the OFSTRUCT information to reopen the file, and the OF_CREATE parameter causes it to truncate the file to 0 length (thus, the new version of the document entirely replaces the previous version).

If, however, FileSave receives a nonzero parameter, it fills the OFSTRUCT structure with zeros and passes the specified file name to OpenFile:

```
memset (&PermFileStruct, 0, sizeof (PermFileStruct));
HPermFile = OpenFile (FileName, &PermFileStruct, OF_CREATE
   | OF_WRITE);
```

FileSave then copies each of the active records (that is, those that have not been deleted), in sorted order, to the permanent file. To understand how the program accesses each of the active records in sorted order, you must know the file structure, which is explained later in the chapter.

Managing Records

The Address Manager file structure was designed to allow the program to store variable-length records and to provide rapid sequential access to the records in sorted order. The format of each record in the file is shown in Figure 7.8. Notice that the first portion of the record stores fixed-length data (this data is fixed in length because the number of characters that the user can enter into the corresponding edit controls is limited). When the CDocument code reads this portion of a record, it reads the fixed data directly into a structure of the following type:

```
struct TagRecord
   {
   long OffNextRec;
   long OffPrevRec;
   char Name [41];
   char Company [41];
   char Address [81];
   char City [27];
   char State [3];
   char Zip [11];
   };
```

FIGURE 7.8

The format of an individual record stored in an Address Manager file

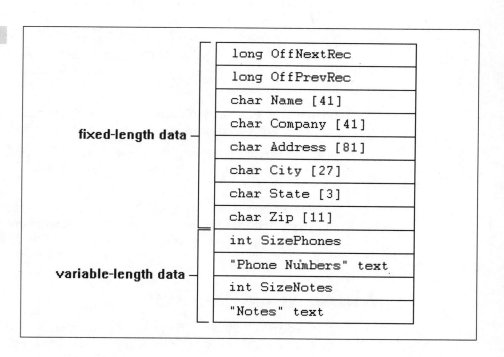

Following the fixed-length data, the record stores the text that the user has entered into the Phone Numbers and Notes text boxes (this data is variable in length because the number of characters that the user can enter into these text boxes is not limited). Both the Phone Numbers text and the Notes text are preceded by an integer value that gives the size of the following text in bytes.

The file consists of a simple sequence of these records; there is no header at the beginning of the file. Notice that each record begins with the offset (that is, the number of bytes from the beginning of the file) of the *next* record in sorted order, followed by the offset of the *previous* record; if there is no next record or no previous record, the offset field is set to –1. Consequently, the records form a doubly-linked list that allows the program to access the records sequentially; that is, the program can rapidly move forward or backward through the records in sorted order. Figure 7.9 illustrates a file with three records. Note that the offset of the *first* record in sorted order is stored in the CDocument data member OffFirstRec, so that the program can quickly locate the beginning of the list.

Table 7.1 lists the public member functions provided by the CDocument class for creating, saving, or retrieving records from the document. The CMainDialog member functions call these functions to implement various program commands.

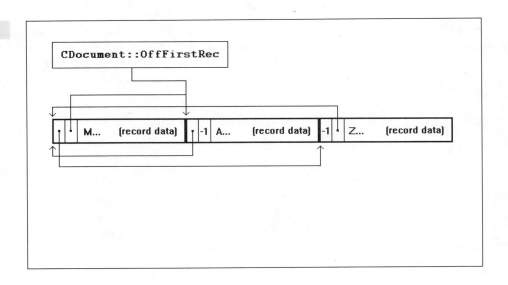

TABLE 7.1: The Public Member Functions Provided by the `CDocument` Class for Managing Records

MEMBER FUNCTION	PURPOSE
RecDelete	Deletes the current record
RecFind	Searches for and displays the next record that matches the current search text (which is stored by the `CFindDialog` class)
RecFirst	Displays the first record in the sorted order
RecNew	Clears the edit controls so that the user can enter a new record
RecNext	Displays the record that *follows* the current record in the sorted order
RecPrevious	Displays the record that precedes the current record in the sorted order
RecSave	Saves the current contents of the edit controls in a record

Adding and Deleting Records

The `RecNew` function clears the edit controls in the main dialog box so that the user can enter data for a new record. It also sets the `CDocument::NewRecord` flag to `TRUE`; this setting indicates that the record that is currently displaying has *not* already been saved in the temporary file.

The `RecSave` function saves the current contents of the edit controls within a record in the temporary file. To do this, it performs the following steps:

- If the record has already been saved in the temporary file (that is, `NewRecord` is `FALSE`), it first deletes the old version of the record. It does this by adjusting the offsets stored within the previous record and the next record, so that the old record is removed from the linked list (actually, the record data is left in place, but the record is effectively deleted because it is not pointed to by any of the records in the linked list).

- It writes the record data (that is, the current contents of the edit controls) at the *end* of the temporary file (it does not write the data for an existing record over the old version of the record because the new version of the record may be *longer*).

- It searches through the linked list for the correct position of the record, and inserts the record into the list at this position by changing the offsets saved in the previous and next records. The new version of an existing record may have a different position than the old version because the user can change the sort key (that is, the Name field).

- It sets the `NewRecord` flag to `FALSE`, because the record has now been saved in the file.

- It assigns the record's offset to the `CDocument::OffCurrentRec` data member. This data member stores the file offset of the *current record* (that is, the record currently displayed in the dialog box).

To delete the current record, the `RecDelete` function removes the record from the linked list by adjusting the offsets stored by the next record and the previous record. The data is left in place, but is no longer part of the linked list used to access the records, and therefore is effectively deleted.

As you have probably observed, the method for deleting and adding records makes no effort to reclaim file space and therefore creates a file that is larger than necessary. To use file space more efficiently, the program could add each deleted record to a linked list of free blocks. When writing a record, the program could search this list for the first block of sufficient size (or the smallest block of sufficient size) and write the record at that position. However, because the file is temporary and is used only during the current program session, the Address Manager employs the simpler method of merely abandoning deleted records and always writing records to the end of the file. When the document is saved in response to the Save or Save As... command, the `FileSave` function writes only the active records (that is, the ones that have not been deleted) to the permanent file, creating a minimum-sized file.

Retrieving Records

The CMainDialog class calls the RecFirst, RecNext, RecPrevious, and RecFind functions to retrieve specific records from the temporary file. Each of these functions calls the private member function ReadRecord to read and display a record at the offset specified by the parameter that it is passed. RecFirst passes ReadRecord the offset stored in CDocument::OffFirstRec to retrieve the first record in the sorted order. RecNext passes the next-record offset stored in the current record to read the next record, and RecPrevious passes the previous-record offset stored in the current record to read the previous record.

RecFind reads through the records in the linked list, starting with the record immediately following the current record, in its search for a record that matches the current search text (if the current record is a new, blank record, it starts searching with the first record in the list). It stops searching when it finds a match or when it has searched all of the records; if it reaches the end of the linked list before searching all records, it resumes searching with the first record. When it finds a match, RecFind reads and displays the record by calling ReadRecord; the found record then becomes the current record.

The search text is stored in the Name and AnyText data members of the FindDialog object, which is a global instance of the CFindDialog class. CFindDialog is derived from the CMDialog class (of the General Windows Classes) so that—in addition to being used to store the search text—it can be used to display a modal dialog box that allows the user to enter the search text. When the user chooses the Find... command, the CMainDialog::OnCommand function (the IDM_FIND branch) first calls CFindDialog::Create to display the Find modal dialog box, which allows the user to enter or edit the search text, and then it calls RecFind. If the user chooses the Find Next command, OnCommand (the IDM_FINDNEXT branch) simply calls RecFind to perform the search, using the current search text (if, however, no search text has been entered, it displays the Find dialog box before calling RecFind). Because RecFind always begins searching with the record immediately *following* the current record, a subsequent call to RecFind in response to the Find Next command searches for the *next* matching record in the linked list; the user can thus repeatedly issue the Find Next command to find *all* matching records in the file, viewing these records in sorted order.

Notice that `RecFind` uses the C++ run-time library function `strstr` to determine whether the search text is contained within a field of a given record. Because `strstr` is case-sensitive, all text is converted to uppercase before calling `strstr` so that the search is *not* case-sensitive.

Notice, also, that `RecFind` considers a record to match only if *both* search strings (`FindDialog.Name` and `FindDialog.AnyText`) are found; that is, the record is considered to match only if both of the following conditions are true:

- The `FindDialog.Name` search string is found within the Name field, or `FindDialog.Name` is empty (an empty search string causes `strstr` to report that the string is found).

- The `FindDialog.AnyText` search string is found within any field (or `FindDialog.Name` is empty; note that the `CFindDialog` code does not allow *both* search strings to be empty).

`RecFind` begins by searching for the `Name` string—which is the faster search—and proceeds to search for the `AnyText` string only if the `Name` string is found. Likewise, when searching for the `AnyText` string, it first quickly searches the fixed-length data and proceeds with the lengthier search of the variable-length data only if the string is not found in the fixed-length data.

Exchanging Data

The Address Manager provides four commands that exchange data or communicate with other programs: Copy Address, Copy Telephone, Print Env/Label, and Dial.

When the user chooses the Copy Address or Copy Telephone command, the branch of the `CMainDialog::OnCommand` function that processes the `IDM_COPYADDRESS` and `IDM_COPYPHONE` messages copies the appropriate text from the edit controls to the Windows Clipboard. The following is a synopsis of the technique that it uses:

1. If the contents of one or more edit controls has changed, the routine calls `CDocument::RecSave`. The reason for this call is that in the process of saving the record, `RecSave` copies the current

contents of the edit controls to the `CDocument::Record` structure; `OnCommand` can then access the data directly from this structure.

2. The routine calls the Windows API function `GlobalAlloc` to allocate a block of memory large enough to hold the address or phone number.

3. It calls `GlobalLock` to obtain a pointer to the global memory block.

4. It uses the pointer to copy the address or phone number to the global memory block.

5. It calls `GlobalUnlock` to unlock the global memory block so that it can be supplied to the Clipboard.

6. It calls `OpenClipboard` to open the Clipboard.

7. It calls `EmptyClipboard` to remove the current Clipboard contents.

8. It calls `SetClipboardData` to supply the handle of the global memory block to the Clipboard, so that the data will be available to other programs.

9. It calls `CloseClipboard` to close the Clipboard.

N O T E

See the section "The Compact Menu Commands" in Chapter 3 for general information on the Clipboard, and see the section "Printing the Text" in Chapter 8 for a description of the procedure for obtaining text *from* the Clipboard.

In response to the Print Env/Label command, the `IDM_PRINTENVELOPE` branch of `OnCommand` calls the `IDM_COPYADDRESS` branch of `OnCommand` to copy the current address into the Clipboard. It calls the Windows API function `WinExec` to run the Envelope and Label Printer program (ENVELOPE, presented in Chapter 8) if this program is not already running, and it obtains a handle to ENVELOPE's main window by calling the API function `FindWindow`. Once it has this handle, it can manipulate the ENVELOPE program's controls and send messages to its window. Specifically, it checks the From Clipboard button (so that ENVELOPE obtains the address from the Clipboard), and it sends it a `WM_COMMAND` message with the same identifier that is sent when the user clicks the Print button within the ENVELOPE window, causing ENVELOPE to extract the address from the Clipboard and print it.

When the user chooses the Dial command, the IDM_DIAL branch of On-Command calls the IDM_COPYPHONE branch to copy the selected phone number from the Phone Numbers edit control to the Clipboard, and then causes the Phone Dialer program (DIAL, presented in Chapter 9) to extract this number from the Clipboard and dial it. The method it uses is exactly analogous to the method used by the IDM_PRINTENVELOPE routine to print an envelope.

Preventing Data Loss

The Address Manager is the first program presented in the book that stores data entered by the user. This section briefly discusses the code that prevents the user's data from being lost as commands are carried out or the program is terminated.

The program uses two flags to indicate the presence of modified data that needs to be preserved: CMainDialog::Modified and CDocument::Modified.

CMainDialog::Modified is TRUE when one or more edit controls contain new data. The CMainDialog code sets this flag to TRUE in response to the EN_CHANGE message, which an edit control sends to the main dialog box whenever its contents change, and it resets the flag to FALSE whenever the current record has been saved in the temporary file (by calling RecSave) or the current record has been deleted. CMainDialog::Modified is tested whenever the edit controls are about to be overwritten (for example, when reading the next record), and whenever the edit controls must be saved prior to an operation such as saving the file; if CMainDialog::Modified is TRUE, the program calls RecSave to save the record before proceeding with the operation.

CDocument::Modified is TRUE when the temporary file contains modified data. It is set to TRUE whenever the temporary file is changed in the CDocument member functions RecDelete or RecSave. It is reset to FALSE whenever a file is first opened (in FileNew or FileOpen), and whenever the temporary file is saved in a permanent file (in FileSave). CMainDocument tests CDocument::Modified before opening a new file (in response to the New or Open... command), and when the program is about to be terminated. If CDocument::Modified is TRUE, the program displays a message and gives the user an opportunity to save the document or cancel the operation.

Enhancing the Address Manager

The following is a list of ways you might enhance the Address Manager program:

- *You could enhance the Find command in several ways.* First, you could allow the user to specify search strings corresponding to specific record fields in addition to the Name field. For example, you might add a search string for the Zip code field, so that the user could search for all addresses that have a specific zip code. Similarly, you might add search strings for the City field, the State field, and other fields. Second, you could provide an option that would make the search case-sensitive. Third, you could add an option that would cause the program to combine the search strings, using OR logic; that is, to cause the Find command to search for all records that match the "Name" search string *or* that match the "Any Text" search string (currently, the program combines search strings, using AND logic).

- *Add a command to the Record menu for duplicating the current record,* so that the user could create a similar record without having to retype all of the text.

- *Add an "Attention" field to the record,* which would be printed at the end of the address.

- *Implement a command that would generate a "merge file."* That is, it would write all of the records to a text file in a format that could be used by a word processor print merge command (for printing multiple, customized copies of a document such as a letter).

- *Provide a command that would print envelopes or labels for an entire set of records* (rather than just a single envelope or label for the current record). The set of records could be based upon the current search text; for example, the user could print envelopes for all records in a specific city or all records having a specific zip code. To implement this command, you might also need to modify the Envelope and Label Printer presented in Chapter 8.

- *Add a special signature to the beginning of each permanent data file saved by the program,* so that the program could identify valid files and not attempt to read a file that it did not save (currently, the program behavior is unpredictable if the user attempts to open an invalid file).

- *Add Cut, Copy, and Paste commands to the Edit menu.* The user could choose these commands while working in an edit control as an alternative to using the keyboard commands for these operations. To carry out the menu command, you would have to determine which edit control has the focus (using the API function GetFocus) and then send the WM_CUT, WM_COPY, or WM_PASTE command to this control.

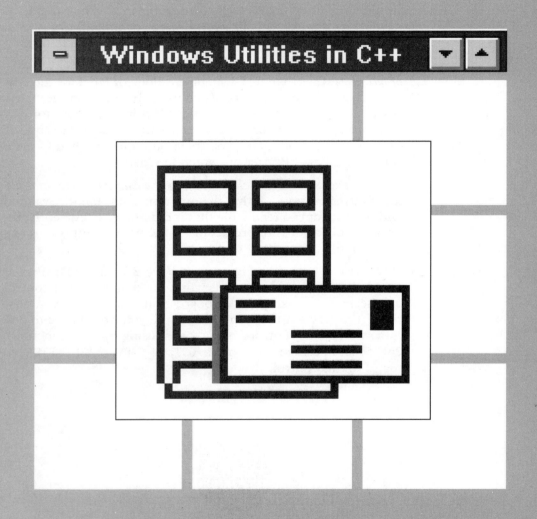

CHAPTER

8

Envelope and Label Printer

THIS chapter presents the Envelope and Label Printer, which is a utility that quickly addresses envelopes and prints mailing labels. As you saw in Chapter 7, the Address Manager program automatically runs the Envelope and Label Printer to print the current address when you issue the print command. You can also use the Envelope and Label Printer by itself, or in conjunction with other programs.

The source code for the Envelope and Label Printer illustrates a variety of programming techniques, including choosing and storing font information, obtaining text from the Clipboard, managing print jobs, and printing text.

How to Use the Envelope and Label Printer

When you first run the Envelope and Label Printer, the program window appears as shown in Figure 8.1. The following sections explain how to use this program. You will learn how to print an envelope or label, how to format an envelope, how to format a label, and how to set the Always on Top option.

FIGURE 8.1

The Envelope and
Label Printer window

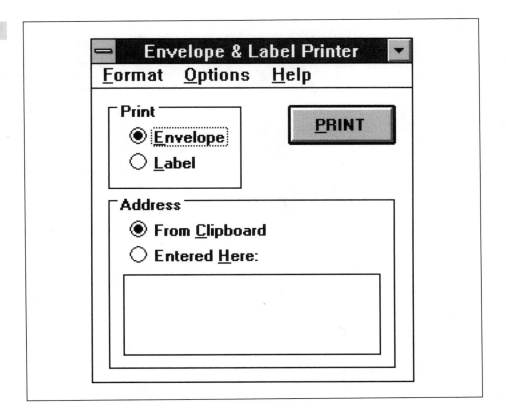

Printing

To print an envelope or label, perform the following three steps:

1. In the Print area, choose the Envelope option to print an envelope, or the Label option to print a label.

2. In the Address area, choose the From Clipboard option if the address is contained in the Clipboard, or the Entered Here: option if you want to manually enter the address. If you choose the Entered Here: option, type or paste the address into the adjoining text box.

3. Issue the print command by clicking the PRINT button or using one of the other methods discussed below.

Once you have specified the desired settings (steps 1 and 2), you can quickly print additional envelopes or labels using these same settings by simply issuing the print command (that is, by performing step 3 only). The Envelope and Label Printer saves all settings, as well as the text entered into the Entered Here: text box, even after you quit the program.

NOTE When typing text into the Entered Here: text box, you can perform cut, copy, and paste operations, using the standard Windows keystrokes for these commands.

Choosing the From Clipboard option allows you to easily print an envelope or label using text from another Windows or MS-DOS program. If, for example, you are writing a letter in a Windows word processor, you could print an envelope or label as follows: Select the address within the document, issue the Copy command on the word processor's Edit menu, and then click the PRINT button in the Envelope and Label Printer. As you will see shortly, you can also *automatically* transfer an address from the Address Manager program to the Envelope and Label Printer.

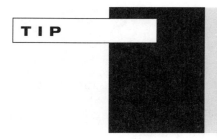

TIP If the text for the address is in the Clipboard and you want to view or edit the text before printing it, choose the Entered Here: option rather than the From Clipboard option and paste the text into the Entered Here: text box, using the standard Ctrl+V or Shift+Insert keystroke.

When you issue the print command, the program immediately prints a single envelope or label, and then ejects the envelope, label, or label sheet from the printer (that is, it sends a form-feed command to the printer).

If you are printing labels on sheets of labels (such as laser printer labels), you can print a *single* label and remove it from the sheet. You can later reinsert the *same* sheet to print another of the labels. The program will automatically advance from label to label (that is, it will first print the label in the upper-left corner of the sheet, and then proceed through the remaining labels on the sheet row-by-row). Later, you will see how to force the program to print a specific label on the sheet.

You can issue the print command (that is, perform step 3 in the list above), using any of the following three methods:

- Click the PRINT button, or press the Alt+P keystroke.
- Choose the Print command on the system menu.
- In the Address Manager utility (presented in Chapter 7), choose the Print Env/Label command on the Record menu, or click the Print E/L button.

If you use the third method, the Address Manager program performs the following steps:

1. It copies the currently displayed address to the Clipboard.

2. It runs the Envelope and Label Printer program, if it is not already running.

3. It automatically chooses the From Clipboard option.

4. It automatically issues the print command to initiate printing. The type of object printed (that is, an envelope or label) as well as the format of the object depend upon the current settings you have made in the Envelope and Label Printer program.

The following sections explain how to specify the way that the Envelope and Label Printer prints envelopes or labels.

Formatting Envelopes

Before you print your first envelope, you should choose the Envelope... command on the Format menu to specify the way that envelopes are to be printed. The program will display the Format Envelope dialog box; the initial appearance of this dialog box is shown in Figure 8.2.

FIGURE 8.2

The Format Envelope dialog box before you specify settings

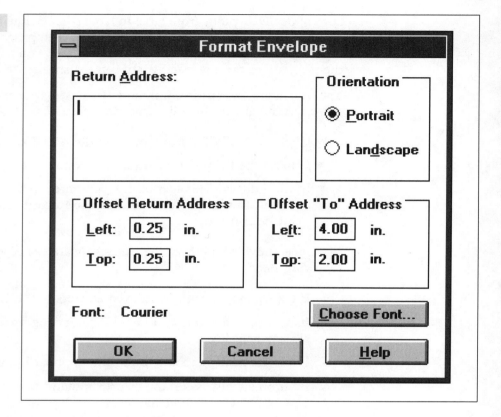

First, enter into the Return Address: box the *return address* (if any) that you want to appear on the envelopes you print. Then, choose the desired printing orientation. If you choose the Portrait option, the lines of text will be printed across the page (that is, at right angles to the direction of feed); if you choose the Landscape option, lines of text will be printed in the vertical direction on the page (that is, parallel to the direction of feed). The difference is illustrated in Figure 8.3. If, for example, you are printing single envelopes on an HP LaserJet II printer, you need to choose the Landscape orientation.

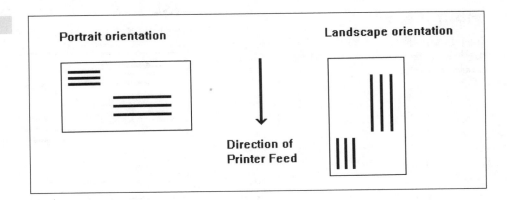

NOTE The orientation you select will be used only while an envelope is being printed. After the envelope is printed, printing will revert to the default orientation-setting made through the Windows Control Panel, so that printed output from other programs will not be affected.

Next, specify the *position* where the return address is to be printed by entering the appropriate measurements into the text boxes in the Offset Return Address area. Enter the distance from the left edge of the envelope to the beginning of the address into the Left: text box, and enter the distance from the top of the envelope to the beginning of the address into the Top: box. All measurements are in inches. In the same way, specify the position where the addressee's address should be printed by entering measurements into the text boxes in the Offset "To" Address area. The offset values are illustrated in Figure 8.4.

It may require some trial and error to arrive at the offset values that print the addresses at the desired positions on the envelope. Because of the way that a particular type of envelope is positioned in the printer, the required offset values might not equal the actual distances between the text and the edges of the envelope itself (as is perhaps implied by Figure 8.4). That is, you may have to adjust the offset values according to the way that the envelopes you are using are aligned in your printer. For example, Figure 8.5

FIGURE 8.4

The address offsets
specified in the Format
Envelope dialog box

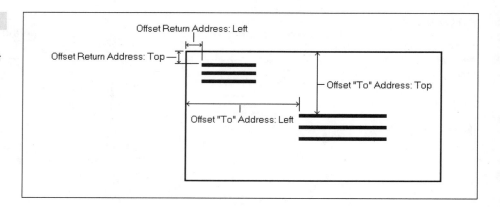

FIGURE 8.4

The address offsets
specified in the Format
Envelope dialog box

shows an appropriate set of offsets for hand-feeding a #10 envelope on an HP LaserJet II printer (when the paper size is set to $8^1/_2'' \times 11''$ through the Windows Control Panel).

TIP

Most Windows printer drivers allow you to specify the paper size by opening the printer setup dialog box through the Windows Control Panel; some drivers even allow you to choose standard envelope sizes from a list. Accordingly, before printing an envelope, you *could* set the paper size to the size of the envelope and then, after printing the envelope, restore the original paper size. However, it is *much easier* to simply leave the paper size set to the most common size that you use (for most users, $8^1/_2'' \times 11''$), and set the offsets in the Format Envelope dialog box of the Envelope and Label program so that the addresses are printed at the desired positions. You can then simply print envelopes without adjusting the page size.

FIGURE 8.5

Appropriate offsets for
hand-feeding #10
envelopes on an HP
LaserJet II printer (with
the paper size set to
8½″ × 11″ in the
Windows Control
Panel)

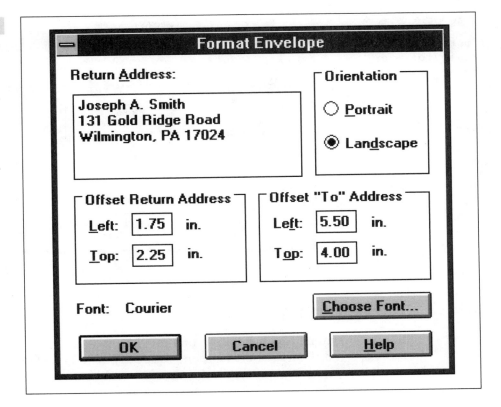

Finally, you can choose the *font* that will be used to print envelopes. The typeface name of the current font is displayed near the bottom of the Format Envelope dialog box. Initially, the font is set to the standard font for your default Windows printer. To choose another font, click the Choose Font... button and the program will display the Font dialog box, which is shown in Figure 8.6. You can use this dialog box to choose the desired font name, style, and size and also to see a sample of the actual font. Note that the Font dialog box lists only the fonts that are available for the current default Windows printer; therefore, the names and styles that you see depend upon your printer and the fonts that you have installed.

All settings that you make in the Format Envelope dialog box are saved, even after you quit the program, and will be used for printing all subsequent envelopes. Therefore, you need reopen the dialog box only if you must change one or more settings.

FIGURE 8.6

The Font dialog box for choosing a printer font

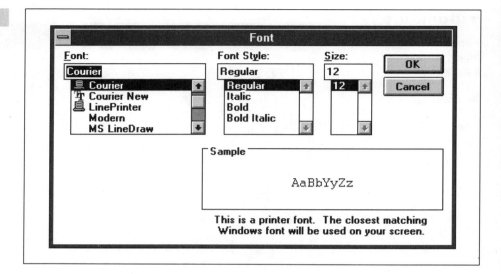

Formatting Labels

Before you print your first label, you should choose the Label... command on the Format menu to specify the way that labels are to be printed. The program will display the Format Label dialog box; the initial appearance of this dialog box is shown in Figure 8.7.

The directions given here assume that you are printing labels on cut sheets, such as laser printer labels. Label sheets typically measure $8\frac{1}{2}'' \times 11''$ and contain varying numbers of labels. The next section provides special instructions for printing continuous-form labels (which are usually printed on dot-matrix or daisy-wheel printers).

First, specify the starting position of the address to be printed on the first label (that is, the label in the upper-left corner of a sheet) by entering values into the Offset of First Label area. Enter the offset of the address from the left edge of the page into the Left: text box, and enter the offset of the address from the top of the page into the Top: text box. It may take some

FIGURE 8.7

The Format Label dialog box before you specify settings

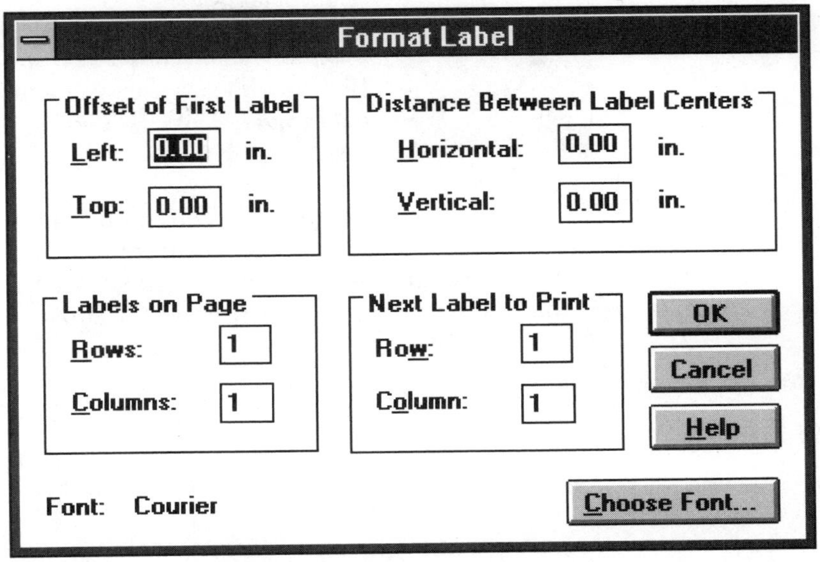

trial and error to place the address at the desired position; the necessary offset values depend upon the distances of the label from the edges of a sheet, the desired indents of the text from the edges of a label, and the way a sheet aligns in the printer.

Next, specify the spacing of the labels on a sheet by entering values into the Distance Between Label Centers area. Enter the horizontal distance between the centers of adjoining labels into the Horizontal: text box, and the vertical distance between centers of adjoining labels into the Vertical: text box. Of course, the easiest way to determine the distance between centers is to measure the distance between corresponding edges; for example, to obtain the horizontal distance between centers, measure the distance between the left edge of one label and the left edge of the adjoining label. Although you can directly measure these values, you may need to fine-tune them to avoid misalignment of labels near the end of the page (small errors will accumulate as the program moves from label to label down the sheet).

NOTE If there is only one column of labels, the value entered into the Horizontal: text box is ignored. Likewise, if there is only one row of labels, the value entered into the Vertical: text box is ignored.

In the Labels on Page area, you should now specify the arrangement of the labels on a sheet. Enter the number of rows of labels on a sheet into the Rows: text box, and the number of columns of labels on a sheet into the Columns: text box. Figure 8.8 illustrates the measurements that have been discussed so far.

FIGURE 8.8

The measurements entered into the Format Label dialog box

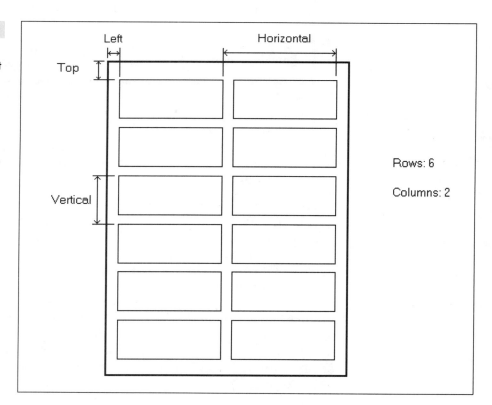

You can now specify the *next* label that is to be printed by entering values into the Next Label to Print area. Enter the row of the label into the Row: text box, and the column of the label into the Column: text box. Initially, these text boxes contain the values 1 and 1, so that the program will first print the label in the upper-left corner of the sheet. Each time you print a label, the program *automatically* adjusts these values to the position of the next label, moving row-by-row, so that the program prints the labels on the sheet in sequence. Before you print a label, however, you can open the Format Label dialog box and enter values into these text boxes to print a *specific* label on the sheet.

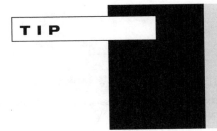

T I P

Most printers allow you to print a single label on a sheet, peel the label off, and then reinsert the sheet into the printer to print another label. If your printer cannot do this, you will have to print *all* the labels that you want to use on a sheet before peeling labels off.

Finally, you can specify the font that is used to print labels by clicking the Choose Font... button. See the discussion on choosing a font in the previous section. Note that the font you choose for printing labels does *not* affect the font selected for printing envelopes (that is, the program allows you to choose two separate fonts, one for envelopes and one for labels).

Figure 8.9 shows a completed Format Label dialog box with settings appropriate for printing Avery laser printer labels that measure $1\frac{1}{3}'' \times 4''$.

All settings that you make in the Format Label dialog box are saved, even after you quit the program, and will be used for printing all subsequent labels. Therefore, you need reopen the dialog box only if you must change one or more settings.

FIGURE 8.9

Settings for printing
Avery $1\frac{1}{3}'' \times 4''$ laser
printer labels

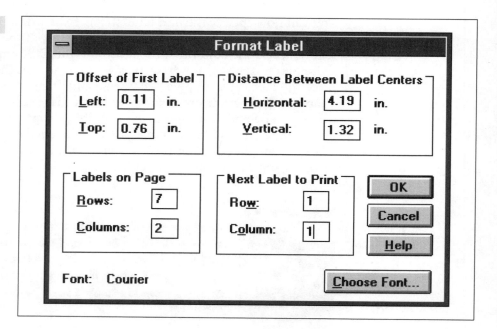

Format Label

Offset of First Label

Left: `0.11` in.

Top: `0.76` in.

Distance Between Label Centers

Horizontal: `4.19` in.

Vertical: `1.32` in.

Labels on Page

Rows: `7`

Columns: `2`

Next Label to Print

Row: `1`

Column: `1`

OK

Cancel

Help

Font: Courier

Choose Font...

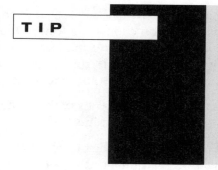

TIP

You can restore *all* program settings (settings made in the main dialog box, in the Format Envelope dialog box, and in the Format Label dialog box) to their default values by renaming the files ENVELOPE.INI and ENVELOPE.LFN (which stores the font descriptions). You will find these files in your Windows directory after the first time you run the program.

Printing Continuous-Form Labels

You can also use the Envelope and Label Printer to print labels on continuous pin-feed forms, which are normally printed on dot-matrix or daisy-wheel printers. Use the general methods for setting the label format that were described in the previous section; however, observe the following special guidelines:

- Enter 1 into the Rows: text box.
- You do *not* need to enter a value into the Vertical: text box.
- Enter the number of labels across the form into the Columns: text box, in the Labels on Page area. For example, for "three-across" labels, enter the value 3.
- Make sure that the value 1 is entered into the Row: text box in the Next Label to Print area.

Setting the Always on Top Option

The Options menu has only a single item: Always on Top. If you enable this option, the program window will always be displayed on top of overlapping windows, even when the window is inactive or minimized.

TIP

You can use the following method to make the Envelope and Label Printer readily accessible on your desktop for quickly printing an envelope or label: Choose the Always on Top option and minimize the program window; the program icon will then always be visible on your desktop while you are working in other programs. Whenever you need to print an envelope or label (using the current settings and format), simply click on the icon to open the system menu, and then click on the Print command or simply press Enter (because the Print command is at the top of the menu, it is automatically highlighted).

How the Envelope and Label Printer Works

The source code for the Envelope and Label Printer program, ENVE-LOPE, is provided in Listings 8.1 through 8.6, and the program icon is shown in Figure 8.10. Listing 8.1 is the program header file (ENVE-LOPE.H), which contains all of the class definitions and is included in both of the C++ source files. Listing 8.2 (ENVELOPE.CPP) contains the C++ source code for `WinMain` and declarations for the global program objects. Listing 8.3 (DIALOG.CPP) defines the member functions belonging to the main window class (`CMainDialog`) as well as the classes that manage the Format Envelope and Format Label modeless dialog boxes (`CFormEnvDialog` and `CFormLabelDialog`).

Listing 8.4 (ENVELOPE.DEF) is the module-definition file, and Listings 8.5 and 8.6 (RESOURCE.H and ENVELOPE.RC) are the program resource files generated by the Microsoft App Studio.

FIGURE 8.10

The ENVELOPE program icon

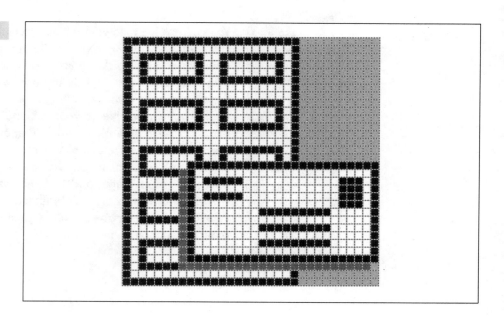

Listing 8.1

```
//////////////////////////////////////////////////////////////
//                                                          //
// ENVELOPE.H:  Header file for the ENVELOPE program.       //
//                                                          //
//////////////////////////////////////////////////////////////

#include "..\wclasses\wclasses.h"
#include "resource.h"

// constant for help topic:
#define HELPFORMENVDLG    100
#define HELPFORMLABELDLG 101
#define MAXADDRESS 512


//////////////////////////////////////////////////////////////
// main dialog box class definition:                        //
//////////////////////////////////////////////////////////////

class CMainDialog : public CMLDialog
{
    HBRUSH HBrushWorkSpace;
    int OnTop;

    virtual BOOL DialogProc (UINT Msg, WPARAM WParam,
                             LPARAM LParam);
    char *GetLine (char *Buffer);
    BOOL OnCommand (int IDItem, HWND HWndCtl, WORD NotifyCode);
    BOOL OnCtlColor (HDC HDCChild, HWND HWndChild, int CtlType);
    BOOL OnDestroy ();
    BOOL OnInitDialog (HWND HWndFocus, LPARAM Data);
    BOOL OnSysColorChange ();
    void PrintEnvelope ();
    void PrintLabel ();
    void WrapUp ();

public:
    CMainDialog ();
    void GetCurrentPrinter (char *PrnDriver, char *PrnName,
```

```
            char *PrnPort, int SizeBuffers);
};


//////////////////////////////////////////////////////////////
// 'Format Envelope' modal dialog box class definition:       //
//////////////////////////////////////////////////////////////

class CFormEnvDialog : public CMDialog
{
   virtual BOOL DialogProc (UINT Msg, WPARAM WParam,
                              LPARAM LParam);
public:
   char Address [MAXADDRESS];
   LOGFONT LogFont;
   BOOL Portrait;
   float RetLeft;
   float RetTop;
   float ToLeft;
   float ToTop;

   CFormEnvDialog ();
   void WrapUp ();
};


//////////////////////////////////////////////////////////////
// 'Format Label' modal dialog box class definition:          //
//////////////////////////////////////////////////////////////

class CFormLabelDialog : public CMDialog
{
   virtual BOOL DialogProc (UINT Msg, WPARAM WParam,
                              LPARAM LParam);
public:
   int Cols;
   LOGFONT LogFont;
   int NextCol;
   int NextRow;
   float OffHoriz;
   float OffLeft;
```

```
    float OffTop;
    float OffVert;
    int Rows;

    CFormLabelDialog ();
    void WrapUp ();
};
```

Listing 8.2

```
///////////////////////////////////////////////////////////
//                                                         //
// ENVELOPE.CPP:  Global object declarations and program entry //
//                point for the ENVELOPE program.          //
//                                                         //
///////////////////////////////////////////////////////////

#include "envelope.h"

///////////////////////////////////////////////////////////
// global object declarations:                            //
///////////////////////////////////////////////////////////

CApplication App;
CMainDialog MainDialog;
CFormLabelDialog FormLabelDialog;
CFormEnvDialog FormEnvDialog;

///////////////////////////////////////////////////////////
// program entry function:                                //
///////////////////////////////////////////////////////////

int PASCAL WinMain
    (HINSTANCE HInstCurrent,
    HINSTANCE HInstPrevious,
    LPSTR CmdLine,
    int CmdShow)
    {
    MSG Msg;

    if (HInstPrevious)
```

```
        {
        HWND HWndPopup;

        GetInstanceData
            (HInstPrevious,
            (BYTE *)&MainDialog.mHDialog,
            sizeof (HWND));
        ShowWindow (MainDialog.mHDialog, SW_SHOWNORMAL);
        HWndPopup = GetLastActivePopup (MainDialog.mHDialog);
        BringWindowToTop (MainDialog.mHDialog);
        BringWindowToTop (HWndPopup);
        return (FALSE);
        }

    App.Initialize (HInstCurrent, HInstPrevious, CmdLine,
                    CmdShow);

    if (!App.LoadAccel ("EnvelopeAccel"))
        return (FALSE);

    if (!MainDialog.SetIcon ("EnvelopeIcon"))
        return (FALSE);

    if (!MainDialog.Create ("MainDlg"))
        return (FALSE);

    while (GetMessage (&Msg, NULL, NULL, NULL))
        if (!TranslateAccelerator (MainDialog.mHDialog,
                                   App.mHAccelTable,
                                   &Msg))
            if (!IsDialogMessage (MainDialog.mHDialog, &Msg))
                {
                TranslateMessage (&Msg);
                DispatchMessage (&Msg);
                }

    return (Msg.wParam);
    }
```

Listing 8.3

```
/////////////////////////////////////////////////////////////
//                                                           //
// DIALOG.CPP:  Dialog class member functions for the        //
//              ENVELOPE program.                            //
//                                                           //
/////////////////////////////////////////////////////////////

#include "envelope.h"
#include <commdlg.h>
#include <fcntl.h>
#include <io.h>
#include <print.h>
#include <stdio.h>
#include <stdlib.h>
#include <string.h>
#include <sys\stat.h>

// define __max and __min because some C++ run-time libraries
// don't include them:
#define __max(a,b)  (((a) > (b)) ? (a) : (b))
#define __min(a,b)  (((a) < (b)) ? (a) : (b))

extern CFormEnvDialog FormEnvDialog;
extern CFormLabelDialog FormLabelDialog;
extern CMainDialog MainDialog;

#define CRCODE '\x9d'  // CR and LF are encoded with unused
#define LFCODE '\x9e'  // ANSI codes
#define SIZENUMBUF 6

/////////////////////////////////////////////////////////////
// CMainDialog member functions:                             //
/////////////////////////////////////////////////////////////

CMainDialog::CMainDialog ()
    {
    HBrushWorkSpace = 0;
    }
```

```cpp
BOOL CMainDialog::DialogProc (UINT Msg, WPARAM WParam,
                             LPARAM LParam)
  {
  switch (Msg)
    {
    case WM_CLOSE:
       Destroy ();
       return (TRUE);

    case WM_COMMAND:
       return OnCommand ((int)WParam, (HWND)LOWORD (LParam),
                         HIWORD (LParam));

    case WM_CTLCOLOR:
       return OnCtlColor ((HDC)WParam, (HWND)LOWORD (LParam),
                          (int)HIWORD (LParam));

    case WM_DESTROY:
       return OnDestroy ();

    case WM_ENDSESSION:
       if (WParam)
          WrapUp ();
       return (TRUE);

    case WM_INITDIALOG:
       return OnInitDialog ((HWND)WParam, LParam);

    case WM_SYSCOLORCHANGE:
       return OnSysColorChange ();

    case WM_SYSCOMMAND:  // user chose command on system menu
       if (WParam == IDM_PRINT)  // Print command chosen
          return OnCommand ((int)WParam, (HWND)LOWORD (LParam),
                            HIWORD (LParam));
       else                     // another command chosen; let
          return (FALSE);  // system do default processing

    default:
       return (FALSE);
    }
```

```
    }

void CMainDialog::GetCurrentPrinter (char *PrnDriver,
    char *PrnName, char *PrnPort, int SizeBuffers)
// supplies information on the current default Windows printer:
// name of driver is copied to PrnDriver, name of printer model
// is copied to PrnName, and printer port is copied to PrnPort;
// SizeBuffers specifies the size of the receiving buffers, all
// of which must be at least the specified size
    {
    char PrnInfo [80];
    LPSTR PtrChar;
    LPSTR PtrPrnDriver;
    LPSTR PtrPrnName;
    LPSTR PtrPrnPort;

    GetProfileString   // obtain default printer information from
        ("windows",    // the [windows] section of WIN.INI, under
        "device",      // the 'device' entry name
        "",
        PrnInfo,
        sizeof (PrnInfo));

    // break the string from WIN.INI into separate strings for
    // the printer name, printer driver name, and port name (the
    // WIN.INI string has the format 'printer_name,driver_name,
    // port_name'):
    PtrChar = PtrPrnName = PrnInfo;
    PtrPrnDriver = PtrPrnPort = 0;
    while (*PtrChar)
        {
        if (*PtrChar == ',')
            {
            *PtrChar++ = 0;
            while (*PtrChar == ' ')
                PtrChar = AnsiNext (PtrChar);   // AnsiNext works even
            if (!PtrPrnDriver)                   // for foreign
                PtrPrnDriver = PtrChar;          // character sets
            else
                {
                PtrPrnPort = PtrChar;
```

```
                        break;
                        }
                }
            else
                PtrChar = AnsiNext (PtrChar);
            }
        // copy the individual strings to the receiving buffers:
        _fmemcpy (PrnDriver, PtrPrnDriver, SizeBuffers);
        _fmemcpy (PrnName, PtrPrnName, SizeBuffers);
        _fmemcpy (PrnPort, PtrPrnPort, SizeBuffers);
        }

char *CMainDialog::GetLine (char *Buffer)
// if Buffer is non-0, extracts the first line from Buffer; if
// Buffer is 0, extracts the next line from the same buffer
// used in previous call to GetLine; if a line consisting of at
// least 1 character is available, returns address of this line;
// otherwise, returns 0
    {
    static char *PtrChar;
    char *PtrLine;

    if (Buffer)  // a new buffer is specified
        PtrChar = Buffer;

    if (*PtrChar == '\0') // end of buffer reached; no line
        return (0);        // available

    PtrLine = PtrChar;   // PtrLine points to beginning of line

    // scan to end of line and insert a '\0' character (assumes
    // that a line can be terminated with a LF, a CR, a LF-CR
    // pair, or a CR-LF pair):
    while (*PtrChar)
        {
        if (*PtrChar == '\r')
            {
            *PtrChar++ = '\0';
            if (*PtrChar == '\n')
                ++PtrChar;
            break;
```

```
         }
      else if (*PtrChar == '\n')
         {
         *PtrChar++ = '\0';
         if (*PtrChar == '\r')
            ++PtrChar;
         break;
         }
      ++PtrChar;
      }
   return PtrLine;
   }

BOOL CMainDialog::OnCommand (int IDItem, HWND HWndCtl,
                             WORD NotifyCode)
   {
   switch (IDItem)
      {
      case IDM_ABOUT:  // Help/About menu command
         {
         CMDialog MDialog;
         MDialog.Create ("AboutDlg", mHDialog);
         return (TRUE);
         }

      case IDM_FORMENVELOPE:  // Format/Envelope menu command
         // display 'Format Envelope' modeless dialog box:
         FormEnvDialog.Create ("FormEnvDlg", mHDialog);
         return (TRUE);

      case IDM_FORMLABEL:  // Format/Label menu command
         // display 'Format Label' modeless dialog box:
         FormLabelDialog.Create ("FormLabelDlg", mHDialog);
         return (TRUE);

      case IDM_HELPCONTENTS:  // Help/Contents menu command
         WinHelp (mHDialog, "ENVELOPE.HLP", HELP_CONTENTS, OL);
         return (TRUE);

      case IDM_HELPHELP:  // Help/How to Use Help menu command
         WinHelp (mHDialog, "ENVELOPE.HLP", HELP_HELPONHELP, OL);
```

```
            return (TRUE);

        case IDM_HELPSEARCH:  // Help/Search for Help On menu
                              // command
            WinHelp (mHDialog, "ENVELOPE.HLP", HELP_PARTIALKEY,
                    (DWORD)(LPCSTR)"");
            return (TRUE);

        case IDM_ONTOP:    // Options/Always on Top menu command
            OnTop = !OnTop;
            CheckMenuItem (GetMenu (mHDialog), IDM_ONTOP,
                          OnTop ? MF_CHECKED : MF_UNCHECKED);
            SetWindowPos (mHDialog,
                          OnTop ? HWND_TOPMOST : HWND_NOTOPMOST,
                          0, 0, 0, 0, SWP_NOMOVE | SWP_NOSIZE);
            return (TRUE);

        case IDM_PRINT:    // System/Print menu command (or
                           // Print button)
            if (IsDlgButtonChecked (mHDialog, IDC_ENVELOPE))
                PrintEnvelope ();
            else
                PrintLabel ();
            return (TRUE);

        default:
            return (FALSE);
        }
    }

BOOL CMainDialog::OnCtlColor (HDC HDCChild, HWND HWndChild,
                             int CtlType)
    {
    COLORREF WorkSpaceColor;

    switch (CtlType)
        {
        case CTLCOLOR_BTN:
        case CTLCOLOR_STATIC:
            WorkSpaceColor = GetSysColor (COLOR_APPWORKSPACE);
            if (GetRValue (WorkSpaceColor) * 2 +
```

```
          GetGValue (WorkSpaceColor) * 5 +
          GetBValue (WorkSpaceColor) > 1020)
        SetTextColor (HDCChild, RGB (0, 0, 0));
      else
        SetTextColor (HDCChild, RGB (255, 255, 255));
      SetBkMode (HDCChild, TRANSPARENT);
      return ((BOOL)HBrushWorkSpace);

    case CTLCOLOR_DLG:
      return ((BOOL)HBrushWorkSpace);

    default:
      return (FALSE);
    }
}

BOOL CMainDialog::OnDestroy ()
  {
  WrapUp ();
  if (HBrushWorkSpace != 0)
     DeleteObject (HBrushWorkSpace);
  WinHelp (mHDialog, "ENVELOPE.HLP", HELP_QUIT, OL);
  PostQuitMessage (0);
  return (TRUE);
  }

BOOL CMainDialog::OnInitDialog (HWND HWndFocus, LPARAM Data)
// obtains the data for the main dialog box; data for the
// Format dialog boxes is obtained by the constructors for the
// CFormEnvDialog and CFormLabelDialog classes
  {
  char Buffer [MAXADDRESS];
  int Result;

  OnTop = (int)GetPrivateProfileInt
     ("options",
     "ontop",
     0,
     "ENVELOPE.INI");
  if (OnTop)
     {
```

```
            CheckMenuItem (GetMenu (mHDialog), IDM_ONTOP, MF_CHECKED);
            SetWindowPos (mHDialog, HWND_TOPMOST, 0, 0, 0, 0,
                          SWP_NOMOVE | SWP_NOSIZE);
        }

    // restore prior status of Envelope and Label radio buttons:
    Result = (BOOL)GetPrivateProfileInt
        ("options",
        "envelope",
        1,
        "ENVELOPE.INI");
    CheckDlgButton
        (mHDialog,
        Result ? IDC_ENVELOPE : IDC_LABEL,
        1);

    // restore prior status of 'From Clipboard' and 'Entered Here'
    // radio buttons:
    Result = (BOOL)GetPrivateProfileInt
        ("options",
        "clipboard",
        1,
        "ENVELOPE.INI");
    CheckDlgButton
        (mHDialog,
        Result ? IDC_CLIPBOARD : IDC_ENTERED,
        1);

    // restore previous address:
    GetPrivateProfileString
        ("options",
        "address",
        "",
        Buffer,
        sizeof (Buffer),
        "ENVELOPE.INI");
    // translate codes for CR and LF characters into actual
    // CR and LF characters (CR and LF characters must be stored
    // in coded format because WritePrivateProfile will store only
    // a single line):
    for (int i = 0; Buffer [i]; ++i)
```

```
        {
        if (Buffer [i] == CRCODE)
            Buffer [i] = '\r';
        if (Buffer [i] == LFCODE)
            Buffer [i] = '\n';
        }
    SetDlgItemText (mHDialog, IDC_ADDRESS, Buffer);

    // add a Print command and a separator to the system menu:
    InsertMenu
        (GetSystemMenu (mHDialog, FALSE),
        0,
        MF_BYPOSITION | MF_SEPARATOR,
        0,
        0);
    InsertMenu
        (GetSystemMenu (mHDialog, FALSE),
        0,
        MF_BYPOSITION | MF_STRING,
        IDM_PRINT,
        "&Print");

    HBrushWorkSpace = CreateSolidBrush
        (GetSysColor (COLOR_APPWORKSPACE));
    return (TRUE);
    }


BOOL CMainDialog::OnSysColorChange ()
    {
    if (HBrushWorkSpace != 0)
        DeleteObject (HBrushWorkSpace);
    HBrushWorkSpace =
        CreateSolidBrush (GetSysColor (COLOR_APPWORKSPACE));
    return (TRUE);
    }


void CMainDialog::PrintEnvelope ()
// prints an envelope using the return address entered into the
// Format Envelope dialog box, and a 'to' address obtained either
// from the Clipboard or from the 'Entered Here' edit control
    {
```

```
char Address [MAXADDRESS];
DOCINFO DocInfo;
char DriverFileName [13];
HANDLE HClipData;
HFONT HFont;
HDC HPrnDC;
HMODULE HPrnModule;
int LineHeight;
char PrnDriver [64];
char PrnName [64];
char PrnPort [64];
char *PtrAddress;
char __far *PtrClipData;
DEVMODE *PtrDevMode;
LPFNDEVMODE PtrExtDeviceMode;
char *PtrLine;
int SizeDevMode;
int WindowUnits;
TEXTMETRIC TM;
int X, Y;

// get information on current default Windows printer:
GetCurrentPrinter (PrnDriver, PrnName, PrnPort,
   sizeof (PrnDriver));

// obtain the current printer settings (in a DEVMODE
// structure) and set the DEVMODE dmOrientation field
// according to the page orientation chosen in the Format
// Envelope dialog box (stored in FormEnvDialog.Portrait):

// first load the printer driver DLL:
strcpy (DriverFileName, PrnDriver);
strcat (DriverFileName, ".DRV");
HPrnModule = LoadLibrary (DriverFileName);

// now obtain the address of the ExtDeviceMode function
// exported by the printer driver DLL:
PtrExtDeviceMode = (LPFNDEVMODE)GetProcAddress (HPrnModule,
   "ExtDeviceMode");
if (PtrExtDeviceMode == NULL)  // older print drivers do NOT
   {                           // provide a ExtDeviceMode
```

```
      MessageBox                    // function
         (mHDialog,
         "Old printer driver. Cannot set page orientation.",
         "Envelope & Label Printer",
         MB_ICONEXCLAMATION | MB_OK);
      PtrDevMode = O;               // indicates that no printer
      }                             // settings are available
else
      {
      // call the DLL's ExtDeviceMode function to obtain the
      // size of the buffer required to hold the printer
      // settings:
      SizeDevMode = (*PtrExtDeviceMode)
         ((HWND)mHDialog,
         (HMODULE)HPrnModule,
         (LPDEVMODE)NULL,
         (LPSTR)PrnName,
         (LPSTR)PrnPort,
         (LPDEVMODE)NULL,
         (LPSTR)NULL,
         (UINT)O);

      // allocate a buffer to hold the printer settings:
      PtrDevMode = (DEVMODE *)new char [SizeDevMode];

      // now call ExtDeviceMode again to copy the settings into
      // the buffer:
      (*PtrExtDeviceMode)
         ((HWND)mHDialog,
         (HMODULE)HPrnModule,
         (LPDEVMODE)PtrDevMode,
         (LPSTR)PrnName,
         (LPSTR)PrnPort,
         (LPDEVMODE)NULL,
         (LPSTR)NULL,
         (UINT)DM_OUT_BUFFER);

      // modify the orientation setting:
      PtrDevMode->dmOrientation = FormEnvDialog.Portrait ?
         DMORIENT_PORTRAIT : DMORIENT_LANDSCAPE;
      } // end else
```

```
FreeLibrary (HPrnModule);  // unload the printer driver DLL

// create the printer device context:
HPrnDC = CreateDC
   (PrnDriver,
    PrnName,
    PrnPort,
    PtrDevMode);  // if PtrDevMode is non-0, the device context
                  // uses the settings it contains

delete [] PtrDevMode;  // free the buffer holding the settings

// set the device context attributes:

// set mapping mode so that units are 0.01 inches:
SetMapMode (HPrnDC, MM_LOENGLISH);

// font height stored in LogFont is in WINDOW units (so that
// the point height will be displayed properly by the Font
// common dialog box); therefore, save the height, temporarily
// convert the height to PRINTER units, and then restore
// the window units after the font has been selected:

// save window units:
WindowUnits = FormEnvDialog.LogFont.lfHeight;
// convert window units to printer units:
FormEnvDialog.LogFont.lfHeight *= 100;
HDC HWndDC = GetDC (mHDialog);
FormEnvDialog.LogFont.lfHeight /= GetDeviceCaps (HWndDC,
   LOGPIXELSY);
ReleaseDC (mHDialog, HWndDC);
// obtain a font handle
HFont = CreateFontIndirect (&FormEnvDialog.LogFont);
// select font into printer device context:
SelectObject (HPrnDC, HFont);
// restore window units:
FormEnvDialog.LogFont.lfHeight = WindowUnits;

// calculate the line height:
GetTextMetrics (HPrnDC, &TM);
```

```
LineHeight = TM.tmHeight + TM.tmExternalLeading;

// initiate the print job and page:
DocInfo.cbSize = sizeof (DocInfo);
DocInfo.lpszDocName = "Envelope";
DocInfo.lpszOutput = 0;
StartDoc (HPrnDC, &DocInfo);
StartPage (HPrnDC);

// display the output:

// print return address:
// calculate coordinates of start of line:
X = (int)(FormEnvDialog.RetLeft * 100.0);
Y = (int)(-FormEnvDialog.RetTop * 100.0);
// copy return address into temporary Address buffer (because
// GetLine modifies the buffer):
memcpy (Address, FormEnvDialog.Address, sizeof (Address));
// print each line:
PtrLine = GetLine (Address);  // get first line
while (PtrLine)
   {
   TextOut (HPrnDC, X, Y, PtrLine, strlen (PtrLine)); // print
   Y -= LineHeight;         // adjust Y coordinate
   PtrLine = GetLine (0);  // get next line
   }

// print 'to' address:
if (IsDlgButtonChecked (mHDialog, IDC_CLIPBOARD))
   { // 'From Clipboard' button is checked; therefore, get
     // text from Clipboard
   if (!IsClipboardFormatAvailable (CF_TEXT) &&
      !IsClipboardFormatAvailable (CF_OEMTEXT) ||
      !OpenClipboard (mHDialog))
      {                              // Clipboard does not
      PtrAddress = new char [1];  // contain text; set
      PtrAddress [0] = '\0';      // PtrAddress to empty
      }                              // string
   else  // Clipboard contains text
      {
      // obtain handle to Clipboard data:
```

```
            HClipData = GetClipboardData (CF_TEXT);
            // obtain pointer to Clipboard data:
            PtrClipData = (char __far*)GlobalLock (HClipData);
            // allocate a private buffer to hold Clipboard data:
            PtrAddress = new char [(int)GlobalSize (HClipData)];
            // copy data into private buffer:
            _fmemcpy (PtrAddress, PtrClipData,
               (size_t)GlobalSize (HClipData));
            // unlock handle to Clipboard data and close Clipboard:
            GlobalUnlock (HClipData);
            CloseClipboard ();
            }
      }
else  // 'Entered Here' button is checked; therefore get text
   {  // from Address edit control:
   int Size = (int)SendDlgItemMessage (mHDialog, IDC_ADDRESS,
      WM_GETTEXTLENGTH, O, OL) + 1;
   PtrAddress = new char [Size];
   GetDlgItemText (mHDialog, IDC_ADDRESS, PtrAddress, Size);
   }

// calculate starting coordinates and print the 'to' address:
X = (int)(FormEnvDialog.ToLeft * 100.0);
Y = (int)(-FormEnvDialog.ToTop * 100.0);
PtrLine = GetLine (PtrAddress);
while (PtrLine)
   {
   TextOut (HPrnDC, X, Y, PtrLine, strlen (PtrLine));
   Y -= LineHeight;
   PtrLine = GetLine (0);
   }

delete [] PtrAddress;

// end the page and print job:
EndPage (HPrnDC);
EndDoc (HPrnDC);

// release device context and font handle:
DeleteDC (HPrnDC);
DeleteObject (HFont);
```

```
    }

void CMainDialog::PrintLabel ()
// prints a mailing label using a 'to' address obtained either
// from the Clipboard or from the 'Entered Here' edit control
    {
    DOCINFO DocInfo;
    HANDLE HClipData;
    HFONT HFont;
    HDC HPrnDC;
    int LineHeight;
    char PrnDriver [64];
    char PrnName [64];
    char PrnPort [64];
    char __far *PtrClipData;
    char *PtrAddress;
    char *PtrLine;
    TEXTMETRIC TM;
    int WindowUnits;
    int X, Y;

    // note: for more detailed comments, see the print
    // routine in CMainDialog::PrintEnvelope, above in
    // file

    // create a device context for the default printer:
    GetCurrentPrinter (PrnDriver, PrnName, PrnPort,
        sizeof (PrnDriver));
    HPrnDC = CreateDC
        (PrnDriver,
        PrnName,
        PrnPort,
        0);

    // mapping mode:
    SetMapMode (HPrnDC, MM_LOENGLISH);

    // convert font height and select font:
    WindowUnits = FormLabelDialog.LogFont.lfHeight;
    FormLabelDialog.LogFont.lfHeight *= 100;
    HDC HWndDC = GetDC (mHDialog);
```

```
FormLabelDialog.LogFont.lfHeight /= GetDeviceCaps (HWndDC,
    LOGPIXELSY);
ReleaseDC (mHDialog, HWndDC);
HFont = CreateFontIndirect (&FormLabelDialog.LogFont);
SelectObject (HPrnDC, HFont);
FormLabelDialog.LogFont.lfHeight = WindowUnits;

// calculate the line height:
GetTextMetrics (HPrnDC, &TM);
LineHeight = TM.tmHeight + TM.tmExternalLeading;

// obtain the text for the 'to' address either from the
// Clipboard or from the 'Entered Here' edit control:
if (IsDlgButtonChecked (mHDialog, IDC_CLIPBOARD))
    {
    if (!IsClipboardFormatAvailable (CF_TEXT) &&
        !IsClipboardFormatAvailable (CF_OEMTEXT) ¦¦
        !OpenClipboard (mHDialog))
        {
        PtrAddress = new char [1];
        PtrAddress [0] = '\0';
        }
    else
        {
        HClipData = GetClipboardData (CF_TEXT);
        PtrClipData = (char __far*)GlobalLock (HClipData);

        PtrAddress = new char [(int)GlobalSize (HClipData)];
        _fmemcpy (PtrAddress, PtrClipData,
            (size_t)GlobalSize (HClipData));
        GlobalUnlock (HClipData);
        CloseClipboard ();
        }
    }
else
    {
    int Size = (int)SendDlgItemMessage (mHDialog, IDC_ADDRESS,
        WM_GETTEXTLENGTH, O, OL) + 1;
    PtrAddress = new char [Size];
    GetDlgItemText (mHDialog, IDC_ADDRESS, PtrAddress, Size);
    }
```

```
// obtain the starting coordinates of the next label to be
// printed:
X = (int)(FormLabelDialog.OffLeft * 100.0 +
    (FormLabelDialog.NextCol - 1) * FormLabelDialog.OffHoriz *
    100.0);
Y = (int)-(FormLabelDialog.OffTop * 100.0 +
    (FormLabelDialog.NextRow - 1) * FormLabelDialog.OffVert *
    100.0);

// initiate the print job and page:
DocInfo.cbSize = sizeof (DocInfo);
DocInfo.lpszDocName = "Label";
DocInfo.lpszOutput = 0;
StartDoc (HPrnDC, &DocInfo);
StartPage (HPrnDC);

// print the address:
PtrLine = GetLine (PtrAddress);
while (PtrLine)
    {
    TextOut (HPrnDC, X, Y, PtrLine, strlen (PtrLine));
    Y -= LineHeight;
    PtrLine = GetLine (0);
    }

delete [] PtrAddress;

// end the page and print job:
EndPage (HPrnDC);
EndDoc (HPrnDC);

// release device context and font handle:
DeleteDC (HPrnDC);
DeleteObject (HFont);

// update position of next label to be printed:
if (FormLabelDialog.NextCol >= FormLabelDialog.Cols)
    {
    FormLabelDialog.NextCol = 1;
    if (FormLabelDialog.NextRow >= FormLabelDialog.Rows)
```

```
            FormLabelDialog.NextRow = 1;
         else
            ++FormLabelDialog.NextRow;
         }
      else
         ++FormLabelDialog.NextCol;
      }

void CMainDialog::WrapUp ()
// saves the all program data; for details, see the comments
// in the CMainDialog::OnInitDialog function
   {
   // save data displayed by the modeless dialog boxes:
   FormEnvDialog.WrapUp ();
   FormLabelDialog.WrapUp ();

   char Buffer [MAXADDRESS];

   WritePrivateProfileString
      ("options",
       "ontop",
        OnTop ? "1" : "0",
       "ENVELOPE.INI");

   WritePrivateProfileString
      ("options",
       "envelope",
        IsDlgButtonChecked (mHDialog, IDC_ENVELOPE) ? "1" : "0",
       "ENVELOPE.INI");

   WritePrivateProfileString
      ("options",
       "clipboard",
        IsDlgButtonChecked (mHDialog, IDC_CLIPBOARD) ? "1" : "0",
       "ENVELOPE.INI");

   GetDlgItemText (mHDialog, IDC_ADDRESS, Buffer,
      sizeof (Buffer));
   for (int i = 0; Buffer [i]; ++i)
      {
      if (Buffer [i] == '\r')  // see the comments in the
```

```
            Buffer [i] = CRCODE;   // CMainDialog::OnInitDialog
       if (Buffer [i] == '\n')   // function
            Buffer [i] = LFCODE;
       }
  WritePrivateProfileString
     ("options",
      "address",
      Buffer,
      "ENVELOPE.INI");
  }


///////////////////////////////////////////////////////////////
// CFormEnvDialog member functions:                           //
///////////////////////////////////////////////////////////////

CFormEnvDialog::CFormEnvDialog ()
// obtains the data that is displayed in the Format Envelope
// dialog box
  {
  GetPrivateProfileString
     ("envelope",
      "address",
      "",
      Address,
      sizeof (Address),
      "ENVELOPE.INI");
  for (int i = 0; Address [i]; ++i)
     {
     if (Address [i] == CRCODE)
        Address [i] = '\r';
     if (Address [i] == LFCODE)
        Address [i] = '\n';
     }

  Portrait = (BOOL)GetPrivateProfileInt
     ("envelope",
      "portrait",
      TRUE,
      "ENVELOPE.INI");

  char NumBuf [SIZENUMBUF];
```

```
GetPrivateProfileString
    ("envelope",
    "retleft",
    "",
    NumBuf,
    sizeof (NumBuf),
    "ENVELOPE.INI");
if (NumBuf [0])
    RetLeft = (float)atof (NumBuf);
else
    RetLeft = 0.25;

GetPrivateProfileString
    ("envelope",
    "rettop",
    "",
    NumBuf,
    sizeof (NumBuf),
    "ENVELOPE.INI");
if (NumBuf [0])
    RetTop = (float)atof (NumBuf);
else
    RetTop = 0.25;

GetPrivateProfileString
    ("envelope",
    "toleft",
    "",
    NumBuf,
    sizeof (NumBuf),
    "ENVELOPE.INI");
if (NumBuf [0])
    ToLeft = (float)atof (NumBuf);
else
    ToLeft = 4.0;

GetPrivateProfileString
    ("envelope",
    "totop",
    "",
```

```
   NumBuf,
   sizeof (NumBuf),
   "ENVELOPE.INI");
if (NumBuf [0])
   ToTop = (float)atof (NumBuf);
else
   ToTop = 2.0;

// initialize the font descriptions:

int HFontFile;
char FontFileName [256] = "";
int Length;

// the descriptions of the envelope and label fonts are stored
// in the file ENVELOPE.LFN, kept in the Windows directory:
Length = GetWindowsDirectory (FontFileName,
   sizeof (FontFileName));
if (FontFileName [Length - 1] == '\\')     // Windows directory
   strcat (FontFileName, "ENVELOPE.LFN"); // is the root
else
   strcat (FontFileName, "\\ENVELOPE.LFN");

// attempt to open the file:
HFontFile = open (FontFileName, O_BINARY | O_RDWR);
if (HFontFile == -1)
   {
   // ENVELOPE.LFN does not exist, because prior font
   // descriptions have not been saved; obtain a description
   // of the default printer font:
   char PrnDriver [64];
   char PrnName [64];
   char PrnPort [64];
   TEXTMETRIC TM;

   // get and set up printer information context:
   MainDialog.GetCurrentPrinter (PrnDriver, PrnName, PrnPort,
      sizeof (PrnDriver));
   HDC HPrnIC = CreateIC
      (PrnDriver,
      PrnName,
```

```
            PrnPort,
            0);
        SetMapMode (HPrnIC, MM_LOENGLISH);

        // obtain metrics for the default printer font and assign
        // metrics to the appropriate fields of the LOGFONT
        // structures used by CFormEnvDialog and CFormLabelDialog
        // to store the fonts used to print envelopes/labels:
        GetTextMetrics (HPrnIC, &TM);
        memset (&LogFont, 0, sizeof (LogFont));
        LogFont.lfHeight =  -(TM.tmHeight - TM.tmInternalLeading);
        LogFont.lfWeight = TM.tmWeight;
        LogFont.lfItalic = TM.tmItalic;
        LogFont.lfUnderline = TM.tmUnderlined;
        LogFont.lfStrikeOut = TM.tmStruckOut;
        LogFont.lfCharSet = TM.tmCharSet;
        LogFont.lfPitchAndFamily = TM.tmPitchAndFamily;
        GetTextFace (HPrnIC, sizeof (LogFont.lfFaceName),
            LogFont.lfFaceName);

        DeleteDC (HPrnIC);   // release the information context

        // convert character height from printer units to window
        // units:
        HDC HWndDC = GetDC (MainDialog.mHDialog);
        LogFont.lfHeight *= GetDeviceCaps (HWndDC, LOGPIXELSY);
        LogFont.lfHeight /= 100;
        ReleaseDC (MainDialog.mHDialog, HWndDC);

        // copy the LOGFONT structure into LOGFONT structure used
        // for labels:
        FormLabelDialog.LogFont = LogFont;
        }
    else  // ENVELOPE.LFN exists; therefore, read the prior font
        { // descriptions into LOGFONT structures:
        read (HFontFile, &LogFont, sizeof (LOGFONT));
        read (HFontFile, &FormLabelDialog.LogFont,
            sizeof (LOGFONT));
        close (HFontFile);
        }
    }
```

```
BOOL CFormEnvDialog::DialogProc (UINT Msg, WPARAM WParam,
                                 LPARAM LParam)
    {
    char NumBuf [SIZENUMBUF];
    static LOGFONT TempLogFont;

    switch (Msg)
        {
        case WM_COMMAND:
            switch (WParam)
                {
                case IDCANCEL:
                    EndDialog (mHDialog, IDCANCEL);
                    return (TRUE);

                case IDC_FONT:  // user clicked 'Choose Font...'
                    {              // button
                    CHOOSEFONT CF;
                    HDC HPrnIC;
                    char PrnDriver [64];
                    char PrnName [64];
                    char PrnPort [64];

                    // obtain an information context for the default
                    // Windows printer:
                    MainDialog.GetCurrentPrinter (PrnDriver, PrnName,
                        PrnPort, sizeof (PrnDriver));
                    HPrnIC = CreateIC
                        (PrnDriver,
                        PrnName,
                        PrnPort,
                        0);
                    SetMapMode (HPrnIC, MM_LOENGLISH);

                    // initialize a CHOOSEFONT structure; the values
                    // assigned to this structure affect the behavior
                    // of the Font common dialog box:
                    memset (&CF, 0, sizeof (CF));
                    CF.lStructSize = sizeof (CF);
                    CF.hwndOwner = mHDialog;
```

```
        CF.lpLogFont = &TempLogFont;
        // display printer fonts and use TempLogFont to
        // initialize the fields of the Font dialog box:
        CF.Flags = CF_PRINTERFONTS |
           CF_INITTOLOGFONTSTRUCT;
        CF.hDC = HPrnIC;

        // display the Font common dialog box:
        ChooseFont (&CF);

        DeleteDC (HPrnIC);

        // display name of newly chosen font:
        SetDlgItemText (mHDialog, IDC_FONTNAME,
           TempLogFont.lfFaceName);
        return (TRUE);
        }

     case IDC_HELP:
        WinHelp (MainDialog.mHDialog, "ENVELOPE.HLP",
              HELP_CONTEXT, HELPFORMENVDLG);
        return (TRUE);

     case IDOK:
        // assign the data that the user entered into the
        // Format Envelope dialog box to the
        // CFormEnvDialog data members; adjust numeric
        // data to proper ranges:
        GetDlgItemText (mHDialog, IDC_ADDRESS, Address,
           sizeof (Address));
        Portrait = (BOOL)IsDlgButtonChecked (mHDialog,
           IDC_PORTRAIT);

        GetDlgItemText (mHDialog, IDC_RETLEFT, NumBuf,
           sizeof (NumBuf));
        RetLeft = (float)atof (NumBuf);
        RetLeft = (float)__max (RetLeft, 0.0);
        RetLeft = (float)__min (RetLeft, 99.99);
        sprintf (NumBuf, "%.2f", RetLeft);
        RetLeft = (float)atof (NumBuf);
```

```
        GetDlgItemText (mHDialog, IDC_RETTOP, NumBuf,
           sizeof (NumBuf));
        RetTop = (float)atof (NumBuf);
        RetTop = (float)__max (RetTop, 0.0);
        RetTop = (float)__min (RetTop, 99.99);
        sprintf (NumBuf, "%.2f", RetTop);
        RetTop = (float)atof (NumBuf);

        GetDlgItemText (mHDialog, IDC_TOLEFT, NumBuf,
           sizeof (NumBuf));
        ToLeft = (float)atof (NumBuf);
        ToLeft = (float)__max (ToLeft, 0.0);
        ToLeft = (float)__min (ToLeft, 99.99);
        sprintf (NumBuf, "%.2f", ToLeft);
        ToLeft = (float)atof (NumBuf);

        GetDlgItemText (mHDialog, IDC_TOTOP, NumBuf,
           sizeof (NumBuf));
        ToTop = (float)atof (NumBuf);
        ToTop = (float)__max (ToTop, 0.0);
        ToTop = (float)__min (ToTop, 99.99);
        sprintf (NumBuf, "%.2f", ToTop);
        ToTop = (float)atof (NumBuf);

        // save the temporary LOGFONT structure (which
        // may contain new values if the user clicked
        // the Choose Font... button):
        LogFont = TempLogFont;

        EndDialog (mHDialog, IDOK);
        return (TRUE);

     default:
        return (TRUE);
     }

case WM_INITDIALOG:
   SendDlgItemMessage (mHDialog, IDC_RETLEFT, EM_LIMITTEXT,
      (WPARAM)SIZENUMBUF - 1, OL);
   SendDlgItemMessage (mHDialog, IDC_RETTOP, EM_LIMITTEXT,
      (WPARAM)SIZENUMBUF - 1, OL);
```

```
        SendDlgItemMessage (mHDialog, IDC_TOLEFT, EM_LIMITTEXT,
            (WPARAM)SIZENUMBUF - 1, OL);
        SendDlgItemMessage (mHDialog, IDC_TOTOP, EM_LIMITTEXT,
            (WPARAM)SIZENUMBUF - 1, OL);

        // initialize fields of Format Envelope dialog box using
        // values stored in CFormEnvDialog member functions:
        SetDlgItemText (mHDialog, IDC_ADDRESS, Address);

        CheckDlgButton
            (mHDialog,
            Portrait ? IDC_PORTRAIT : IDC_LANDSCAPE,
            1);

        sprintf (NumBuf, "%.2f", RetLeft);
        SetDlgItemText (mHDialog, IDC_RETLEFT, NumBuf);

        sprintf (NumBuf, "%.2f", RetTop);
        SetDlgItemText (mHDialog, IDC_RETTOP, NumBuf);

        sprintf (NumBuf, "%.2f", ToLeft);
        SetDlgItemText (mHDialog, IDC_TOLEFT, NumBuf);

        sprintf (NumBuf, "%.2f", ToTop);
        SetDlgItemText (mHDialog, IDC_TOTOP, NumBuf);
        SetDlgItemText (mHDialog, IDC_FONTNAME,
            LogFont.lfFaceName);

        // if user clicks the Choose Font... button, the Font
        // dialog box will be initialized with and will modify
        // a TEMPORARY LOGFONT structure, so that the permanent
        // structure is not altered if the user clicks Cancel
        // button in Format Envelope dialog box:
        TempLogFont = LogFont;

        return (TRUE);

    default:
        if (Msg == mHelpMessage)
            {
            SendMessage (mHDialog, WM_COMMAND, IDC_HELP, OL);
```

```
            return (TRUE);
            }
        else
            return (FALSE);
        }
    }

void CFormEnvDialog::WrapUp ()
// saves the data displayed by the 'Format Envelope' dialog box
    {
    for (int i = 0; Address [i]; ++i) // encode CR and LF
        {                             // characters; see comments
        if (Address [i] == '\r')      // in CMainDialog::
            Address [i] = CRCODE;     // OnInitDialog function
        if (Address [i] == '\n')
            Address [i] = LFCODE;
        }
    WritePrivateProfileString
        ("envelope",
        "address",
        Address,
        "ENVELOPE.INI");

    WritePrivateProfileString
        ("envelope",
        "portrait",
        Portrait ? "1" : "0",
        "ENVELOPE.INI");

    char NumBuf [SIZENUMBUF];

    sprintf (NumBuf, "%.2f", RetLeft);
    WritePrivateProfileString
        ("envelope",
        "retleft",
        NumBuf,
        "ENVELOPE.INI");

    sprintf (NumBuf, "%.2f", RetTop);
    WritePrivateProfileString
        ("envelope",
```

```
        "rettop",
        NumBuf,
        "ENVELOPE.INI");

    sprintf (NumBuf, "%.2f", ToLeft);
    WritePrivateProfileString
        ("envelope",
        "toleft",
        NumBuf,
        "ENVELOPE.INI");

    sprintf (NumBuf, "%.2f", ToTop);
    WritePrivateProfileString
        ("envelope",
        "totop",
        NumBuf,
        "ENVELOPE.INI");

    // save font descriptions in LOGFONT structures within
    // ENVELOPE.LFN, in the Windows directory:
    int HFontFile;
    char FontFileName [128] = "";
    int Length;

    Length = GetWindowsDirectory (FontFileName,
        sizeof (FontFileName));
    if (FontFileName [Length - 1] == '\\')
        strcat (FontFileName, "ENVELOPE.LFN");
    else
        strcat (FontFileName, "\\ENVELOPE.LFN");

    HFontFile = open (FontFileName,
        O_BINARY | O_CREAT | O_TRUNC |
        O_RDWR, S_IREAD | S_IWRITE);
    if (HFontFile == -1)
        {
        MessageBox
            (0,
            "_open failed for font file",
            "Envelope & Label Printer",
            MB_ICONEXCLAMATION | MB_OK);
```

```
    return;
    }
write (HFontFile, &LogFont, sizeof (LOGFONT));
write (HFontFile, &FormLabelDialog.LogFont,
    sizeof (LOGFONT));
close (HFontFile);
}


/////////////////////////////////////////////////////////////////
// CFormLabelDialog member functions:                          //
/////////////////////////////////////////////////////////////////

CFormLabelDialog::CFormLabelDialog ()
// reads in the data that is displayed by the Format Label
// dialog box
    {
    // read in the ints:

    Cols = GetPrivateProfileInt
        ("label",
        "cols",
        1,
        "ENVELOPE.INI");

    NextCol = GetPrivateProfileInt
        ("label",
        "nextcol",
        1,
        "ENVELOPE.INI");

    NextRow = GetPrivateProfileInt
        ("label",
        "nextrow",
        1,
        "ENVELOPE.INI");

    Rows = GetPrivateProfileInt
        ("label",
        "rows",
        1,
        "ENVELOPE.INI");
```

```
// read in the floats:

char NumBuf [SIZENUMBUF];

GetPrivateProfileString
   ("label",
   "offhoriz",
   "",
   NumBuf,
   sizeof (NumBuf),
   "ENVELOPE.INI");
if (NumBuf [0])
   OffHoriz = (float)atof (NumBuf);
else
   OffHoriz = 0.0;

GetPrivateProfileString
   ("label",
   "offleft",
   "",
   NumBuf,
   sizeof (NumBuf),
   "ENVELOPE.INI");
if (NumBuf [0])
   OffLeft = (float)atof (NumBuf);
else
   OffLeft = 0.0;

GetPrivateProfileString
   ("label",
   "offtop",
   "",
   NumBuf,
   sizeof (NumBuf),
   "ENVELOPE.INI");
if (NumBuf [0])
   OffTop = (float)atof (NumBuf);
else
   OffTop = 0.0;
```

```
    GetPrivateProfileString
        ("label",
        "offvert",
        "",
        NumBuf,
        sizeof (NumBuf),
        "ENVELOPE.INI");
    if (NumBuf [0])
        OffVert = (float)atof (NumBuf);
    else
        OffVert = 0.0;
    }

BOOL CFormLabelDialog::DialogProc (UINT Msg, WPARAM WParam,
                                        LPARAM LParam)
    {
    char NumBuf [SIZENUMBUF];
    static LOGFONT TempLogFont;

    switch (Msg)
        {
        case WM_COMMAND:
            switch (WParam)
                {
                case IDCANCEL:
                    EndDialog (mHDialog, IDCANCEL);
                    return (TRUE);

                case IDC_FONT:              // see comments in the
                    {                       // IDC_FONT routine in
                    CHOOSEFONT CF;          // CFormEnvDialog::
                    HDC HPrnIC;             // DialogProc function
                    char PrnDriver [64];    // (earlier in file)
                    char PrnName [64];
                    char PrnPort [64];

                    MainDialog.GetCurrentPrinter (PrnDriver, PrnName,
                        PrnPort, sizeof (PrnDriver));
                    HPrnIC = CreateIC
                        (PrnDriver,
                        PrnName,
```

```
                    PrnPort,
                    O);
                SetMapMode (HPrnIC, MM_LOENGLISH);

                memset (&CF, O, sizeof (CF));
                CF.lStructSize = sizeof (CF);
                CF.hwndOwner = mHDialog;
                CF.lpLogFont = &TempLogFont;
                CF.Flags = CF_PRINTERFONTS |
                    CF_INITTOLOGFONTSTRUCT;
                CF.hDC = HPrnIC;

                ChooseFont (&CF);

                DeleteDC (HPrnIC);

                SetDlgItemText (mHDialog, IDC_FONTNAME,
                    TempLogFont.lfFaceName);
                return (TRUE);
                }

        case IDC_HELP:
            WinHelp (MainDialog.mHDialog, "ENVELOPE.HLP",
                    HELP_CONTEXT, HELPFORMLABELDLG);
            return (TRUE);

        case IDOK:
            // get the ints:
            GetDlgItemText (mHDialog, IDC_COLS, NumBuf,
                sizeof (NumBuf));
            Cols = abs (atoi (NumBuf));

            GetDlgItemText (mHDialog, IDC_NEXTCOL, NumBuf,
                sizeof (NumBuf));
            NextCol = abs (atoi (NumBuf));

            GetDlgItemText (mHDialog, IDC_NEXTROW, NumBuf,
                sizeof (NumBuf));
            NextRow = abs (atoi (NumBuf));

            GetDlgItemText (mHDialog, IDC_ROWS, NumBuf,
```

```
            sizeof (NumBuf));
Rows = abs (atoi (NumBuf));

// get the floats:
GetDlgItemText (mHDialog, IDC_OFFHORIZ, NumBuf,
    sizeof (NumBuf));
OffHoriz = (float)atof (NumBuf);
OffHoriz = (float)__max (OffHoriz, 0.0);
OffHoriz = (float)__min (OffHoriz, 99.99);
sprintf (NumBuf, "%.2f", OffHoriz);
OffHoriz = (float)atof (NumBuf);

GetDlgItemText (mHDialog, IDC_OFFLEFT, NumBuf,
    sizeof (NumBuf));
OffLeft = (float)atof (NumBuf);
OffLeft = (float)__max (OffLeft, 0.0);
OffLeft = (float)__min (OffLeft, 99.99);
sprintf (NumBuf, "%.2f", OffLeft);
OffLeft = (float)atof (NumBuf);

GetDlgItemText (mHDialog, IDC_OFFTOP, NumBuf,
    sizeof (NumBuf));
OffTop = (float)atof (NumBuf);
OffTop = (float)__max (OffTop, 0.0);
OffTop = (float)__min (OffTop, 99.99);
sprintf (NumBuf, "%.2f", OffTop);
OffTop = (float)atof (NumBuf);

GetDlgItemText (mHDialog, IDC_OFFVERT, NumBuf,
    sizeof (NumBuf));
OffVert = (float)atof (NumBuf);
OffVert = (float)__max (OffVert, 0.0);
OffVert = (float)__min (OffVert, 99.99);
sprintf (NumBuf, "%.2f", OffVert);
OffVert = (float)atof (NumBuf);

LogFont = TempLogFont;

EndDialog (mHDialog, IDOK);
return (TRUE);
```

```
                default:
                   return (TRUE);
                }

        case WM_INITDIALOG:
           // limit edit controls for ints:
           SendDlgItemMessage (mHDialog, IDC_COLS, EM_LIMITTEXT,
              (WPARAM)2, OL);
           SendDlgItemMessage (mHDialog, IDC_NEXTCOL, EM_LIMITTEXT,
              (WPARAM)2, OL);
           SendDlgItemMessage (mHDialog, IDC_NEXTROW, EM_LIMITTEXT,
              (WPARAM)2, OL);
           SendDlgItemMessage (mHDialog, IDC_ROWS, EM_LIMITTEXT,
              (WPARAM)2, OL);

           // limit edit controls for floats:
           SendDlgItemMessage (mHDialog, IDC_OFFHORIZ,
              EM_LIMITTEXT, (WPARAM)SIZENUMBUF - 1, OL);
           SendDlgItemMessage (mHDialog, IDC_OFFLEFT, EM_LIMITTEXT,
              (WPARAM)SIZENUMBUF - 1, OL);
           SendDlgItemMessage (mHDialog, IDC_OFFTOP, EM_LIMITTEXT,
              (WPARAM)SIZENUMBUF - 1, OL);
           SendDlgItemMessage (mHDialog, IDC_OFFVERT, EM_LIMITTEXT,
              (WPARAM)SIZENUMBUF - 1, OL);

           // assign values to edit controls for ints:
           SetDlgItemInt (mHDialog, IDC_COLS, Cols, TRUE);
           SetDlgItemInt (mHDialog, IDC_NEXTCOL, NextCol, TRUE);
           SetDlgItemInt (mHDialog, IDC_NEXTROW, NextRow, TRUE);
           SetDlgItemInt (mHDialog, IDC_ROWS, Rows, TRUE);

           // assign values to edit controls for floats:
           sprintf (NumBuf, "%.2f", OffHoriz);
           SetDlgItemText (mHDialog, IDC_OFFHORIZ, NumBuf);
           sprintf (NumBuf, "%.2f", OffLeft);
           SetDlgItemText (mHDialog, IDC_OFFLEFT, NumBuf);
           sprintf (NumBuf, "%.2f", OffTop);
           SetDlgItemText (mHDialog, IDC_OFFTOP, NumBuf);
           sprintf (NumBuf, "%.2f", OffVert);
           SetDlgItemText (mHDialog, IDC_OFFVERT, NumBuf);
```

```
        SetDlgItemText (mHDialog, IDC_FONTNAME,
           LogFont.lfFaceName);

        TempLogFont = LogFont;

        return (TRUE);

    default:
        if (Msg == mHelpMessage)
            {
            SendMessage (mHDialog, WM_COMMAND, IDC_HELP, OL);
            return (TRUE);
            }
        else
            return (FALSE);
    }
  }

void CFormLabelDialog::WrapUp ()
// saves the data displayed by the Format Label dialog box
  {
  char NumBuf [SIZENUMBUF];

  // save the ints:
  sprintf (NumBuf, "%d", Cols);
  WritePrivateProfileString
     ("label",
     "cols",
     NumBuf,
     "ENVELOPE.INI");

  sprintf (NumBuf, "%d", NextCol);
  WritePrivateProfileString
     ("label",
     "nextcol",
     NumBuf,
     "ENVELOPE.INI");

  sprintf (NumBuf, "%d", NextRow);
  WritePrivateProfileString
     ("label",
```

```
        "nextrow",
        NumBuf,
        "ENVELOPE.INI");

    sprintf (NumBuf, "%d", Rows);
    WritePrivateProfileString
        ("label",
        "rows",
        NumBuf,
        "ENVELOPE.INI");

    // save the floats:

    sprintf (NumBuf, "%.2f", OffHoriz);
    WritePrivateProfileString
        ("label",
        "offhoriz",
        NumBuf,
        "ENVELOPE.INI");

    sprintf (NumBuf, "%.2f", OffLeft);
    WritePrivateProfileString
        ("label",
        "offleft",
        NumBuf,
        "ENVELOPE.INI");

    sprintf (NumBuf, "%.2f", OffTop);
    WritePrivateProfileString
        ("label",
        "offtop",
        NumBuf,
        "ENVELOPE.INI");

    sprintf (NumBuf, "%.2f", OffVert);
    WritePrivateProfileString
        ("label",
        "offvert",
        NumBuf,
        "ENVELOPE.INI");
    }
```

Listing 8.4

```
;;;;;;;;;;;;;;;;;;;;;;;;;;;;;;;;;;;;;;;;;;;;;;;;;;;;;;;;;;;;;;;;;;;;;;;;
;                                                                    ;
; ENVELOPE.DEF:  Module-definition file for the ENVELOPE             ;
;                program.                                            ;
;                                                                    ;
;;;;;;;;;;;;;;;;;;;;;;;;;;;;;;;;;;;;;;;;;;;;;;;;;;;;;;;;;;;;;;;;;;;;;;;;


NAME ENVELOPE

DESCRIPTION  'Envelope & Label Printer'

EXETYPE WINDOWS

CODE PRELOAD MOVEABLE DISCARDABLE

DATA PRELOAD MOVEABLE MULTIPLE

HEAPSIZE 1024

STACKSIZE 10240
```

Listing 8.5

```
//////////////////////////////////////////////////////////////////////
//                                                                  //
// RESOURCE.H:  Constant definitions for the ENVELOPE program       //
//              resources (generated by Microsoft App Studio).      //
//                                                                  //
//////////////////////////////////////////////////////////////////////

//{{NO_DEPENDENCIES}}
// App Studio generated include file.
// Used by ENVELOPE.RC
//
#define IDC_HELP                    100
#define IDC_TEXT                    101
#define IDC_ENVELOPE                102
#define IDC_LABEL                   103
```

```
#define IDC_CLIPBOARD                    104
#define IDC_ENTERED                      105
#define IDC_ADDRESS                      106
#define IDC_PORTRAIT                     108
#define IDC_LANDSCAPE                    109
#define IDC_RETLEFT                      110
#define IDC_RETTOP                       111
#define IDC_TOLEFT                       112
#define IDC_TOTOP                        113
#define IDC_FONT                         114
#define IDC_FONTNAME                     115
#define IDC_OFFLEFT                      117
#define IDC_OFFTOP                       118
#define IDC_OFFHORIZ                     119
#define IDC_OFFVERT                      120
#define IDC_ROWS                         121
#define IDC_COLS                         122
#define IDC_NEXTROW                      123
#define IDC_NEXTCOL                      124
#define IDM_ABOUT                        1000
#define IDM_HELPHELP                     1001
#define IDM_HELPSEARCH                   1002
#define IDM_HELPCONTENTS                 1003
#define IDM_SHOWDIALOG                   1004
#define IDM_ONTOP                        1005
#define IDM_FORMENVELOPE                 1006
#define IDM_FORMLABEL                    1007
#define IDM_PRINTSETUP                   1008
#define IDM_PRINT                        1009
#define IDC_STATIC                       -1

// Next default values for new objects
//
#ifdef APSTUDIO_INVOKED
#ifndef APSTUDIO_READONLY_SYMBOLS

#define _APS_NEXT_RESOURCE_VALUE         103
#define _APS_NEXT_COMMAND_VALUE          1010
#define _APS_NEXT_CONTROL_VALUE          119
```

```
#define _APS_NEXT_SYMED_VALUE          101
#endif
#endif
```

Listing 8.6

```
//////////////////////////////////////////////////////////////
//                                                            //
// ENVELOPE.RC:  Resource-definition file for the ENVELOPE    //
//               program (generated by Microsoft App Studio). //
//                                                            //
//////////////////////////////////////////////////////////////

//Microsoft App Studio generated resource script.
//
#include "resource.h"

#define APSTUDIO_READONLY_SYMBOLS
//////////////////////////////////////////////////////////////
//
// Generated from the TEXTINCLUDE 2 resource.
//
#include "windows.h"


//////////////////////////////////////////////////////////////
#undef APSTUDIO_READONLY_SYMBOLS


//////////////////////////////////////////////////////////////
//
// Accelerator
//

ENVELOPEACCEL ACCELERATORS DISCARDABLE
BEGIN
    VK_F1,          IDM_HELPCONTENTS,        VIRTKEY,NOINVERT
END
```

```
///////////////////////////////////////////////////////////////
//
// Dialog
//

MAINDLG DIALOG DISCARDABLE  177, 148, 137, 141
STYLE WS_MINIMIZEBOX | WS_POPUP | WS_VISIBLE | WS_CAPTION |
    WS_SYSMENU
CAPTION "Envelope & Label Printer"
MENU EnvelopeMenu
FONT 8, "MS Sans Serif"
BEGIN
    CONTROL         "&Envelope",IDC_ENVELOPE,"Button",
                    BS_AUTORADIOBUTTON | WS_GROUP | WS_TABSTOP,
                    16,18,42,10
    CONTROL         "&Label",IDC_LABEL,"Button",
                    BS_AUTORADIOBUTTON,16,30,34,10
    CONTROL         "From &Clipboard",IDC_CLIPBOARD,"Button",
                    BS_AUTORADIOBUTTON | WS_GROUP | WS_TABSTOP,
                    16,63,61,10
    CONTROL         "Entered &Here:",IDC_ENTERED,"Button",
                    BS_AUTORADIOBUTTON,16,75,60,10
    EDITTEXT        IDC_ADDRESS,13,89,110,39,ES_MULTILINE |
                    ES_AUTOVSCROLL | ES_AUTOHSCROLL | WS_GROUP |
                    0x1000
    DEFPUSHBUTTON   "&PRINT",IDM_PRINT,84,8,46,19,WS_GROUP
    GROUPBOX        "Print",IDC_STATIC,7,5,57,43
    GROUPBOX        "Address",IDC_STATIC,7,50,123,84
END

ABOUTDLG DIALOG DISCARDABLE  12, 24, 130, 100
STYLE DS_MODALFRAME | WS_POPUP | WS_VISIBLE | WS_CAPTION |
    WS_SYSMENU
CAPTION "About"
FONT 8, "MS Sans Serif"
BEGIN
    CTEXT           "Windows Envelope && Label Printer",-1,7,10,
                    116,8
    CTEXT           "by Michael J. Young",-1,7,28,116,8
    ICON            "EnvelopeIcon",-1,55,47,18,20
    DEFPUSHBUTTON   "OK",IDOK,43,80,40,14
```

```
END

FORMENVDLG DIALOG DISCARDABLE  12, 24, 190, 174
STYLE DS_MODALFRAME ¦ WS_POPUP ¦ WS_VISIBLE ¦ WS_CAPTION ¦
    WS_SYSMENU
CAPTION "Format Envelope"
FONT 8, "MS Sans Serif"
BEGIN
        LTEXT           "Return &Address:",IDC_STATIC,7,6,53,9,
                        NOT WS_GROUP
        EDITTEXT        IDC_ADDRESS,8,21,112,47,ES_MULTILINE ¦
                        ES_AUTOVSCROLL ¦ ES_AUTOHSCROLL ¦ 0x1000
        CONTROL         "&Portrait",IDC_PORTRAIT,"Button",
                        BS_AUTORADIOBUTTON ¦ WS_GROUP,131,26,40,10
        CONTROL         "Lan&dscape",IDC_LANDSCAPE,"Button",
                        BS_AUTORADIOBUTTON,131,44,50,10
        LTEXT           "&Left:",IDC_STATIC,15,89,17,9
        EDITTEXT        IDC_RETLEFT,36,87,20,12,ES_AUTOHSCROLL ¦
                        WS_GROUP
        LTEXT           "&Top:",IDC_STATIC,15,106,17,9
        EDITTEXT        IDC_RETTOP,36,104,20,12,ES_AUTOHSCROLL
        LTEXT           "Le&ft:",IDC_STATIC,105,89,17,9
        EDITTEXT        IDC_TOLEFT,126,87,20,12,ES_AUTOHSCROLL
        LTEXT           "T&op:",IDC_STATIC,105,106,17,9
        EDITTEXT        IDC_TOTOP,126,104,20,12,ES_AUTOHSCROLL
        PUSHBUTTON      "&Choose Font...",IDC_FONT,124,132,58,14
        DEFPUSHBUTTON   "OK",IDOK,9,153,50,14
        PUSHBUTTON      "Cancel",IDCANCEL,71,153,50,14
        GROUPBOX        "Orientation",IDC_STATIC,126,7,56,60
        GROUPBOX        "Offset Return Address",IDC_STATIC,8,73,84,52
        LTEXT           "in.",IDC_STATIC,62,89,11,9
        LTEXT           "in.",IDC_STATIC,63,105,11,9
        GROUPBOX        "Offset ""To"" Address",IDC_STATIC,98,73,84,
                        52
        LTEXT           "in.",IDC_STATIC,153,89,11,9
        LTEXT           "in.",IDC_STATIC,153,105,11,9
        LTEXT           "Font:",IDC_STATIC,8,135,19,9
        LTEXT           "<font name>",IDC_FONTNAME,32,135,89,9
        PUSHBUTTON      "&Help",IDC_HELP,132,153,50,14
END
```

```
FORMLABELDLG DIALOG DISCARDABLE  0, 0, 214, 149
STYLE DS_MODALFRAME | WS_POPUP | WS_VISIBLE | WS_CAPTION |
    WS_SYSMENU
CAPTION "Format Label"
FONT 8, "MS Sans Serif"
BEGIN
    LTEXT           "&Left:",IDC_STATIC,15,24,17,9
    EDITTEXT        IDC_OFFLEFT,36,21,20,12,ES_AUTOHSCROLL |
                    WS_GROUP
    LTEXT           "&Top:",IDC_STATIC,15,40,17,9
    EDITTEXT        IDC_OFFTOP,36,39,20,12,ES_AUTOHSCROLL
    LTEXT           "&Horizontal:",IDC_STATIC,104,24,37,9
    EDITTEXT        IDC_OFFHORIZ,148,21,20,12,ES_AUTOHSCROLL |
                    WS_GROUP
    LTEXT           "&Vertical:",IDC_STATIC,104,40,29,9
    EDITTEXT        IDC_OFFVERT,148,39,20,12,ES_AUTOHSCROLL
    LTEXT           "&Rows:",IDC_STATIC,14,84,22,9
    EDITTEXT        IDC_ROWS,55,81,14,12,ES_AUTOHSCROLL |
                    WS_GROUP
    LTEXT           "&Columns:",IDC_STATIC,14,100,32,9
    EDITTEXT        IDC_COLS,55,99,15,12,ES_AUTOHSCROLL
    LTEXT           "Ro&w:",IDC_STATIC,97,85,22,9
    EDITTEXT        IDC_NEXTROW,137,82,14,12,ES_AUTOHSCROLL |
                    WS_GROUP
    LTEXT           "C&olumn:",IDC_STATIC,97,101,32,9
    EDITTEXT        IDC_NEXTCOL,137,100,15,12,ES_AUTOHSCROLL
    DEFPUSHBUTTON   "OK",IDOK,172,72,36,14,NOT WS_TABSTOP
    PUSHBUTTON      "Cancel",IDCANCEL,172,89,36,14,NOT WS_TABSTOP
    PUSHBUTTON      "&Help",IDC_HELP,172,107,36,14,NOT WS_TABSTOP
    GROUPBOX        "Offset of First Label",IDC_STATIC,8,8,75,52
    LTEXT           "in.",IDC_STATIC,62,24,11,9
    LTEXT           "in.",IDC_STATIC,63,40,11,9
    GROUPBOX        "Distance Between Label Centers",IDC_STATIC,
                    90,8,117,52
    LTEXT           "in.",IDC_STATIC,175,24,11,9
    LTEXT           "in.",IDC_STATIC,175,40,11,9
    GROUPBOX        "Labels on Page",IDC_STATIC,7,68,75,52
    GROUPBOX        "Next Label to Print",IDC_STATIC,90,69,75,52
    PUSHBUTTON      "&Choose Font...",IDC_FONT,149,130,58,14,
                    NOT WS_TABSTOP
    LTEXT           "Font:",IDC_STATIC,7,132,19,9
```

```
    LTEXT              "<font name>",IDC_FONTNAME,31,132,89,9
END

#ifdef APSTUDIO_INVOKED
/////////////////////////////////////////////////////////////////
//
// TEXTINCLUDE
//

1 TEXTINCLUDE DISCARDABLE
BEGIN
    "resource.h\0"
END

2 TEXTINCLUDE DISCARDABLE
BEGIN
    "#include ""windows.h""\r\n"
    "\0"
END

3 TEXTINCLUDE DISCARDABLE
BEGIN
    "\r\n"
    "\0"
END


/////////////////////////////////////////////////////////////////
#endif    // APSTUDIO_INVOKED


/////////////////////////////////////////////////////////////////
//
// Icon
//

ENVELOPEICON            ICON    DISCARDABLE    "ENVELOPE.ICO"

/////////////////////////////////////////////////////////////////
//
// Menu
//
```

```
ENVELOPEMENU MENU DISCARDABLE
BEGIN
    POPUP "&Format"
    BEGIN
        MENUITEM "&Envelope...",               IDM_FORMENVELOPE
        MENUITEM "&Label...",                  IDM_FORMLABEL
    END
    POPUP "&Options"
    BEGIN
        MENUITEM "Always on &Top",             IDM_ONTOP
    END
    POPUP "&Help"
    BEGIN
        MENUITEM "&Contents...\tF1",           IDM_HELPCONTENTS
        MENUITEM "&Search for Help On...",     IDM_HELPSEARCH
        MENUITEM "&How to Use Help...",        IDM_HELPHELP
        MENUITEM SEPARATOR
        MENUITEM "&About...",                  IDM_ABOUT
    END
END


#ifndef APSTUDIO_INVOKED
/////////////////////////////////////////////////////////////////////
//
// Generated from the TEXTINCLUDE 3 resource.
//


/////////////////////////////////////////////////////////////////////
#endif    // not APSTUDIO_INVOKED
```

Organization of the Program

The primary duties of the ENVELOPE program are divided among the three dialog box classes, CMainDialog, CFormEnvDialog, and CFormLabelDialog.

The following are the responsibilities of the CMainDialog class:

- To display the main program dialog box, which allows the user to change program options and issue commands
- To respond to the menu commands and the PRINT button and to perform the appropriate actions
- At program initialization, to read the settings of the main program options (that is, the options displayed in the main dialog box) from the initialization file
- At program exit, to write the settings of the main program options to the initialization file

The CFormEnvDialog class has the following responsibilities:

- To store the envelope format settings (the return address, offsets, font, and so on) in public data members, so that these settings can be directly accessed by the CMainDialog code
- To display the Format Envelope modal dialog box (when the CMainDialog code calls CFormEnvDialog::Create), which allows the user to change the envelope format settings (it is derived from the CMDialog class so that it can be used to display a modal dialog box)
- At program initialization, to read the envelope format settings from the initialization file
- At program exit, to write the envelope format settings to the initialization file

Finally, the CFormLabelDialog class has these responsibilities:

- To store the label format settings (the offsets, font, and so on) in public data members, so that these settings can be directly accessed by the CMainDialog code
- To display the Format Envelope modal dialog box (when the CMainDialog code calls CFormLabelDialog::Create), which allows the user to change the label format settings (it is derived from the CMDialog class so that it can be used to display a modal dialog box)

- At program initialization, to read the label format settings from the initialization file

- At program exit, to write the label format settings to the initialization file

Initializing

When the main dialog box is first displayed at program startup, the `CMainDialog::OnInitDialog` function (defined in DIALOG.CPP of Listing 8.3) reads the main program option settings from the initialization file. It reads only the settings maintained or displayed by the main dialog box (namely, the state of the Envelope, Label, From Clipboard, and Entered Here: radio buttons, the text in the Entered Here: text box, and the state of the `OnTop` flag).

Notice that when `OnInitDialog` reads the text to be stored in the Entered Here: text box, it translates all characters that have the value `CRCODE` (9D hex) into CR (carriage-return) characters, and all characters that have the value `LFCODE` (9E hex) into LF (line-feed) characters, as follows:

```
GetPrivateProfileString
   ("options",
   "address",
   "",
   Buffer,
   sizeof (Buffer),
   "ENVELOPE.INI");
for (int i = 0; Buffer [i]; ++i)
   {
   if (Buffer [i] == CRCODE)
      Buffer [i] = '\r';
   if (Buffer [i] == LFCODE)
      Buffer [i] = '\n';
   }
SetDlgItemText (mHDialog, IDC_ADDRESS, Buffer);
```

This translation is necessary because the routine that saves the text at program exit (in `CMainDialog::WrapUp`) translates each CR character into a `CRCODE` character, and each LF character into a `LFCODE` character. The reason `WrapUp` translates CR and LF characters is that the API function used to write the text to the initialization file, `WritePrivateProfileString`, will write only a *single line* of text. The Entered Here: text box, however, may contain several lines, each of which is terminated with a CR-LF pair. If CR and LF characters were not translated, all characters following the first CR-LF pair would be lost. (The encoded hex values 9D and 9E were chosen because they are not used to represent printable characters in the ANSI character set.)

OnInitDialog also adds a Print command, followed by a separator, to the system menu by calling the Windows API function InsertMenu:

```
InsertMenu
   (GetSystemMenu (mHDialog, FALSE),
   0,
   MF_BYPOSITION | MF_SEPARATOR,
   0,
   0);
InsertMenu
   (GetSystemMenu (mHDialog, FALSE),
   0,
   MF_BYPOSITION | MF_STRING,
   IDM_PRINT,
   "&Print");
```

The CFormEnvDialog class constructor reads the settings for the envelope format from the initialization file. This task is performed in the constructor rather than by the OnInitDialog function because the constructor is called *once*, at program startup, while the OnInitDialog function is called *every time* the Format Envelope modal dialog box is displayed. The CFormEnvDialog constructor also initializes the program font descriptions, as explained in the next section.

Likewise, the CFormLabelDialog class constructor reads the settings for the label format from the initialization file. Later in the chapter (in the section "Wrapping Up") you will see how the program option settings are saved in the initialization file.

Choosing the Fonts

As you will see later in the chapter, if you want to print text using a specific font, you must provide a description of that font contained in a LOGFONT structure. This section explains how the program obtains and stores the descriptions of the fonts that it uses for printing envelopes and labels.

The description of the font used for envelopes is stored in the CFormEnvDialog::LogFont public data member, and the description of the font used for labels is stored in the CFormLabelDialog::LogFont public data member; both of these data members are LOGFONT structures. At program startup, the CFormEnvDialog constructor attempts to read the contents of both of these data members from the file ENVELOPE.LFN (which is written to the Windows directory at program termination). If the file is not found (because either it was deleted or the program is being run for the first time), the constructor initializes the data members with the description of the default font for the current default Windows printer. To obtain this description, the constructor performs the following steps:

1. It calls the helper function CMainDialog::GetCurrentPrinter to obtain the information on the current default Windows printer that is stored in the "[windows]" section of the WIN.INI file, under the "device" entry. Note that the user designates the *default printer* through the Windows Control Panel.

2. It passes the printer information to the Windows API function CreateIC to obtain an information context for the printer. An information context can be used to get information on a particular device; unlike a device context, however, it cannot be used to send output to that device.

3. It calls the API function SetMapMode to select the MM_LOENGLISH mapping mode for the printer information context, because this mapping mode is used for printing. Mapping modes will be explained later, in the section "Printing Labels."

4. It calls the API function GetTextMetrics to obtain measurements for the default printer font; the measurements are assigned to the fields of a TEXTMETRIC structure. The *default* printer font is the one that is automatically used to print text until you explicitly choose a different font; normally, it is a standard font built into the printer.

5. It copies the applicable font measurements from the TEXTMETRIC structure to the LogFont LOGFONT structure.

6. It calls the API function `GetFaceName` to obtain the name of the default font, copying this name into the `lfFaceName` field of `LogFont`.

7. It calls the API function `DeleteDC` to release the information context. Because a limited number of information contexts are available, the program releases it as soon as it has finished using it.

8. The font height that is now stored in `LogFont.lfHeight` is in *printer units*. The constructor converts these units to *window units*, because the API function that displays the Font common dialog box (`ChooseFont`, which will be described later) assumes that the font height is in window units. The conversion will be explained later, in the section "Selecting the Font."

9. It copies the contents of `CFormEnvDialog::LogFont` to `CFormLabelDialog::LogFont`, so that *both* of the program font descriptions contain information on the default printer font.

NOTE

Ideally—in the spirit of object-oriented programming—the `CFormEnvDialog` class and the `CFormLabelDialog` class should each initialize their own font description. However, to make the program simpler and faster, both font descriptions are initialized within a single routine in the `CFormEnvDialog` class constructor. Also, for the same reasons, the `CFormEnvDialog::WrapUp` function (described later) writes *both* font descriptions to the font description file (ENVELOPE.LFN) at program termination.

When the user clicks the Choose Font... button while the Format Envelope dialog box is displayed, the `CFormEnvDialog::DialogProc` function (the `IDC_FONT` branch) displays the Font common dialog box, which allows the user to choose a new font for printing envelopes. Similarly, when the user clicks the Choose Font... button while the Format Label dialog box is displayed, `CFormLabelDialog::DialogProc` displays the Font common dialog box, which allows the user to choose a new font for printing labels.

Both `DialogProc` member functions display the Font dialog box by assigning values to a `CHOOSEFONT` structure, and then passing the address of this structure to the API function `ChooseFont`, which handles all the details of displaying and managing the dialog box. In general, the values assigned to the `CHOOSEFONT` structure affect the behavior of—and the initial data displayed by—the Font dialog box. The `Flags` field is assigned two values:

```
CF.Flags = CF_PRINTERFONTS | CF_INITTOLOGFONTSTRUCT;
```

The `CF_PRINTERFONTS` flag causes the Font dialog box to display the fonts that are available for the *printer* (rather than those available for the screen). `DialogProc` identifies the specific printer by assigning a handle to an information context for the default printer to the `hDC` field:

```
CF.hDC = HPrnIC;
```

The information context handle is obtained by calling the `CreateIC` API function, as described previously.

The `CF_INITTOLOGFONTSTRUCT` flag causes `ChooseFont` to initialize the Font dialog box controls, using the `LOGFONT` structure pointed to by the `lpLogFont` field of the `CHOOSEFONT` structure. The `lpLogFont` field is assigned the address of `TempLogFont`, which contains a copy of the `LogFont` data member of `CFormEnvDialog` or `CFormLabelDialog` (the copy was made in the `WM_INITDIALOG` routine):

```
CF.lpLogFont = &TempLogFont;
```

As a result of the `CF_INITTOLOGFONTSTRUCT` flag and the `lpLogFont` assignment, when the Font dialog box is first displayed, it contains a description of the font that the program is currently using. After the user closes the Font dialog box and the `ChooseFont` function returns, `TempLogFont` contains a description of the font that the user selected. Then, if the user clicks the OK button in the Format Envelope or Format Label dialog box, `TempLogFont` is copied to the permanent font description that is stored in the `LogFont` data member:

```
case IDOK:

    // other code ...

    LogFont = TempLogFont;
```

```
EndDialog (mHDialog, IDOK);
return (TRUE);
```

N O T E

The `ChooseFont` function expects the font height that you initially assign to the `lfHeight` field of the `LOGFONT` structure to be in window units (that is, screen pixels). Likewise, the font height that `ChooseFont` assigns to this field after the user closes the Font dialog box (based upon the point size that the user specified) is in window units. As you will see in the section "Printing Labels," the height must be temporarily converted to printer units immediately prior to selecting the font for printing, and restored to screen units after printing is complete.

Finally, the `WrapUp` member function of `CFormEnvDialog` saves the contents of both `CFormEnvDialog::LogFont` and `CFormLabelDialog::LogFont` in the ENVELOPE.LFN file. In the next section, you will see how the font descriptions are used to select the actual font when printing labels or envelopes.

Printing

When the user clicks the PRINT button or chooses the Print command on the system menu, the `CMainDialog::OnCommand` function calls `CMainDialog::PrintLabel` to print a label, if the Label radio button is checked, or it calls `CMainDialog::PrintEnvelope` to print an envelope, if the Envelope button is checked.

N O T E

Because the PRINT command is on the *system* menu rather than on the main menu belonging to the window, the program receives a WM_SYSCOMMAND message rather than a WM_COMMAND message when the user chooses the command. Accordingly, when the main window receives a WM_SYSCOMMAND message with WParam equal to IDM_PRINT, CMain-Dialog::DialogProc calls CMainDialog::On-Command, passing it the IDM_PRINT identifier, so that the routine that processes the PRINT button will receive control.

Printing Labels

The CMainDialog::PrintLabel function is simpler than the CMainDialog::PrintEnvelope function and is therefore described first. The label printing routine in PrintLabel performs the following basic steps (which are typical of the steps required to print text from a Windows program):

1. It creates a printer device context.

2. It sets the mapping mode.

3. It obtains a font handle and selects the font.

4. It initiates the print job and the page.

5. It prints the text on the label.

6. It terminates printing by ending the page and the print job, and by releasing the font handle and the printer device context.

After completing these steps, PrintLabel updates the row and column position of the *next* label to be printed, assigning these values to Form-LabelDialog.NextRow and FormLabelDialog.NextCol.

Creating a Printer Device Context PrintLabel first calls CMainDialog::GetCurrentPrinter (described previously) to obtain information on the current default printer, and then passes this information to the

Windows API function `CreateDC` to obtain a handle to a device context for the printer.

Setting the Mapping Mode Next, `PrintLabel` calls the API function `SetMapMode` to change the mapping mode for the printer device context to the `MM_LOENGLISH` setting. The mapping mode determines the units and the coordinate system used to specify the position of each item that is printed (via a Windows display function such as `TextOut`). Under the default mapping mode (known as `MM_TEXT`), the units are pixels; the x-coordinates (that is, horizontal coordinates) increase as you move right, and the y-coordinates (that is, vertical coordinates) increase as you move down. The problem with the default mapping mode is that the size of a pixel differs from printer to printer. Under the `MM_LOENGLISH` mapping mode, the size of a unit is 0.01 inch (on *any* printer); the x-coordinates increase as you move right, and the y-coordinates increase as you move up. Under both mapping modes, the origin (the point 0, 0) is—by default—at the upper-left corner of the window. Note, therefore, that to make a point visible in the `MM_LOENGLISH` mapping mode, it must be given a zero or negative y-coordinate. These two mapping modes are illustrated in Figure 8.11.

FIGURE 8.11

The default (MM_TEXT) mapping mode and the MM_LOENGLISH mapping mode

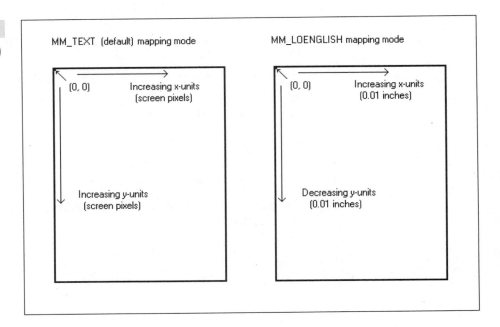

MM_TEXT (default) mapping mode

(0, 0) Increasing x-units (screen pixels)

Increasing y-units (screen pixels)

MM_LOENGLISH mapping mode

(0, 0) Increasing x-units (0.01 inches)

Decreasing y-units (0.01 inches)

Selecting the Font Before using the font description contained in the FormLabelDialog.LogFont data member, PrintLabel saves the value of the lfHeight field (which stores the font height), temporarily converts the value of lfHeight from window units (that is, screen pixels) to printer units (that is, units equaling 0.01 inch), so that the font will have the correct size on the printed page. After making this conversion, it restores the original value of the lfHeight field (so that LogFont can be used to initialize the Font dialog box). The following is the code that performs the conversion:

```
FormLabelDialog.LogFont.lfHeight *= 100;
HDC HWndDC = GetDC (mHDialog);
FormLabelDialog.LogFont.lfHeight /= GetDeviceCaps (HWndDC,
    LOGPIXELSY);
ReleaseDC (mHDialog, HWndDC);
```

This code performs the following calculation (expressed in pseudocode):

```
lfHeight = lfHeight * 100 * 1/WindowUnitsPerInch
```

where WindowUnitsPerInch, the number of window units per inch in the vertical direction, is obtained by passing the value LOGPIXELSY to the API function GetDeviceCaps (notice that the routine must obtain a handle to a window device context in order to call GetDeviceCaps).

PrintLabel then passes the font description to the API function CreateFontIndirect to obtain a font handle:

```
HFont = CreateFontIndirect (&FormLabelDialog.LogFont);
```

To select the font into the printer device context, it then passes the font handle to the SelectObject API function:

```
SelectObject (HPrnDC, HFont);
```

After the call to SelectObject, all text will be printed, using the font matching the description in FormLabelDialog.LogFont.

Finally, PrintLabel calculates the total height of a line of text displayed in the newly selected font:

```
GetTextMetrics (HPrnDC, &TM);
LineHeight = TM.tmHeight + TM.tmExternalLeading;
```

Initiating the Print Job and Page Before it can begin sending text to the printer, the PrintLabel function must initiate the print job by passing job information to the API function StartDoc, as follows:

```
DOCINFO DocInfo;

//...

DocInfo.cbSize = sizeof (DocInfo);
DocInfo.lpszDocName = "Label";
DocInfo.lpszOutput = 0;
StartDoc (HPrnDC, &DocInfo);
```

It must also initialize a new page by calling the StartPage API function:

```
StartPage (HPrnDC);
```

Printing the Text If the Entered Here: button is checked, PrintLabel obtains the text for the address from the Entered Here: text box (which has the identifier IDM_ADDRESS). The text is stored in a buffer allocated with the new operator, the address of which is assigned to PtrAddress.

If, however, the From Clipboard button is checked, PrintLabel obtains the address text from the Clipboard, using the following steps:

1. It calls the API function IsClipboardFormatAvailable to determine whether the Clipboard currently contains text (passing CF_TEXT to IsClipboardFormatAvailable tests for the presence of text from a Windows program, and passing CF_OEMTEXT tests for the presence of text from an MS-DOS session).

2. It calls the OpenClipboard API function to open the Clipboard. If steps 1 and 2 are both successful, it proceeds to step 3; otherwise it simply assigns PtrAddress the address of an empty string.

3. It calls the GetClipboardData API function to obtain a handle to the block of global memory containing the Clipboard text.

4. It calls the GlobalLock API function to obtain a pointer to the block of global memory.

5. It uses the new operator to allocate a block of local memory large enough to hold the text, assigning the address of this block to

`PtrAddress`. It determines the size of the text by calling the API function `GlobalSize`.

6. It calls the run-time function `_fmemcpy` to copy the text from the global memory to the local memory. (The text is copied into a local block because `PrintLabel` alters it; a program must not modify a memory block belonging to the Clipboard. Also, it is easier and faster to access the text in a local-memory allocation, using a near pointer, than text in a global memory block, using a far pointer.)

7. It calls the API function `GlobalUnlock` to unlock the global memory block before closing the Clipboard.

8. It calls the API function `CloseClipboard` to close the Clipboard.

N O T E

For a description of the procedure for adding text *to* the Clipboard, see the section "Exchanging Data" in Chapter 7.

Before it begins printing the text, `PrintLabel` also calculates the starting coordinates of the text, which are stored in the `int` variables `X` and `Y`:

```
X = (int)(FormLabelDialog.OffLeft * 100.0 +
    (FormLabelDialog.NextCol - 1) * FormLabelDialog.OffHoriz *
    100.0);
Y = (int)-(FormLabelDialog.OffTop * 100.0 +
    (FormLabelDialog.NextRow - 1) * FormLabelDialog.OffVert *
    100.0);
```

These calculations use the label format information maintained by the `CFormLabelDialog` class to determine which label on the page is to be printed and to derive the offset of the beginning of the text on this label. Because the printer device context is set to the `MM_LOENGLISH` mapping mode (described previously), the coordinates are calculated in 0.01-inch units and the vertical coordinate (`Y`) is made negative (recall that the origin is at the upper-left corner of the screen and that vertical coordinates increase, moving up).

PrintLabel finally proceeds to print each line contained in the address text, using the API function TextOut:

```
char *PtrLine;

// ...

PtrLine = GetLine (PtrAddress);
while (PtrLine)
    {
    TextOut (HPrnDC, X, Y, PtrLine, strlen (PtrLine));
    Y -= LineHeight;
    PtrLine = GetLine (0);
    }
```

Notice that the helper function CMainDialog::GetLine is used to extract each line from the buffer (PtrAddress); when no more lines are available, GetLine returns 0.

Terminating Printing When it has finished printing the label, Print-Label calls the API function EndPage to signal the device driver that the page is complete; the device driver then ejects the label (or label sheet) from the printer:

```
EndPage (HPrnDC);
```

PrintLabel also calls the EndDoc API function to terminate the print job:

```
EndDoc (HPrnDC);
```

Finally, PrintLabel releases the printer device context,

```
DeleteDC (HPrnDC);
```

and frees the font handle:

```
DeleteObject (HFont);
```

Printing Envelopes

The CMainDialog::PrintEnvelope function prints an envelope using the same basic procedure as the PrintLabel function. Before printing the addressee's address, however, it prints the return address, using the text stored in the FormEnvDialog.Address data member.

Also, when creating the printer device context, PrintEnvelope performs a series of steps to set the page orientation according to the current value of the FormEnvDialog.Portrait data member; this data member is set to TRUE when the user has checked the Portrait radio button in the Format Envelope dialog box, and it is set to FALSE when the user has checked the Landscape radio button. See the description of the page orientation given previously in the chapter, in the section "Formatting Envelopes."

Recall that when PrintLabel calls CreateDC to create the printer device context, it passes 0 as the fourth parameter; this causes the device context to use the *default* printer settings (that is, the settings that the user has assigned through the Windows Control Panel), including the default page orientation. In contrast, PrintEnvelope passes the address of a DEVMODE structure as the fourth parameter, which causes the device context to use the printer settings that are contained in this structure rather than the default ones:

```
HPrnDC = CreateDC
   (PrnDriver,
   PrnName,
   PrnPort,
   PtrDevMode);
```

PrintEnvelope needs to specify *only* the page orientation; all other printer settings contained in the DEVMODE structure (such as the paper size and the number of copies) should have their default values. Therefore, Print-Envelope first obtains a DEVMODE structure that contains all of the default printer settings, and then—before passing this structure to CreateDC—it assigns the appropriate value to the field that specifies the page orientation (dmOrientation).

The following is a summary of the procedure that PrintEnvelope uses to obtain a DEVMODE structure initialized with the default printer settings:

1. It calls the helper function CMainDialog::GetCurrentPrinter to obtain information on the current default Windows printer, including the name of the printer driver.

2. It passes the name of the printer driver to the LoadLibrary API function, to load the printer driver so that the functions it provides can be called. (A printer driver is a type of dynamic-link

library; as such, it contains functions that a program can call
once the library file has been loaded.)

3. It calls the API function GetProcAddress to obtain the address of
    the ExtDeviceMode function within the device driver, and it stores
    this address in a function pointer. (ExtDeviceMode is not part of
    the Windows API proper; rather, each printer driver exports its
    own version of this function.)

4. It uses the function pointer to call the ExtDeviceMode function,
    passing 0 as the last parameter (fwMode). This causes ExtDevice-
    Mode to return the *size* of the printer data. (The size of the data
    varies because some printer drivers supply printer-specific infor-
    mation following the standard DEVMODE structure.)

5. It allocates a buffer to hold the printer data and stores the address
    of this buffer in the DEVMODE pointer PtrDevMode.

6. It calls ExtDeviceMode again, passing DM_OUT_BUFFER as the last pa-
    rameter, which causes the function to fill the PtrDevMode buffer
    (passed as the third parameter) with the default printer settings.

After obtaining the initialized DEVMODE structure, PrintEnvelope sets the
dmOrientation field,

```
PtrDevMode->dmOrientation = FormEnvDialog.Portrait ?
    DMORIENT_PORTRAIT : DMORIENT_LANDSCAPE;
```

and then passes the structure to CreateDC to obtain the printer device
context, as shown previously in this section. Note that the printer settings
passed to CreateDC affect *only* printing performed with the supplied device context; they do *not* alter the default printer settings set through the
Control Panel or affect subsequent print jobs that a program performs,
using different device contexts. PrintEnvelope then proceeds with the
print job and prints the envelope, using techniques that were explained
earlier, in the section "Printing Labels."

Wrapping Up

As usual, the CMainDialog code calls the CMainDialog::WrapUp function
to save the program settings in the initialization file at program termination (that is, whenever the user quits the program or terminates Windows).

In the ENVELOPE program, however, the `CMainDialog::WrapUp` routine begins by calling the `WrapUp` routines belonging to each of the classes that manage format settings, so that each class can save the settings that it manages:

```
FormEnvDialog.WrapUp ();
FormLabelDialog.WrapUp ();
```

Because the code for reading settings is contained in the `CFormEnvDialog` and `CFormLabelDialog` class constructors, it might seem logical to place the code for saving settings in the class destructors, eliminating the need for the program to explicitly call a `WrapUp` function. Under Windows, however, the destructor is called only if the user quits the program; it is *not* called if the program is terminated because the user has quit Windows. (This feature limits the usefulness of destructors in Windows programs. In MS-DOS programs, you can normally assume that the destructor will be called unless there is a disaster such as a power outage or system crash.)

Enhancing the Envelope and Label Printer

The following are some ways that you might enhance the Envelope and Label Printer:

- *Provide an option that would print more than one label* without ejecting the label sheet after each label, so that the user could more easily print a set of labels. If this option were selected, the label sheet would be ejected only after all labels on the sheet have been printed *or* the user has clicked a button (which would be labeled "Eject Sheet" or "Form Feed," for example). To implement this option, the program would withhold the calls to the `EndPage` and `EndDoc` functions until the sheet is to be ejected.

- *Implement options for printing postal bar codes* on envelopes or labels. A postal bar code is a machine-readable representation of the addressee's zip code; printing it on an envelope or label may expedite mail handling or save postage costs in some circumstances. The program could extract the zip code from the address and then translate it into the proper sequence of long and short bars. An explanation of the encoding scheme should be available from the U.S. Postal Service.

- Expand the Format Label dialog box and the printing routine to *allow the user to include a return address on a label, so that the user could print on labels that have a space for a return address.*

CHAPTER

9

Phone Dialer

THIS chapter presents the Phone Dialer utility, which automatically dials phone numbers, using a Hayes-compatible modem. You can quickly dial simple phone numbers, or you can automate the dialing of complex sequences, such as those required for charging calls to your calling card. You can have the program dial a number once, or you can have it repeatedly redial a number to help you get through a busy phone line. You can enter a number into the program manually, have it extract a number that you copied into the Clipboard from another program, or automatically dial a phone number stored in the Address Manager utility presented in Chapter 7.

In studying the source code for the Phone Dialer, you will learn how to use Windows API functions to access a serial port, how to send commands to a modem attached to a serial port, how to use a modeless dialog box to display messages and receive commands, and how to use timing loops and Windows timer messages to create pauses or perform periodic actions.

How to Use the Phone Dialer

The Phone Dialer program window is shown in Figure 9.1. In the following sections, you will learn how to enter and dial a phone number, and how to set program options to customize the way that numbers are dialed.

The Phone Dialer
program window

```
┌─────────────────────────────────────────────┐
│  ┌───────────────────────────────────────┐   │
│  │ ▬      Phone Dialer              ▼ │   │
│  ├───────────────────────────────────────┤   │
│  │ Options   Help                        │   │
│  │                                       │   │
│  │  ┌─Telephone Number──────────────┐    │   │
│  │  │ ◉ From Clipboard              │    │   │
│  │  │ ○ Entered Here:  ┌──────────┐ │    │   │
│  │  │                  └──────────┘ │    │   │
│  │  └───────────────────────────────┘    │   │
│  │                                       │   │
│  │  ☐ Use Prefix    ┌──────────────┐    │   │
│  │                  │     DIAL     │    │   │
│  │  ☐ Use Suffix    └──────────────┘    │   │
│  │                                       │   │
│  │  ☐ Auto Repeat                        │   │
│  └───────────────────────────────────────┘   │
└─────────────────────────────────────────────┘
```

Dialing

To initiate dialing of a phone number, perform the following two basic
steps:

1. In the Telephone Number box, either choose the From Clipboard
    option to dial a number contained in the Windows Clipboard, or
    choose the Entered Here: number and manually type or paste a
    number into the adjoining text box.

2. Issue the dial command by clicking the DIAL button or using one
    of the other methods discussed below.

NOTE

To use the Phone Dialer, you need a Hayes-
compatible modem with an audible speaker. The
modem and telephone must be simultaneously
connected to the same phone line.

When you issue the dial command, the program displays a box with the "Dialing…" message, and you will hear the modem dialing the phone number. After four seconds (sufficient time to dial a simple phone number), the program displays the dialog box show in Figure 9.2. If you wish to speak, *first* pick up your phone and *then* click the OK button (or press Enter or Escape). If you do not wish to speak (for example, if the line is busy), simply leave your phone on the hook; after 25 seconds, the program will automatically hang up.

FIGURE 9.2

The dialog box displayed after the program has initiated dialing

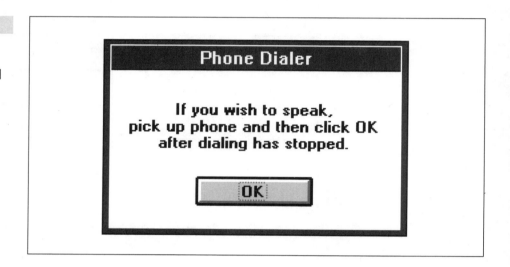

Phone Dialer

If you wish to speak,
pick up phone and then click OK
after dialing has stopped.

[OK]

NOTE

The program causes the modem to hang up (1) when you click the OK button, or (2) after 25 seconds have elapsed since it initiated dialing. If the modem hangs up *after* you have picked up your phone, the connection is preserved. If, however, the modem hangs up *before* you pick up your phone, the connection is terminated.

WARNING

The OK button will not appear until four seconds after dialing has been initiated. This is sufficient time for the modem to dial most common phone numbers. However, if the phone number is long or contains pauses (which are described later), the modem may still be dialing when the OK button appears. In this case, you can pick up the phone, but you must *not* click OK (or press Enter or Esc) until dialing is complete; otherwise, you will cause the modem to hang up *before* it has completed dialing.

Choosing the From Clipboard option allows you to dial a number contained in another application. To do this, select the number in the other program, issue the program's copy command (usually the Copy command on the Edit menu or the Ctrl+C keystroke), and then issue the dial command in the Phone Dialer. As discussed shortly, you can *automatically* transfer and dial a number appearing in the Address Manager program by simply placing the insertion point on the number and clicking the Address Manager's Dial button.

Choosing the Entered Here: option allows you to manually enter or edit a phone number. The next section discusses guidelines for entering phone numbers.

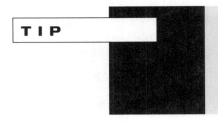

TIP

If you want to inspect and possibly edit a phone number contained in the Clipboard before dialing it, choose the Entered Here: option rather than the From Clipboard option, and paste the number into the Entered Here: text box.

You can use any of the following methods to issue the dial command:

- Click the DIAL button or press Alt+D.

- Choose the Dial command on the system menu.

- While running the Address Manager utility, place the insertion point on the line in the Phone Numbers text box that contains the phone number you want to dial (or select the line), and choose the Dial command on the Record menu or click the Dial button.

If you use the third method, the Address Manager runs the Phone Dialer (if it is not already running), extracts and copies the number to the Clipboard, chooses the From Clipboard option in the Phone Dialer, and issues the Phone Dialer's dial command. The number is dialed using the current option settings that you have made in the Phone Dialer.

Guidelines for Phone Numbers

The phone number that is contained in the Clipboard, or that you type into the Entered Here: text box, may contain the digits 0–9, as well as comma, *, or # characters. These characters are sent directly to the modem.

The number may also contain the separator characters (,), -, or /. However, there may not be more than one separator between any two of the phone number characters listed in the previous paragraph. The separator characters enhance readability, but are not sent to the modem.

Finally, the phone number may be preceded or followed by additional text, provided that no valid phone number character precedes the phone number itself (the program extracts the *first* sequence of valid phone number characters from the text).

Each comma (,) embedded in the phone number generates a pause. On Hayes-compatible modems, the pause is two seconds by default, although the period can be programmed. You might, for example, enter a number such as the following to dial a phone number, pause for eight seconds, and then dial a voice-mail extension:

```
1-956-983-9821,,,,284
```

The * and # characters can be included to initiate telephone commands. For example, the following number would disable call waiting (assuming that this is the appropriate command for your telephone system), pause for two seconds, and then dial a phone number:

```
*70,1-487-981-9972
```

As you will see in the next section, you can also define a general-purpose prefix and a general-purpose suffix, and optionally include either or both of them when you dial a phone number.

Using Program Options

In the following sections, you will learn how to define and use telephone number prefixes and suffixes, how to perform auto-repeat dialing, how to configure the program for your modem, and how to use the Always on Top option.

Using Prefixes and Suffixes

The prefix is dialed immediately before the telephone number if you select the Use Prefix check box, and the suffix is dialed immediately after the telephone number if you select the Use Suffix check box.

To define a prefix, suffix, or both, choose the Dialing Options... command on the Options menu. The program will open the Dialing Options dialog box, shown in Figure 9.3. Enter any desired prefix into the Prefix:

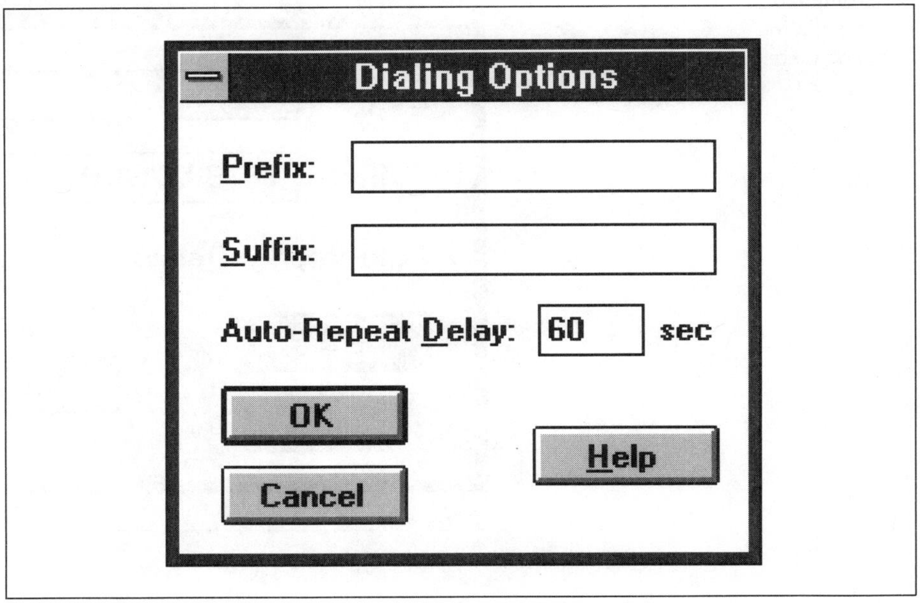

FIGURE 9.3

The Dialing Options dialog box

text box, and any desired suffix into the Suffix: text box. The program will send all characters, exactly as you type them, directly to the modem; therefore, you should *not* include separator characters or extraneous text.

You could, for example, define the prefix

```
*70,
```

and then select the Use Prefix option before dialing a number to disable call waiting during the call. As another example, you might define the prefix

```
9,
```

to activate an outside phone line. You would then select the Use Prefix option whenever making an outside call.

As a third example, you could define a prefix and a suffix for charging a call to your calling card; an example is shown in Figure 9.4. Then, to charge a call, you would select both the Use Prefix and the Use Suffix options before dialing the number.

FIGURE 9.4

An example of a prefix and a suffix for charging a call to a calling card

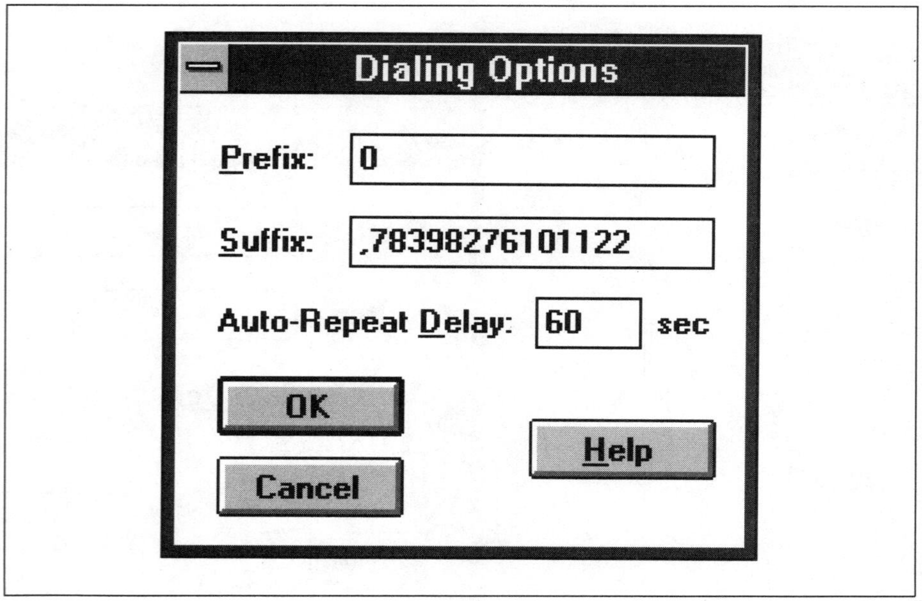

In general, to dial characters in addition to the basic phone number, either you can define a prefix or suffix, or you can store the additional characters directly in the phone number (for example, when you enter a phone number into the Address Manager or other program). Defining a prefix or suffix is best for general-purpose dialing characters that you want to be able to switch on or off (such as the characters for charging a call to a calling card). Storing characters within the number itself is best for characters that are unique to a given phone number or that are *always* used when dialing the number (for example, a voice-mail extension).

Using Auto-Repeat Dialing

You can have the Phone Dialer automatically redial the current number at regular intervals by choosing the Auto Repeat option. If you choose this option, the phone dialer works as follows: After the program dials the number, it displays—as usual—the dialog box show in Figure 9.2, which contains an OK button.

If the other party's phone begins ringing or is answered (which you can hear through the modem speaker), pick up the receiver and click OK, as usual. In this case, the number will *not* be redialed.

If, however, the phone line is busy (that is, you hear a busy signal on the modem speaker), do not do anything. (Specifically, you should *not* click the OK button, because this tells the program that you have accepted the call and terminates auto-repeat dialing.) After 25 seconds, the program will hang up the modem and it will display the dialog box shown in Figure 9.5, which indicates the number of seconds before the number will be redialed. While this box is displayed, you can cancel auto-repeat dialing by clicking the Cancel button (or by pressing Enter or Esc). When the auto-repeat delay has elapsed, the program dials the number again and the sequence described here begins again.

By default, the delay before the program redials the number is 60 seconds. To specify a different delay, choose the Dialing Options... command on the Options menu and enter the desired number of seconds into the Auto-Repeat Delay: text box. You can enter a value between 1 and 9999.

FIGURE 9.5

The dialog box
displayed during the
delay before the
program redials a
phone number

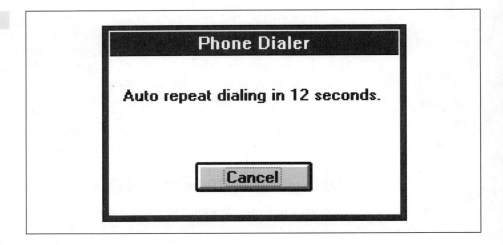

Setting the Modem Options

Before using the Phone Dialer for the first time, you should configure the program for your modem by choosing the Modem Settings... command on the Options menu. The program will display the Modem Settings dialog box, shown in Figure 9.6.

In the Dial Type area, select the Tone option if your phone line uses tone dialing, or select the Pulse option if your phone line uses pulse dialing (the initial setting is Tone).

In the Port area, choose the serial port to which your modem is connected (the initial port setting is COM1).

Setting the Always on Top Option

If you enable the Always on Top option on the Options menu, the program window will always be displayed on top of overlapping windows, even when the window is inactive or minimized.

FIGURE 9.6

The Modem Settings
dialog box

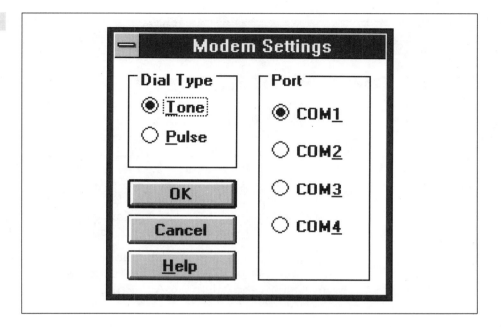

T I P

You can use the following method to make the
Phone Dialer readily accessible on your desktop for
quickly dialing a number: Choose the Always on
Top option, choose the From Clipboard option and
any other options you want to use, and minimize
the program window; the program icon will then
always be visible on your desktop while you are
working in other programs. Whenever you need to
dial a number, copy it to the Clipboard, click on the
Phone Dialer icon to open the system menu, and
then click on the Dial command or simply press
Enter (because the Dial command is at the top of the
menu, it is automatically highlighted).

How the Phone Dialer Works

Listings 9.1 through 9.6 provide the source code for the Phone Dialer program, DIAL, and the program icon is shown in Figure 9.7. Listing 9.1 is the program header file (DIAL.H), which defines each of the classes used in the program and is included in the two C++ source files. Listing 9.2 (DIAL.CPP) defines the WinMain function and declares the global program objects. Listing 9.3 (DIALOG.CPP) defines the member functions belonging to the main window class (CMainDialog) as well as the classes that manage the other modal and modeless dialog boxes.

Listing 9.4 (DIAL.DEF) is the module-definition file, and Listings 9.5 and 9.6 (RESOURCE.H and DIAL.RC) are the program resource files generated by the Microsoft App Studio.

FIGURE 9.7

The DIAL program icon

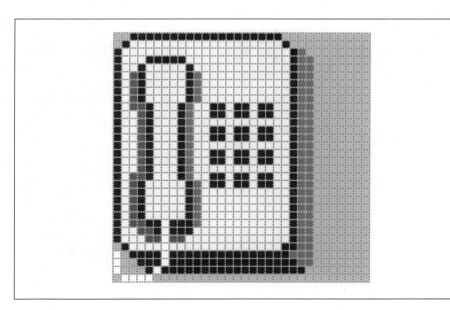

Listing 9.1

```
///////////////////////////////////////////////////////////////
//                                                             //
// DIAL.H:  Header file for the DIAL program.                  //
//                                                             //
///////////////////////////////////////////////////////////////

#include "..\wclasses\wclasses.h"
#include "resource.h"

// constant for help topic:
#define HELPDIALOPTIONSDLG 100
#define HELPMODEMDLG        101


///////////////////////////////////////////////////////////////
// main dialog box class definition:                           //
///////////////////////////////////////////////////////////////

class CMainDialog : public CMLDialog
{
   HBRUSH HBrushWorkSpace;
   UINT HTimer;
   int OnTop;

   void DialIt ();
   BOOL IsPhoneDigit (char Ch);
   BOOL IsPhoneSep (char Ch);
   virtual BOOL DialogProc (UINT Msg, WPARAM WParam,
                            LPARAM LParam);
   BOOL OnCommand (int IDItem, HWND HWndCtl, WORD NotifyCode);
   BOOL OnCtlColor (HDC HDCChild, HWND HWndChild, int CtlType);
   BOOL OnDestroy ();
   BOOL OnInitDialog (HWND HWndFocus, LPARAM Data);
   BOOL OnSysColorChange ();
   BOOL OnTimer ();
   void WrapUp ();

public:
   CMainDialog ();
};
```

```
//////////////////////////////////////////////////////////////
// 'Dialing Options' modal dialog box class definition:      //
//////////////////////////////////////////////////////////////

class CDialOptionsDialog : public CMDialog
{
    virtual BOOL DialogProc (UINT Msg, WPARAM WParam,
                             LPARAM LParam);
public:
    int Delay;
    char Prefix [32];
    char Suffix [32];

    CDialOptionsDialog ();
    void WrapUp ();
};


//////////////////////////////////////////////////////////////
// Message modeless dialog box class definition:             //
//////////////////////////////////////////////////////////////

class CMessageDialog : public CMLDialog
{
    virtual BOOL DialogProc (UINT Msg, WPARAM WParam,
                             LPARAM LParam);
public:
    BOOL ButtonClicked;

};


//////////////////////////////////////////////////////////////
// 'Modem Settings' modal dialog box class definition:       //
//////////////////////////////////////////////////////////////

class CModemDialog : public CMDialog
{
    virtual BOOL DialogProc (UINT Msg, WPARAM WParam,
                             LPARAM LParam);
public:
    char Port [5];        // "COM1", "COM2", "COM3", or "COM4"
```

```
    char DialType [2];   // "T" or "P"

    CModemDialog ();
    void WrapUp ();
};
```

Listing 9.2

```
/////////////////////////////////////////////////////////////
//                                                           //
// DIAL.CPP:  Global object declarations and program entry   //
//            point for the DIAL program.                    //
//                                                           //
/////////////////////////////////////////////////////////////

#include "dial.h"

/////////////////////////////////////////////////////////////
// global object declarations:                              //
/////////////////////////////////////////////////////////////

CApplication App;
CMainDialog MainDialog;
CDialOptionsDialog DialOptionsDialog;
CModemDialog ModemDialog;
CMessageDialog MessageDialog;

/////////////////////////////////////////////////////////////
// program entry function:                                  //
/////////////////////////////////////////////////////////////

int PASCAL WinMain
    (HINSTANCE HInstCurrent,
    HINSTANCE HInstPrevious,
    LPSTR CmdLine,
    int CmdShow)
    {
    MSG Msg;

    if (HInstPrevious)
        {
```

```
      HWND HWndPopup;

      GetInstanceData
         (HInstPrevious,
          (BYTE *)&MainDialog.mHDialog,
          sizeof (HWND));
      ShowWindow (MainDialog.mHDialog, SW_SHOWNORMAL);
      HWndPopup = GetLastActivePopup (MainDialog.mHDialog);
      BringWindowToTop (MainDialog.mHDialog);
      BringWindowToTop (HWndPopup);
      return (FALSE);
      }

   App.Initialize (HInstCurrent, HInstPrevious, CmdLine,
                   CmdShow);

   if (!App.LoadAccel ("DialAccel"))
      return (FALSE);

   if (!MainDialog.SetIcon ("DialIcon"))
      return (FALSE);

   if (!MainDialog.Create ("MainDlg"))
      return (FALSE);

   while (GetMessage (&Msg, NULL, NULL, NULL))
      if (!TranslateAccelerator (MainDialog.mHDialog,
                                 App.mHAccelTable,
                                 &Msg))
         // add extra call to IsDialogMessage to handle
         // message dialog if it is displayed:
         if (!IsDialogMessage (MainDialog.mHDialog, &Msg) &&
             (!MessageDialog.mHDialog ||
             !IsDialogMessage (MessageDialog.mHDialog, &Msg)))
             {
             TranslateMessage (&Msg);
             DispatchMessage (&Msg);
             }

   return (Msg.wParam);
   }
```

Listing 9.3

```cpp
///////////////////////////////////////////////////////////////
//                                                           //
// DIALOG.CPP:  Dialog class member functions for the        //
//              DIAL program.                                 //
//                                                           //
///////////////////////////////////////////////////////////////

#include "dial.h"
#include <ctype.h>
#include <stdio.h>
#include <string.h>

#define SIZENUMBER 64 // size of buffer to hold phone number

#define __max(a,b)  (((a) > (b)) ? (a) : (b))
#define __min(a,b)  (((a) < (b)) ? (a) : (b))

extern CMainDialog MainDialog;
extern CDialOptionsDialog DialOptionsDialog;
extern CMessageDialog MessageDialog;
extern CModemDialog ModemDialog;


///////////////////////////////////////////////////////////////
// CMainDialog member functions:                             //
///////////////////////////////////////////////////////////////

CMainDialog::CMainDialog ()
   {
   HBrushWorkSpace = 0;
   }

void CMainDialog::DialIt ()
// dials the phone number obtained from the Clipboard or entered
// into the IDC_NUMBER edit control
   {
   char CommandBuf [4 + sizeof (DialOptionsDialog.Prefix)-1 +
      SIZENUMBER-1 + sizeof (DialOptionsDialog.Suffix)-1 + 2];
   COMSTAT ComStatInfo;
   DCB DCBPort;
```

```
HANDLE HClipData;
int IDPort;
char Message [128];
MSG Msg;
char NumBuf [SIZENUMBER];
DWORD OldTime;
char __far *PtrClipData;
int Result;

// display the message modeless dialog box if it is not
// already displayed, set "Dialing..." message, and hide
// button (user can't cancel operation until later):
if (MessageDialog.mHDialog == 0)
   MessageDialog.Create ("MessageDlg", mHDialog);
SetDlgItemText (MessageDialog.mHDialog, IDC_MESSAGE,
   "Dialing...");
ShowWindow (GetDlgItem (MessageDialog.mHDialog, IDOK),
   SW_HIDE);

// build up the command string, CommandBuf, that will be
// sent to the modem to dial the phone number:

strcpy (CommandBuf,"ATD");  // Hayes dial command
strcat (CommandBuf, ModemDialog.DialType);  // add 'T' or 'P'

// if 'Use Prefix' box is checked, add prefix:
if (IsDlgButtonChecked (mHDialog, IDC_PREFIX))
   strcat (CommandBuf, DialOptionsDialog.Prefix);

// add the digits of the phone number
if (IsDlgButtonChecked (mHDialog, IDC_CLIPBOARD))
   {  // 'From Clipboard' is checked; get number (NumBuf) from
      // Clipboard:
   if (!IsClipboardFormatAvailable (CF_TEXT) &&
      !IsClipboardFormatAvailable (CF_OEMTEXT) ||
      !OpenClipboard (mHDialog))
      {                        // Clipboard does not contain text;
      NumBuf [0] = '\0';   // set NumBuf to empty string
      }
   else  // Clipboard contains text
      {
```

```
                // obtain handle to Clipboard data:
                HClipData = GetClipboardData (CF_TEXT);
                // obtain pointer to Clipboard data:
                PtrClipData = (char __far*)GlobalLock (HClipData);
                // calculate size of data and copy data into NumBuf:
                int Size = __min ((int)GlobalSize (HClipData),
                   SIZENUMBER);
                _fmemcpy (NumBuf, PtrClipData, Size);
                NumBuf [SIZENUMBER-1] = '\0';
                // unlock handle to Clipboard data and close Clipboard:
                GlobalUnlock (HClipData);
                CloseClipboard ();
                }
        }
else   // 'Entered Here' is checked;
   {  // get number (NumBuf) from IDC_NUMBER edit control:
   GetDlgItemText (mHDialog, IDC_NUMBER, NumBuf,
      sizeof (NumBuf));
   }

// copy only the valid phone digits from the number (in
// NumBuf) into the command string (CommandBuf):

// move to first phone digit:
int NIdx = 0;
while (NumBuf [NIdx] &&
   !IsPhoneDigit (NumBuf [NIdx]))
   ++NIdx;

// scan thru remainder of phone number:
BOOL PrevSeparator = FALSE;
int CIdx = strlen (CommandBuf);
while (NumBuf [NIdx])
   {
   if (IsPhoneDigit (NumBuf [NIdx]))
      {
      CommandBuf [CIdx++] = NumBuf [NIdx]; // copy phone digit
      PrevSeparator = FALSE;              // reset flag
      }
   else if (IsPhoneSep (NumBuf [NIdx]))   // skip separator but
      {                                   // keep scanning;
```

```
          if (PrevSeparator)  // quit scanning if more than one
             break;           // contiguous separator is found
          PrevSeparator = TRUE;
          }
       else                   // quit scanning on first character
          break;              // that is neither a valid phone
       ++NIdx;                // digit nor a separator
       }
CommandBuf [CIdx] = '\0';

// if 'Use Suffix' box is checked, add suffix:
if (IsDlgButtonChecked (mHDialog, IDC_SUFFIX))
   strcat (CommandBuf, DialOptionsDialog.Suffix);

strcat (CommandBuf, "\r");  // terminate with CR and NULL

// open the serial port:
IDPort = OpenComm ((LPSTR)ModemDialog.Port, 256, 256);
if (IDPort < 0)  // a return value < 0 means an error occurred
   {
   sprintf (Message, "Communication error (line %d).",
      __LINE__);
   MessageBox
      (mHDialog,
      Message,
      "Phone Dialer",
      MB_ICONEXCLAMATION | MB_OK);
   CloseComm (IDPort);
   MessageDialog.Destroy ();
   return;
   }

// get the current communication parameters:
Result = GetCommState (IDPort, &DCBPort);
if (Result != 0)
   {
   sprintf (Message, "Communication error (line %d).",
      __LINE__);
   MessageBox
      (mHDialog,
      Message,
```

```
            "Phone Dialer",
            MB_ICONEXCLAMATION | MB_OK);
        CloseComm (IDPort);
        MessageDialog.Destroy ();
        return;
        }

    // set the desired communication parameters:
    DCBPort.BaudRate = 300;
    DCBPort.Parity = NOPARITY;
    DCBPort.ByteSize = 8;
    DCBPort.StopBits = ONESTOPBIT;
    Result = SetCommState (&DCBPort);
    if (Result != 0)
        {
        sprintf (Message, "Communication error (line %d).",
            __LINE__);
        MessageBox
            (mHDialog,
            Message,
            "Phone Dialer",
            MB_ICONEXCLAMATION | MB_OK);
        CloseComm (IDPort);
        MessageDialog.Destroy ();
        return;
        }

    GetCommError (IDPort, NULL);  // clear error status

    // write the modem command string to the serial port:
    Result = WriteComm (IDPort, (LPSTR)CommandBuf,
        strlen (CommandBuf));
    if (Result < 0)
        {
        sprintf (Message, "Communication error (line %d).",
            __LINE__);
        MessageBox
            (mHDialog,
            Message,
            "Phone Dialer",
            MB_ICONEXCLAMATION | MB_OK);
```

```
      CloseComm (IDPort);
      MessageDialog.Destroy ();
      return;
      }

// pause for 4 seconds to permit data to reach modem and
// modem to complete dialing a typical phone number:
OldTime = GetCurrentTime();
while (GetCurrentTime () - OldTime < 4000)
      ;

// make sure that all characters have been sent from the
// transmit queue:
GetCommError (IDPort, &ComStatInfo);
if (ComStatInfo.cbOutQue)  // if characters are STILL in
      {          // transmission queue, an error has occurred
      sprintf (Message, "Communication error (line %d).",
         __LINE__);
      MessageBox
         (mHDialog,
         Message,
         "Phone Dialer",
         MB_ICONEXCLAMATION ¦ MB_OK);
      CloseComm (IDPort);
      MessageDialog.Destroy ();
      return;
      }

// change message to indicate that phone has been dialed:
SetDlgItemText (MessageDialog.mHDialog, IDC_MESSAGE,
   "If you wish to speak,\npick up phone and then click OK\n"
   "after dialing has stopped.");
// show OK button to allow user to dismiss message dialog box:
SetDlgItemText (MessageDialog.mHDialog, IDOK, "OK");
ShowWindow (GetDlgItem (MessageDialog.mHDialog, IDOK),
   SW_SHOW);
MessageDialog.ButtonClicked = FALSE;  // initialize flag
// disable main dialog box to prevent user from issuing a
// command before current message has been processed:
EnableWindow (mHDialog, FALSE);
```

```
// pause for 25 seconds or until the user clicks OK button in
// the message dialog box; this pause gives the user time to
// pick up the phone (or to determine that the line is busy
// and decide NOT to pick up the phone) before the modem
// hangs up:
OldTime = GetCurrentTime();
while (!MessageDialog.ButtonClicked && GetCurrentTime () -
   OldTime < 25000)
   {
   // process messages during loop so that other windows
   // (including the message dialog box with OK button!)
   // can receive messages:
   while (PeekMessage (&Msg, NULL, NULL, NULL, PM_REMOVE))
      {
      if (!IsDialogMessage (MessageDialog.mHDialog, &Msg)
         && !IsDialogMessage (mHDialog, &Msg))
         {
         TranslateMessage (&Msg);
         DispatchMessage (&Msg);
         }
      }
   }

// write a command that causes the modem to hang up (if the
// user has picked up the phone, the phone will remain
// connected; otherwise the connection is terminated):
Result = WriteComm (IDPort, "ATH0\r", 5);
if (Result < 0)
   {
   sprintf (Message, "Communication error (line %d).",
      __LINE__);
   MessageBox
      (mHDialog,
      Message,
      "Phone Dialer",
      MB_ICONEXCLAMATION | MB_OK);
   CloseComm (IDPort);
   EnableWindow (mHDialog, TRUE);
   MessageDialog.Destroy ();
   return;
   }
```

```
// allow 3 seconds for the transmission queue to clear:
OldTime = GetCurrentTime ();
while (TRUE)
   {
   GetCommError (IDPort, &ComStatInfo);
   if (GetCurrentTime () - OldTime > 3000)
      {
      // 3 seconds have elapsed before transmission queue
      // has cleared; an error must have occurred
      sprintf (Message, "Communication error (line %d).",
         __LINE__);
      MessageBox
         (mHDialog,
         Message,
         "Phone Dialer",
         MB_ICONEXCLAMATION | MB_OK);
      CloseComm (IDPort);
      EnableWindow (mHDialog, TRUE);
      MessageDialog.Destroy ();
      return;
      }
   if (!ComStatInfo.cbOutQue)  // quit loop if transmission
      break;                   // queue is clear
   }

CloseComm (IDPort);  // close the serial port

// if user has not clicked OK button to begin speaking and
// Auto Repeat is checked, start timer to initiate repeat
// dialing (see OnTimer function):
if (IsDlgButtonChecked (mHDialog, IDC_REPEAT) &&
   !MessageDialog.ButtonClicked)
   {
   HTimer = SetTimer (mHDialog, 1, 1000, 0);
   // change text in message dialog box:
   sprintf (Message, "Auto repeat dialing in %d seconds.",
      DialOptionsDialog.Delay);
   SetDlgItemText (MessageDialog.mHDialog, IDC_MESSAGE,
      Message);
   // button can now be used to Cancel auto repeat dialing:
```

```
            SetDlgItemText (MessageDialog.mHDialog, IDOK, "Cancel");
            }
    // if no auto repeat, reenable main dialog box and remove
    // message dialog box:
    else
        {
        EnableWindow (mHDialog, TRUE);
        MessageDialog.Destroy ();
        }
    return;
    }

BOOL CMainDialog::DialogProc (UINT Msg, WPARAM WParam,
                                    LPARAM LParam)
    {
    switch (Msg)
        {
        case WM_CLOSE:
            Destroy ();
            return (TRUE);

        case WM_COMMAND:
            return OnCommand ((int)WParam, (HWND)LOWORD (LParam),
                            HIWORD (LParam));

        case WM_CTLCOLOR:
            return OnCtlColor ((HDC)WParam, (HWND)LOWORD (LParam),
                            (int)HIWORD (LParam));

        case WM_DESTROY:
            return OnDestroy ();

        case WM_ENDSESSION:
            if (WParam)
                WrapUp ();
            return (TRUE);

        case WM_INITDIALOG:
            return OnInitDialog ((HWND)WParam, LParam);

        case WM_SYSCOLORCHANGE:
```

```
            return OnSysColorChange ();

    case WM_SYSCOMMAND:  // user chose command on system menu
        if (WParam == IDM_DIAL)  // Dial command chosen
            return OnCommand ((int)WParam, (HWND)LOWORD (LParam),
                              HIWORD (LParam));
        else                    // another command chosen; let
            return (FALSE);  // system do default processing

    case WM_TIMER:
        return (OnTimer ());

    default:
        return (FALSE);
    }
}

BOOL CMainDialog::IsPhoneDigit (char Ch)
// returns TRUE if Ch is a character that can be sent to the
// modem as part of a phone number, and FALSE otherwise
    {
    if (isdigit (Ch) || Ch == ',' || Ch == '*' || Ch == '#')
        return (TRUE);
    else
        return (FALSE);
    }

BOOL CMainDialog::IsPhoneSep (char Ch)
// returns TRUE if Ch is a valid separator character that can be
// inserted within a phone number, and FALSE otherwise
    {
    if (Ch == '(' || Ch == ')' || Ch == '-' || Ch == '/')
        return (TRUE);
    else
        return (FALSE);
    }

BOOL CMainDialog::OnCommand (int IDItem, HWND HWndCtl,
                            WORD NotifyCode)
    {
    switch (IDItem)
```

```
{
case IDM_ABOUT:   // Help/About menu command
   {
   CMDialog MDialog;
   MDialog.Create ("AboutDlg", mHDialog);
   return (TRUE);
   }

case IDM_DIAL:   // system/Dial menu command or Dial button
   DialIt ();
   return (TRUE);

case IDM_DIALING:   //Options/Dialing Options menu command
   DialOptionsDialog.Create ("DialOptionsDlg", mHDialog);
   return (TRUE);

case IDM_MODEM:   // Options/Modem Settings menu command
   ModemDialog.Create ("ModemDlg", mHDialog);
   return (TRUE);

case IDM_HELPCONTENTS:   // Help/Contents menu command
   WinHelp (mHDialog, "DIAL.HLP", HELP_CONTENTS, OL);
   return (TRUE);

case IDM_HELPHELP:   // Help/How to Use Help menu command
   WinHelp (mHDialog, "DIAL.HLP", HELP_HELPONHELP, OL);
   return (TRUE);

case IDM_HELPSEARCH:   // Help/Search for Help On menu
                       // command
   WinHelp (mHDialog, "DIAL.HLP", HELP_PARTIALKEY,
            (DWORD)(LPCSTR)"");
   return (TRUE);

case IDM_ONTOP:    // Options/Always on Top menu command
   OnTop = !OnTop;
   CheckMenuItem (GetMenu (mHDialog), IDM_ONTOP,
                  OnTop ? MF_CHECKED : MF_UNCHECKED);
   SetWindowPos (mHDialog,
                 OnTop ? HWND_TOPMOST : HWND_NOTOPMOST,
                 0, 0, 0, 0, SWP_NOMOVE | SWP_NOSIZE);
```

```
                    return (FALSE);

            default:
                return (FALSE);


            }
        }


BOOL CMainDialog::OnCtlColor (HDC HDCChild, HWND HWndChild,
                                int CtlType)
    {
    COLORREF WorkSpaceColor;

    switch (CtlType)
        {
        case CTLCOLOR_BTN:
        case CTLCOLOR_STATIC:
            WorkSpaceColor = GetSysColor (COLOR_APPWORKSPACE);
            if (GetRValue (WorkSpaceColor) * 2 +
                GetGValue (WorkSpaceColor) * 5 +
                GetBValue (WorkSpaceColor) > 1020)
                SetTextColor (HDCChild, RGB (0, 0, 0));
            else
                SetTextColor (HDCChild, RGB (255, 255, 255));
            SetBkMode (HDCChild, TRANSPARENT);
            return ((BOOL)HBrushWorkSpace);

        case CTLCOLOR_DLG:
            return ((BOOL)HBrushWorkSpace);

        default:
            return (FALSE);
        }
    }

BOOL CMainDialog::OnDestroy ()
    {
    WrapUp ();
    if (HBrushWorkSpace != 0)
        DeleteObject (HBrushWorkSpace);
    WinHelp (mHDialog, "DIAL.HLP", HELP_QUIT, OL);
```

```
    PostQuitMessage (0);
    return (TRUE);
    }

BOOL CMainDialog::OnInitDialog (HWND HWndFocus, LPARAM Data)
    {
    char Buffer [SIZENUMBER];
    int Result;

    SendDlgItemMessage (mHDialog, IDC_NUMBER, EM_LIMITTEXT,
        (WPARAM)SIZENUMBER-1, OL);

    // obtain values of options displayed by main dialog box
    // (options displayed by the 'Dialing Options' and 'Modem
    // Settings' dialog boxes are obtained by the constructors for
    // the classes that manage these dialog boxes):

    OnTop = (int)GetPrivateProfileInt
        ("options",
        "ontop",
        0,
        "DIAL.INI");
    if (OnTop)
        {
        CheckMenuItem (GetMenu (mHDialog), IDM_ONTOP, MF_CHECKED);
        SetWindowPos (mHDialog, HWND_TOPMOST, 0, 0, 0, 0,
                    SWP_NOMOVE | SWP_NOSIZE);
        }

    // restore prior status of 'From Clipboard' and 'Entered Here'
    // radio buttons:
    Result = (BOOL)GetPrivateProfileInt
        ("options",
        "clipboard",
        1,
        "DIAL.INI");
    CheckDlgButton
        (mHDialog,
        Result ? IDC_CLIPBOARD : IDC_ENTERED,
        1);
```

```
// restore previous phone number:
GetPrivateProfileString
   ("options",
   "number",
   "",
   Buffer,
   sizeof (Buffer),
   "DIAL.INI");
SetDlgItemText (mHDialog, IDC_NUMBER, Buffer);

// restore status of check boxes:
if (GetPrivateProfileInt ("options", "useprefix", O,
   "DIAL.INI"))
   CheckDlgButton (mHDialog, IDC_PREFIX, 1);

if (GetPrivateProfileInt ("options", "usesuffix", O,
   "DIAL.INI"))
   CheckDlgButton (mHDialog, IDC_SUFFIX, 1);

if (GetPrivateProfileInt ("options", "repeat", O, "DIAL.INI"))
   CheckDlgButton (mHDialog, IDC_REPEAT, 1);

// add a Dial command and a separator to the system menu:
InsertMenu
   (GetSystemMenu (mHDialog, FALSE),
   O,
   MF_BYPOSITION | MF_SEPARATOR,
   O,
   O);
InsertMenu
   (GetSystemMenu (mHDialog, FALSE),
   O,
   MF_BYPOSITION | MF_STRING,
   IDM_DIAL,
   "&Dial");

HBrushWorkSpace = CreateSolidBrush
   (GetSysColor (COLOR_APPWORKSPACE));

return (TRUE);
}
```

```
BOOL CMainDialog::OnSysColorChange ()
   {
   if (HBrushWorkSpace != 0)
      DeleteObject (HBrushWorkSpace);
   HBrushWorkSpace =
      CreateSolidBrush (GetSysColor (COLOR_APPWORKSPACE));
   return (TRUE);
   }

BOOL CMainDialog::OnTimer ()
// when the DialIt function creates a timer, this function is
// called once each second; it manages automatic repeat dialing
   {
   char Message [64];
   static DWORD TimeDue = 0;

   // if user has clicked Cancel button in message modeless
   // dialog box, terminate timer, reenable main dialog box, and
   // remove message dialog box:
   if (MessageDialog.ButtonClicked)
      {
      KillTimer (mHDialog, 1);
      TimeDue = 0;
      EnableWindow (mHDialog, TRUE);
      MessageDialog.Destroy ();
      return (TRUE);
      }

   // if TimeDue == 0, this is the first invocation of OnTimer
   // since the timer was set; therefore, calculate and save
   // the time when redialing is due in the static variable
   // TimeDue:
   if (TimeDue == 0)
      TimeDue = GetCurrentTime () + (DWORD)1000 *
         (DWORD)DialOptionsDialog.Delay;

   if (GetCurrentTime () < TimeDue)
      {  // redial not yet due; just update message
      sprintf (Message, "Auto repeat dialing in %d seconds.",
         (TimeDue - GetCurrentTime ()) / 1000);
```

```
            SetDlgItemText (MessageDialog.mHDialog, IDC_MESSAGE,
                Message);
            }
        else  // redial is due; kill timer and call DialIt to dial
            {
            KillTimer (mHDialog, 1);
            TimeDue = 0;
            DialIt ();
            }
        return (TRUE);
        }

void CMainDialog::WrapUp ()
// saves all program option settings
    {
    // save settings maintained by the modeless dialog box
    // classes:
    ModemDialog.WrapUp ();
    DialOptionsDialog.WrapUp ();

    char Buffer [SIZENUMBER];

    WritePrivateProfileString
        ("options",
         "ontop",
         OnTop ? "1" : "0",
         "DIAL.INI");

    WritePrivateProfileString
        ("options",
         "clipboard",
         IsDlgButtonChecked (mHDialog, IDC_CLIPBOARD) ? "1" : "0",
         "DIAL.INI");

    GetDlgItemText (mHDialog, IDC_NUMBER, Buffer,
        sizeof (Buffer));
    WritePrivateProfileString
        ("options",
         "number",
         Buffer,
         "DIAL.INI");
```

```
WritePrivateProfileString
    ("options",
    "useprefix",
    IsDlgButtonChecked (mHDialog, IDC_PREFIX) ? "1" : "0",
    "DIAL.INI");

WritePrivateProfileString
    ("options",
    "usesuffix",
    IsDlgButtonChecked (mHDialog, IDC_SUFFIX) ? "1" : "0",
    "DIAL.INI");

WritePrivateProfileString
    ("options",
    "repeat",
    IsDlgButtonChecked (mHDialog, IDC_REPEAT) ? "1" : "0",
    "DIAL.INI");
    }

/////////////////////////////////////////////////////////////////
// CDialOptionsDialog member functions:                         //
/////////////////////////////////////////////////////////////////

CDialOptionsDialog::CDialOptionsDialog ()
    {
    Delay = GetPrivateProfileInt
        ("dialoptions",
        "delay",
        60,
        "DIAL.INI");

    GetPrivateProfileString
        ("dialoptions",
        "prefix",
        "",
        Prefix,
        sizeof (Prefix),
        "DIAL.INI");

    GetPrivateProfileString
```

```
                 ("dialoptions",
                 "suffix",
                 "",
                 Suffix,
                 sizeof (Suffix),
                 "DIAL.INI");
    }

BOOL CDialOptionsDialog::DialogProc (UINT Msg, WPARAM WParam,
                                              LPARAM LParam)
    {
    switch (Msg)
        {
        case WM_COMMAND:
            switch (WParam)
                {
                case IDCANCEL:
                    EndDialog (mHDialog, IDCANCEL);
                    return (TRUE);

                case IDC_HELP:
                    WinHelp (MainDialog.mHDialog, "DIAL.HLP",
                             HELP_CONTEXT, HELPDIALOPTIONSDLG);
                    return (TRUE);

                case IDOK:
                    {
                    int TempInt = GetDlgItemInt (mHDialog, IDC_DELAY,
                        0, TRUE);
                    if (TempInt < 1 || TempInt > 9999)
                        {
                        MessageBox
                            (mHDialog,
                            "Delay must be between 1 and 9999 seconds.",
                            "Phone Dialer",
                            MB_ICONEXCLAMATION | MB_OK);
                        SetFocus (GetDlgItem (mHDialog, IDC_DELAY));
                        return (TRUE);
                        }
                    Delay = TempInt;
```

```
                    GetDlgItemText
                        (mHDialog,
                        IDC_PREFIX,
                        Prefix,
                        sizeof (Prefix));
                    GetDlgItemText
                        (mHDialog,
                        IDC_SUFFIX,
                        Suffix,
                        sizeof (Suffix));

                    EndDialog (mHDialog, IDOK);
                    return (TRUE);
                    }

            default:
                return (TRUE);
            }

    case WM_INITDIALOG:
        SendDlgItemMessage (mHDialog, IDC_PREFIX, EM_LIMITTEXT,
            (WPARAM)(sizeof (Prefix) - 1), OL);
        SendDlgItemMessage (mHDialog, IDC_SUFFIX, EM_LIMITTEXT,
            (WPARAM)sizeof (Suffix) - 1, OL);
        SendDlgItemMessage (mHDialog, IDC_DELAY, EM_LIMITTEXT,
            (WPARAM)4, OL);

        SetDlgItemText (mHDialog, IDC_PREFIX, Prefix);
        SetDlgItemText (mHDialog, IDC_SUFFIX, Suffix);
        SetDlgItemInt (mHDialog, IDC_DELAY, Delay, TRUE);
        return (TRUE);

    default:
        if (Msg == mHelpMessage)
            {
            SendMessage (mHDialog, WM_COMMAND, IDC_HELP, OL);
            return (TRUE);
            }
        else
            return (FALSE);
    }
```

```
    }

void CDialOptionsDialog::WrapUp ()
// saves option settings maintained by the CDialOptionsDialog
// class
    {
    char NumBuf [5];
    sprintf (NumBuf, "%d", Delay);
    WritePrivateProfileString
        ("dialoptions",
        "delay",
        NumBuf,
        "DIAL.INI");

    WritePrivateProfileString
        ("dialoptions",
        "prefix",
        Prefix,
        "DIAL.INI");

    WritePrivateProfileString
        ("dialoptions",
        "suffix",
        Suffix,
        "DIAL.INI");
    }

//////////////////////////////////////////////////////////////////
// CMessageDialog member function:                              //
//////////////////////////////////////////////////////////////////

BOOL CMessageDialog::DialogProc (UINT Msg, WPARAM WParam,
                                 LPARAM LParam)
    {
    switch (Msg)
        {
        case WM_INITDIALOG:
            return (TRUE);

        case WM_COMMAND:            // user has clicked button or
            ButtonClicked = TRUE;   // pressed Enter or Esc;
```

```
          return (TRUE);              // therefore, set flag

      default:
          return (FALSE);
      }
   }


////////////////////////////////////////////////////////////////
// CModemDialog member functions:                             //
////////////////////////////////////////////////////////////////

CModemDialog::CModemDialog ()
   {
   GetPrivateProfileString
      ("modem",
      "dialtype",
      "T",
      DialType,
      sizeof (DialType),
      "DIAL.INI");

   GetPrivateProfileString
      ("modem",
      "port",
      "COM1",
      Port,
      sizeof (Port),
      "DIAL.INI");
   }

BOOL CModemDialog::DialogProc (UINT Msg, WPARAM WParam,
                                LPARAM LParam)
   {
   switch (Msg)
      {
      case WM_COMMAND:
         switch (WParam)
            {
            case IDCANCEL:
               EndDialog (mHDialog, IDCANCEL);
               return (TRUE);
```

```
            case IDC_HELP:
                WinHelp (MainDialog.mHDialog, "DIAL.HLP",
                        HELP_CONTEXT, HELPMODEMDLG);
                return (TRUE);

            case IDOK:
                DialType [0] = IsDlgButtonChecked (mHDialog,
                    IDC_TONE) ? 'T' : 'P';
                DialType [1] = '\0';

                if (IsDlgButtonChecked (mHDialog, IDC_COM1))
                    strcpy (Port, "COM1");
                else if (IsDlgButtonChecked (mHDialog, IDC_COM2))
                    strcpy (Port, "COM2");
                else if (IsDlgButtonChecked (mHDialog, IDC_COM3))
                    strcpy (Port, "COM3");
                else
                    strcpy (Port, "COM4");

                EndDialog (mHDialog, IDOK);
                return (TRUE);

            default:
                return (TRUE);
            }

    case WM_INITDIALOG:
        CheckDlgButton
            (mHDialog,
            DialType [0] == 'T' ? IDC_TONE : IDC_PULSE,
            1);
        CheckDlgButton
            (mHDialog,
            IDC_COM1 + Port [3] - '1',
            1);
        return (TRUE);

    default:
        if (Msg == mHelpMessage)
            {
```

```
                SendMessage (mHDialog, WM_COMMAND, IDC_HELP, OL);
                return (TRUE);
                }
            else
                return (FALSE);
        }
    }

void CModemDialog::WrapUp ()
// saves option settings maintained by the CModemDialog class
    {
    WritePrivateProfileString
        ("modem",
        "dialtype",
        DialType,
        "DIAL.INI");

    WritePrivateProfileString
        ("modem",
        "port",
        Port,
        "DIAL.INI");
    }
```

Listing 9.4

```
;;;;;;;;;;;;;;;;;;;;;;;;;;;;;;;;;;;;;;;;;;;;;;;;;;;;;;;;;;;;;;;;;;;;;;
;                                                                  ;
; DIAL.DEF:  Module-definition file for the DIAL program           ;
;                                                                  ;
;;;;;;;;;;;;;;;;;;;;;;;;;;;;;;;;;;;;;;;;;;;;;;;;;;;;;;;;;;;;;;;;;;;;;;


NAME DIAL

DESCRIPTION  'Phone Dialer'

EXETYPE WINDOWS

CODE PRELOAD MOVEABLE DISCARDABLE
```

```
DATA PRELOAD MOVEABLE MULTIPLE

HEAPSIZE 1024

STACKSIZE 10240
```

Listing 9.5

```
///////////////////////////////////////////////////////////////////////
//                                                                     //
// RESOURCE.H:  Constant definitions for the DIAL program              //
//              resources (generated by Microsoft App Studio).         //
//                                                                     //
///////////////////////////////////////////////////////////////////////

//{{NO_DEPENDENCIES}}
// App Studio generated include file.
// Used by DIAL.RC
//
#define IDC_HELP                        100
#define IDC_TEXT                        101
#define IDC_PREFIX                      102
#define IDC_SUFFIX                      103
#define IDC_CLIPBOARD                   104
#define IDC_ENTERED                     105
#define IDC_NUMBER                      106
#define IDC_REPEAT                      107
#define IDC_DELAY                       110
#define IDC_TONE                        111
#define IDC_PULSE                       112
#define IDC_COM1                        113
#define IDC_COM2                        114
#define IDC_COM3                        115
#define IDC_COM4                        116
#define IDC_MESSAGE                     117
#define IDM_ABOUT                       1000
#define IDM_HELPHELP                    1001
#define IDM_HELPSEARCH                  1002
#define IDM_HELPCONTENTS                1003
#define IDM_ONTOP                       1005
#define IDM_DIALING                     1006
```

```
#define IDM_MODEM                       1007
#define IDM_DIAL                        1008
#define IDC_STATIC                      -1

// Next default values for new objects
//
#ifdef APSTUDIO_INVOKED
#ifndef APSTUDIO_READONLY_SYMBOLS

#define _APS_NEXT_RESOURCE_VALUE        104
#define _APS_NEXT_COMMAND_VALUE         1009
#define _APS_NEXT_CONTROL_VALUE         119
#define _APS_NEXT_SYMED_VALUE           101
#endif
#endif
```

Listing 9.6

```
/////////////////////////////////////////////////////////////////
//                                                             //
// DIAL.RC:  Resource-definition file for the DIAL             //
//           program (generated by Microsoft App Studio).      //
//                                                             //
/////////////////////////////////////////////////////////////////

//Microsoft App Studio generated resource script.
//
#include "resource.h"

#define APSTUDIO_READONLY_SYMBOLS
/////////////////////////////////////////////////////////////////
//
// Generated from the TEXTINCLUDE 2 resource.
//
#include "windows.h"


/////////////////////////////////////////////////////////////////
#undef APSTUDIO_READONLY_SYMBOLS


/////////////////////////////////////////////////////////////////
```

```
//
// Accelerator
//

DIALACCEL ACCELERATORS DISCARDABLE
BEGIN
    VK_F1,           IDM_HELPCONTENTS,         VIRTKEY,NOINVERT
END


/////////////////////////////////////////////////////////////////
//
// Dialog
//

MAINDLG DIALOG DISCARDABLE  177, 0, 157, 101
STYLE WS_MINIMIZEBOX ¦ WS_POPUP ¦ WS_VISIBLE ¦ WS_CAPTION ¦
    WS_SYSMENU
CAPTION "Phone Dialer"
MENU DialMenu
FONT 8, "MS Sans Serif"
BEGIN
    CONTROL         "From &Clipboard",IDC_CLIPBOARD,"Button",
                    BS_AUTORADIOBUTTON ¦ WS_GROUP ¦ WS_TABSTOP,
                    12,21,61,10
    CONTROL         "Entered &Here:",IDC_ENTERED,"Button",
                    BS_AUTORADIOBUTTON,12,33,60,10
    EDITTEXT        IDC_NUMBER,72,32,72,12,ES_AUTOHSCROLL ¦
                    WS_GROUP ¦ 0x1000
    CONTROL         "Use &Prefix",IDC_PREFIX,"Button",
                    BS_AUTOCHECKBOX ¦ WS_TABSTOP,7,58,48,10
    CONTROL         "Use &Suffix",IDC_SUFFIX,"Button",
                    BS_AUTOCHECKBOX ¦ WS_TABSTOP,7,72,48,10
    CONTROL         "Auto &Repeat",IDC_REPEAT,"Button",
                    BS_AUTOCHECKBOX ¦ WS_TABSTOP,7,86,54,10
    DEFPUSHBUTTON   "&DIAL",IDM_DIAL,85,67,50,19
    GROUPBOX        "Telephone Number",IDC_STATIC,7,8,143,43
END

ABOUTDLG DIALOG DISCARDABLE  12, 24, 116, 100
STYLE DS_MODALFRAME ¦ WS_POPUP ¦ WS_VISIBLE ¦ WS_CAPTION ¦
```

```
    WS_SYSMENU
CAPTION "About"
FONT 8, "MS Sans Serif"
BEGIN
    CTEXT           "Windows Phone Dialer",-1,0,10,116,8
    CTEXT           "by Michael J. Young",-1,0,28,116,8
    ICON            "DialIcon",-1,48,48,18,20
    DEFPUSHBUTTON   "OK",IDOK,36,80,40,14
END

DIALOPTIONSDLG DIALOG DISCARDABLE  12, 24, 122, 107
STYLE DS_MODALFRAME | WS_POPUP | WS_VISIBLE | WS_CAPTION |
    WS_SYSMENU
CAPTION "Dialing Options"
FONT 8, "MS Sans Serif"
BEGIN
    LTEXT           "&Prefix:",IDC_STATIC,9,11,23,9
    EDITTEXT        IDC_PREFIX,37,9,78,12,ES_AUTOHSCROLL
    LTEXT           "&Suffix:",IDC_STATIC,9,31,22,9
    EDITTEXT        IDC_SUFFIX,37,29,78,12,ES_AUTOHSCROLL
    LTEXT           "Auto-Repeat &Delay:",IDC_STATIC,9,50,67,9
    EDITTEXT        IDC_DELAY,77,48,23,12,ES_AUTOHSCROLL
    DEFPUSHBUTTON   "OK",IDOK,9,67,40,14,NOT WS_TABSTOP
    PUSHBUTTON      "Cancel",IDCANCEL,9,86,40,14,NOT WS_TABSTOP
    LTEXT           "sec",IDC_STATIC,103,50,15,8
    PUSHBUTTON      "&Help",IDC_HELP,76,77,40,14,NOT WS_TABSTOP
END

MODEMDLG DIALOG DISCARDABLE  12, 24, 117, 113
STYLE DS_MODALFRAME | WS_POPUP | WS_VISIBLE | WS_CAPTION |
    WS_SYSMENU
CAPTION "Modem Settings"
FONT 8, "MS Sans Serif"
BEGIN
    CONTROL         "&Tone",IDC_TONE,"Button",BS_AUTORADIOBUTTON
                    | WS_GROUP | WS_TABSTOP,12,18,34,10
    CONTROL         "&Pulse",IDC_PULSE,"Button",
                    BS_AUTORADIOBUTTON,12,32,34,10
    CONTROL         "COM&1",IDC_COM1,"Button",BS_AUTORADIOBUTTON
                    | WS_GROUP | WS_TABSTOP,68,21,33,9
    CONTROL         "COM&2",IDC_COM2,"Button",BS_AUTORADIOBUTTON,
```

```
                            68,39,33,9
    CONTROL             "COM&3",IDC_COM3,"Button",BS_AUTORADIOBUTTON,
                            68,57,33,9
    CONTROL             "COM&4",IDC_COM4,"Button",BS_AUTORADIOBUTTON,
                            68,75,33,9
    DEFPUSHBUTTON       "OK",IDOK,6,58,47,14,WS_GROUP |
                            NOT WS_TABSTOP
    PUSHBUTTON          "Cancel",IDCANCEL,6,75,47,14,NOT WS_TABSTOP
    GROUPBOX            "Dial Type",IDC_STATIC,6,4,47,48
    GROUPBOX            "Port",IDC_STATIC,62,4,48,102
    PUSHBUTTON          "&Help",IDC_HELP,6,92,47,14,NOT WS_TABSTOP
END

MESSAGEDLG DIALOG DISCARDABLE  12, 24, 125, 76
STYLE DS_MODALFRAME | WS_POPUP | WS_VISIBLE | WS_CAPTION
CAPTION "Phone Dialer"
FONT 8, "MS Sans Serif"
BEGIN
    DEFPUSHBUTTON       "OK",IDOK,37,51,50,14
    CTEXT               "Static",IDC_MESSAGE,4,15,116,26
END

#ifdef APSTUDIO_INVOKED
/////////////////////////////////////////////////////////////////
//
// TEXTINCLUDE
//

1 TEXTINCLUDE DISCARDABLE
BEGIN
    "resource.h\0"
END

2 TEXTINCLUDE DISCARDABLE
BEGIN
    "#include ""windows.h""\r\n"
    "\0"
END

3 TEXTINCLUDE DISCARDABLE
BEGIN
```

```
    "\r\n"
    "\0"
END


////////////////////////////////////////////////////////////
#endif    // APSTUDIO_INVOKED


////////////////////////////////////////////////////////////
//
// Icon
//

DIALICON                ICON    DISCARDABLE     "DIAL.ICO"

////////////////////////////////////////////////////////////
//
// Menu
//

DIALMENU MENU DISCARDABLE
BEGIN
    POPUP "&Options"
    BEGIN
        MENUITEM "&Dialing Options...",         IDM_DIALING
        MENUITEM "&Modem Settings...",          IDM_MODEM
        MENUITEM "Always on &Top",              IDM_ONTOP
    END
    POPUP "&Help"
    BEGIN
        MENUITEM "&Contents...\tF1",            IDM_HELPCONTENTS
        MENUITEM "&Search for Help On...",      IDM_HELPSEARCH
        MENUITEM "&How to Use Help...",         IDM_HELPHELP
        MENUITEM SEPARATOR
        MENUITEM "&About...",                   IDM_ABOUT
    END
END


#ifndef APSTUDIO_INVOKED
////////////////////////////////////////////////////////////
```

```
//
// Generated from the TEXTINCLUDE 3 resource.
//


/////////////////////////////////////////////////////////////////////////
#endif    // not APSTUDIO_INVOKED
```

Organization of the Program

To give you an overview of the organization of the program, this section summarizes the responsibilities of the four classes that manage the modeless and modal dialog boxes and perform the main program actions: CMainDialog, CDialOptionsDialog, CModemDialog, and CMessageDialog.

The following are the responsibilities of the CMainDialog class:

- To display the main program window, which allows the user to change program options and issue commands

- To respond to the menu commands and the DIAL button and perform the appropriate actions

- At program initialization, to read the settings of the main program options (that is, the options displayed in the main dialog box) from the initialization file; this task is performed by the CMainDialog::OnInitDialog function

- At program exit, to write the settings of the main program options to the initialization file; this task is performed by the CMainDialog::WrapUp function

The CDialOptionsDialog class has the following responsibilities:

- To store the dialing settings (the prefix, suffix, and auto-repeat delay) in public data members, so that these settings can be directly accessed by the CMainDialog code

- To display the Dialing Options modal dialog box (when the user chooses the Dialing Options... menu command and the CMainDialog code calls CDialOptionsDialog::Create), which allows the user to change the dialing settings

- At program initialization, to read the dialing settings from the initialization file; this task is performed in the `CDialOptionsDialog` constructor

- At program exit, to write the dialing settings to the initialization file; this task is performed in the `CDialOptionsDialog::WrapUp` function (which is called by `CMainDialog::WrapUp` at program termination)

The `CModemDialog` class has these responsibilities:

- To store the modem settings (the dial type—tone or pulse—and the serial port) in public data members, so that these settings can be directly accessed by the `CMainDialog` code

- To display the Modem Settings modal dialog box (when the user chooses the Modem Settings... menu command and the `CMain-Dialog` code calls `CModemDialog::Create`), which allows the user to change the modem settings

- At program initialization, to read the modem settings from the initialization file; this task is performed in the `CModemDialog` constructor

- At program exit, to write the modem settings to the initialization file; this task is performed in the `CModemDialog::WrapUp` function (which is called by `CMainDialog::WrapUp` at program termination)

Finally, the `CMessageDialog` class has these responsibilities:

- To display a modeless dialog box for showing various messages during dialing or while the program is waiting to redial

- To set its `ButtonClicked` public data member to `TRUE` if the user clicks the button that is displayed in the dialog box; the `CMainDialog` code can examine this data member to determine whether the button was clicked

The DIAL program saves and retrieves program settings from the initialization file (DIAL.INI), using the same techniques as the ENVELOPE program presented in Chapter 8. For a discussion on these methods, see the sections "Initializing" and "Wrapping Up" in Chapter 8.

Dialing a Number

When the user clicks the DIAL button or chooses the Dial command on the system menu, the CMainDialog::OnCommand function calls the CMainDialog member function DialIt to dial the phone number. This section discusses the basic steps that DialIt performs to access the serial port and to send command strings to the modem that cause it to dial the number. The next section discusses the logic in the DialIt and CMainDialog::OnTimer functions that supports auto-repeat dialing.

DialIt begins by calling CMessageDialog::Create to display the modeless dialog box that is used for showing messages (hereafter, this modeless dialog box will be called simply the *message dialog box*). Note that DialIt calls Create *only* if the message dialog box is not already displayed (it would already be displayed if auto-repeat dialing were active, as discussed in the next section). It also sets the text displayed in the message dialog box to "Dialing…" and hides the button. (When the message dialog box was designed in App Studio, it was assigned a single static text control and a single button. The program changes the text as required; it also hides, shows, and changes the button text as appropriate.)

DialIt next builds up the command string that it sends to the modem to dial the number, which it copies to the CommandBuf character array. It first copies the characters "ATD" (the standard Hayes dialing command) to CommandBuf. It then copies the character stored in ModemDialog.DialType, which is either 'T' to initiate tone dialing or 'P' to initiate pulse dialing. Then, if the user has selected the Use Prefix option, it copies the prefix contained in DialOptionsDialog.Prefix.

Next, DialIt copies the phone number itself to CommandBuf. If the user has selected the From Clipboard option, it obtains the number from the Clipboard; if, however, the user has selected the Entered Here: option, it obtains the number from the edit control adjoining the Entered Here: radio button (which has the identifier IDC_NUMBER). When it copies the number to CommandBuf, it copies the first sequence of valid phone characters (that is, '0' - '9', '*', '#', and ',') that it finds in the text; while copying this sequence of characters, it skips all separator characters (that is, '(', ')', '-', and '/').

NOTE For a description of the technique for obtaining text from the Clipboard, see the section "Printing the Text" in Chapter 8.

Then, if the user has selected the Use Suffix option, it copies the suffix text from DialOptionsDialog.Suffix to CommandBuf. Finally, it terminates the text in CommandBuf with a carriage-return and a NULL character.

DialIt now begins accessing the serial port to which the modem is attached. It first calls the Windows API function OpenComm to open the port:

```
IDPort = OpenComm ((LPSTR)ModemDialog.Port, 256, 256);
```

Notice that the name of the port ("COM1" through "COM4") is contained in ModemDialog.Port, which stores the value that the user chose through the Modem Options dialog box.

DialIt next sets the serial port communications parameters to the appropriate values. To do this, it first calls the API function GetCommState to obtain the complete set of default communications parameters within DCBPort, which is a DCB (device control block) structure:

```
Result = GetCommState (IDPort, &DCBPort);
```

It then assigns appropriate values to the DCB fields that store the primary communications parameters, leaving all other fields set to their default values, and calls the API function SetCommState to apply the parameters to the serial port:

```
DCBPort.BaudRate = 300;
DCBPort.Parity = NOPARITY;
DCBPort.ByteSize = 8;
DCBPort.StopBits = ONESTOPBIT;
Result = SetCommState (&DCBPort);
```

DialIt next calls the API function WriteComm to send the command string in CommandBuf to the modem, via the serial port that has been opened:

```
Result = WriteComm (IDPort, (LPSTR)CommandBuf,
    strlen (CommandBuf));
```

After sending the dial command, DialIt pauses four seconds to give the serial port time to transfer the command string to the modem, and the modem time to dial a typical phone number:

```
OldTime = GetCurrentTime();
while (GetCurrentTime () - OldTime < 4000)
    ;
```

GetCurrentTime is an API function that returns the number of milliseconds that have elapsed since Windows was started.

Before proceeding, DialIt checks to make sure that the *transmission queue* is empty. When you send a string to the serial port by calling WriteComm, the characters are stored temporarily in the transmission queue, from which they are written one at a time to the serial port. The queue becomes empty when all characters have been successfully sent to the modem via the serial port. To determine whether the transmission queue is empty, DialIt calls the API function GetCommError, which fills the fields of ComStatInfo (COMSTAT structure):

```
GetCommError (IDPort, &ComStatInfo);
```

The cbOutQue field of this structure is assigned the number of characters remaining in the transmission queue. If the number is zero, all is well and DialIt continues. If the number is not zero, an error must have occurred because all characters should have been sent to the modem within the four-second delay; in this case DialIt reports the error and quits.

DialIt now changes the text in the message dialog box to indicate that the user can pick up the phone, and it displays the OK button within this dialog box:

```
SetDlgItemText (MessageDialog.mHDialog, IDC_MESSAGE,
    "If you wish to speak,\npick up phone and then click OK\n"
    "after dialing has stopped.");
SetDlgItemText (MessageDialog.mHDialog, IDOK, "OK");
ShowWindow (GetDlgItem (MessageDialog.mHDialog, IDOK),
    SW_SHOW);
```

After displaying this message DialIt pauses for 25 seconds *or* until the user clicks the OK button. This pause gives the user time to pick up the phone (or to decide not to pick up the phone if the line is busy) before the modem hangs up.

Before entering the delay loop, DialIt resets the MessageDialog.Button-Clicked flag:

```
MessageDialog.ButtonClicked = FALSE;
```

The CMessageDialog code will set this flag to TRUE if the user clicks the OK button, as a signal to terminate the delay loop. DialIt also disables the main program window:

```
EnableWindow (mHDialog, FALSE);
```

Because the delay loop processes messages, the user would be able to activate program commands (including the dial command) *while* the dial command is being processed, producing results that are hard to predict. Therefore, the main window is disabled so that the user cannot choose commands during this time.

The following is the delay loop:

```
OldTime = GetCurrentTime ();
while (!MessageDialog.ButtonClicked && GetCurrentTime () -
   OldTime < 25000)
   {
   while (PeekMessage (&Msg, NULL, NULL, NULL, PM_REMOVE))
      {
      if (!IsDialogMessage (MessageDialog.mHDialog, &Msg)
         && !IsDialogMessage (mHDialog, &Msg))
         {
         TranslateMessage (&Msg);
         DispatchMessage (&Msg);
         }
      }
   }
```

Notice that messages are retrieved and dispatched on each pass of the loop. This is done to allow other programs to receive control and to permit normal message processing to continue during the pause; in particular, it allows CMessage::DialogProc to set the ButtonClicked to TRUE if the user clicks the OK button in the message dialog box.

N O T E   The Setup Saver program contains a similar delay loop, which is explained in the section "Terminating the Current Programs" in Chapter 4.

At the end of the pause, DialIt sends a command string to the modem to cause the modem to hang up:

```
Result = WriteComm (IDPort, "ATHO\r", 5);
```

If the user picked up the phone during the pause, the connection is preserved; otherwise, it is lost.

Finally, DialIt closes the serial port:

```
CloseComm (IDPort);
```

If the Auto Repeat check box is not checked (or if it is checked but the user clicked the OK button to accept the call), DialIt now reenables the main program window and destroys the message dialog box:

```
EnableWindow (mHDialog, TRUE);
MessageDialog.Destroy ();
```

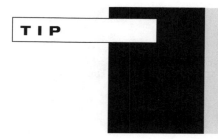

T I P   The main window must be reenabled *before* the message dialog box is destroyed, so that Windows will activate the main window. If the dialog box were destroyed first, Windows would activate the window belonging to a *different program*, because it cannot activate a disabled window.

Generating Auto-Repeat Dialing

After closing the serial port, if the Auto Repeat check box is checked *and* the user did not click the OK button in the message dialog box to accept the call, DialIt proceeds to initiate automatic redialing, as follows:

- It calls the API function SetTimer to start a Windows timer, causing the CMainDialog::OnTimer function (which processes WM_TIMER messages) to receive control each second. As you will see, OnTimer keeps track of the elapsed time and initiates redialing.

- It leaves the main window disabled (the user must not attempt to issue a program command, such as the dial command, while auto-repeat dialing is active).

- It leaves the message dialog box displayed, but changes the message to indicate that the program is waiting to redial and to specify the number of seconds before redialing will occur.

- It changes the label on the button in the message dialog box to Cancel, because clicking the button at this stage will cancel auto-repeat dialing.

Each time OnTimer receives control, it first tests the MessageDialog.ButtonClicked flag to see whether the user has clicked the Cancel button in the message box. If the flag is TRUE, it terminates auto-repeat dialing by stopping the timer, enabling the main window, and removing the message dialog box:

```
if (MessageDialog.ButtonClicked)
    {
    KillTimer (mHDialog, 1);
    TimeDue = 0;
    EnableWindow (mHDialog, TRUE);
    MessageDialog.Destroy ();
    return (TRUE);
    }
```

Notice that when OnTimer stops auto-repeat dialing, it also sets TimeDue to 0. TimeDue is a static variable that is used to store the time when redialing is due (the time is stored as the number of milliseconds since the Windows session started); it is initialized to 0 and is reset to 0 whenever the auto-repeat delay ends and the timer is stopped. If OnTimer is being called for the *first* time after the timer has been set, TimeDue will equal 0;

in this case, OnTimer sets TimeDue to the time when redialing is due:

```
if (TimeDue == 0)
    TimeDue = GetCurrentTime () + (DWORD)1000 *
        (DWORD)DialOptionsDialog.Delay;
```

OnTimer then tests whether redialing is currently due. If redialing is not yet due, it simply updates the text in the message dialog box to indicate the number of seconds until redialing will be performed. If redialing is due, it stops the timer, resets TimeDue to 0, and initiates dialing by calling DialIt:

```
if (GetCurrentTime () < TimeDue)
    {
    sprintf (Message, "Auto repeat dialing in %d seconds.",
        (TimeDue - GetCurrentTime ()) / 1000);
    SetDlgItemText (MessageDialog.mHDialog, IDC_MESSAGE,
        Message);
    }
else
    {
    KillTimer (mHDialog, 1);
    TimeDue = 0;
    DialIt ();
    }
```

Enhancing the Phone Dialer

The following are some suggestions for enhancing the Phone Dialer:

- *Allow the user to define a* set *of prefixes and a* set *of suffixes*, rather than a single prefix and a single suffix. Each prefix could be identified by a name or descriptive string. For example, the user might define prefixes with the descriptions "Activate outside line" and "Start charge to calling card," and might define a suffix with the description "End charge to calling card." Then, before dialing a number, the user could choose a specific prefix from one list box, and a specific suffix from another list box. Each list box should contain a "None" item to disable the prefix or suffix.

- *Allow the user to set the timeout period* before the program causes the modem to hang up after initiating dialing. Currently, the timeout period is fixed at 25 seconds. A short period would be useful for rapidly redialing with the auto-repeat feature; a longer period might be necessary for dialing a long number (especially one containing pauses).

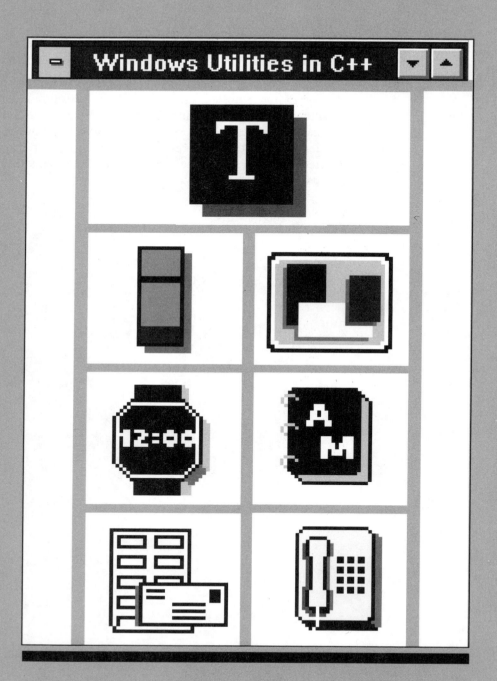

The General Windows Classes

THE General Windows Classes (GWC) are a collection of C++ classes, written by the author, that make it easier to write utility-like Windows programs. The source code for the GWC is provided on the companion disk and is printed in this appendix. All of the utility programs presented in this book make use of these classes; you can also use them when writing your own utilities or other types of Windows programs.

This appendix explains how to use the General Windows Classes to write Windows programs. It also presents the GWC source code and describes the inner workings of these classes.

How to Use the General Windows Classes

The General Windows Classes provide three classes that you can use for writing Windows programs: CApplication, for storing information on the current program instance and for loading accelerator tables; CMLDialog, for creating and managing the main program window as well as the modeless dialog boxes that your program displays; and CMDialog, for creating and managing the modal dialog boxes that your program displays. In general, these classes handle many of the routine tasks required of Windows programs and simplify the writing of the code. Also, a class derived from CMLDialog or CMDialog can define a member function to handle all messages sent to the dialog box; you can thus fully encapsulate all code and data required to handle a particular dialog box within the C++ object that manages the dialog box.

The following are the basic steps for using the General Windows Classes when developing a Windows program (the next sections provide detailed information on using the individual public member functions and data members of each class):

- Include the WCLASSES.H header file in any source or header file that references the GWC, and add WCLASSES.CPP to the list of source code files in your project file (see the instructions for creating project files near the end of Chapter 1). WCLASSES.H and WCLASSES.CPP are contained in the \WCLASSES subdirectory within the directory in which you installed the companion disk files.

- If necessary, derive one or more custom classes from CMLDialog or CMDialog, adding new members and overriding inherited members as needed. As discussed later, you will need to derive your own class for a main window or dialog box if you want to provide custom message-handling or if you want to add members for storing information or performing tasks required in managing the window.

- Declare a single global instance of the CApplication class. You must also call the Initialize member function of this instance *before* calling any of the member functions of the other GWC classes.

- Declare an instance of CMLDialog for the main program window and for each modeless dialog box that you want to display. Declare an instance of CMDialog for each modal dialog box that you want to display.

- Call the public member functions and access the public data members of the objects you have declared, according to the instructions given in the following sections.

N O T E

For a description of how the General Windows Classes are used in an actual Windows application, see Chapter 2.

Using the CApplication Class

You must declare exactly one global instance of the CApplication class in your program, as in the following example:

```
CApplication App;
```

Before calling any of the other GWC member functions, you must initialize the CApplication object by calling the CApplication::Initialize function; for example:

```
App.Initialize (HInstCurrent, HInstPrevious, CmdLine, CmdShow);
```

The four parameters passed to Initialize are the same as the four parameters that are passed to the WinMain function when the program begins running. HInstCurrent is the handle to the current program instance, HInstPrevious is the handle to the previous program instance (or 0 if there is no previous instance), CmdLine is a pointer to the command line passed to the program, and CmdShow is a flag indicating how the main window is to be initially displayed (that is, whether it is to be minimized, maximized, or displayed in its normal size).

Initialize stores the values you pass to it in the following public data members:

```
HINSTANCE mHInstCurrent;
HINSTANCE mHInstPrevious;
LPSTR mCmdLine;
int mCmdShow;
```

Because these data members are public and the CApplication instance is declared globally, you can access this data from anywhere in the program. For example, a function in the program might use the following code to test whether the command line contains the string "/s":

```
if (strstr (App.mCmdLine, "/s"))
    // then command line contains "/s" ...
```

The values saved in the CApplication data members are also used internally by the GWC code.

To load an accelerator table for the program, you can call the CApplication::LoadAccel function, as in the following example:

```
if (!App.LoadAccel ("TemplateAccel"))
    return (FALSE);
```

You should pass LoadAccel a string containing the name that you assigned to the accelerator table when you defined it, using your resource editor. The function returns TRUE if successful, or FALSE if an error occurs.

N O T E Chapter 2 discusses defining, loading, and using accelerator tables.

LoadAccel stores the handle of the accelerator table in the public data member mHAccelTable. You can use this data member to access the accelerator table, for example, when calling the TranslateAccelerator API function in a message loop (see Chapter 2).

Using the CMLDialog Class

To display a modeless dialog box—or to create a main program window based upon a dialog box template—either you can declare an instance of the CMLDialog class, or you can derive your own class from CMLDialog and declare an instance of the derived class. You should derive your own class if you want to do one or more of the following:

- Provide custom processing for the messages sent to the dialog box
- Define additional data members to store information on the dialog box
- Define additional member functions to perform tasks related to the dialog box

For a very simple modeless dialog box (for example, one that just displays a message), you could use an instance of CMLDialog itself. To create a more complex modeless dialog box or a main program window, you will almost certainly have to derive your own class from CMLDialog.

The `CMLDialog` class provides a virtual member function, `DialogProc`, that receives control whenever the dialog box is sent a message. This function processes messages as follows:

- When the user chooses the Close command on the system menu, clicks the OK button (that is, a push button with the identifier `IDOK`), or clicks the Cancel button (that is, a push button with the identifier `IDCANCEL`), it destroys the dialog box.

- For all other messages, it allows Windows to perform default message processing.

To provide custom message processing for a modeless dialog box, you must derive a class from `CMLDialog` and define a `DialogProc` member function that overrides the default version of this function inherited from `CMLDialog`. This function should have the following declaration within your class:

```
virtual BOOL DialogProc (UINT Msg, WPARAM WParam, LPARAM LParam);
```

For information and examples showing how to process messages from the `DialogProc` function, see Chapter 2, as well as Chapters 3 through 9.

The remainder of this section discusses the public members provided by `CMLDialog`, which you can use for your modeless dialog box or main window, whether or not you have derived your own class.

You can assign an icon to the dialog box by calling the `SetIcon` member function, as in the code,

```
if (!MainDialog.SetIcon ("TemplateIcon"))
   return (FALSE);
```

where `MainDialog` is an instance of a class derived from `CMLDialog`. You must pass `SetIcon` a string containing the name that you assigned the icon resource when you created it, using your resource editor. `SetIcon` returns `TRUE` if successful, or `FALSE` if an error occurred. Assigning an icon is useful primarily for a modeless dialog box that is used as a main program window; the icon will be displayed whenever the window is minimized. Note that during the course of the program you can call `SetIcon` to assign a different icon, or pass it `0` to remove the icon. If no icon is assigned to a main window, Windows will display a plain white square when the window is minimized.

To display a modeless dialog box, call the `Create` member function of the `CMLDialog` class. For example, the following call would create a modeless dialog box that a program displays in addition to its main window:

```
MessageDialog.Create ("MessageDlg", mHDialog);
```

In this example, `MessageDialog` is an instance of `CMLDialog` or a class derived from `CMLDialog`. The first parameter is a string containing the name of the template for the dialog box (you design and name the dialog template using your resource editor). The second parameter supplies the handle of the window that owns the dialog box—in this case, the main program window.

To display a modeless dialog box that serves as the main program window, you can omit the second parameter:

```
if (!MainDialog.Create ("MainDlg"))
   return (FALSE);
```

This example assumes that `MainDialog` is an instance of a class derived from `CMLDialog`. Omitting the second parameter causes it to revert to its default value, 0, indicating that the dialog box does not have an owner (because it is a main window).

`Create` returns a nonzero value if successful, or 0 if an error occurs. `Create` also assigns the handle of the dialog box that it creates to the `CMLDialog` public data member `mHDialog`. You can use this member to access the handle whenever you need it.

To remove the dialog box, call the `Destroy` member function. For instance, the call

```
MessageDialog.Destroy ();
```

would destroy the dialog box that was displayed in the example above.

WARNING   Do *not* destroy a dialog box created using `CMLDialog::Create` by calling the API function `DestroyWindow`. Rather, call `CMLDialog::Destroy`, which performs important clean-up tasks in addition to destroying the dialog box.

Using the CMDialog Class

To display a modal dialog box, either you can declare an instance of the CMDialog class, or you can derive your own class from CMDialog and declare an instance of the derived class. The reasons for deriving your own class are the same as those listed for the CMLDialog class in the previous section. To display a very simple modal dialog box—such as an "About" dialog box—you can probably get away with using a CMDialog instance; for displaying a typical dialog box that displays and allows the user to enter data, you will most likely have to derive your own class.

The default message processing provided by the CMDialog class is the same as that provided by CMLDialog (see the previous section). To provide custom message processing for a modal dialog box, you must derive a class from CMDialog and define a DialogProc member function that overrides the default version of this function inherited from CMDialog. This function should have the following declaration within your class:

```
virtual BOOL DialogProc (UINT Msg, WPARAM WParam, LPARAM LParam);
```

The version of DialogProc that you define will receive control whenever a message is sent to the dialog box. Information and examples showing how to process these messages are given in Chapters 2 through 9.

To display a modal dialog box, call the Create member function of the CMDialog class, as in the statement,

```
MDialog.Create ("AboutDlg", mHDialog);
```

where MDialog is an instance of CMDialog. The first parameter is a string containing the name that you assigned to the dialog box template in the resource editor, and the second parameter is the handle of the window that is to own the dialog box (normally, the main program window or another dialog box).

Because CMDialog::Create displays a modal dialog box (which suspends normal message processing), it does not return until the user issues a command to close the dialog box and the DialogProc message handling function calls the EndDialog API function to remove the dialog box. If successful, Create returns the value that DialogProc passed to EndDialog; if an error occurs, it returns -1.

`Create` assigns the dialog box handle to the public data member `mHDialog`. `Create` also sets up a *hook* function, which sends a message to the dialog box whenever the user presses the F1 key. The identifier of this message is stored in the `CMDialog` public data member `mHelpMessage`. If the identifier of a message that `DialogProc` processes is equal to `mHelpMessage`, then `DialogProc` can display context-sensitive help information on the dialog box. This technique is illustrated in the following code excerpt from the TEMPLATE program, which was explained in Chapter 2 (in the section "Displaying Context-Sensitive Help"):

```
default:
    if (Msg == mHelpMessage)
        {
        SendMessage (mHDialog, WM_COMMAND, IDC_HELP, OL);
        return (TRUE);
        }
    else
        return (FALSE);
```

How the General Windows Classes Work

The source code for the General Windows Classes is given in Listings 1 and 2. Listing 1 (WCLASSES.H) is the header file, which contains the definitions of all of the classes. Listing 2 (WCLASSES.CPP) is the C++ source file, which implements the member functions of the classes.

Listing 1

```
/////////////////////////////////////////////////////////////////
//                                                             //
// WCLASSES.H:  Header file for the WCLASSES general Windows   //
//              classes.                                       //
//                                                             //
/////////////////////////////////////////////////////////////////
```

```
#define STRICT
#include <windows.h>

//////////////////////////////////////////////////////////////////
// Application class definition:                                  //
//////////////////////////////////////////////////////////////////

class CApplication
{
public:
    LPSTR mCmdLine;
    int mCmdShow;
    HACCEL mHAccelTable;
    HINSTANCE mHInstCurrent;
    HINSTANCE mHInstPrevious;

    CApplication ();

    void Initialize (HINSTANCE HInstCurrent,
                     HINSTANCE HInstPrevious,
                     LPSTR CmdLine,
                     int CmdShow)
        {
        mHInstCurrent = HInstCurrent;
        mHInstPrevious = HInstPrevious;
        mCmdLine = CmdLine;
        mCmdShow = CmdShow;
        }

    BOOL LoadAccel (LPCSTR AccelTableName)
        {
        if (mHInstCurrent == 0)
           return (FALSE);
        mHAccelTable = LoadAccelerators (mHInstCurrent,
                                         AccelTableName);
        return ((BOOL)mHAccelTable);
        }

}; // end CApplication
```

```
////////////////////////////////////////////////////////////////
// Modal dialog box class definition:                          //
////////////////////////////////////////////////////////////////

class CMDialog
{
    virtual BOOL DialogProc (UINT Msg, WPARAM WParam,
                             LPARAM LParam);
    virtual void Remove ()
        {
        EndDialog (mHDialog, -1);
        }

protected:
    HICON mHIcon;

public:

    HWND mHDialog;
    static UINT mHelpMessage;

    CMDialog ();
    ~CMDialog ();

    virtual int Create
        (LPCSTR DlgTemp,
        HWND HWndOwner = NULL);

    friend BOOL CALLBACK _export GenDlgProc (HWND HWndDlg,
                                             UINT Msg,
                                             WPARAM WParam,
                                             LPARAM LParam);
};

////////////////////////////////////////////////////////////////
// Modeless dialog box class definition:                       //
////////////////////////////////////////////////////////////////

class CMLDialog : public CMDialog
{
```

```
        virtual BOOL DialogProc (UINT Msg, WPARAM WParam,
                                 LPARAM LParam);

        virtual void Remove ()
           {
           DestroyWindow (mHDialog);
           }

    public:

        virtual int Create
           (LPCSTR DlgTemp,
           HWND HWndOwner = NULL);

        void Destroy ();

        BOOL SetIcon (char *IconName);
    };


    ///////////////////////////////////////////////////////////////
    // CQueue class definitions:                                 //
    ///////////////////////////////////////////////////////////////

    struct SQueue
    {
       HWND HWnd;
       void *PObject;
       SQueue *Next;
    };

    class CQueue
    {
       SQueue *mPQueue;

    public:
       CQueue ()
          {
          mPQueue = 0;
          }
```

```
    void FreePObject (HWND HWnd);
    void *GetPObject (HWND HWnd);
    BOOL SetPObject (HWND HWnd, void *PObject);
};
```

Listing 2

```
/////////////////////////////////////////////////////////////////////
//                                                                   //
// WCLASSES.CPP:  C++ source code for the WCLASSES general           //
//                Windows classes.                                   //
//                                                                   //
/////////////////////////////////////////////////////////////////////

#include "wclasses.h"


/////////////////////////////////////////////////////////////////////
// global definitions & initializations:                            //
/////////////////////////////////////////////////////////////////////

UINT CMDialog::mHelpMessage = 0; // initialize static data member
static CApplication *PApp = 0;
static CQueue Queue;

BOOL CALLBACK _export GenDlgProc (HWND HWndDlg, UINT Msg,
                                  WPARAM WParam, LPARAM LParam)
    {
    CMDialog *PObject;  // base class pointer used to access
                        // CMDialog, CMLDialog, & derived objects

    // attempt to obtain object address (should be available for
    // all messages sent AFTER WM_INITDIALOG):
    PObject = (CMDialog *)Queue.GetPObject (HWndDlg);

    if (PObject == 0)  // WM_INITDIALOG message not yet processed
        {
        if (Msg == WM_INITDIALOG)  // on WM_INITDIALOG, LParam
            {                      // contains object address
            PObject = (CMDialog *)LParam;
            // save dialog handle in data member:
```

```
            PObject->mHDialog = HWndDlg;
            // save the dialog handle and object address in queue:
            if (!Queue.SetPObject (HWndDlg, PObject))
                {                        // insufficient memory to add
                PObject->Remove ();  // element to queue; destroy
                return (TRUE);       // dialog box
                }
            }
    else  // some message has been sent BEFORE WM_INITDIALOG;
        return (FALSE);  // perform default processing
    }

// draw icon for a modeless dialog box (for a modal dialog
// box, icon is not available and mHIcon is always 0):

// user is dragging icon; if an icon has been created,
// return its handle to Windows:
if (Msg == WM_QUERYDRAGICON && PObject->mHIcon != 0)
    return (BOOL)PObject->mHIcon;

// dialog box needs to be drawn and is minimized; if icon
// has been created, draw the icon:
if (Msg == WM_PAINT && PObject->mHIcon != 0 &&
    IsIconic (PObject->mHDialog))
    {
    PAINTSTRUCT PS;
    // get device context:
    BeginPaint (PObject->mHDialog, &PS);
    // force Windows to draw the icon background:
    SendMessage (PObject->mHDialog, WM_ICONERASEBKGND,
                (WPARAM)PS.hdc, 0L);
    // draw the icon itself:
    DrawIcon (PS.hdc, 0, 0, PObject->mHIcon);
    // release the device context:
    EndPaint (PObject->mHDialog, &PS);
    return (TRUE);
    }
// call the DialogProc member function of the dialog box
// object to process the message:
return (PObject->DialogProc (Msg, WParam, LParam));
}
```

```
LRESULT CALLBACK _export MessageProc (int Code, WPARAM WParam,
                                      LPARAM LParam)
// while this function is enabled as a hook function, it is
// called whenever a message is sent to a window belonging to
// the program; it is called before the window procedure
    {
    HWND HWnd;
    MSG *PMsg = (MSG *)LParam;

    if (Code == MSGF_DIALOGBOX &&
        PMsg->message == WM_KEYDOWN &&
        PMsg->wParam == VK_F1)
    // user pressed F1 while the modal dialog box or one of
    // its controls has the focus; send the help message to
    // the dialog box:
        {
        HWnd = PMsg->hwnd; // handle of the dialog box or of a
                           // control that is a child of the dialog
                           // box and currently has the focus

        // get the handle of the dialog box itself (rather than
        // the handle of a control with the focus); while handle
        // is for a child, get the parent window handle (the
        // dialog box itself is not a child of another window):
        while (GetWindowLong (HWnd, GWL_STYLE) & WS_CHILD)
            HWnd = (HWND)GetWindowWord (HWnd, GWW_HWNDPARENT);

        // place help message in queue, with handle of dialog box:
        PostMessage (HWnd, CMDialog::mHelpMessage, O, OL);
        return (1);   // 1 return value indicates that message has
        }             // been processed and should not be passed on
    else              // to the dialog procedure;
        return (0);   // O return value means to pass message on
    }                 // to the dialog procedure


/////////////////////////////////////////////////////////////////
// CApplication member function:                               //
/////////////////////////////////////////////////////////////////

CApplication::CApplication ()
```

```
   {
   ::PApp = this;   // save address of object in global pointer
   mHInstCurrent = 0;
   mHInstPrevious = 0;
   mCmdLine = 0;
   mCmdShow = 0;
   mHAccelTable = 0;
   }

////////////////////////////////////////////////////////////////
// CMDialog member functions:                                 //
////////////////////////////////////////////////////////////////

CMDialog::CMDialog ()
   {
   mHDialog = 0;
   mHIcon = 0;
   }

CMDialog::~CMDialog ()
   {
   if (mHIcon != 0)
      DestroyIcon (mHIcon);
   }

int CMDialog::Create
   (LPCSTR DlgTemp,
   HWND HWndOwner /* = NULL */)
   {
   HHOOK HHook;
   int ReturnVal;

   // make sure that a CApplication object has been declared
   // and initialized:
   if (PApp == 0 || PApp->mHInstCurrent == 0)
      return (-1);

   if (mHelpMessage == 0)  // a help message ID has not yet
      {                    // been obtained
      // get a unique ID for the help message
      mHelpMessage = RegisterWindowMessage ("WCLASSESMSG");
```

```
   if (mHelpMessage == 0)
      return (-1);
   }

// enable the MessageProc hook function for capturing F1
// keystrokes:
HHook = SetWindowsHookEx
   (WH_MSGFILTER,
   MessageProc,
   PApp->mHInstCurrent,
   GetCurrentTask ());
if (HHook == 0)
   return (-1);

// display the modal dialog box:
ReturnVal = DialogBoxParam
   (PApp->mHInstCurrent,
   DlgTemp,
   HWndOwner,
   GenDlgProc,
   (LPARAM)(void far *)this);   // supply the object address

// disable the MessageProc hook function:
UnhookWindowsHookEx (HHook);

// remove the queue element storing the object address:
Queue.FreePObject (mHDialog);

mHDialog = 0;
return (ReturnVal);
}

BOOL CMDialog::DialogProc (UINT Msg, WPARAM WParam,
                           LPARAM LParam)
   {
   switch (Msg)
      {
      case WM_INITDIALOG:
         return (TRUE);

      case WM_COMMAND:
```

```
                      // user clicked OK or Cancel button, pressed Esc, or
                      // chose Close command on system menu:
                      if (WParam == IDOK || WParam == IDCANCEL)
                         {
                         EndDialog (mHDialog, TRUE);  // close the dialog box
                         return (TRUE);
                         }
                      else
                         return (FALSE);  // perform default processing

                default:
                   return (FALSE);  // perform default processing
                }
          }

//////////////////////////////////////////////////////////////////
// CMLDialog member functions:                                    //
//////////////////////////////////////////////////////////////////

int CMLDialog::Create
   (LPCSTR DlgTemp,
   HWND HWndOwner /* = NULL */)
   {
   if (PApp == 0 || PApp->mHInstCurrent == 0)
      return (0);

   // create the modeless dialog box:
   return (int)CreateDialogParam
      (PApp->mHInstCurrent,
      DlgTemp,
      HWndOwner,
      GenDlgProc,
      (LPARAM)(void far *)this);  // supply object address
   }

void CMLDialog::Destroy ()
   {
   if (mHDialog == 0)
      return;
   // destroy the modeless dialog box:
   DestroyWindow (mHDialog);
```

```
    // remove the queue element storing the object address:
    Queue.FreePObject (mHDialog);
    mHDialog = 0;
    }

BOOL CMLDialog::DialogProc (UINT Msg, WPARAM WParam,
                              LPARAM LParam)
    {
    switch (Msg)
        {
        case WM_INITDIALOG:
            return (TRUE);

        case WM_CLOSE:
            Destroy ();
            return (TRUE);

        case WM_COMMAND:
            if (WParam == IDOK || WParam == IDCANCEL)
                {
                Destroy ();
                return (TRUE);
                }
            else
                return (FALSE);

        default:
            return (FALSE);
        }
    }

BOOL CMLDialog::SetIcon (char *IconName)
    {
    HICON HIconHold;

    if (IconName == 0)
    // program passed 0; therefore, destroy the current icon:
        {
        if (mHIcon != 0)
            DestroyIcon (mHIcon);
        mHIcon = 0;
```

```
      return (TRUE);
      }

   if (PApp == 0 || PApp->mHInstCurrent == 0)
      return (FALSE);

   // load the specified icon from program resources:
   HIconHold = LoadIcon (PApp->mHInstCurrent, IconName);
   if (HIconHold == 0)
      return (FALSE);

   // destroy the previous icon, if any:
   if (mHIcon != 0)
      DestroyIcon (mHIcon);

   mHIcon = HIconHold;  // store the icon handle
   return (TRUE);
   }


//////////////////////////////////////////////////////////////////
// CQueue member functions:                                     //
//////////////////////////////////////////////////////////////////

void CQueue::FreePObject (HWND HWnd)
// remove the queue element that contains the handle HWnd
   {
   SQueue *PQueueTemp;
   SQueue *PQueueTemp1;

   if (mPQueue == 0)
      return;
   // examine first element in linked list:
   if (mPQueue->HWnd == HWnd)  // first element has HWnd;
      {                         // remove it from linked list
      PQueueTemp = mPQueue;
      mPQueue = mPQueue->Next;
      delete PQueueTemp;
      return;
      }
   PQueueTemp = mPQueue;
```

```
    while (PQueueTemp->Next != 0)   // search linked list for
       {                            // element with HWnd
       if (PQueueTemp->Next->HWnd == HWnd)
          {                              // found the element;
          PQueueTemp1 = PQueueTemp->Next;   // remove it
          PQueueTemp->Next = PQueueTemp->Next->Next;
          delete PQueueTemp1;
          return;
          }
       PQueueTemp = PQueueTemp->Next;
       }
    return;
    }


void * CQueue::GetPObject (HWND HWnd)
// returns the object address stored in the queue element that
// contains the handle HWnd
    {
    SQueue *PQueueTemp;

    // search through linked list:
    PQueueTemp = mPQueue;
    while (PQueueTemp != 0)
       {
       if (PQueueTemp->HWnd == HWnd)
          return (PQueueTemp->PObject);
       PQueueTemp = PQueueTemp->Next;
       }
    return (0);
    }


BOOL CQueue::SetPObject (HWND HWnd, void *PObject)
// adds a new element to the queue
    {
    SQueue *PQueueTemp;

    // allocate memory for the new element:
    PQueueTemp = new SQueue;
    if (PQueueTemp == 0)
       return (FALSE);
```

```
// assign values to fields of new element (it is placed at
// the beginning of the linked list):
PQueueTemp->HWnd = HWnd;
PQueueTemp->PObject = PObject;
PQueueTemp->Next = mPQueue;

// adjust the mPQueue data member to point to the new
// element at beginning of linked list:
mPQueue = PQueueTemp;
return (TRUE);
}
```

The following sections explain the key programming techniques used by the General Windows Classes.

How CApplication Works

When the program creates the single global instance of the CApplication class, the class constructor saves the address of the object in the global variable PApp, so that the GWC code can access the information on the current program instance that is stored in this object:

```
::PApp = this;
```

The application data is stored in the CApplication object when the program calls the CApplication::Initialize function.

The LoadAccel member function loads the accelerator table by calling the API function LoadAccelerators.

How CMLDialog and CMDialog Work

The following sections explain the main tasks performed by the CMLDialog and CMDialog classes. Note that these two classes are related: CMLDialog is the derived class and CMDialog is the base class.

Creating and Destroying the Dialog Box

The CMLDialog version of the Create function creates the modeless dialog box simply by calling the CreateDialogParam API function. CreateDialog-Param creates and displays the dialog box and returns immediately, so that the program can continue normal message processing while the dialog box remains displayed. The CMLDialog::Destroy function removes the dialog box by calling the DestroyWindow API function.

The CMDialog version of Create creates the modal dialog box by calling the DialogBoxParam API function. DialogBoxParam does not return until the user has closed the dialog box (while the dialog box is displayed, the main program window is disabled and the dialog box code provided by Windows handles all messages). Windows destroys the modal dialog box when the dialog procedure calls the API function EndDialog; thus, the CMDialog class does not need to provide a special member function for destroying a modal dialog box.

Routing the Messages

When the dialog box is created, the CreateDialogParam or DialogBox-Param API function must be passed the address of the dialog procedure, which is the function that is to be called whenever a message is sent to the dialog box. The specified dialog procedure must be a normal global function, *not* a member function of a class (the dialog procedure is called from the Windows system code; a call to a member function, however, must originate from a C++ module and must contain an object specification).

The goal of the GWC, however, is to allow messages to be processed by a member function of the object that manages the dialog box (so that all code and data for managing the dialog box can be encapsulated in the object that manages the dialog box). To achieve this goal, both versions of the Create member function pass to the API function (CreateDialog-Param or DialogBoxParam) the address of GenDlgProc, which is a global dialog function that is defined at the beginning of the WCLASSES.CPP file. For example, the following is the call to CreateDialogParam:

```
return (int)CreateDialogParam
    (PApp->mHInstCurrent,
```

```
DlgTemp,
HWndOwner,
GenDlgProc,   // address of the global dialog procedure
(LPARAM)(void far *)this);
```

When `GenDlgProc` is called to process a message, it calls the `DialogProc` member function of the object that manages the dialog box, passing it the message information so that `DialogProc` can perform the actual message processing.

Thus, `GenDlgProc` is the first function to be called whenever a message is sent to any modeless or modal dialog box created by the program using the GWC. `GenDlgProc`'s main task is to route the message to the appropriate object. This is accomplished through the following mechanism:

- When either version of `Create` creates the dialog box, it passes the address of the object that manages the dialog box to the API function (`CreateDialogParam` or `DialogBoxParam`). This address is obtained from the predefined pointer `this` and is passed as the last parameter. For example, the following is the call to the `Create-DialogParam` function:

```
return (int)CreateDialogParam
   (PApp->mHInstCurrent,
   DlgTemp,
   HWndOwner,
   GenDlgProc,
   (LPARAM)(void far *)this);   // address of the object
                                // associated with the dialog box
                                // being created
```

- The API function (`CreateDialogParam` or `DialogBoxParam`) passes the object address as the `LParam` parameter to the dialog procedure, `GenDlgProc`, when the `WM_INITDIALOG` message is sent (the `WM_INIT-DIALOG` message is sent immediately before the dialog box is displayed).

- When `GenDlgProc` processes the `WM_INITDIALOG` message, it uses the object address to call the object's `DialogProc` member function. Before doing so, however, it stores the object address together with the window handle in a queue that is maintained by the `CQueue` class. This queue will be described later; its important feature is that for each dialog box, it stores the dialog box handle together with the object address, and it allows you to retrieve the object address by specifying the handle. GenDlgProc must store the object address because this address is *not* supplied with subsequent messages (messages sent after WM_INITDIALOG supply only the handle). (When GenDlgProc processes WM_INITDIALOG, it also stores the dialog box handle in the object's mHDialog data member.)

- When GenDlgProc processes a message that is sent *after* WM_INIT-DIALOG, it obtains the object address from the queue and then uses this address to call the object's DialogProc member function.

The queue that is maintained by the CQueue class is implemented as a linked list and is shown in Figure A.1. Each element in the queue contains

FIGURE 1

The queue maintained by the CQueue class; the example queue has three elements

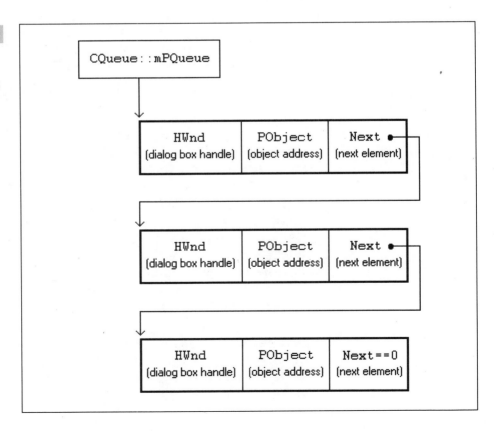

a dialog box handle and an object address (that is, the address of the object managing the dialog box). The SetPObject member function adds an element to the queue. The GetPObject is passed a dialog box handle and returns the associated object address. The FreePObject function is passed a dialog box handle and deletes the associated element from the queue.

When a dialog box is destroyed, the GWC calls FreePObject to delete the associated queue element. For CMLDialog, this is done in the Destroy member function, and for CMDialog, this is done in the Create function after control returns from the call to DialogBoxParam.

Hooking F1 Keystrokes

As explained previously, when you create a modal dialog box, the CMDialog class defines a hook function. Whenever the user presses F1 while the dialog box is displayed, the hook function sends the dialog box a unique message (the identifier of this message is stored in CMDialog::mHelpMessage), so that the dialog procedure can display context-sensitive help.

To establish this mechanism, the GWC performs the following steps:

- The first time you call CMDialog::Create to display a modal dialog box, Create calls the API function RegisterWindowMessage to obtain a unique message identifier that it can safely use for passing private messages (namely, the F1-key help message). It saves this identifier in the public data member mHelpMessage.

- Before Create calls DialogBoxParam to display the dialog box, it calls the SetWindowsHookEx API function to install the hook function, MessageProc (which is defined near the beginning of WCLASSES.CPP). As a result, whenever a message is sent to any window in the program (including the dialog box or any control that it contains), the system calls MessageProc *before* it calls the normal window procedure.

- If the message indicates that the user pressed F1, MessageProc calls the PostMessage API function to place the help message in the program's message queue. This message has the identifier CMDialog::mHelpMessage, and it contains the handle of the modal dialog box so that it will be processed by the dialog box procedure.

- After control returns from DialogBoxParam, Create calls the API function UnhookWindowsHookEx to deactivate the hook function.

Drawing the Icon

The CMLDialog::SetIcon function loads the specified icon resource by calling the LoadIcon API function, and it stores the icon handle in the protected data member mHIcon. The icon handle in mHIcon is then used for displaying the icon whenever the modeless dialog box managed by the CMLDialog object (or the object of a class derived from CMLDialog) is reduced to an icon. The CMLDialog class destructor calls the DestroyIcon API function to relinquish the icon handle when the dialog box object is destroyed.

The icon is drawn by the GenDlgProc dialog procedure, which was described previously. GenDlgProc draws the icon whenever the dialog box receives the WM_PAINT message (indicating that the window area needs painting), the dialog box is minimized (that is, the IsIconic API function returns TRUE), *and* an icon has been defined (that is, mHIcon is nonzero). To draw the icon, it performs the following steps:

1. It calls the BeginPaint function to obtain a handle to a device context.

2. It sends the dialog box the WM_ICONERASEBKGND message. When Windows provides default processing for this message, it draws the background area of the icon.

3. It calls the DrawIcon API function, passing it the icon handle, to draw the icon itself over the background drawn in step 2.

4. It calls the EndPaint API function to release the device context.

Also, whenever the user starts dragging the icon on the screen, Windows sends the dialog box a WM_QUERYDRAGICON message. In response to this message, GenDlgProc returns the icon handle (provided that one has been obtained). Windows then displays a black-and-white version of this icon as it moves the icon on the screen.

INDEX

Note to the Reader: **Boldfaced** numbers indicate pages where you will find the principal discussion of a topic or the definition of a term. *Italic* numbers indicate pages where a topic is illustrated in a figure.

Numbers and Symbols

386 Enhanced mode, global memory and, 80, 135
:: (scope-resolution operator), 49

A

About command
    Microsoft Windows, 80
    Template program Options menu, 26, 57
About dialog box, Template program, 26, *27*
    displaying, 57
accelerator tables, 49, 535
activating
    previous program instance in Template program, 48–49

Screen Saver, 284–286, *285*
Address Manager program, **316–391**, *317. See also* Template program; Windows utilities
    API functions, **378–381**
    GetOpenFileName function, 380
    OpenFile function, 378–379, 380, 381
    CDocument class, 377
    for File New command, 378–379
    for File Open command, 379–380
    for File Save and Save As commands, 381
    file structure and, 381–383, *382, 383*
    FileOpen function, 380
    FileSave function, 381
    Modified function, 389–390

H

P

A Book Full of Sound and Fury.

500pp. ISBN:1199-8.

The Audible PC is the complete guide to multimedia sound production with Windows. This book is a must for anyone who wants to explore the infinite possibilities of sound.

You'll find product reviews and descriptions, a survey of animation and presentation software, in-depth information on MIDI, sequencers, digital audio, sound cards, and more.

You'll also find a FREE 5¼" disk containing demo versions of two popular PC sound applications—Master Tracks Pro for Windows and Sound Forge.

SYBEX. Help Yourself.

2021 Challenger Drive
Alameda, CA 94501
1-800-227-2346

SYBEX

YOUR GUIDE TO A WORLD OF CONVENIENCE.

321 pp. ISBN: 798-3.

Finally there's a guide that helps you fulfill the promises of computer convenience you've always heard about —*Exploring the World of Online Services.*

With the help of this book, you can discover the myriad conveniences you can enjoy by using your computer and a modem. Find out how to send electronic mail and messages, or tap into over 5,500 public online databases. Get money-saving advice for choosing modems and communication software, and for saving money on your online bills.

Online veterans will especially enjoy the in-depth coverage of WinCIM, the new Windows version of the CompuServe Information Manager (CIM), and the in-depth discussion of a range of online service providers.

SYBEX. Help Yourself.

GET A FREE CATALOG JUST FOR EXPRESSING YOUR OPINION.

Help us improve our books and get a **FREE** full-color catalog in the bargain. Please complete this form, pull out this page and send it in today. The address is on the reverse side.

Name _____   Company _____

Address _____   City _____ State ____ Zip _____

Phone (____) _____

1. How would you rate the overall quality of this book?

- ❏ Excellent
- ❏ Very Good
- ❏ Good
- ❏ Fair
- ❏ Below Average
- ❏ Poor

2. What were the things you liked most about the book? (Check all that apply)

- ❏ Pace
- ❏ Format
- ❏ Writing Style
- ❏ Examples
- ❏ Table of Contents
- ❏ Index
- ❏ Price
- ❏ Illustrations
- ❏ Type Style
- ❏ Cover
- ❏ Depth of Coverage
- ❏ Fast Track Notes

3. What were the things you liked *least* about the book? (Check all that apply)

- ❏ Pace
- ❏ Format
- ❏ Writing Style
- ❏ Examples
- ❏ Table of Contents
- ❏ Index
- ❏ Price
- ❏ Illustrations
- ❏ Type Style
- ❏ Cover
- ❏ Depth of Coverage
- ❏ Fast Track Notes

4. Where did you buy this book?

- ❏ Bookstore chain
- ❏ Small independent bookstore
- ❏ Computer store
- ❏ Wholesale club
- ❏ College bookstore
- ❏ Technical bookstore
- ❏ Other _____

5. How did you decide to buy this particular book?

- ❏ Recommended by friend
- ❏ Recommended by store personnel
- ❏ Author's reputation
- ❏ Sybex's reputation
- ❏ Read book review in _____
- ❏ Other _____

6. How did you pay for this book?

- ❏ Used own funds
- ❏ Reimbursed by company
- ❏ Received book as a gift

7. What is your level of experience with the subject covered in this book?

- ❏ Beginner
- ❏ Intermediate
- ❏ Advanced

8. How long have you been using a computer?

years _____

months _____

9. Where do you most often use your computer?

- ❏ Home
- ❏ Work

- ❏ Both
- ❏ Other _____

10. What kind of computer equipment do you have? (Check all that apply)

- ❏ PC Compatible Desktop Computer
- ❏ PC Compatible Laptop Computer
- ❏ Apple/Mac Computer
- ❏ Apple/Mac Laptop Computer
- ❏ CD ROM
- ❏ Fax Modem
- ❏ Data Modem
- ❏ Scanner
- ❏ Sound Card
- ❏ Other _____

11. What other kinds of software packages do you ordinarily use?

- ❏ Accounting
- ❏ Databases
- ❏ Networks
- ❏ Apple/Mac
- ❏ Desktop Publishing
- ❏ Spreadsheets
- ❏ CAD
- ❏ Games
- ❏ Word Processing
- ❏ Communications
- ❏ Money Management
- ❏ Other _____

12. What operating systems do you ordinarily use?

- ❏ DOS
- ❏ OS/2
- ❏ Windows
- ❏ Apple/Mac
- ❏ Windows NT
- ❏ Other _____

13. On what computer-related subject(s) would you like to see more books?

_____

_____

_____

_____

14. Do you have any other comments about this book? (Please feel free to use a separate piece of paper if you need more room)

_____

_____

_____

_____

PLEASE FOLD, SEAL, AND MAIL TO SYBEX

SYBEX INC.
Department M
2021 Challenger Drive
Alameda, CA
94501

SYBEX®

About the Disk

What's on the Disk?

The companion disk includes the following components:

- All of the utility programs presented in this book
- An online help file for each utility
- All of the source files required to create the utilities and the online help

What about Installation?

To install the utility programs, the program source files, or both, run the automated install program, INSTALL.EXE, on the disk. For complete installation instructions, see Chapter 1. (A high-density drive is required.)

How Can I Get a 5¼" Disk?

Send $5.00, plus proof of purchase, and your written request to:

SYBEX Inc.
Customer Service Department
2021 Challenger Drive
Alameda, CA 94501
(800) 227-2346

Please include your name, complete mailing address, and the following reference number: 1286-2. Without the reference number, your request cannot be processed. Allow six weeks for delivery.